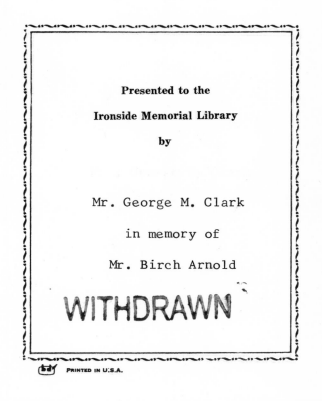

Presented to the

Ironside Memorial Library

by

Mr. George M. Clark

in memory of

Mr. Birch Arnold

WITHDRAWN

PRINTED IN U.S.A.

W9-AOX-833

IN
DEFENSE
OF
PROPERTY

Books by

GOTTFRIED DIETZE

ÜBER FORMULIERUNG DER MENSCHENRECHTE
Duncker & Humblot, Berlin, 1956

THE FEDERALIST—A CLASSIC ON FEDERALISM
AND FREE GOVERNMENT
The Johns Hopkins Press, Baltimore, 1960

IN DEFENSE OF PROPERTY

BY

GOTTFRIED DIETZE

Professor of Political Science
The Johns Hopkins University

HENRY REGNERY COMPANY · CHICAGO 1963

Manufactured in the United States of America
© 1963 Henry Regnery Company
LIBRARY OF CONGRESS CATALOG CARD NUMBER: 63-12890

TO THE MEMORY OF
WILLIAM VOLKER

30550

CONTENTS

		Page
PREFACE		ix
INTRODUCTORY REMARK		1

Chapter

I PROPERTY, ETHICS AND CIVILIZATION

Introduction	
Appreciation in Languages	9
Property in Antiquity	12
Property in Christian Thought	15
Property and The Enlightenment	19
Property, a Universal Value	34
Conclusion	37

II PROPERTY, FREEDOM AND CIVIL RIGHTS

Introduction	40
Freedom and Liberties	41
The Vital Importance of Property Rights	48
The Importance of Property in More Advanced Societies	51
Property and Liberal Rights in the Democratic Revolutions	57
Conclusion	63

III THE RISE OF PROPERTY IN THE NINETEENTH CENTURY

Introduction	65
Defense by Various Schools	66
Protection Through Legislation and Adjudication	71
Protection Through Jurisprudence	84
Conclusion	90

IV   THE FALL OF PROPERTY IN THE TWENTIETH CENTURY

Introduction   93
Attacks by Non-Jurists   95
Attacks by Jurists   100
Restriction Through Interpretation   108
Restriction Through Legislation   115
Conclusion   125

V   PROPERTY AND DEMOCRACY

Introduction   128
Property and New Liberal Rights   131
Democracy, Absolute Democracy and Property:
    The Theory   139
Democracy, Absolute Democracy and Property:
    The Practice   149
Conclusion   161

VI   THE DECLINE OF PROPERTY—SCOPE, CONSEQUENCES
     AND PROSPECTS

Introduction   164
The Decline of Property in International Law   165
Consequences of the Decline of Property Rights   172
Suggestions for Improvement   181
Prospects of Property in Europe and America   190

CONCLUDING REMARK   200

NOTES   210

SELECTED BIBLIOGRAPHY   259

INDEX   263

PREFACE

I wrote this book not in order to defend my material goods, of which I possess only a few, but from the belief that the protection of private property is a prerequisite for a free and moral society and that progress can be best assured if we are permitted to keep and liberally dispose of what we acquire by means of the free and honest use of our faculties.

A book written in defense of an institution which has become discredited by social legislation challenges modern democratic trends and thus is a political work. Its main argument invites criticism because it contests prevalent academic and popular sentiments. However, the task of a professional student of social affairs is not only to state undisputable data, but also to publish whatever he believes as a result of his studies. The latter duty may be even more obligatory if it might serve a good cause. If the appreciation of private property is essential to our civilization, a defense of property must be a worthwhile endeavor when that civilization is threatened—all the more so if it reveals fallacies present in many of our beliefs and if it exposes perversions in our democratic forms of government which have resulted from the revolt of the masses and have led us on a road to serfdom.

I am grateful to Messrs. Lindsey Cowen, Lawrence S. Grow, and Murray N. Rothbard for valuable criticisms of the manuscript; to the Law School of the University of Virginia, the Brookings Institution, the Johns Hopkins University, and to the Relm Foundation for facilitating my research and writing. Miss Myra E. Moss kindly assisted me with my editorial work. I hope that the final product will not disappoint her.

GOTTFRIED DIETZE

Washington, D. C.
February 22, 1963

INTRODUCTORY REMARK

THE IDEA OF WRITING this essay occurred to me in the last months of the 1950's. At that time, America was full of glowing forecasts. Only a week after the Soviets had hit the moon, the "roaring sixties" were hailed. A veritable millennium was prophesied. For someone who, like myself, was burdened with a European experience, these predictions looked strange in the face of the danger of nuclear war. They seemed as impious as perhaps Emperor William's prophesy to lead the Germans on to glorious times had appeared to my grandparents,[1] and as blasphemous as the phantasies about the thousand years of national-socialist rule had been to my parents after the further advance of the masses.

We all think about the past, the present and the future, even though in these days most of us seem to be concerned with our present existence rather than with our past or future. We reflect upon our situation especially when a decade draws to a close, and even more when a century finishes. The last weeks of the fifties did not mark the end of a century, but merely that of a decade. And yet it was the end of a decade which was unique in the history of mankind. For in that decade, the possibility of a destruction of man had become obvious. There was good cause for reflection.

At that time I was at one of the sacred places in the history of freedom, the University of Virginia, which had been founded by the author of the Declaration of Independence. Here, I often thought of that decla-

1

ration and its essential feature—freedom, and wondered how freedom
had fared in our time. Why, I began to ask, was I so shocked by the
optimism that surrounded me? Had not Jefferson himself envisaged
happiness for America at a time when the foundations of the young
nation had been frail indeed? Had not his hopes been shared by his
contemporaries? Had not Alexander Hamilton, disagreeing with Jefferson on many another score, also foreseen a great and happy American
empire?[2] Had not the American Revolution, from the beginning believed
to be permanent,[3] become truly glorious through its achievements? The
American empire was built, and the freedom and happiness Americans
enjoyed played an important role in its construction. But was there freedom and happiness now? Would the empire last? I wondered.

When I arrived from Europe in 1949, America appeared as the very
embodiment of freedom. I had entered secondary school a few months
after Hitler had ascended to power, and soon experienced persecution.
The war increased the awareness that there was no freedom in Germany.
Small wonder, then, that after the conflagration I delved into a study of
free government. I became impressed by the American form of government, and my enthusiasm for American institutions became reflected
in my dissertation.[4] A few months after I had received my doctorate,
when the post-war misery in Germany had ended, I embarked for the
United States, full of expectation.

Now, ten years later, I wondered whether a re-evaluation of this country was due. Materially, I was in a better situation than ever before.
Though my days at Princeton, UCLA and Harvard were spent in poverty, they were wonderful years, filled with intellectual challenge and
an abundance of new impressions. I made many friends, and found
understanding everywhere. The frugality of scholarship aid prompted
me to complete my studies quickly. After having taught shortly in a
small college which had been founded by Benjamin Rush and named
after John Dickinson, I was appointed to the Johns Hopkins faculty.
I had every reason to be satisfied. And yet, I was worried. I asked myself whether Goethe's optimism concerning America, expressed in a
poem dedicated to the United States, was still justifiable.[5] Having been
under the spell of *Faust* from the days of my youth, the poet's opinion
of America had always impressed me, as also the statement by a Span-
iard, that the discovery of the new world was the greatest event since
the birth of Christ.[6] Now, after having lived in the United States for a
whole decade, I asked myself whether Goethe's optimism was still war-

ranted, or whether a "re-discovery" of America might be appropriate.[7]

In many respects, the United States appeared to me as an idyll. She had hardly been touched by wars and had been spared the uprooting of social values from which the European nations had not been able to escape. She was a land of plenty and enjoyment. It appeared quite fitting that the author of *Enjoy, enjoy!* had also written *Only in America*, and that both books were bestsellers.[8] However, I wondered whether these volumes would have been popular at an earlier period. Didn't they describe the very over-optimism that bothered me? The question arose in my mind whether the modern American way of life was actually what I thought the American way of life was when I came to this country.

Goethe's poem obviously had been prompted by the fact that America was not burdened with the traditions of Europe, that the American way of life could be that of free men.[9] Other Europeans lauded America for the same reason. However, one should not believe that they considered the American way of life to be an easy one. Used to many comforts, they did not identify life in the new world with comfortable living. For a long time, Americans scarcely felt differently. All the American way of life meant to them was the freedom of the individual from traditional fetters.[10]

They were justified in that feeling. For hardly anywhere else in the world were there as many people as free to make the most of their opportunities. The liberties Americans possessed stimulated their drive for progress and created what soon became known as the American type, the man of action, the doer.[11] A man in pursuit of happiness was conceived to be using his freedom for the sake of progress, a Faustian indeed, a frontiersman. Living comforts were considered to be nothing but by-products of effort and diligence. In this atmosphere of activity nothing was taken for granted. On the other hand, a whole world could be conquered if an individual found the effort to do so worthwhile. Small wonder then that America became the empire that had been envisaged by her founders. Never in the history of mankind had a free nation risen so quickly to so eminent a position.

With this thought, I shuddered. During the past decade, I had witnessed an enormous decline of the United States. When I arrived in 1949, her pre-eminence in world politics had been undisputed. Today many people believe that the United States is no longer as powerful as the Soviet Union, a nation which first caught up with the United States on nuclear weapons and then overtook her with missiles.

And yet, although most Americans were aware of this dangerous shift in the balance of power, many of them did not seem to be disturbed. There was general agreement that prosperity had never been greater. One enjoyed "the American way of life." Reflecting once again upon that way of life, I began to wonder whether it has not been responsible for the American plight. But such responsibility presupposed that the former Amercian way of life had changed. Obviously, a way of life which permitted the decline of America could not very well be identical with one that brought about the development of the United States to the most powerful nation on earth.

Upon closer inspection, I found that the present American way of life differs indeed from what it had been prior. Much of the former spirit of activity has vanished. Things are taken for granted. Comforts are enjoyed without much effort. Security is rated higher than opportunity. The frontiersman has been replaced by the men of the "new frontiers."[12] In short, the American way of life has deteriorated into an easy way of living.

This change appeared to me so enormous that I felt that only a new interpretation of something as fundamental as freedom could have caused it. Naturally, the New Freedom came to mind. Wasn't here indeed as new a concept of freedom as any which had been conceived? Had not its originator Woodrow Wilson—though perhaps unconsciously —done the spade work for the undermining of traditional American values? Clearly, the New Freedom implied not merely a variation of the old conception of freedom, as some people may have believed. *The New Freedom* suggested the total rejection of that conception. Its stupendous importance becomes obvious in the movement that is recognized as deriving from it—the New Deal.[13]

The generation which permitted American greatness to wane within the short period of a decade appeared to be mainly the result of the New Deal. It will be argued that the height of American power was reached at the end of the New Deal period, namely, in World War II. However, it would be wrong to refer to the generation that won that war as a New Deal generation. For it had, on the whole, grown up before the New Deal. It had learned how to fight for a living and how to master adversity. After all, it survived the Depression and won the war. The situation changed with the generation that came of age during and after the war. Indeed these were children of the New Deal! Born in the late twenties and thirties, they grew up in the atmosphere of the welfare state. The state was more or less helping their parents and themselves. This help, appreciated by their parents as a temporary relief, was taken for granted by the children who had known no other milieu. When they had grown up, hardly anything counteracted that feeling. There were, as a result of the war boom, plenty of jobs. The young, leaving their homes, stepped into an easy life. Hardly ever before had such a thing happened in America. For never before had young adults so greatly desired to be taken care of. The New Deal had created a veritable New Generation.

By the middle of the twentieth century, a century which had been heralded as the American century,[14] the American concept of the pursuit of happiness had changed. Originally implying the freedom to get ahead according to one's ability and effort, it now meant the right to stand still and get things irrespective of ability and effort by leaning upon the state. Disability and laziness had come to be rewarded. People enjoy things without being able to call them their own. If I recall correctly, J. P. Morgan once said that as long as one had to worry about what one owns, one could not really afford it. Today, people no longer merely buy things for the cash which they worry about. They buy articles for which they are not able to pay cash. Still worse: they do not worry about buying on credit. They not only have become debtors on a larger scale than ever before, but also more careless about debts than before!

These considerations led me to reflect once again upon the excessive optimism which surrounded me. Of course, Americans always have been optimistic. But wasn't their traditional optimism more justifiable than that which I found today? Previously, it seemed to me, American optimism was one which implied an ability to master adversity, an optimism which had for its corollary a confidence in the future growth of the nation. Didn't today's optimism, by contrast, verge on carelessness? Didn't people live day by day, thinking little of their future, let alone that of their country? Hadn't the freedom to build America against adversity degenerated into a feeling of the right to live off her?

What, I asked, was the essence of this tremendous reorientation? Just having become aware, in a study of the *Federalist,* of how much the Founding Fathers emphasized the need for a protection of property,[15] the idea occurred to me that the existing dilemma might be due to an absence of the appreciation of private property. If one enjoys the comforts of life without much effort, if one buys on credit and does not worry about incurring debts, if one carelessly assumes that things will be taken care of in some way, then it is likely that private property is not sufficiently appreciated. For all the factors which are conducive to an appreciation of property are missing: the effort that makes one value what is gained through it; the pride of owning what one enjoys; the feeling of responsibility and strength resulting from ownership.

The absence of an appreciation of property appeared to me the negation of the philosophy which had been instrumental in the creation of the United States—the philosophy of John Locke. For this philosophy considered property a natural right and made its protection the primary end of government. The American Constitution and the Declaration of Independence reflect this idea.

Thinking of the Declaration of Independence, my thoughts were once again with Thomas Jefferson. While that great student of Locke had been a defender of property rights, he had been also an advocate of popular government, believing that the latter was a good means for protecting those rights. However, whereas the appreciation of property was now slight, popular government was stronger and more popular than ever before. The question naturally occurred as to whether the growth of democracy was connected with the decline of property. In the Declaration of Independence, Jefferson had not indicated a conflict between popular government and the protection of property. His statements implied that there was as much propriety in the former as there was in the latter. But is this still true today? Is not, on the contrary, such a conflict obvious? If an expansion of popular government was matched by a decline of property rights, was there not some connection between the growth of democracy and the growing disregard for property? Had not Jefferson himself recognized a conflict between the propriety of democracy and that of property in his *Notes on Virginia?*[16]

Propriety, property, democracy; the relation of these values fascinated me. I wondered if our age was not characterized by democracy, impropriety, and a disregard for property. As a transplanted European, I also felt curious about the situation in Europe. Having lived for some time in the old and new worlds, I increasingly had become aware of the spiritual community of the two continents. And my frequent visits to Europe during the past decade made me recognize that this commonness included also the plight from which I saw America suffering. For in Europe I perceived the same easygoing attitude and carelessness which I had noticed in the United States. Perhaps the disregard for property with its undesirable results was a Western phenomenon? This question prompted me to extend my inquiries beyond the United States and to undertake a more general examination of attitudes toward property and the consequences of its disparagement.

This essay is the result of these efforts. Its aim is to show the tragedy involved in the decline of property. It is thus a brief for the protection of free property. It is up to the reader to agree or disagree with the arguments advanced. Though I am not a relativist, I am too much aware of human shortcomings to claim to know the absolute truth. My chief purpose is the modest one of arousing some awareness of the dangers confronting our existence as free individuals. Such an undertaking is likely to meet with criticism, the more so since its main arguments run counter to current intellectual fashions. But I have always had my doubts about fashions. By definition, they lack permanency and thus truth. And I always felt that individuals should challenge what was fashionable and common. My major thesis then, is that the institution of private property is basic to our culture and constitutes an important part of freedom; that recent infringements upon property rights, irrespective of how minor they may have been in the beginning, increased by leaps and bounds with the growth of egalitarian democracy; that just as previously social and socialist regulations of property, undertaken in democratic societies, contributed to the rise of national socialism, so in the present world in which fascism has become discredited, they are likely to end up—evolutionary as the process may be—in communism. It is also asserted that the protection of private property is a prerequisite for what Jefferson called "natural aristocracy,"[17] and that restrictions of free property are tantamount to the elimination of the cream of the human race on both the national and international levels. A lot has been said, during the past years, against persecution on grounds of race. Regrettable as such persecution is, it is felt that the persecution of those who own property, which is the essence of social legislation, is just as bad.[18]

The first part of this study is concerned with the appreciation of property over the ages. Then the relation of property rights to human freedom and its various aspects will be demonstrated. It will be maintained that property rights are superior to democratic rights and at least on a par with all liberal rights of the individual. Finally, the manner in which the general appreciation of property was reflected in law as well as how this trend has become reversed will be shown. Our emphasis upon the law is based upon the consideration that the law, being "essentially the embodiment of the established forms of recurrent social behavior patterns,"[19] is probably the safest barometer of human trends. Due to its conservative character, it will only embody ideas that have become definitely accepted by society. Therefore, if it can be shown that the disparagement of property is sanctioned by that "ethical minimum," the law,[20] then there is reason to believe that such disparagement has actually progressed even further in spheres outside the law.

Accordingly, the study deals with the lawmaker in modern Western society, namely, with democratic government. The manner in which the degeneration of democracy resulted in a disregard for property as well as the illegitimacy of that process will be discussed. It will be revealed how property has been protected under higher law[21] and legislation; how the latter originally conformed to higher law and reflected that law's disposition in favor of a protection of property; how since the end of the nineteenth century democratic lawmakers rejected higher law to a greater and greater extent; how that rejection, combined with trends toward equality, resulted in a social outlook on property rights that led to infringements upon these rights. The decline of property will thus be revealed as the result of the march of democracy.

No attempt will be made to define property rights. Different historical periods and societies have offered a great variety of definitions. Moreover, within a certain society, people have not been able to agree at any given time upon one definite concept of property. Even the Roman lawyers, renowned for their juristic abilities, refrained from defining property rights, and their wisdom has been praised by those who followed. However, in spite of an omission to define property, the reader should be aware that in the absence of a specific qualification the term "property" is used in its original sense, i.e., in the sense of private property. This does not imply, however, that references to property could not refer to its narrower and broader concepts, i.e., to merely static property as well as to the right of the free acquisition and use of property. For, like the scope of other rights of the individual, that of property rights was not always the same. It depended on time and circumstances, and expanded with the growth of civilization.

I

PROPERTY, ETHICS
AND CIVILIZATION

INTRODUCTION

PROPERTY is related to propriety, and is an ethical institution. It is a feature of our civilization.

The kinship of property with what is proper has been recognized from early times. It has been acknowledged by the people themselves in that genuine expression of popular feeling—language. It has been seen by our great thinkers. No matter what period or aspect of our civilization we may consider, we find that the institution of private property has been defended on grounds of justice, freedom, progress, peace and happiness. Often attacked and suppressed, ultimately free property emerged victorious. Common ownership, although enjoying temporary vogues, has been rejected as utopian, as incompatible with the good of society and the individual, as productive of quarrels, as retarding development, as restraining freedom, as arbitrary and unjust. Always, property has been defended on ethical grounds—be they of an idealistic or materialistic kind[1]—and provided with ample justifications.

Wherever we turn, we find that property has been considered as proper and that proper people have respected property.

APPRECIATION IN LANGUAGES

The popular appreciation of property can be seen in our languages.

9

Words as well as proverbs suggest the intimate connection of property with propriety.

The Oxford dictionary defines "proper" as one's "own," but also as "decent, decorous, respectable, correct." Similarly, "propriety" is described as "property" and as "in conformity with good manners or polite usage; correctness of behavior or morals." "Property" is said to be now rarely used for "propriety," implying that previously it was used more frequently in that sense. Indeed, former English authors often spoke of "propriety" when they meant "property." Thomas Hobbes, an advocate of absolute monarchy and yet a defender of private property, spoke of "propriety," "dominion," and "mine and thine" as meaning identical things. In a similar vein John Locke, the champion of limited government who felt that property was a natural right, considered "property" as "properly" belonging to man.[2]

The Oxford dictionary states that "propriety" is derived from the old French *propriété*. That word connoted something good and proper, but, also, something owned. Today, while mainly having the latter meaning, sometimes *propriété* is employed for "correctness" and "goodness." Frenchmen, when speaking properly, speak *avec propriété*. *Propre* means "own." A thing has its *propre substance*, a person his *nom propre*. Victor Hugo used the word in this sense when he wrote, *"le propre du despotisme, c'est de niveler."*[3] However, *propre* is used also in the sense of *bienséant, bien arrangé,* meaning "right," "correct," "good." A gentleman uses *expressions propres*, and wears a *habit propre*. As if to make sure that the connection between property and what is good and proper is not overlooked, the French language has another word which shows the close connection between the notions. That word is *bien*. Movables are *biens meubles*, and real estate is *biens immeubles*. The same word is used for "the good" and "goods." The public good is *le bien public*, and the goods of the earth are *les biens de la terre*. *Bien* is also an adverb. Its adjectival form, *bon*, means "good."

The situation is similar in Italian and Spanish. In the former tongue, *proprio* means "own," but also "proper, genuine, right." *Proprietà* is the word for both "property" and "propriety." In Spanish, the noun *buena* was formerly used for "property." Today, the adjective *bueno* means "good." *Proprio* stands for "own," but also, for *justo*, "right." Something done *al proprio* is something done *justamente*, done correctly, with propriety, *con propiedad*. *Propiedad,* in turn, has also the meaning of "fortune," "wealth," and "property."

It may be argued that the close connection between property and propriety in the languages mentioned is due to the fact that all these words are derived from Latin. However, this argument cannot refute our thesis. It is acknowledged that the Latins used *proprietas* for "propriety" as well as "property," and *proprius* for "good" and "proper" as well as for "own." Thus they showed that the connection between property and propriety existed a long time before the creation of modern languages. However, no one forced the nations that were emerging from the Roman empire to adopt that relationship. If the English, the French, the Italians and the Spaniards had not believed in an affinity of propriety and property, they would not have taken over the Latin usage and continued to use it to this day.

Furthermore, modern languages show the affinity of property and propriety in words which are not derived from Latin. In English, for instance, another word for property is "goods," the noun of "good." A German word for property is *Gut*. When not capitalized, *gut* means "good." Moreover, the word *eigen* is used not only in the sense of "own," but also in that of "fitting, befitting, good." Examples from other languages could be added to support our thesis of the close connection between property and propriety.

The connection is evident also in proverbs. Formulated and used over the ages, proverbs are as good a barometer of popular feeling as are words. Everywhere, they express the value of property. More than that: no matter in what language they might occur, they laud property for identical reasons, often even employing the same phraseology. What is the cause of these coincidences? Did one linguistic group adopt proverbs used by another? Or were these proverbs created spontaneously by a specific group only? The answer to these questions is not relevant. Our assertion of the universal recognition of the value of property is supported by both theories.

The value of property is generally stated in the different languages —in nearly identical sentences! *A chacun oiseau son nid lui semble beau,* say the French, and their brethren across the Rhine claim *Eignes Nest hält wie die Mauer fest*—"Every bird thinks his own nest charming!"

But consensus extends beyond a mere agreement that property in general is something good. It also extends to specific features of its goodness. For instance, ownership is considered a prerequisite for status. The Latin *tanti quantum habeas sis* found its equivalent in modern languages. *Chi ha, è—chi non ha, non è* the Italians put it. The French as well as the English prefer a play on words: *Celui est homme de bien qui est homme de biens*—he is a good man who is a man of goods. Cervantes, perhaps too proud to adopt a saying which was in use in Italy and France, the Latin sisters of Spain, used his own words: *Tanto vales cuanto tienes.* Was he aware that the Germans were employing the phrase, *Jeder gilt so viel als er hat,* which is a literal translation of the above?

Property is also considered conducive to the individual's independence, freedom and happiness. The English saying, "A man's house is his castle," has its counterpart in the French *chacun est roi en sa maison.* The Germans, adding a note of *Gemütlichkeit,* put it, *Eigen Heim, Glück allein.*

Furthermore, property is considered a means for the acquisition of more property and thus connected with progress. The general agreement expressed about that point, symbolized by the use of literal translations, is indeed striking. The saying, "money breeds money," reads, in German, *Geld gibt Geld,* and, in Italian, *danari fanno danari,* and, in Spanish, *dinero llama dinero.* All of these translations are proverbs in their own right.

As in the case of words which show the close connection between property and propriety, we could mention many more proverbs which show that connection, and which prove that there has existed and still exists a popular belief that property is something ethical. In the following pages, we will demonstrate that this belief has been shared by great thinkers throughout the history of Western civilization.

PROPERTY IN ANTIQUITY

Property was defended in Greece and Rome. In antiquity the institution of private property, implying an unequal possession of goods, demonstrated its value by enduring its first major challenge. It survived what was thought to be such a startling and complete change that it was considered "the dividing-line between the ancient and modern political theory,"[4] namely, the transition from a social atmosphere which was founded upon the notion of the inequality of human beings, to one which assumed the equality of men.

Aristotle expounded a strong defense of property. Basing his ideas on a study of existing societies, he took issue with Plato's "communism,"[5] which had resulted from a somewhat unrealistic examination of the legends of the golden age. Aristotle maintained that individuals are the prerequisites of society, and advanced the idea that private property is ordained by natural law and sanctioned by the ages.[6] As an instrument of the highest life, it is necessary for the sake of society as much as for that of the individual. Stressing that labor is one of the justifications of property,[7] Aristotle recognized that in a communistic society men would have no incentive: "That which is common to the greatest number has the least care bestowed upon it," he wrote. "Everyone thinks chiefly of his own, hardly at all of the common interest, and only when he is himself concerned as an individual. For besides other considerations, everybody is more inclined to neglect the duty which he expects another to fulfil; as in families many attendants are often less useful than a few."[8] Ownership is conducive to progress. It promotes the growth of character, because two important virtues, self-control and liberality, result from it. It is a source of pleasure. The pleasure of owning for oneself is complemented by the joy of being able to give to others. A common use of property would give rise to disputes and endanger peace and order.[9] Afraid of revolution, Aristotle opposed an expropriation of the rich.[10] His writings contain a comprehensive enumeration of the reasons for the desirability of private property. Aristotle's justification of property through natural law and usage; his arguments as to the usefulness of property: all these are defenses of property which have been used to our day.

The Stoic ideal of equality, combined with the idea that men have a common right to use the goods of nature, exercised a strong egalitarian influence upon Roman thinking. However, it could not prevent the advent of the most individualistic and property-conscious of all legal systems—Roman law. Cicero, although sympathetic to the Stoic ideal of equality and common ownership,[11] recognized the utopian nature of such ideas. Human society being what it is, he felt, needed the institution of private property. A fragment of Cicero's *Republic* reveals that Plato's communism was discussed in that work.[12] Since the citizens of the good state, as described in the *Republic,* owned unequal amounts of property, we may assume that he rejected Plato's communism. This assumption seems to be borne out by his other writings. In book two of *De Officiis,* Cicero condemns agrarian laws, property taxes, laws abolishing debts, confiscations and other measures tending to bring about an equal distribution of property. He states that government, being established primarily for the protection of the property of the individuals, should not encroach upon it.[13] There is reason to believe that Cicero favored an unequal distribution of property because he hoped it would bring about a well-to-do class which would maintain authority and prevent society from degenerating into anarchy. His advocacy of the protection of property is thus closely connected with his well-known apprehension that democracy might become too democratic for its own good.[14]

Like Cicero, the Roman jurists believed that in the state of nature there existed equality and communal property. But they also recognized the utopian character of such a state and advocated the institution of private property. On the whole, they defended property on approximately the same grounds as Cicero had. The liberal character of the Roman law of property is "so manifest and so well known" that it suffices to mention only a few features which attest to the high degree of protection property enjoyed. The loss of property by prescription was kept within narrow limits. If a thing was alienated without the owner's consent, not even *bona fide* recipients acquired ownership. The argument that legal security required the protection of *bona fide* recipients did not impress Roman lawyers, who "did not even hold it worth while to discuss the question whether it might be in the interest of commerce to protect the *bona fide* recipient, for what was dear to the lawyers was not security of commerce and business intercourse but security of vested rights." This comprehensive protection of property from alienation was matched by far-reaching guaranties of the free use and employment of property. "The liberal principle demanded that ownership should be as unrestricted as possible and that the greatest possible latitude should be given to individual action and initiative." To the Roman, property rights included not only the right to use (*ius utendi*) and the right to draw fruit (*ius fruendi*) but also the right to abuse (*ius abu-*

tendi). In as much as Roman law was very individualistic, it did not favor a community of property.[15]

PROPERTY IN CHRISTIAN THOUGHT

The transition from paganism to Christianity was a significant event in the history of our civilization. However, it did not challenge the institution of private property. As a matter of fact, Christian ideas on property, Catholic and Protestant alike, came to complement those features of Greek and Roman thought that favored the protection of property.

The Christian philosophers of the Middle Ages, like their pagan predecessors, considered common ownership utopian and defended private property for the sake of the individual as well as for that of society.

The distrust of riches and the emphasis on advantages of poverty in the New Testament, combined with the gospel of the equality of all the children of God and the brotherhood of man, suggest an egalitarian theory of property. Also, the way of life of the first Christians in Jerusalem and of the persecuted followers of the new faith in Rome shows a belief in communistic principles. However, once the Christian religion was acknowledged and became the official religion of the empire, communistic practices disappeared. Common ownership was considered utopian. Private property became recognized as a good institution.

The church fathers did not have to develop their own philosophy of property. They could employ what had been said on that subject by the Greeks and Romans. The golden age came to correspond to the Garden of Eden, and the idea of the equality of the faithful. After the Fall, men were compelled to accept certain institutions of social domination. The dominance of some people over others, resulting from an unequal distribution of property, was such an institution.[16] Private property was thus a prerequisite for the existence of society. It was a "method by which the blind greed of human nature may be controlled and regulated."[17] It was to prevent anarchy and to provide a means for the preservation of law and order.

Later, property was defended by the scholastic philosophers. Whereas the church fathers tended to assert that the protection of property was due to human rather than natural law, the scholastics emphasized that property rights were based on natural law. Early representatives of that school, stressing the blessings of property for the individual and society, broadened the basis of its justification. In his *Summa Decretorum,* published about 1158, Rufinus wrote that good customs and written law, providing for private property, complement the law of nature and make it more perfect. Furthermore, he said that, although the institution of property might have originated in the Fall, it now is sanctioned not only by convention, but also by usage, and therefore is as legitimate as if it had been sanctioned by natural law.[18] The philosophers who preceded St. Thomas usually followed this line of reasoning. Alexander of Hales even stated that private ownership is included in natural law.[19] Albertus Magnus, the teacher of St. Thomas, felt that private ownership is natural.[20]

St. Thomas proclaimed that property is natural and good. In his *Treatise on Law,* he defended the Old Testament's provisions on property and emphasized their conformity with Aristotelian thinking. He justified property along the lines of Aristotle, recognizing property as legitimate and necessary, because men are more careful to procure things for themselves than anything which would belong to all; because human affairs will be better ordered if each man has his own particular job in procuring things; and because human life will be more peaceful, since common ownership produces quarrels.[21]

Clerics after St. Thomas did not feel differently about the value of property. Thomas' most famous student, Aegidius Romanus, elaborated Thomas' theory of property with quotations from Aristotle. He objected to Plato's communism by employing Aristotelian arguments, and emphasized that property is natural because it is representative of civilization. Thus he connected the advance of civilization and natural law, and made civilization appear an institution of natural law in which private property figures prominently. Property, existing before government and sanctioned by natural law, cannot be abrogated by legislation.[22]

The scholastics' defense of property was matched by that of the Catholic doctors a few generations later. Luis de Molina asserted that without private property one cannot preserve society.[23] Leonardo Lessius wrote that if common ownership had prevailed, the world would have remained uncivilized and been plagued by wars.[24] Juan de Lugo considered private property as something convenient and necessary for social life.[25]

In Catholic thought then, a continuous, if not a growing, appreciation of property is present. Private property was felt to be desirable on the grounds of utility and law, and considered an institution that indicated a state of civilization.

The Reformation was probably the most revolutionary event in modern church history. It challenged the most powerful church on the earth. It brought forth strong denunciations of the wealth of that church combined with exhortations that the clergy lead a more modest life. It seemed, by threatening an institution that owned great material wealth and by criticizing the use of that wealth, to question the institution of property. But it did not do so. Throughout the Reformation, private property continued to be considered an ethical value. As a matter of fact, the bases for its protection were expanded. Catholic thinkers had contented themselves with claiming that property was protected mainly by natural law. Protestant theologians also emphasized that property was sanctioned by the Scriptures. Not merely a broader justification was rendered, but also, the function of property to promote progress was stressed to a greater extent. By means of this emphasis, the Reformation stimulated the industry and energy of men, and had no small influence upon the rise of such powers as the Netherlands, England, Sweden, the United States and Germany.

It is not surprising that some reformers, denouncing the wealth of the Catholic church and its use, desired a more equal distribution of property. John Wycliffe's ideas on property, introduced into Bohemia by John Hus, brought about communistic revolts.[26] The situation was similar in other nations. However, these extremist movements did not succeed, because the great leaders of the Reformation recognized the danger of communistic utopias.

In Germany, radical elements attempted to push the Reformation beyond its original aims. Anabaptists and peasants did not hesitate to use violence in order to bring about a more equal distribution of property. Luther's reaction was unequivocal. He denounced the rebels as devils and called their aim to seize other people's goods unchristian. His disgust with communistic ideas was so extreme that he advised his countrymen to kill the rebels on sight. He refuted the idea that common ownership was advocated in the Scriptures. The passage in Genesis, that God gave the earth and its fruits to all men, could, so he felt, not be cited as a justification of common property, since the Old Testament was revised by the New, which does not require common ownership. The fact that the early Christians pooled their resources, he argued, had been overemphasized. Common ownership was not compulsory then, and would not be compulsory for later generations. Human nature being what it is, private property is indispensable. Luther gave many reasons for this assertion. For example, there is the argument of incentive. Modern men are unlikely to work under a communistic system, Luther said, stressing that from among the needy, only those who deserve it should be helped. Property is a prerequisite for the raising of families. Property, acquired through work, was and should be a means for the stimulation of production. It helps to preserve peace. Men advocating common property act like the shepherd who puts lions, wolves, eagles and sheep in one pen.[27]

Luther's support of private property was matched by John Calvin. Calvin was so emphatic about the value of property that he was said to have enthroned the doctrine of the divine right of property.[28] He realized that common ownership is utopian and denounced the Anabaptists' plan to abolish property and inequality. God, the supreme legislator, by decreeing "Thou shalt not steal," ordained the protection of property. What each individual possesses has not fallen to him by chance, but by the distribution of the Sovereign Lord of all. Criticizing idleness as sinful, Calvin felt that God ordained the possessions of property as a reward for labor. Property gives man incentive and provides the basis for human progress. It can and should be used to acquire more property. It gives man a vocation, enables him to provide for his family and to help others. It is necessary for the peace of society. In view of its extensive blessings, Calvin urged that the institution of property be maintained and that counsel and aid be loaned to those who want to retain their belongings. The state should see to it that every person may enjoy his property without molestation. The prince who squanders the property of his subjects is a tyrant.[29]

Calvin's ideas on property found elaboration in Puritanism, which contributed greatly to the development of England and the United States. The Puritans rejected the idea of common ownership as utopian and dangerous.[30] In Elizabethan England, Hooker and Whitgift attacked the anarchy of the communistic Anabaptists.[31] Later on, Presbyterians and constitutional sectarians repudiated the extravagancies of the Levellers.[32] Common ownership was considered to be conducive to quarreling, destructive of happiness, and preventive of progress.[33] Wealth properly accumulated, is a divine institution and a sign of the grace of God. Property is prescribed by God himself, and his rules are laid down in the Scriptures. "It is no sin but a duty," wrote Richard Baxter, a representative of the early Puritans, "to labour not for labour sake, formally resting in the act done, but for that honest increase and provision which is the end of our labour; and therefore *to choose a gainful calling rather than another,* that we may well be able to do good and relieve the poor."[34] John Wesley expressed similar thoughts. "Gain all you can," he preached, "by common sense, by using in your business all the understanding which God has given you. It is amazing to observe how few do this; how men run on in the same dull track with their forefathers. But whatever they do who know not God, this is no rule for you. It is a shame for a Christian not to improve upon *them,* in whatever he takes in hand. You should be continually learning from the experience of others, or from your own experience, reading and reflection, to do everything you have to do better to-day than you did yesterday. And see that you practise whatever you learn; that you make the best of all that is in your hand."[35] It would be difficult to imagine a more thorough endorsement of the temper which has made modern industry! For the Puritan, the "making of the best of all that is in your hand" does not mean only the promotion of one's own interests but also in a truly Christian fashion to do good to others. Private property is a blessing for the individual as well as for society. Its importance is so paramount that it is considered the essence of justice.[36]

PROPERTY AND THE ENLIGHTENMENT

The Reformation emancipated Christians from the Roman church. Under Protestant doctrine, God would give grace not to a church, but to the individual himself. Here was a revolution of the first magnitude. Not only was the unity of the church destroyed, but also the political unity of the West. As a result of the movement toward national states, philosophical thinking, which had been involved mainly with religious thinking and had been of a rather universal character, now became secularized and nationalistic. However, in spite of the revolutionary character of the Reformation, the institution of private property not only survived unharmed, but emerged stronger than before.

The trend toward a greater appreciation of property continued during the age of reason. Although this epoch was as revolutionary in the realm of thought as the Reformation had been in that of religion, the appreciation of property rights remained untouched. Probably the belief that the individualistic atmosphere of the era increased that appreciation to an extent greater than ever before is not exaggerated. No matter what kind of government writers might have advocated—absolute monarchy, absolute democracy or limited government—they stressed the value of property. Of course, the age of reason was not without plans which advocated common ownership. However, although these plans may have had adherents, they were, on the whole, recognized as unrealistic and then discarded.

Private property was defended by the advocates of absolute monarchy. In the beginning of his *Republic,* Jean Bodin emphasized that he did not plan to deal with the "imaginary forme and Idea of Commonweale, without effect to substance, as have Plato and Sir Thomas More . . . vainly imagined."[37]—a clear refutation of communistic thinking. Common ownership, Bodin argued, is incompatible with divine and natural law. It tends, as the Anabaptist experience demonstrated at Münster, toward anarchy. It destroys the family and, since the family is the basis of the state, the state itself. Things belonging to no one in particular will be neglected by everyone. Bodin also denied that there had been a golden age in which communism existed under the law of nature. Rather, men lived as beasts and robbery went unpunished. Gradually, men became civilized and law-abiding. Property is such a fundamental institution that the degree of civilization can be measured by the severity of punishment for infringements upon property, such as theft. The abolition of property would ruin the foundation of all commonwealths. The state is founded chiefly for the protection of property.[38] A prince, no matter how great his authority—and certainly Bodin, the originator of the modern concept of sovereignty, wanted a monarch to be as powerful as possible—could not justify infringements upon private property. The claim that the king exercises *dominium* over all things within his *imperium* is based upon a misinterpretation of Roman law, for "every subject hath the true proprietie of his own things, and may therefore dispose at his pleasure."[39] The king, no matter how great his temporal powers may be, is still bound by the law of nature and the laws of the realm, and cannot arbitrarily infringe upon property rights.[40]

In line with Bodin's thinking, property was defended by *Ligueurs,* Huguenots, and other French advocates of royal absolutism. One François Grimaudet indicated that though the king can tax, he is not free to confiscate.[41] Pierre de Belloy felt that God confers power upon kings in order that they might "render to each what belongs to him."[42] William Barclay's famous defense of the divine right of kings, published in 1600, expressly denied an intention to abolish private property, saying that all possessions would be protected by the king.[43] This general appreciation of property did not change throughout the *ancien régime*. No matter how much royalists, including Louis XIV, might proclaim that the king owned all the property of the realm, they considered private property to be protected by divine and natural law or the fundamental laws of France, and thus guarded it from arbitrary confiscations.[44]

Also the advocates of absolute monarchy on the other side of the Channel appreciated private property. James I, although maintaining that as a monarch by divine right he owned all the property in the land, recognized that the law of God ordains private property.[45] He stressed that he intended neither to deprive anyone of his possessions nor to replace the property-protecting common law through civil law. "If the fundamental Lawes of any Kingdome should be altered," he asked, "who should discerne what is *Meum* and *Teum,* or how should a King governe?"[46] This attitude is characterisic of the Stuart period. No matter how strongly royal absolutism might be asserted, private property, conceived to be protected by natural law, was considered sacrosanct. In 1678, a pamphleteer maintained, in view of the fact that during the Civil Wars parliament had passed more laws inimical to property than any Stuart, that liberty and property were better protected by absolute kings than under popular government.[47]

The protection of property plays an important role in the reflections of the great English defender of absolute monarchy, Thomas Hobbes. Significantly, he began his study of society with an examination of the origins of property rights.[48] While Hobbes admitted that in the state of nature there existed common ownership, he denied that this was a state of happiness. In contrast to concepts of common ownership which implied that everyone could take from the common stock what he needed, Hobbes stated that every man has a right to everything, i.e., to the whole of the common stock. Men could try to get as much as they wanted, and keep their goods as long as possible.[49] "One man invadeth with right, and another with right resisteth."[50] The state of nature is a "war of all against all" in which private propery is far from being safe. In order to change this condition, men set up political authority transferring all their rights to a sovereign who would redistribute them. Although property rights are created by the state, they are protected by the absolute ruler who guarantees to rich and poor alike the right to acquire and hold property.[51] Hobbes emphasized that there exists equal opportunity to acquire property. Every subject may "exercise and have the benefit of his own industry."[52] People should have the right "to buy, and sell, and otherwise contract with one another, to choose their own abode, their own diet, their own trade of life."[53] Unequal property, inevitable under a system of equal opportunity for all, would enjoy the protection of the state in a very comprehensive manner. Property will be necessary not only for the "bare preservation" of the individual, but also for the protection of "all other contentments of life, which every man by lawfull industry without danger, or hurt to the Commonwealth, shall acquire himself."[54] Like Bodin's sovereign, Hobbes' monarch by divine right is not restricted by any human law. However, he is bound by higher law to secure the protection of property and to insure the safety of the individuals. Should he fail to do so, he would forfeit his sovereignty.[55]

The defense of property by the proponents of absolute monarchy was matched by that of the advocates of absolute democracy. Just as absolute monarchs, although maintaining that in principle they exercise *dominium* over all things in the commonwealth, realized the value of private property and acknowledged its protection under higher law, in a similar manner the friends of absolute democracy considered property necessary for the well-being of individuals and society, and protected by the law. This fact was evident throughout the period under consideration. It is revealed in the democratic revolutions in England and France, as well as in the writings of the modern father of absolute democracy, Jean Jacques Rousseau.

The English revolution was the first democratic revolution in modern times. It was the first major challenge to the divine right of kings. But, in spite of the incisive changes it brought about, the institution of private property survived without difficulty. Even the more radical reformers opposed common ownership. When Gerrard Winstanley, the Digger, advocated the abolition of private property, the Levellers repudiated his communism and decried "parity" as a "Utopian fiction."[56] Their petitions, pamphlets and plans of government demanded that

Parliament should not abolish private property, and emphasized the need for a protection of proprietors against tyranny.[57] In view of this, it is not surprising that the more conservative forces of the revolution, headed by Cromwell and his son-in-law Ireton, should take an even stronger stand for the protection of property. In the Putney debates, held in 1647 on the future constitution of England, they opposed Leveller proposals for equal suffrage on the ground that such suffrage would endanger property. An equal distribution of property was considered destructive of the English constitution and conducive to anarchy. Private property appeared as a cornerstone of civilization.

Despite the fact that Rousseau's philosophy, by elevating the general will to something sublime, potentially was dangerous to private property, he recognized the value of that institution. In his *Discourse on the Origin of Inequality*, published in 1755, he described a golden age in which men are equal and without property, living off the gifts of nature. However, their increasing appetite, combined with the development of families, the creation of permanent living quarters, the invention of weapons and the cooperation in agriculture and industry, brought about the institution of private property as an important part of civilization.[58]

In his *Discourse on Political Economy*, Rousseau defended private property in a more direct manner. Taking political organization for granted, he considered property rights as sacred, "because property is the true foundation of civil society."[59] His advocacy of property is even more evident in the *Social Contract*. The social state with its institution of private property now is no longer merely taken for granted, but considered more desirable than the state of nature in which property could be owned by usurpation only. Using arguments similar to those of Hobbes, Rousseau advanced the idea that under absolute democracy property is well protected. The individuals, when leaving the state of nature and establishing civil society, give up all they own to the sovereign general will, who then regrants to them their property. Thus legitimized, private property enjoys the greatest possible degree of safety. The democratic sovereign, although creating property rights and thus being able also to abolish them, would refrain from doing the latter.[60]

Finally, property was defended by the democratic revolution which owed so much to the teachings of Rousseau, the French Revolution. The importance of that revolution can be scarcely overemphasized. It was an event that, as Kant put it, "could never be forgotten,"[61] an event

which, according to Burke, amounted to a negation of all old values.[62]
It abolished the *ancien régime* in France and ushered in democratic
movements all over the continent. It overthrew the remnants of feudalism. It challenged the position of the Church. And yet, the institution
of private property survived quite easily. As a matter of fact, the French
Revolution, in spite of its tendencies toward democratic absolutism and
its disregard for human lives, provided private property with an even
better justification than had Rousseau. The latter had maintained that
property was based on convention. The revolutionaries, on the other
hand, proclaimed that property was a natural right. Of course, Rousseau's
idea was not without followers. A first draft of a declaration of the rights
of man, read by Mirabeau, assumed the principle of the conventional
nature of property. It was emphasized therein that although the law
must recognize civil equality, there was no need for equal property. The
general will, while sovereign, would be obliged to assure the welfare of
the people and to protect private property.[63] However, this first draft was
rejected in favor of one which stated that property is a natural right.[64]
The latter, in a slightly different form, became embodied in the Declaration of the Rights of Man and Citizen of August 26, 1789. After stating
in the preamble that it intended to define the "natural, inalienable, and
sacred rights of man," that declaration declared in article two: "The aim
of every political association is the preservation of the natural and imprescriptible rights of man. These rights are liberty, property, security
and resistance to oppression." Article seventeen called property a sacred
and inviolable right. In a similar vein title one of the constitution of 1791
guaranteed the inviolability of property.

When in the following years agrarians attempted to eliminate the
unequal distribution of landed property, the leaders of the revolution
hastened to disassociate themselves from such radical plans and reaffirmed the rights of property. The day the monarchy was abolished,
Danton suggested that the Convention declared "that all property,
landed, personal, and industrial, will be maintained for ever."[65] In conformity with this suggestion, the Convention voted in March, 1793,
capital punishment for anyone proposing agrarian laws. Three months
later, the Jacobins proclaimed that they favored the protection of private
property and that they were willing to die in its defense.[66] Their constitution of June 24, 1793, rejected Robespierre's suggestion that property
rights are conventional and listed property among the inviolable rights of
man. When Jacobin egalitarians proceeded to favor the expropriation

of rich landowners, the small landowners, afraid that their own possessions might be expropriated next, joined the wealthy in guillotining
the egalitarians. After Robespierre had been executed, the Convention
reaffirmed its respect of property rights. These rights were declared
natural rights by the constitution of the year III, adopted in 1795. This
final document of the revolution reasserted strongly that private property is a distinct feature of civilization, maintaining in article eight that
"it is upon the maintenance of property that the cultivation of the land,
all the production, all means of labor, and the whole social order rest."
It even provides that the electorate should be limited to property owners
because "a country governed by property-owners is a true civil society."[67]
As if. to affirm that constitution's strong protection of property, the
Directory decreed on April 16, 1796, the year of Babeuf's communist
uprising, that those proposing "the pillage or partition of individual
properties, under the name of an agrarian law, or in any other manner,"
shall be punished by death or deportation.[68]

The French Revolution is thus characterized by continuous assertions of property rights. Of course, there were attempts to bring about
a more equal division of property in such an important egalitarian event.
Some property, notably that of the Church and the nobles, was subjected
to restrictions. However, these restrictions were undertaken with caution. They were permitted mainly because such property was considered representative of the *ancien régime* and feudalism, which were
believed to have prevented individuals from acquiring property.[69]
Once men had become emancipated and free to acquire property, poor
and rich alike became careful, even fanatic, to protect property. Property was recognized to be of great value not only for the individual, but
also for society. Plans advocating common ownership and communism
were attacked and discarded as dangerous utopias. In the end, private
property emerged as a sacrosanct institution. As such, it was embodied
in the masterpiece of Napoleonic legislation. The Civil Code was called
a "code of property."[70]

During the Enlightenment, the advocates of absolute monarchy
and absolute democracy, no matter how strong their belief in the in-
fallibility of their respective sovereigns was, favored private property
which the sovereign is to respect. In view of this, it is not surprising
that the friends of limited government would support private property
even more strongly. They no longer claimed that the sovereign exercises

dominium as well as *imperium*. They did not maintain that individuals, when forming a government, surrender all their rights. Rather, they held that these rights, being inalienable, would remain with the individuals. The sovereign would no longer be bound merely under higher law to protect private property. Individuals themselves possess subjective rights which they could assert. Of course, the concept of property as a natural right was not conceived spontaneously. Like the concept of limited government, it developed gradually, until it came to fruition in the American Revolution.

Private property was already advocated by the defenders of limited government in the seventeenth century. Hugo Grotius, often thought of as the father of international law, was also representative of the political aspirations of the Dutch middle class against Spanish absolutism. He discarded common ownership as something belonging to the unrealistic golden age of the poets. Ambitious men could not be expected to be content with feeding on the products of the earth. Desiring a more refined mode of life, they strive to acquire as many things as possible. Consequently, unless private property was safe, society would be shaken by quarrels. According to Grotius, private property preceded government, and the latter is bound by natural law to respect property. Government exercises *imperium,* but not *dominium*—sovereignty over the realm, but not ownership over things in the realm.[71]

Pufendorf also issued statements on the blessings of property. Joint ownership, he felt, might exist in the utopias of More and Campanella. Real people, however, cannot live without private property. Property was established by human convention and protected by the law of nature and the Decalogue. Agreements establishing property were established prior to the creation of government. Government was bound by the contract through which it had been created to respect property and to guarantee to all individuals equal rights to acquire and exchange property.[72]

Toward the end of the seventeenth century, the rights of property were advocated by John Locke. The defender of the Glorious Revolution justified property on an ever broader scale than had his predecessors. His *Second Treatise of Government* is as much a treatise on private property as on limited government. Property appears as a feature of civilization. Established "to the use of the industrious and rational," and "not to the fancy or covetousness of the quarrelsome and contentious," it is instituted for the benefit and enjoyment of the individual.

A prerequisite for incentive and human progress, property guarantees peace not only among individuals, but also among nations. However, Locke was not content with mere statements on the blessings of property. Having realized that considerations of convenience and right are complementary with one another, Locke also provided property with highest justification. Previous authors had been content with justifying property under government-made law, under conventions concluded prior to the establishment of society, or under natural law which was binding upon the sovereign. Locke went further. The individual himself possesses a natural right of property, a right he could claim against the government. Maintaining that an individual acquires property as soon as he mixes his labor with things, Locke made it clear that property does not need human convention in order to be protected. It enjoys protection as a natural right. Government, being instituted primarily for the protection of property, could be abolished by revolution if it arbitrarily infringes upon property.[73]

After Locke had established property as a natural right, its value was seen by eighteenth century advocates of limited government. In Locke's own country, his ideas were assumed by the outstanding commentator on English law, Blackstone. Feeling that common ownership is utopian, Blackstone defended private property on grounds of expediency and law. He accepted Locke's ideas on the origin of property, but also maintained that property is based upon convention, and made an attempt to reconcile that doctrine with the notion of natural right. Property, Blackstone felt, although originally resting on natural law, could, under conventions concluded by individuals, be regulated by the government.[74] However, by means of regulatory measures, it could be expanded rather than restricted. The English government, whenever regulating private property, was bound by natural law. English law itself was part of the law of nature. The latter was "coeval with mankind, and dictated by God himself, . . . binding over all the globe, in all countries, and at all times. No human laws are of any validity, if contrary to this; and such of them as are valid derive all their force, and all their authority, mediately or immediately, from this original."[75] This subordination of the law of England to the law of nature and the resultant protection of private property was based mainly upon Blackstone's high evaluation of property. Considering property a remedy for sin, he felt that it was a positive good and characteristic for the advance of civilization. Property is necessary "in order to maintain peace and harmony," to promote "the great ends of civil society" and the common good for "the public good is in nothing more essentially interested than in the protection of every individual's private rights," and "experience has shown that property best answers the purpose of civil life, especially in commercial countries, when its transfers and circulation are totally free and unfettered." "So great, moreover, is the regard of the law for private property, that it will not authorize the least violation of it; no, not even for the general good of the whole community."[76]

Property was defended also by the Scottish advocate of limited government, David Hume. He felt that property exists by convention. Conventions were agreed upon and obeyed for no other reason than that of the common interest which leads the individual, "in concurrence with others, into the general plan or system of actions, which tends to public utility."[77] While Hume considered the protection of property a matter of justice, he felt that it should and could be defended on utilitarian grounds, since justice derives its merit and moral obligation merely from its usefulness to the public. Rejecting the idea of equal ownership as "impracticable" and "pernicious," Hume, who never considered communistic ideas seriously, maintained that the institution of private property is necessary in civil society. The varying industry and thrift of men result necessarily in an unequal possession of property, and the oppression of these virtues would end in misery for all. A government favoring communism would be either a tyranny that would inquire into everyone's belongings and punish those who have too much, or an anarchy in which the individuals, possessing equal amounts of property, also would have equal power and in which no real authority could exist.[78] "Who sees not," he asked, "that whatever is produced or improved by a man's art or industry, ought, for ever, to be secured to him, in order to give encouragement to such *useful* habits and accomplishments? That the property ought also to descend to children and relations, for the same *useful* purpose? That it may be alienated by consent, in order to beget that commerce and intercourse which is so *beneficial* to human society? And that all contracts and promises ought carefully to be fullfilled, in order to secure mutual trust and confidence, by which the general *interest* of mankind is so much promoted?"[79]

On the continent, the value of property was seen by the famous French observer of English institutions, the champion of the separation of powers, Montesquieu. In a sense similar to that expressed by Hume, Montesquieu felt that property is protected by the civil laws which are made by men. Rejecting abstract thinking and basing his ideas mainly on his observation of existing institutions, Montesquieu could scarcely be expected to assert that property rights are protected under natural law. His protection of these rights merely under civil law did not, however, diminish his appreciation of property. Although he felt that men could have been equal and owned property in common in a state of nature, he declared that common ownership is not possible in civil society.[80] Private property is to be respected under that *"Palladium* of property," the civil law, because it secures the prosperity and happiness of the people. Montesquieu referred to the idea that the good of the individual should give way to that of the public as a "paralogism," and was willing to admit it only in such exceptional cases as "when the government of the community, or in other words, the liberty of the subject is concerned." Even in these cases, however, he did not admit infringements upon private property, "because the public good consists in every one's having his property, which was given him by the civil laws, invariably preserved." After citing Cicero as a man who objected to infringements upon property, Montesquieu continued: "Let us, therefore, lay down a certain maxim, that whenever the public good happens to be a matter in question, it is not for the advantage of the public to deprive an individual of his property, or even to retrench the least part of it by law, or a political regulation."[81]

By the middle of the eighteenth century, the ideas of all these authors were known in the new world. Therefore, it is not surprising that when the property of the Americans was threatened by Parliament, they repeatedly cited European advocates of limited government in defense of private property. Likewise, it is not surprising that America, blessed as she was during her formative period with statesmen that deserve to be called philosopher kings, came forth with assertions of private property that climaxed the Enlightenment's appreciation of property and made America appear as a haven for property rights.

This emphatic defense of property was supported by American tradition. Locke's statement that "in the beginning, all the world was America," implying that originally there existed a community of ownership in the new world, tends to be misleading about the colonists' attitude toward property. Actually, colonial mercantilist restrictions and provisions for the communal form of production made the colonists aware of the value of private property. The experience at Plymouth Rock, for instance, demonstrated the practical impossibility of common ownership at an early stage. Irrespective of what each one of the colonists produced, everything went into a common warehouse and the government doled out the proceeds of the warehouse as need seemed to require. However, this system soon proved to be unsatisfactory. The warehouse was constantly running out of provisions, and many of the colonists were starving. In view of this emergency, Governor Bradford and the remaining members of the colony agreed during the third winter to give up common ownership and to permit each colonist to keep the products of his work. This gave incentive to all. Came spring, reported Governor Bradford, "the women now wente willingly into ye feild, and tooke their little-ones with them to set corne, which before would aledg weaknes, and inabilitie; whom to have compelled would have bene thought great tiranie and oppression." The result of these efforts was a happy one: "By this time harvest was come, and in stead of famine, now God gave them plentie, and ye face of things was changed, to ye rejoicing of ye harts of many, for which they blessed God. And ye effect of their particular planting was well seene, for all had, one way & other, pretty well to bring ye year aboute, and some of ye abler sorte and more industrious had to spare, and sell to others, so as any generall wante or famine hath not been amongest them since to this day."[82] On the whole, it may be said that Americans were well aware of the value of private property from the beginning. Thus it is not surprising that when property rights were threatened in the second half of the eighteenth century, the Americans rallied in defense of these rights and that the American Revolution became, to a great extent, a movement for the protection of property.

The causes for the first phase of that revolution, the struggle against England, were of course many. To mention only a few, there was the distaste for British militarism, caused in large part by the contact in the French and Indian wars; there was the factor of political discrimination due to the inability to work out some form of equitable colonial representation; there was fear of Anglicanism in the New England colonies, and especially after the Quebec Act of 1774, of Roman Catholicism. Still, in a large measure, the struggle against the mother country was a struggle for the protection of the colonists' property. Feeling that property was infringed upon by acts of Parliament, the colonists advanced many arguments which show their appreciation of property and are as revealing as the revolutionary slogan, "no taxation without representation." James Otis' treatise, *The Rights of the British Colonies Asserted and*

Proved, published in 1764, requests the right to participate in Parliament as a means for the protection of the colonists' liberty and property. The resolutions of the Stamp Act Congress of 1765, as well as John Dickinson' *Farmer's Letters,* show that the colonists considered property rights as an important part of freedom.[83] A Massachusetts circular letter of 1768, drafted by Samuel Adams, stated that "it is an essential, unalterable right in nature, ungrafted into the British Constitution, as a fundamental law, and ever held sacred and irrevocable by the Subjects within the Realm, that what a man has honestly acquired is absolutely his own, which he may freely give, but cannot be taken from him without his consent."[84] Many more statements which reveal how dear the institution of private property was to the colonists could be cited.[85] The first concerted action before Independence, the Continental Congress of 1774, expressed a general sentiment when it declared that the colonists are entitled to their property "by the immutable laws of nature" and that no sovereign has the right to infringe upon it without their consent.[86] The same sentiment prevailed in the Second Continental Congress that declared Independence.[87]

The Declaration of Independence is, to a great extent, a document in defense of property. The question has been raised as to why Jefferson spoke of the unalienable rights of "life, liberty, and the pursuit of happiness" rather than of "life, liberty and property" as Locke had stated. However, this substitution does not imply that Jefferson cared less about property than Locke. The strong influence of the *Second Treatise of Government* on the Declaration is undisputed. There is no reason why Jefferson, who admired Locke so greatly that "the Declaration, in its form, in its phraseology, follows closely certain sentences in Locke's second treatise on government,"[88] should not have believed in the truth of the treatise's major idea, namely, that property is sacrosanct and that government is instituted mainly for its protection. It may be argued that the substitution of "pursuit of happiness" for "property," in view of the close resemblance of the Declaration to the *Second Treatise,* must have been made for urgent reasons and that it demonstrates a deviation from Locke's emphasis on property. However, this argument is scarcely convincing. If Jefferson had wanted to omit an emphasis on property, then he would have refrained from denouncing the king's infringements upon the colonists' property so emphatically. The substitution of "pursuit of happiness" for "property" is probably merely a proof of how well Jefferson knew the *Second Treatise.* He simply read it carefully enough to know that the protection of property is the major prerequisite of, and perhaps even identical with, happiness. His phrase "pursuit of happiness" is thus nothing but a summary statement of the various Lockean ideas on the ethical purposes of private property. It strengthens rather than weakens the case for property. This assumption is verified by Jefferson's statements in later years. Even the Jefferson who had been influenced by the egalitarian French Revolution made it clear that in the Declaration "he only attempted to express the ideas of the Whigs,"[89] and that he did not intend to introduce a new social concept that would endanger or even replace the idea of the value of private property. A year before his death, the man who preferred to be remembered for his authorship of the Declaration of Independence rather than for having served twice as President of the United States, gladly passed up a chance of being remembered for having introduced, by speaking of the "pursuit of happiness," a new and stirring idea. When drafting the Declaration, his aim was, in his own words, "not to find out new principles, or new arguments, never before thought of, not merely to say things which had never been said before; but to place before mankind the common sense of the subject, in terms so plain and firm as to command their assent. . . . Neither aiming at originality of principles or sentiments, nor yet copied from any particular and previous writing, it was intended to be an expression of the American mind. . . . All its authority rests then on the harmonizing sentiments of the day, whether expressed in conversation, in letters, printed essays, or the elementary books of public right, as Aristotle, Cicero, Locke, Sidney, etc."[90] Significantly, Jefferson referred to the great defenders of property in Greece and Rome and modern times—to Aristotle, Cicero and Locke. This was a very natural reference, since these philosophers had formulated theories which provided for a protection of property rights.[91]

The close connection between property and happiness is also evident in the state constitutions which were adopted during the struggle for independence. While these constitutions assert the protection of private property,[92] some of them mention property in a manner which indicates its close connection with happiness. Thus the constitution of Virginia of 1776 proclaims in section one that "all men are by nature equally free and independent, and have certain inherent rights, . . . namely, the enjoyment of life and liberty, with the means of acquiring and possessing property, and pursuing and obtaining happiness and safety." The constitution of Vermont, adopted during the following year, contains a similar provision. The constitutions of Massachusetts of 1780 and of New Hampshire of 1784 are even more outspoken in their assertions that the protection of property is a prerequisite of, if not identical with, the happiness of men. The former states in article one that "all men are born free and equal, and have certain natural, essential and unalienable rights; among which may be reckoned the right of enjoying and defending their lives and liberties; that of seeking and obtaining their safety and happiness." In a similar vein, the constitution of New Hampshire reads in article two that "all men have certain natural, essential and inherent rights; among which are—the enjoying and defending life and liberty—acquiring, possessing and protecting property—and in a word, of seeking and obtaining happiness."

The concern of Americans about the protection of property can be seen also in later stages of the revolution. During and after the war, the social implications of the revolution became evident, and trends toward an equal distribution of property came to the fore. In some States, the debtor faction, composed largely of small farmers and artisans, obtained control of the legislature, and passed laws infringing upon property rights, such as stay-laws, laws making paper money legal tender, and other laws impairing the obligation of contracts. These tendencies aroused severe criticism from men who felt that one of the aims of the struggle against England, security of private property, was now endangered by Americans themselves. Jefferson, writing his *Notes on Virginia,* was angered by conditions in his home state. Benjamin Rush of Pennsylvania, the father of American medicine, voiced concern lest "the liberty, the property and life of every individual in the State are laid prostrate."[93] John Adams, in his *Defense of the Constitutions of Government of the United States of America,* admonished his countrymen to recognize the need for the protection of private property. The movement toward an equal distribution of property came to a head with Shays's Rebellion when the debtor element, unable to capture the legislature of Massachusetts, revolted.[94] Since "the property of the United States has been protected from the confiscations of Britain by the joint exertions of all," the revolutionaries felt that it "ought to be common property of all," and were "determined to annihilate all debts public and private," Henry Knox, the Secretary of War at that time, wrote, suggesting the creation of a stronger national government which would be in a better position to protect private property.[95] His view was shared by other Americans.

The Federal Convention was convened largely because of a belief in the ethics of property. John Adams' opinion that "property is surely a right of mankind as really as liberty. . . . The moment the idea is admitted into society that property is not as sacred as the laws of God, and that there is not a force of law and public justice to protect it, anarchy and tyranny commence,"[96] was shared by many. The wisdom of that opinion was demonstrated by Shays's Rebellion. Thus the Founding Fathers by no means devised the new Constitution only in order to protect their own interests, but mainly because they recognized that property rights were an essential part of freedom and that their protection was basic to public peace and order, conducive to progress, a prerequisite for the individual's as well as society's welfare and happiness, and for justice.[97]

In the struggle for ratification, the idea that under the Constitution property would enjoy greater protection played a prominent role. The Federalist Papers, written to rally support for the adoption of the Constitution, emphasized that under that agreement property would be safeguarded.[98] Although we do not know with certainty the extent to which these essays caused ratification, it is not disputed that the adoption of the Constitution was due in a large measure to the desire to have property protected.[99] Once the Constitution had been adopted, the *Federalist* with its emphasis on the sacrosanctity of property came to be considered the classic commentary to the Constitution, a sacred text which was second only to the Declaration of Independence and to the Constitution.

Thus the idea of the protection of private property, one of the major themes of the American Revolution, became one of the outstanding principles of the final document of that revolution, the Constitution. Years before the French adopted the Napoleonic code, their "code of property," America had a "constitution of property."

PROPERTY — A UNIVERSAL VALUE

In the preceding pages, an attempt was made to show the appreciation of private property throughout the course of our civilization, down to the events that emancipated man from absolutism. It was not intended to write a history of property. Due to the importance of that institution, this task has been accomplished before. It was intended merely to show how our thinkers felt about the merits of private property. Needless to say, our list of names is not exhaustive. Other men deserve mention, men who were as enthusiastic about the protection of property as those named, and who frequently were more effective in actually securing such protection. Last, but not least, there were the people who, following or prompting their leaders, saw to it that property was safely held. The ethical connotation of property has always pervaded every strata of society. It is a truly universal idea.

The authors mentioned were influential not merely during their lifetime; their ideas endured and influenced later generations.[100] Aristotle's thoughts on property had their bearing upon subsequent thinking. They can be seen in the ideas of the Romans; they were revived by St. Thomas; Protestant theologians recognized them; they were present throughout the Enlightenment and the nineteenth century; they are referred to as a classical justification of property today.

Roman law, characterized by a far-reaching protection of property, was valid not only in the Roman empire. It has influenced many other countries and still affects them today.[101] Its general impact was so great that it has been likened to that of Christianity.[102] Even Germanic codes were not free from its influence. Many of the principles of Roman law had been adopted by the Germanic tribes that traded with the Romans. Once Rome had been conquered, its law was not totally discarded.[103] Furthermore, that law survived in the practice of notaries through the continued use of Roman forms. And the Church, characteristically referred to as *vivit lege romana,* contributed largely to its lasting influence.[104]

In the twelfth century, the jurists of Bologna revived Roman law. This occurred on such a large scale that it is described as a veritable renaissance.[105] Shortly afterwards, the universities of Valencia, Salamanca and Lerida were founded and spread the Roman law in the Iberian peninsula. It strongly influenced that famous codification of Castile, the *Siete Partidas.*[106] During that period, Roman law had an impact also upon the laws of France and England.[107] In spite of popular reactions against the foreign intruder, it was never totally annihilated in these nations. North of the Alps, Roman law was widely adopted. It was accepted in the Netherlands, where the University of Leyden, founded in 1575, became a center for its study.[108] In Germany, it was received to such a great extent that the beginning of the "reception" of the Roman law was identified as the dividing-line between the Middle Ages and modern times.[109] Roman law was elaborated by the *Pandektenwissen-*

schaft down to the nineteenth century. The impact of that school upon other nations can scarcely be overestimated.[110]

The influence of the Roman law did not remain confined to these countries. From Spain it travelled across the Atlantic to Spanish America and across the Pacific to the Philippines; from France it came to Louisiana and Quebec and other French possessions. From the Netherlands it was introduced into the Dutch colonies and has survived in Ceylon and South Africa until today; from England it was carried to the British Empire and America.[111]

Thus in both the old and new worlds, Roman law exercised an influence over the ages. It still appeals today. Recently a trend toward a revival of Roman law occurred in connection with the unification of Europe.[112] What accounts for this lasting appeal? Perhaps the high degree of protection Roman law offers to the individual and his property: "It is just the liberal character of the Roman law which makes it a lasting document."[113]

The cleric's ideas on property also influenced later generations. Roman Catholic defenses of private property, expounded by St. Thomas and the theologians of the following generations, continued to be accepted. Never substantially changed, they influenced the general attitude toward property which prevailed during the seventeenth and eighteenth centuries, and were relevant in the democratic revolutions in England and France.

The same is true of Protestant thinking. After the Reformation, the gospel of the virtue of acquiring and increasing property came to be a successful creed on a victorious march. It had a substantial share in the development of Protestant countries and of capitalism.[114] Although this is true of the Lutheran creed, it is even more so in the case of Calvinism. At its birthplace, Geneva, there were quickly established, with the support of the *Vénérable Compagnie* which was composed of Calvinist ministers and teachers, a banking business and industries. Similar developments can be seen during the early capitalist periods in such countries as Holland, England, the United States, and among the Huguenots.[115] Besides being advocated by the two major Protestant faiths, the protection of private property was supported by other groups, such as Baptists, Mennonites, Quakers, Pietists, and Methodists.[116]

The influence of the Enlightenment upon later generations will not be considered now. It will be revealed in subsequent chapters which concern the nineteenth and twentieth centuries. In everyday life, we are too aware of that influence to justify a specific discussion. Concepts like popular government and constitutionalism issue from the Enlightenment, as does our modern belief in the rights of the individual, including those of property.

As the preceding pages show, the idea that private property is good is lasting. Furthermore, it is not necessarily connected with any specific place or discipline. Aristotle was a philosopher and Cicero, a jurist. St. Thomas, Luther and Calvin were theologians. Locke and Hume were philosophers; Blackstone and Grotius, jurists. The idea of favoring the protection of property is also interreligious. It was advanced in pagan antiquity, and by Christians of various denominations. Not confined to national boundaries, it is a truly international idea. Alexander of Hales was English; Aegidius, Italian; Lessius, Belgian; de Lugo, Spanish. Montesquieu, the great commentator on English government, was French. Rousseau, the spiritual father of the French Revolution, came from Calvinist Geneva. Jefferson, Hamilton and John Adams were American. A veritable portrait of the West is revealed when one examines the advocacy of private property! Finally, recognition of private property proved to be independent of the social status of individuals. Just as property was defended by Aristotle on the premise that men were unequal, it was advocated, from the days of the Stoics, on the assumption of the equality of men.

CONCLUSION

The foregoing was not intended to give the impression that from antiquity to the end of the eighteenth century, the protection of property was guaranteed. This was far from being the case. If property had been protected, then continuous assertions of the value of such protection would not have been necessary. Everywhere and at any time, in Greece, Rome, during the Middle Ages and throughout the Enlightenment, property rights were tenuous. They were often regulated and severely infringed upon.

On the other hand, voices favoring private property were constantly raised during the history of our civilization. Thus, just as there existed, in spite—or because—of perpetual infringements upon the freedom of the individual, a continual striving for freedom, continuous attacks upon private property resulted in defenses of that institution. It is probably fair to say that on the whole, private property was victorious. For its merits were not only never forgotten, but even recognized to a greater and greater extent.

Common ownership was generally rejected as incompatible with human nature and as unethical. Recognizing the utopian character of that type of ownership, the defenders of property gave a variety of reasons for their position. Private property was defended on such grounds as peace and justice, as an essential part of freedom, as a prerequisite for progress, as conducive to the individual's happiness and the welfare of society, and as a landmark of civilization.[117]

There were justifications of property through many types of law. Though any of them may have prevailed at given periods, often diverse types of justification existed at the same time. Property was defended from the time of Aristotle up to the present day under natural law and, ever since John Locke, as a natural right. Throughout the same period, defenses of property were presented also on the grounds of convention or, later on, those of legislation. Moreover, Aristotle advanced the idea that private property must be good because it had been respected in the past. That idea was not forgotten until it was particularly emphasized by Burke and the historical school. Thus every source of law—natural and customary as well as conventional—sanctioned private property.

Property rights were considerably expanded. Over the years, more and more things could be owned, until finally even intangible things, like rights, were considered as property. Last, but not least, the right to acquire property freely and the right to use property as one pleases, were acknowledged to a greater and greater extent.

There were recognized different justifications for the act of acquisition. In earlier times, the idea was generally accepted that property resulted from occupation. This theory contains the germ of the idea that labor justifies property, since the act of occupation implies labor on the side of the occupier. In time, the labor theory replaced that of occupation. The idea that the acquisition of property was more or less accidental was replaced by the belief that property was a reward for diligence. The ethical connotation of property was thereby strengthened.

The increasing amount of value imputed to property was matched by an increase in the legitimization of property. The latter increase was closely connected with the elevation of individuals from the status of subjects to that of citizens. Whereas formerly property had received its highest sanction from natural law which was binding upon the rulers but did not afford the subject any enforceable claim, the consideration changed during the Enlightenment. Property rights, as ingredient parts of human freedom, came to be considered natural rights that could be claimed by the individuals against the government.

The institution of private property thus truly reflects the growth of civilization, a growth that is largely characterized by the expansion of freedom. This evolution reached a first climax in the latter part of the eighteenth century when the idea of the natural rights of man—including those of property—came to be universally accepted.

II

PROPERTY, FREEDOM
AND CIVIL RIGHTS

INTRODUCTION

IN THE preceding chapter, an attempt was made to show the respect which the concept of private property enjoyed. It appeared as an ethical institution, reflecting civilization and its progress. The relation of property to that main feature of civilization—freedom—must now be shown. But the investigation cannot end here. Trends have recently appeared to distinguish between the components of freedom, i.e., between property rights and so-called "civil" rights, and to emphasize that the latter are more of a prerequisite for democracy than the former. Since democracy is often identified with freedom, it is also asserted that "civil" rights are more important to freedom than property rights. In view of this development, it is imperative to examine whether these trends are sound. Therefore, not only the relation of property to freedom will be discussed, but also, its relation to the component parts of freedom.

The notion of freedom will be examined. Its major components and its relation to democracy will be dealt with. It will be shown that whereas the democratic rights to participate in government are generally conducive to freedom, they are nothing but a means for the attainment of freedom. As such, they are inferior to freedom and its component parts, i.e., the liberal rights of the individual which include those of property.

After democratic rights have been demonstrated to be inferior to liberal rights, then the position of property among liberal rights will be examined. It will be shown that property rights are original and natural rights, the importance of which has been recognized by early societies, by great documents of antiquity and of the Middle Ages, as well as by the modern democratic revolutions.

Discrimination against property rights, due to their alleged irrelevance for the democratic process, will be revealed as unjustified, not only because such discrimination contradicts our traditional concepts of freedom and civilization, but also because it was rejected by the very ideologies that constitute the source of our democratic credo—the ideologies of the democratic revolutions.

FREEDOM AND LIBERTIES

The freedom of men consists of particular, specific rights or liberties. These rights can be classified into two major categories, namely, the liberal rights to be free from coercion and the democratic rights to participate in government. Property rights, constituting a prominent part of the first group, are superior to the rights of the latter group.

As demonstrated elsewhere, the freedom of the individual comprises a great variety of liberties.[1] Freedom can be compared to a tree, and its parts, to the branches. And just as stem and branches are interdependent, so are freedom and its liberties. If too many branches are cut off a tree, it will wither and die. Similarly, if too many of the individual's rights are restricted, freedom will suffer. Where there is no freedom, there can be no liberties.

The fact that freedom consists of particular liberties has been generally recognized.[2] It is evident in the documents that highlight the continuous struggle of men for freedom. Although enumerating various rights, the Magna Carta as well as the English Bill of Rights are great charters of freedom.[3] The Declaration of Independence states clearly that the various rights which it enumerates are nothing but parts of that unalienable right—liberty.[4] After proclaiming liberty as a right of man, the French Declaration of the Rights of Man and Citizen specifies its various components.[5] The Virginia Bill of Rights of 1776 says that "all men are by nature equally free," and then states that they have "certain inherent rights." Likewise the oldest of present constitutions, that of the United States, after proclaiming the desire "to secure the blessings of liberty," proceeds to enumerate specific rights. The form of these classic documents, which distinguishes between freedom and its parts, has been followed by constitution-makers ever since.[6]

From what has been said it follows that property rights, as particular rights of the individual, can be only part of his freedom. Otherwise they would be equal, if not superior, to freedom, and the whole would be subordinated to the part. Although it can scarcely be claimed that without the institution of property we would have reached our present stage of civilization, and although it is evident that property and its blessings survived those who put it to creative use, we must never forget that men were able to acquire property and to create only because they were free. Our civilization, although to a great extent a result of the recognition of property rights, is above all, due to the existence of freedom. In a free society, property rights, important as they are, can never be an end in themselves. If they were, they could not be conducive to some further good, and we might be reduced to misers and live in misery.[7]

Since property is nothing but a part of freedom, its importance vis-à-vis freedom can scarcely be further enhanced. However, its importance can be emphasized by showing its relation to other liberties which are also mere parts of, and thus inferior to, freedom. For an equal status of property rights and of other liberties does not follow necessarily from their quality as parts of freedom. In fact, it has been maintained that property rights are inferior to other liberties.[8] The question as to whether such a position is sound will be examined in the following pages.

The liberties of the individual were not always felt to be of equal importance. Many of them were unknown at primitive stages of human development and could not be considered equal to those which were known. Only with the gradual progress of civilization, did men become aware of their rights. Thus the invention of printing created a desire for a free press, industrialization brought forth the right to strike and to work, and so on. The history of human rights shows how the awareness of a specific right usually resulted from attempts to restrict that right, and how such attempts were combated until the right was safe.[9]

This fact explains why the evaluation of various rights differed under changing conditions. Rights that appeared to be threatened were usually rated higher than those which were taken for granted. A person who, although able to do other things, cannot worship his own way, is probably more anxious to secure freedom of religion than any other liberty. Someone whose property is threatened tends to be interested in the protection of property rather than other rights. We want things we do not have, and do not so much appreciate what we possess.

A temporarily stronger appreciation of a particular right does not, however, change its enduring value. In an absolute sense, such a right is not more important than other rights. Freedom is so important and, at the same time, so vulnerable, that each one of its parts is essential to its existence. Consequently, no part can fall below a certain minimum standard of relevance. This is demonstrated by empirical evidence. Once a right, which during the struggle for its recognition had assumed an importance that appeared to be out of proportion to that of other rights, has won protection, then it loses its temporary significance. It becomes merely another right, an equal among equals.[10] Furthermore, certain liberties became so firmly established and were taken for granted to such a great extent that they seemed to be forgotten. Nevertheless, they retained their value. Whenever they were challenged, they were awakened from their dormancy and re-emerged in the foreground.[11]

Freedom cannot exist if only some rights are acknowledged. A government which guarantees freedom of religion is not free if it permits arbitrary arrests or interference with learning and discussion. Even if all these liberties enjoyed protection, still society would not be free if property rights were restricted. Likewise, the protection of property would be incompatible with free government if, for instance, freedom of speech was curtailed. Freedom also could not exist if any particular liberty were so expanded that it infringed upon another part of freedom. For example, if freedom of speech degenerated into the freedom of libel, or if the right to join unions eliminated the right to work, then freedom would be jeopardized. In a free society, all particular rights must be protected. Any expansion which makes them hinder other rights must be prevented. The protection of particular liberties exists for the sake of freedom, not for that of license; for the protection of freedom, and not for its limitation. This raises the questions as to what rights are necessary to freedom and whether there are rights which, although believed to be conducive to freedom, are not essential to it.

Freedom, considered freedom from coercion by individuals or institutions, is fundamentally something negative.[12] It signifies our freedom to act or not to act. We believe in God or not, or being more active, ask others to believe in God or not to believe; we may be idle or diligent and make little or ample use of our abilities; we may harbor political convictions, or communicate them to others. Thus our enjoyment of "negative" rights does not necessarily condemn us to passivity, but may open the way for action, opportunity and progress. "Negative" rights may thus imply something very positive. Therefore, we shall replace this possibly misleading term by a phrase which better expresses the idea of liberty, and refer to them as "liberal rights."[13]

These rights ought to be distinguished from so-called "positive" rights, i.e., the right to participate in government.[14] The latter are not as conducive to freedom as the former since they do not permit us to engage in a broad range of activities. They allow merely a few things, such as voting and running for public office. When we vote or run for office, we are bound by rules and regulations, and are aware of many restrictions.[15] Although suffrage gives us a sense of importance and flatters our egos, it does not provoke that feeling of freedom which we have when we enjoy such rights as freedom of religion, of speech and employment. Many of us, anxious to possess the latter liberties, consider voting a chore rather than a pleasure. Due to this attitude, countries have even felt obligated to punish non-voting.[16] In short, our rights to participate in government do not seem to be genuinely related to our freedom from coercion. It has been argued that the right to participate in government is the best means for securing freedom. This argument is for the most part true. However, although the right to participate is an important means for securing freedom, it is not infallible. There were many democracies which oppressed individuals.[17] "Positive" rights may thus imply something very negative. Therefore, we shall replace this rather misleading term by a phrase which better expresses the idea of participation in government, and refer to them as "democratic rights."

Although democratic rights will probably be conducive to freedom, they are, in contrast to liberal rights, no prerequisite for freedom. It would be absurd to maintain that Americans in the early days of the republic were less free than they are today or that Germans in the Empire enjoyed less freedom than under Hitler, although in both cases suffrage had greatly expanded. Likewise, it will not be questioned that resident aliens of the United States, although they do not have the right to vote, are as free as American citizens in the fifty states. The inferiority of democratic rights follows from still another consideration. Since government is a means for the protection of men, also popular government as well as its prerequisites—democratic rights—must be such a means. In fact, democratic rights were invented in hopes that they would assure the protection of liberal rights.[18] As a mere means for the achievement of certain ends, they must be inferior to those ends. Furthermore, since they were created by man, they cannot possess the value of liberal rights which are instituted by nature and by higher law and which exist prior to society and government.[19] Since free men created democratic rights for the sake of their unalienable liberal rights, it would be absurd to elevate what was instituted for the promotion of freedom over freedom itself.

The relation between democratic and liberal rights is sufficiently clear to preclude doubts about the superiority of the latter. However, a problem arises because of recent tendencies to discriminate among liberal rights themselves. A distinction has been made during the past decades between property and non-economic rights, including such rights as freedom of speech, of assembly and association, which are referred to as "civil" rights.[20]

This term already reveals the arbitrariness of the distinction. If non-economical rights are civil and are distinguished from property rights, then the latter, by definition, can't be civil. They might even be anti-civil or a-civil. They must be incompatible with civilization. But this is simply not the case. As was shown, each liberal right is essential to freedom. Liberal rights are so essential that all of them have to maintain a minimum standard. Consequently, none of them can be uncivil or acivil, since in those cases they would be incompatible with freedom, the very landmark of civilization. Therefore, property rights are as civil as other rights. The civil nature of property is also demonstrated by historical evidences. As was shown, throughout the ages, irrespective of such factors as the inequality or equality of men, religion, language, belief in natural, customary, or conventional law, property has been considered conducive and basic to civilization.

It is argued that the favoring of "civil" rights is justified on the grounds that these rights are most important for the functioning of democracy. This argument is easily refuted. Although it is admitted that "civil" rights are necessary for democracy, the reason why they should be more necessary for democracy than other liberal rights cannot be understood. Indeed, "civil" rights are no more required for popular government than are such rights as, for example, freedom from arbitrary arrest or execution. A person who has been executed has been deprived not only of his life, but also of his ability to participate in the democratic process. A man who is imprisoned is deprived not only of his freedom of movement, but also of his democratic rights. The situation is not different in the case of infringements upon property. A person who has lost his property usually does not have the same voice in public affairs as before. The loss has a damaging effect upon his prestige. The fact that he has become poor will adversely affect the exercise of his democratic rights. The person who is deprived of his property through legislation and not by his own fault nor by accident, is in a worse situation. A stigma becomes attached to his property. Doubts about its honest acquisition will be raised. He is not only punished through expropriation, but also through an impairment of his honor. Both lessen his effective participation in the democratic process. The clearest example of this situation occurs in communist countries where those who are expropriated are virtually reduced to second-class citizenship and are often excluded from participating in government. Although the deprivation of property in free nations does not assume such drastic forms and, as social legislation, appears to be more palatable, it signifies a difference in degree only from communist practice. Deprivations of property through social legislation are indeed as subtle as they are outrageous negations of that cherished principle, no punishment without law.[21]

The truth of the proposition that "civil" rights are more important for the functioning of democracy than are property rights is dubious from still another point of view. Those who prefer those rights because they are supposed to be conducive to the working of democracy, want, by their own admission, a *working* democracy. Their neglect of property rights is, however, apt to produce the very opposite. Overemphasis on such rights as freedom of speech, association and assembly will make men intoxicated with power and create those hallucinations about their political ability that often have resulted in anarchy and despotism.[22] A working democracy is an orderly democracy.[23] And order in a democracy is achieved to no small extent by permitting those who own property to have an ample share in government. Having something at stake, and in general being the more intelligent, industrious and progressive part of the population, their actions will not be motivated by passion, and they will not be apt to make experiments which might endanger the foundations of government and order. Therefore, only if private property enjoys the same degree of protection as "civil" rights, does there exist the guaranty for a working democracy.

The argument that such rights as freedom of speech, assembly and association are more important for democracy than are property rights is thus not convincing and not valid as a basis for assigning priority to the former rights. Even if one could not prove that property rights are as much a prerequisite for democracy as are "civil" rights; even if "civil" rights might be a more essential prerequisite, then a discrimination against property still would not be justified. For no discrimination against any liberal right can be justified on the grounds that that right is not a prerequisite for democracy. The decisive factor is compatibility with freedom, not with democracy. Otherwise, a means would be elevated over the end, and liberty might be lost.

The proponents of the idea that "civil" rights are more important than other liberal rights because they are more essential for the functioning of democracy defeat their own purposes. Instead of advancing the prestige of "civil" rights, they lessen it. Democratic rights are inferior to liberal rights. Therefore, an emphasis upon the fact that "civil" rights are more conducive to democracy cannot enhance their importance. On the contrary, if one stresses that such rights are more relevant for democracy, then he asserts that they are more democratic. This amounts to transforming liberal rights into democratic rights, degrading them from superior to inferior status, from an essential part of freedom to a mere prerequisite for that which is considered a mere means for the realization of freedom—democracy.[24]

This does not imply that property rights are necessarily undemocratic. None of the liberal rights are incompatible with democracy. They cannot oppose without difficulty a form of government which is likely to guarantee freedom. Since they permit positive action, they also allow for participation in government. Freedom of speech, for example, does not imply only the freedom to express one's thought merely for the sake of talking, but also the right to advance certain ideas for one's own benefit, or for that of society, and to participate in the shaping of public policy. The situation is similar in the case of other liberal rights, including those of property. The protection of private property does not imply merely something static. It also guarantees the free use of property to one's advantage as well as that of the public, and opens the way for the owner's participation in government. Since the protection of property frequently is believed to result mainly from egoistic motives, the blessings of property for the welfare of society are overlooked as often as the blessings of "civil" rights are overemphasized. The latter is due to the belief that these rights do not stem from egoistic considerations to any great extent. However, there is no compelling reason to believe that a man who uses his freedom of speech and association is less interested in his own advancement than a man who uses his property. Furthermore, it is not evident why freedom of expression or of rabble-rousing should be more valuable for the functioning of democracy than the ability to acquire and use property. Property rights as well as other liberal rights are not opposed to democracy. It is true that they are less likely to degenerate into democratic rights than are "civil" rights.[25] However, that relative immunity from democratic vogues does not make them necessarily undemocratic.

Thus the position of property in the scale of human rights is clear. Like other liberal rights, those of property are superior to democratic rights. Property rights do not occupy an inferior position among liberal rights and definitely are equal to so-called "civil" rights. As a matter of fact, one is tempted to ask whether or not property rights, being very important for civilization and as civil as any rights can be, being as relevant for a working democracy as "civil" rights, are superior to those rights. For they do not seem to be as prone, as are "civil" rights, to degenerate into mere democratic rights. They are thus, unlike "civil" rights, immune from being reduced to mere prerequisites for a means for the achievement of freedom, and are likely to remain an essential part of freedom.

THE VITAL IMPORTANCE OF PROPERTY RIGHTS

Property rights are very fundamental rights. This conclusion follows from an examination of the living process and of primitive associations.

Scholars have demonstrated that property is an institution of nature and prior to all human organization, and that its naturalness is evident in an examination of plant and animal life. Even the most primitive forms of life have been found to possess property. A plant has a particular piece of earth for its property, which is occupied by its roots. If deprived of its soil, the plant will die. A plant defends its property. Its roots protect the piece of ground which they occupy from invasions. Some plants protect themselves still more vigorously. Possessing thorns and bristles, or the capacity to secrete fluids which kill approaching animals, they protect the very space above the ground in which they grow. Thus on the most rudimentary level of life, property is essential to life itself, and protected accordingly.[26]

The situation is analogous in animal life. An animal has its cover, refuge, or cave as a prerequisite for its existence.[27] It defends this property. Whether vegetarian or carnivorous, animals have their own territory, and they keep out those that attempt to encroach upon it. Food is not only collected for immediate consumption, but often is stored and defended as property. The apiarist who takes honey from hives shields his skin to avoid being stung for a deprivation of property. Most of us have learned a lesson when trying to take away a dog's bone.

Finally, property is one of the first values of which men are aware. By instinct or reasoning, a child wants to have things. Primitive men have their dwelling and a territory on which they feed, be it through hunting or agricultural pursuits. They are prerequisites of their existence. A primitive man collects his livelihood in excess of what he can consume for the sake of "saving it for a rainy day" or for that of exchanging it for other goods. Aware of the value of his property and the necessity for its protection, he will put it in a safe place.

Property is essential also for freedom. The plant which is uprooted has not only its life endangered, but also, its freedom to grow is threatened. An animal deprived of food not only starves to death, but also lacks freedom of action. If a man is deprived of his property, then the development of his personality is retarded. It does not matter whether only his immediate necessities, or what he has stored for later consumption or exchange are taken away. Although depriving him of his immediate necessities threatens his life, the removal of any property would be just as detrimental, because it would threaten his free development and thus his freedom of existence.

Property is intimately related to life and freedom. It is a prerequisite of the freedom to be and to act. It is as old as life and freedom, and also as important. Property rights are thus distinguishable from such rights as freedom of religion, of speech, of the press, of assembly and association, freedom from arbitrary arrest, and so forth. For these rights were not present at the beginning of life. Furthermore, originally they did not enjoy a status equal to that of life and of freedom. It is not necessary to prove this assertion in the cases of plant and animal life. And it scarcely seems required with respect to man. While men may have been aware of the value of these rights at a primitive stage of their development, they did not consider them as immediate necessities for their existence.

The importance of property from a biological point of view is matched by its importance for society. It may be argued that the mere fact that property is a prerequisite for the survival of men and is thus a truly natural right, does not entail that the institution of private property must also be sanctioned once men have formed societies, since under the new conditions the survival of the species might be better secured under some form of communism or other regulations of property. As a matter of fact, it was asserted that a communistic form of society preceded the institution of private property. Laveleye in Belgium, Sumner Maine in England, and Friedrich Engels in Germany are among the major exponents of this theory.[28] They had many disciples.[29] But these men probably brought forth their ideas because they liked to indulge in generalizations or because such ideas fitted their social beliefs.[30] Recent research reveals different facts. Documentary evidence is far too sketchy to permit the generalization that communism was characteristic of old primitive societies. Even contemporary primitive societies usually recognize some form of private property.

The collectivism in old Egypt, China, and India, indicates nothing to the contrary. These societies resulted from a long evolution, and we have no proof that they accepted complete collectivism in the earlier stages of their development. Besides, there is evidence that they accepted the institution of private property.[31] As far as the early peoples of Europe are concerned, a number of historians reject the proposition that their societies were communistic.[32] Although there existed certain forms of public ownership in Greece, private property also was recognized, and in all probability preceded public ownership.[33] In Rome, private property was always recognized. The public land *(ager publicus)* never existed when private property was not also acknowledged. The former was permanently fed by conquests and constantly eaten up by the inroads of private property.[34] The Gauls allowed for private property, as also did the Germanic tribes.[35] Modern historical evidence suggests the type of ownership that is likely to be adopted under primitive conditions. In the French as well as in the English colonies in the new world, originally there was an extensive "no man's land" which was *res nullius* rather than *res communis*—nobody's rather than everybody's property. However, more and more plots of land became privately owned. It was only later that the state, becoming more firmly established in these virgin lands, seized some of the remaining no man's land as so-called public lands *(domaines publics)* which were nothing but interstices between sections of land which were privately owned. Thus private ownership preceded public ownership.[36]

Whereas the importance of private property was recognized in primitive societies, there is no evidence that other rights of the individual enjoyed similar protection. An exception to the above is the right to the security of life. A person could not arbitrarily be deprived of his life. Procedures existed also for the protection of the individual's physical freedom. But such rights as freedom of religion and conscience; of speech; of assembly and association were not recognized. The fact that private property enjoyed a recognition which was granted only to the physical freedom and to the life of the individual, indicates its importance.

THE IMPORTANCE OF PROPERTY IN MORE ADVANCED SOCIETIES

The relative importance of property is evident also in more advanced societies, and demonstrated by famous codes.

Whereas property rights were recognized as a major characteristic of our civilization, this acknowledgement is not prevalent in regard to other rights. The Decalogue is a case in point. It provides for the protection of life by commanding "Thou shalt not kill," and it grants the same degree of protection of our belongings by ordering, "Thou shalt not steal."[37] None of the other rights of men are mentioned. As a matter of fact, it is suggested that those rights might be rightfully restricted. The prohibition of apostacy and the statement that there is just one God amount to a denial of freedom of religion, a freedom considered by many the most important and fundamental of the individual's rights. The Decalogue's provisions appear to be symbolic. For the absence of freedom of religion seems to be as characteristic a feature of our civilization as the recognition of private property.

Greece is not famous for having championed religious liberty. In Rome, where private property enjoyed great protection, the early Christians were horribly persecuted.[38] The Christian church, which advocated private property, opposed religious freedom. Once Christianity became the religion of Rome, it withheld from heretics the liberty for which Christians of previous generations had fought. Augustine favored freedom of religion as long as heretics held a position of hegemony in Africa. Later, he attempted to consolidate orthodoxy. His doctrines became the foundation for persecutions in the name of Christianity.[39] Bluntschli remarked sarcastically that the Augustinian doctrine holds that when error prevails, it is right to invoke liberty of conscience, but when the truth predominates, it is just to use coercion.[40] And the truth consisted in that what the Church asserted to be true. Intolerance characterized the Middle Ages. In 1184, Emperor Frederick Barbarossa assured Pope Lucius III at Verona that the Church's attempts to preserve religious unity would have the support of the secular power. This agreement was supplemented by enactments in various countries during the centuries which followed. When St. Thomas and other scholastics stressed the value of private property, Popes Innocent III, Gregory IX and Innocent IV devised severe methods of religious persecution. When the Spanish doctors issued defenses of property, the inquisition raged. Vitoria justified the *conquista* by claiming that the Indians would be forced to convert to the Catholic faith.[41] Other nations experienced similar suppressions of religious freedom during the Reformation and Counter-Reformation. In Italy, Giordano Bruno and Galileo Galilei were martyred. The intolerance of the Catholic church did not change greatly in later days. As late as the nineteenth century, freedom of religion was opposed. Gregory XVI, in his encyclical *Mirari* of 1832, declared freedom of conscience in the lay sense to be nothing but the freedom to err. In 1864, Pius IX's *Quanta Cura* denounced freedom of religion as *libertatem perditionis*. It was condemned in the Syllabus of that year. Leo XIII, an advocate of private property in his encyclicals *Quod Apostoli Muneris* and *Rerum Novarum,* in *Libertas Protestantissimum* acknowledged freedom of speech, writing and instruction in religious matters only if it served the truth as conceived by the Roman church.

Nor did the Protestants, who also had advocated private property, favor religious tolerance. They were intolerant not only of Catholics. Their major groups, engaged in a life-and-death struggle with the Catholic church, counteracted internal tendencies that threatened disintegration, and imposed standards of conformism which were scarcely more flexible than those imposed by Rome. This occurred even in places where Protestant groups were not immediately challenged. In New England, for instance, the Puritans abandoned the idea of religious liberty for which their ancestors had fought in spite of the relative security from inimical churches. The intolerance of a Nathaniel Ward and a John Winthrop testify to this fact.

Even during the Enlightenment, when property rights received high sanction, freedom of religion, although it became more and more recognized, did not win general approval. Milton favored toleration for Protestant sects, but not for the more radical nonconformists and Catholics. The era's greatest defender of private property, John Locke, was not very enthusiastic about religious freedom. His *Letter Concerning Toleration,* frequently praised as a defense of religious freedom, is a qualified defense only. Locke claimed that liberty of conscience and of worship are natural rights. However, he excluded from the blessings of religious freedom people who professed politically subversive ideas or atheism, and thus opened the way for state intervention in ecclesiastical affairs. Rousseau's "civil religion" was as intolerant in form as that of the existing churches.[42]

The attitude of Catholics, Protestants and enlightened thinkers was matched by the laws of temporal authorities. The compromise of Augsburg of 1555, under which the subjects had to confess the religion of their rulers, was not abandoned for some time. The Edict of Nantes, issued by Henry IV of France in 1598 and granting freedom to the Huguenots, was revoked by Louis IV of France in 1685. Although Elizabethan England permitted recusants to worship in private, they were deprived of certain rights. Later, in the seventeenth century, when religious animosities grew, the situation became worse. Dissident Protestants and Catholics were suspected not only because their ideas conflicted with those of the Anglican church, but also because the anti-absolutist beliefs of the nonconformists and the papism of the Catholics were considered dangerous to the Stuart regime. Cromwell's constitution, while protecting property rights as well as securing freedom of worship for Protestant sects, still was intolerant of Catholics.[43] The Declaration of Indulgence of 1672, although revealing a more conciliatory attitude toward Catholics, did not grant them full equality. Similarly, the Act of Toleration, issued by William III in 1689, discriminated against them. Other governments also were reluctant to recognize religious freedom. Joseph II of Austria permitted only limited rights of worship to the followers of the Augsburg and Helvetic confessions and the Uniate Greek church in his Patent of Toleration. The Prussian Territorial Code of 1794 guaranteed equal privileges to the Lutheran, Reformed and Catholic churches, but withheld similar rights from other religious groups.[44]

The Ten Commandments cannot be justly blamed for the religious intolerance throughout history. Although its provisions probably facilitated that intolerance, other factors also must have influenced it. If there had existed an urgent desire for religious freedom, then that freedom would have become established at an early stage. However, whereas the necessity for a protection of life and of property was recognized, that for freedom of religion was not acknowledged. Likewise, it would be unfair to blame the Decalogue for not mentioning other rights of the individual. On the other hand, that omission was not conducive to a future protection of these rights since it seemed to imply their irrelevance or non-existence. Yet, if there had existed an urgent need for the protection of such rights as freedom of speech or assembly, then they would have been recognized in the same way in which property rights were acknowledged. Furthermore, the Decalogue is not the only classic document that, while protecting life and property, did not command respect before other rights.

The situation is the same with regard to the classic English charter of liberty in the Middle Ages. The name *Magna Carta Libertorum*—great charter of liberties—should not suggest incorrect conclusions with respect to the actual content of the charter. Not by any means are all the rights of Englishmen mentioned in it. The veneration it later enjoyed provoked interpretations of its clauses which would have surprised the drafters. "Seventeenth century lawyers, ignorant of the law of the early 13th century, knowing nothing of the conditions of the time, saw in the charter a solemn grant to the people of England of rights which the Stuart kings were withholding. Trial by jury, the principle of habeas corpus, the right of parliament to control taxation, all these were thought to have been secured by Magna Carta. Even the great historians of the 19th century wrote of the charter with more enthusiasm than judgment."[45] Actually, neither the rights mentioned above are listed in the charter, nor are more modern rights, such as freedom of religion, speech, assembly or association. On the other hand, Magna Carta abounds with statements securing property rights. It provides that justice be done in the case of wrongful dispossessions by the monarch, and that illegal fines be remitted. No constable or bailiff is to take a man's corn or other chattels without immediate payment. No sheriff, bailiff or other person shall take a freeman's horses or carts for carriage duty. Neither the king nor his bailiffs are permitted to take a man's timber for castle-building or any other royal work. The land of the debtor is not to be seized if the debtor has sufficient chattels to pay the debt. The debtor's sureties are not to be distrained as long as the debtor himself can pay. If the sureties are called on they are to hold the debtor's land until their payment has been restored to them. No scutage or aid is to be taken without the matter being brought before the feudal council of tenants in chief, except for the ransoming of the king's body, the knighting of his eldest son or the first marriage of his eldest daughter.[46] In view of all these recognitions of the rights of private property one is tempted to ask whether or not the provision of clause forty, "To no one will we sell, deny, or delay right or justice," primarily amounts to a protection of property rights. At any rate, the high rank assigned to these rights is obvious in clause thirty-nine: "No freeman shall be taken, or imprisoned, or disseised, or outlawed, or exiled or in any way destroyed, nor will we go upon him, nor will we send upon him, except by the legal judgment of his peers or by the law of the land." Property is valued as highly as life and physical freedom!

In spite of the fact that they both emphasized the protection of life and property and neglected other rights, the Ten Commandments and Magna Carta show differences which indicate an increasing recognition of human rights from antiquity to the Middle Ages. The Decalogue only mentions the rights of life and property. Magna Carta mentions many more. Although it omits several of the modern rights of Englishmen and emphasizes those of life and property, it protects many other rights. Thus freedom of movement is guaranteed and is extended to foreigners.[47] It is provided that amercements are to be in proportion to the seriousness of the offence. In the case of grievous crimes, they are not to be so heavy that they deprive the offender of his means of livelihood. Writs of enquiry touching life or limb shall be granted freely. No one is to be arrested upon the appeal of a woman for the death of any other than her husband.[48] The relatively greater appreciation of life and property in Magna Carta can probably be concluded from the fact that, in contrast to the framing of the Decalogue, these rights are described in greater detail. Although it may be debatable whether or not short commands like "Thou shalt not kill" or "Thou shalt not steal" are better guaranties of life and property than the wordy phrases of Magna Carta, it can, on the other hand, be argued that the detailed prescriptions of the English charter indicate that these rights were so generally accepted and were taken for granted to such a great extent that one could offer instead of short, slogan-like phrases, more detailed descriptions of how these rights would be protected.[49] Finally, the greater protection afforded to human rights by Magna Carta is evident in the fact that whereas the Decalogue restricts an important right like freedom of religion, Magna Carta refrains from putting restrictions upon the rights it mentions.

The tendency toward a more comprehensive recognition of human rights continued after Magna Carta. In spite of the general atmosphere of intolerance, freedom of religion was by no means rejected by everyone. Maximus of Madaura had defended it at the time of Augustine. Marsilius of Padua, living shortly after Innocent III and Thomas Aquinas, favored it, as also did the monarchomarchs and Bodin at the time of the inquisition. In the Netherlands, Grotius inspired the first edict of toleration that was promulgated by the States General in 1614. A hundred years later, Bayle published his important work on universal tolerance. In the meantime, the Arminian Baptists, headed by Hanserd Knollys, had promoted the idea of religious freedom in America. In 1644, Roger Williams had published *The Bloudy Tenant of Persecution*, and, nineteen years later, Rhode Island had attained religious freedom.[50] Similar tendencies could be observed in Europe throughout the seventeenth century. Protestant groups, or the governments influenced by them, had shown a great amount of intolerance. However, the Reformation stimulated the desire for freedom and, challenging religious orthodoxy, advanced the cause of religious liberty.

The increasing emancipation of men was not confined to the religious sphere. Freedom of speech and the press, for some time as severely restricted as freedom of religion, also became more and more recognized. Although the works of heterodox writers were proscribed by the Apostolic Constitutions and were opposed by the Council of Nicea; although indexes of prohibited books were issued by the papacy from 1559; although censorship was established not only in the Catholic world, but also by temporal governments; yet there existed the desire for free speech and for freedom of the press. Finally, these rights were guaranteed by the governments of the various states. As one author said of freedom of speech and the press: "Milton anticipates it, but Locke, Voltaire, Rousseau, Wilkes, Paine, Camden, Erskine and Jefferson are of it, while Cobbett, Carlile and Mill carry on its issues."[51]

Besides freedom of speech and of the press, other rights were increasingly recognized and protected. Habeas corpus, freedom of assembly, and any other particular rights—all of them were considered essential parts of human freedom. However, the acknowledgement of more and more parts of freedom did not impair the recognition of property rights. But the names of Milton and Locke, Voltaire and Rousseau, Jefferson and Paine suggest revolutions which played an important part in the emancipation of men. Therefore, we will now examine how property fared in relation to other liberal rights in these revolutions.

PROPERTY AND LIBERAL RIGHTS IN THE
DEMOCRATIC REVOLUTIONS

Private property was recognized as being at least equal to other liberal rights in the English, American and French Revolutions.

Property is valued in the documents which resulted from the struggle against absolute monarchy in England, namely, the Petition of Right, the Instrument of Government, and the Bill of Rights.

Significantly the Petition of Right, drafted in 1628 under the guidance of Sir Edward Coke, quotes only that clause of Magna Carta that, more than any other provision of the famous charter, demonstrates the parity of property with life and liberty: "No freeman may be taken or imprisoned or be disseised of his freehold or liberties, or his free customs, or be outlawed or exiled, or in any manner destroyed, but by the lawful judgment of his peers, or by the law of the land." Illegal taxation is denounced at the beginning, and at the end of the enumeration of complaints the fact that people have been unjustly condemned and subsequently executed is mentioned. Thus the impairment of property and deprivation of life form the framework for the denunciation of the king's abuses. In the middle portions of this document, arbitrary imprisonment and the billeting of soldiers are criticized. The same order of enumeration is employed in the actual petition to the king: "That no man hereafter be compelled to make or yield any gift, loan, benevolence, tax or such like charge, without common consent by Act of Parliament; and that none be called to make answer, or take such oath, or to give attendance, or be confined, or otherwise molested or disquieted concerning the same, or for refusal thereof; and that no freeman, in any such manner as is before-mentioned, be imprisoned or detained; and that your Majesty will be pleased to remove the said soldiers and mariners, and that your people may not be so burdened in time to come; and that the aforesaid commissions for proceeding by martial law, may be annulled; and that thereafter no commissions of like nature may issue forth to any person whatsoever, to be executed as aforesaid, lest by colour of them any of your Majesty's subjects be destroyed or put to death, contrary to the laws and franchise of the land."

Although in the 1640's the Puritan revolution resorted to bloodshed and abolished the monarchy, it did not oppose the institution of private property. Cromwell's Instrument of Government, issued in 1653, demonstrates that fact. The document assigns a superior position to property rights. Aside from property, only one right is mentioned, namely, freedom of religion. Although the latter is expanded for Protestants, it is considerably restricted for members of other confessions.[52] On the other hand, even though article eighteen of the Instrument of Government established property qualifications for the right to vote, yet it does not restrict property rights. Article six prescribes that no tax, charge, or imposition shall be laid upon the people without the consent of Parliament. Article thirty provides that money for the armed forces must be raised by Parliament. Article thirty-nine appears as a bulwark for vested rights.[53] Since the Instrument of Government mentions only the right of property and that of religion, and since the latter right is restricted whereas the former is not, property rights seem to rank the highest among liberal rights.

In the Bill of Rights of 1689, property rights are considered equal to other rights. First, James II is accused of having endeavored to subvert and to extirpate the liberties of the English. Among such accusations as raising and keeping a standing army in time of peace without the consent of Parliament, quartering soldiers contrary to law, having prosecuted people in the Court of King's bench, for matters and causes cognizable only in Parliament, disarming Protestants, demanding excessive bail from persons committed in criminal cases and eluding the benefit of the laws for the liberty of the subjects, permitting excessive fines and illegal and cruel punishments, there can be found the accusation that the king arbitrarily infringed upon the property of his subjects "by levying money for and to the use of the Crown, by pretence of prerogative, for other time, and in other manner than the same was granted by Parliament." Property rights appear similarly in the latter part of the Bill, where the "ancient rights and liberties" of Englishmen are reaffirmed. Among clauses providing for more religious freedom and for the right of Protestants to bear arms, and prohibiting the raising and keeping of standing armies in time of peace, and the requisition of excessive bail or the imposition of excessive fines or the infliction of cruel and unusual punishments, there can be found the provision "that levying money for or to the use of the Crown, by pretence or prerogative, without grant of parliament, for longer time or in other manner than the same is or shall be granted, is illegal." At the end, the Commons pledge themselves to maintain their Majesties "to the utmost of their powers, with their lives and estates."

The American Revolution, largely influenced by the Whig revolution, recognized the importance of property among liberal rights. This is evident in the Declaration of Independence, the bills of rights of the states, and the Constitution.

Property rights occupy a prominent position in the Declaration of Independence. The "pursuit of happiness," meaning mainly the free acquisition, possession and use of property,[54] is proclaimed as one of the unalienable rights of man at the very beginning of the Declaration, besides those of life and liberty. Even if one does not accept the idea that the pursuit of happiness means the protection of property, property rights still appear to be valued as equal to other rights. First, it could be claimed that they are included in that other unalienable right proclaimed at the outset—liberty. Obviously liberty, meaning the individual's general liberty, in the absence of specific exclusions, would embrace all the particular liberties of men, including the rights of property. Second, property rights are ranked on a par with other liberal rights in later passages. Thus the accusation that British officers harass the colonists is mentioned in the same breath as the complaint that these officers eat out the colonists' substance. The statement that British troops are not being punished for murdering Americans is followed by a note that the king extinguished the colonists' trade with other parts of the world. The complaint about the imposition of taxes without consent is followed by one about the deprivation of the benefits of trial by jury. The king "has plundered our seas, ravaged our coasts, burnt our towns, and destroyed the lives of our people" is written in another passage which indicates that property is considered as valuable as life itself. Finally, the very last sentence of the document states that the colonists pledge their lives, fortunes and honor to support the Declaration.

Occasionally, the Declaration of Independence is considered to favor the poor over the rich and a "fair" distribution of property rather than its protection. It is said that the statement, "all men are created equal," elevates equality over freedom. However, this is hardly the case. "Life, liberty and the pursuit of happiness" are considered unalienable rights of man, while equality is not. The most significant principle of the Declaration is not equality, but freedom. And nowhere in this document can there be found any indication that the value of property is not equal to any of the particular liberties which the Declaration asserts.

The parity of property with other liberal rights is also evident in the bills of rights which were adopted by the new states. The classic example of Virginia is a case in point. In its first section, "the enjoyment of life and liberty, with the means of acquiring and possessing property," are proclaimed as inherent rights of men. Apart from this general statement, property rights are valued equally with other rights in the more specific clauses which follow. Section six provides that men "cannot be taxed or deprived of their property for public uses, without their own consent, . . . nor bound by any law to which they have not, in like manner, assembled, for the public good." Laws which infringe upon property are considered as detrimental as laws which interfere with other rights! Under section eleven, trial by jury is prescribed not only in criminal cases, but also "in controversies respecting property, and in suits between man and man."

Similar provisions can be found in the bills of rights which were adopted by other states. Also here, property ranks with liberty and life as an inherent right of man.[55] Controversies over property enjoy the privilege of trial by jury.[56] No less can a person be deprived of his property than can his life or liberty be taken away from him.[57] Property is as secure from search and seizure as the person is.[58] Every member of society is entitled to enjoy his property as much as his life and liberty.[59]

The equality of private property with other liberal rights thus is evident in the wording of specific articles. However, the fact that these articles are just a few among many other provisions securing various liberties, such as freedom of religion, speech, the press, also demonstrates the truth of this assertion. The bills of rights do not suggest that property rights are inferior to these liberties. The egalitarian character which frequently has been attributed to the early state constitutions is not present in their bills of rights.

Finally, property appears as an important right in the Constitution of the United States, a right that is definitely on a par with, if not superior to, other liberal rights. Although the word "property" is not expressly mentioned in the preamble, nevertheless the protection of property is included in the statement regarding the aims of the people. The assertion that the Constitution is ordained and established to secure the blessings of liberty implies that property should be protected, for "liberty" is a general concept and includes all particular liberties which are not specifically exempted. It includes property rights. The intent of the framers to protect property in the preamble can be concluded also from the declaration that a more perfect union is formed in order to establish justice and insure domestic tranquility, since these values, at the time at which the Constitution was framed, were threatened mainly by actions which were endangering property rights.[60]

The protection of property can be seen also in the articles of the Constitution. Section nine of article one, besides providing for the writ of habeas corpus and prohibiting bills of attainder and ex post facto laws, prohibits arbitrary tax laws. The following section is even more outspoken. Keeping the states from passing bills of attainder and ex post facto laws, it prohibits also, due to infringements upon property through state legislation, the passage of laws impairing the obligation of contracts.

Finally, property, like such rights as freedom of religion, speech, the press and of assembly as well as the right to keep and bear arms and to be free from cruel and unusual punishment, is protected in the amendments of the Constitution. Following the pattern set by some of the states, the United States bill of rights grants under the fourth amendment the same degree of protection from search and seizure to property as it does to the person of the individual. The right of trial by jury is not only guaranteed for criminal prosecutions, but also for suits at common law which involve property.[61] The fifth amendment, besides making provision for indictment by grand jury, and guaranteeing protection against double jeopardy and self-incrimination, states that no person shall "be deprived of life, liberty or property, without due process of law." Later, this "due process clause" was made applicable to the states in the fourteenth amendment.

While there can be no doubt that throughout the Constitution property rights are valued as highly as other liberal rights, it could be argued that they were even dearer to the framers than were such rights as freedom of religion, speech and assembly and other liberties mentioned in amendments, because their protection was already provided for in the original text of the Constitution.

The great document of freedom produced by the French Revolution is the Declaration of the Rights of Man and Citizen of 1789.[62] It protects property as much as other liberal rights.

As Americans had drawn upon the ideas of the Whigs, the French were influenced by American political thought. The colonists' struggle with the mother country was followed with interest. Frenchmen not only rallied to the American cause by enlisting in the new nation's armed forces, but, upon their return home, also helped to acquaint their compatriots with ideologies which had developed on the other side of the Atlantic.[63] Books on the United States were printed.[64] These influences came to bear upon the formulation of the Declaration of the Rights of Man and Citizen.

Earlier drafts show that property was considered equal to other liberal rights. Condorcet mentioned the safety and liberty of property along with personal safety and liberty.[65] Mirabeau's declaration of rights of 1788, besides guaranteeing freedom of speech, the press, of public meeting, the right of speedy, free and impartial justice, provides for protection from attacks upon person, house, papers and property, from banishment or deprivation of life, liberty and property.[66]

Property rights were not neglected in the deliberations of the Constituent Assembly. Lafayette, back from America, suggested a bill of rights which was modeled after that of Virginia. He included property among the unalienable rights of man, next to freedom of opinion, the care of honor and life, the entire disposition of his person, business and faculties, the free communication of thought, the pursuit of happiness and the right to resist oppression.[67] Mounier's proposal differed only slightly from that of Lafayette. It added provisions concerning the prohibition of ex post facto laws, arbitrary arrests and fines, and guaranteeing freedom of religion and of the press, but the proposal did not minimize the protection of property.[68] The plan advanced by the Abbé Siéyès maintained that each man is the sole proprietor of his person and free to exercize his faculties. Freedom of thought and of the press are guaranteed. Men may engage in any occupation, dispose of their property as seems best, and go or remain wherever they please.[69] Finally, the report of the Committee of Five, a committee composed of Mirabeau, Demeunier, De la Luzerne, Rhédon and Tronchet, protects property as much as other liberal rights. The individual's right to employ his powers, his industry, and his property appears as protected as is his liberty of thought and expression. Property is no more under the jurisdiction of the general will than is the person. It is as safeguarded under law as is liberty. Besides guaranteeing resistance to unlawful oppression, public trial, legal forms of accusation, arrest and imprisonment, punishment according to law and in proportion to the offence, the right of free movement, of petition, of public meeting—it protects private property.[70]

In the Declaration of the Rights of Man and Citizen itself, property rights appear to be as natural, unalienable and sacred as other liberal rights. After the first article has affirmed that men are born and continue free and equal in their rights, article two states that the end of all political associations is the preservation of the natural and imprescriptible rights—liberty, property, security and resistance to oppression. In the following articles, various rights of the individual are specified. Arbitrary accusations, arrests and confinements, cruel punishments and punishments under ex post facto laws are prohibited. Freedom of religion, speech, writing and publication, are guaranteed. In the last article of the Declaration, property is considered inviolable, sacred and protected from arbitrary interference. Of all the rights mentioned in the document, only property is declared "inviolable and sacred." It is mentioned, with liberty, security and resistance to oppression, among the "natural and imprescriptible" rights of men. Furthermore, unlike other rights, property is referred to twice, and is mentioned in the most conspicuous passages of the Declaration, at the beginning and the end.[71] No further proof is needed to demonstrate the importance of property among the rights which are enumerated in the Declaration!

The Declaration of the Rights of Man and Citizen has been considered a document of egalitarianism. It cannot be doubted that the idea of equality is prominent in it. However, one should remember that, like the slogan of the revolution, "Liberty, Equality, Fraternity," the first article of the Declaration mentions the idea of freedom before that of equality; that in the second article, equality is not mentioned among the "natural and imprescriptible" rights of men, said to be the end of all political association; and that the most egalitarian provision of the Declaration, article six, does not aspire to an equality that could be interpreted to mean an equal distribution of property. On the contrary: When it stipulates the equality of all men before the law, it also recognizes distinctions that are due to virtue and talent.

CONCLUSION

The great documents of the democratic revolutions, be they written in the seventeenth or eighteenth century, in England, America or France, consider property rights as being definitely equal to such other liberal rights as freedom of speech, the press and assembly. This fact is not surprising. By assigning property rights a position which is not inferior to that held by other rights, the democratic revolutions merely recognized what was obvious and had been hallowed throughout the ages, namely, that property was a natural right, a prerequisite of life and freedom. This attitude reflects approval not only of natural law, but also of custom. For although the overthrow of the *ancien régime* meant rejection of many traditional institutions, nevertheless the institution of private property survived. It proved to be too natural and too essential to life and freedom to be rejected. It was considered as being too intrinsic to civilization—and thus too civil—to be discarded. Furthermore, since the democratic revolutions instituted democracy merely as a means for the protection of freedom, their ideologists did not maintain that the fact that some rights are more relevant to democracy than others implies that the former are more valuable than the latter.

Accordingly, the very events which led to modern democracy support our assertion that property rights are as important a part of freedom as are other liberal rights, not to mention their superiority over democratic rights. Therefore, the distinction between property rights and so-called "civil" rights and the assertion that the latter are entitled to greater protection because they are more necessary for the working of democracy, are unwarranted not only because they misconceive the nature of freedom, disregard the nature of man, and do not take into account the experience of ages, but also because they were rejected by the very people that are usually quoted in their support, namely, by the founders of modern democracy.

III

THE RISE OF PROPERTY IN THE NINETEENTH CENTURY

INTRODUCTION

By THE END of the eighteenth century, the appreciation of property reached a climax. The Reformation had freed the individual to pursue his own religious beliefs and, through its unfaltering protection of private property, its stress upon the ethics of work and its elevation of wealth to a God-willed institution, provided men with extra incentive toward working for greater and greater progress. Still, men had not yet become fully liberated. Authoritarianism in the temporal sphere continued to exist. Consequently, the following generations fought for a further emancipation of the individual. As far as property rights are concerned, people felt that their protection should be comprehensive and not imply merely the right to acquire and possess, but also the right to use property freely. However, there existed considerable restrictions on the latter right until the second part of the eighteenth century. The idea of an unrestricted use of property became generally accepted only after the publication of Adam Smith's *Wealth of Nations*. The appearance of that work in the very year in which the American Revolution— the first major revolt against colonialism and probably the most property-conscious of the modern democratic revolutions—began is no mere coincidence.[1] It is symbolic of the fact that the free acquisition and use of property are as much essential ingredients of free property as is the safety of static property. At that time, property can be said to have come of age. It was defended as a natural right. It was considered necessary

65

on utilitarian grounds. It was conceived to be an essential part of freedom.[2] Last, but not least, its free use had received a classic defense.

In view of this, it was unlikely that property would receive additional sanction. The nineteenth century assimilated the heritage of its predecessor and made the most of it. The fruits of experience, produced by past generations and sometimes involving sacrifices, were now consolidated. The ideas of prior defenders of property, having influenced the formation of eighteenth century thought, persisted in the nineteenth century. A century that was made aware of Greek values by Winckelmann was not likely to overlook the Aristotelian concept of property. Roman law with its protection of property was appreciated in centuries that were on the whole inimical to the freedom of the individual, and thus was not likely to be rejected after freedom had been established in the democratic revolutions.[3] Christian thought on property, having survived the challenge of the Enlightenment, was apt to be welcome in the century of the *bourgeoisie*.[4] Needless to say, the ideas of the Enlightenment and of the democratic revolutions had their own impact. Accordingly, the century is like a receptacle of ideas on the defense of property which were ripened throughout the preceding centuries. As the century of liberalism in which the freedom of the individual attained great dimensions, the nineteenth century abounds in statements of the value of private property.

It would be wrong to believe that property was entirely protected during that period. As in previous centuries, it was often challenged. After all, there were many people who saw in the French Revolution with its emphasis upon the superiority of the general will, primarily a signal for a thorough egalitarianism. Nevertheless, the forces favoring a protection of property maintained the upper hand. From among these forces, some are of a mainly theoretical, others of a mainly practical kind. Among the former, new schools of thought played a major role. The more practical acknowledgement of property can be seen particularly in legislation, adjudication and jurisprudence.

DEFENSE BY VARIOUS SCHOOLS

Private property was defended by utilitarians, idealists, by the historical school, and the adherents of *laissez-faire*.

Probably the outstanding utilitarian was Jeremy Bentham. Generally speaking, he consolidated the ideas on the desirability of property on grounds of utility by making Hume's statements more palatable to the public. "Secure to the cultivator the fruits of his labor, and you probably have done enough," Bentham wrote in his *Principles of the Civil Code*.[5] He stressed that a workman should enjoy the rewards of his work and that the achievement of equality was of secondary concern. Like Hume, he rejected the equal division of wealth as absurd. Afraid of egalitarian revolutions, Bentham emphasized that any existing system was better than the anarchy that would result from its subversion.[6] Other utilitarians were as emphatic as Bentham in their defense of private property.[7]

The utilitarians' advocacy of property was matched by that of the idealists. In his *Principles of Political Right,* Kant maintained that justice, although based upon equal rights, also requires inequality of possessions because these are the rewards for unequal talents.[8] Hegel advanced similar thoughts. He held that justice means inequality of property because the natural inequality of men requires them to have unequal amounts of property so that they might realize their fullest development. The individual achieves external freedom by means of the appropriation of things. Thus, property is essential for the liberty of the individual. All systems proposing some form of common ownership restrict that liberty. Hegel felt that the destruction of monasticism and feudalism were great triumphs for freedom, because they permitted more people to own property.[9]

Property was also defended by the historical school. Toward the end of the eighteenth century, Edmund Burke had defended private property with historicist arguments. He felt that an equality of mankind is a "monstrous fiction," that inequality of possessions is inherent in human society and could never be removed.[10] It is something "which the order of civil life established as much for the benefit of those whom it must leave in a humble state, as those whom it is able to exalt to a condition more splendid."[11] Property is a prerequisite of civilization,[12] and conducive to the common welfare. Consequently, Burke defended property on a broad scale, irrespective of how it is acquired or abused.[13] Property, he argued, is sanctioned by prescription, "the most solid of all titles, not only to property, but which is to secure that property, to government."[14] Its confiscation "cannot be justified under any form it may assume," even if it occurs under the pretext of serving the public good.[15]

In a similar manner, property was defended by the historical school on the continent. Characteristically, its outstanding representative, von Savigny, believed in Roman law. Recognizing that legislation might be dangerous to traditional values, among which those of property figured prominently, Savigny opposed codification.[16] He denied that property could be defended on any *a priori* principles or on grounds of natural law, but held that this was not actually detrimental to its protection, since property was safe under the rule of tradition and prescription. Savigny's school exercised a great influence. In England, one of its outstanding followers was Sir Henry Maine. Writing after Savigny's death, at a time when the controversy about ownership in primitive societies was at its height, Maine advanced the argument that private property is synonymous with civilization and progress. "Nobody is at liberty," he wrote, "to attack several property and to say at the same time that he values civilization. The history of the two cannot be disentangled. Civilization is nothing more than a name for the old order of the Aryan world, dissolved but perpetually reconstituting itself under a vast variety of solvent influences, of which infinitely the most powerful have been those which have slowly . . . . substituted several property for collective ownership."[17]

The school of *laissez-faire* provided another defense of private property. For fundamentally, it supports the idea that men can use their abilities freely in order to attain property, and employ their property according to their ability for the sake of increasing their wealth. *Laissez-faire* was conceived when people struggled to free themselves from the bonds of the *ancien régime* with its limitations upon the free development of the human personality. It signified a reaction to Colbertism and mercantilism as well as to restrictions imposed by local customs and guilds. Mercier de la Rivière, a physiocrat, advanced the idea that the world would improve through the free use of one's own ability and property.[18] In a similar vein, Adam Smith felt that such free play corresponded to the "natural order" and to "natural liberty."[19] In the nineteenth century, *laissez-faire* achieved its greatest popularity. It was identified with the progress of the industrial age. In England, it found expression in the Manchester School and Cobdenism, and was advocated by Ricardo and McCulloch, by the two Mills and Herbert Spencer. Its major repre-

sentatives in France were Say, Dunoyer and Bastiat as well as de Tocqueville, Prévost-Paradol and Tarde. Later in the century, the doctrines
of the Austrian school, headed by Menger and Böhm-Bawerk, were
conducive to *laissez-faire* views.

Due mainly to Herbert Spencer, the idea of *laissez-faire* exercised a
great influence upon the United States.[20] Spencer stoutly defended free
property. In his *Social Statics,* he even attempted to excel Locke. He
argued against the latter's statement that the earth and all inferior
creatures are common to all men, on the ground that it might challenge private property. Also, he criticized Locke's idea that a claim
to property exists only "when there is enough and as good left in common for others," saying that "a condition like this gives birth to such
a host of queries, doubts, and limitations, as practically to neutralize
the general proposition entirely."[21] Thus Spencer recognized the importance of a clear title and of an unrestricted right of property. Denying Proudhon's proposition that property is theft as absurd, Spencer
was not content to recognize property rights merely with regard to physical objects, but advocated also the right of property with respect to
ideas.[22] With this qualitative as well as quantitative advocacy of private
property, Spencer, who was strongly influenced by Darwin, emphasized
that property should be used freely and that *laissez-faire* is something
very natural. Feeling that society requires security for life, liberty and
property, he resented all state interference that might endanger these
values. His *Social Statics,* "an attempt to strengthen *laissez-faire* with
the strict imperatives of biology, was intended as an attack upon . . .
the positive role of legislation in social reform."[23] Spencer felt that state
interference would be detrimental to freedom and progress, even if it
came from representatives of the people. He proposed a return to natural
rights. Everyone ought to be free to do as he pleases, as long as he does
not interfere with the equal rights of others. The only function of the
state is to insure this freedom.[24]

The emergence of utilitarianism, idealism and the historical school due
to a reaction against natural law does not mean that the followers of these
schools entirely rejected the idea of natural law. A utilitarian will be
unable to detach himself completely from the notion that what he sup-
poses to be useful does not also possess a higher sanction, nor will he
want to claim that it does not. Even if he restricts such a sanction to
positive law, he could not absolutely reject higher law without difficulty,

since frequently it is hard to distinguish between what is right under positive law and what is sanctioned by higher law. An idealist is in a similar situation. It is doubtful whether idealism and higher law can be precisely distinguished from one another. With regard to the historical school, it is difficult to see how something sanctioned through the ages would not also enjoy the blessing of nature and God. Also *laissez-faire* was probably a result of rather than a reaction to the natural rights school, and thus was not likely to challenge the idea that free property is a natural right. In summary, it may be said that the philosophies of the nineteenth century discussed above, be they conceived as a reaction against the *Naturrecht* of the preceding century or not, did not detract from the high evaluation private property enjoyed at the end of the eighteenth century. On the contrary, they enhanced that evaluation.

The encyclicals issued in the latter part of the nineteenth century sound like a *résumé* of the various doctrines that stressed the need for a protection of property. They range from a refutation of common ownership as being unnatural, to the advocacy of private property because such property is sanctioned by nature and by society, because it gives man incentive, serves human progress, creates the ability to do good to others, and is essential to freedom. In 1878, Pope Leo XIII wrote in his encyclical *Quod Apostoli Muneris* that the church enjoins that the right of property and of its disposal, being derived from nature, should in every case remain inviolate. His famous encyclical of 1891, *Rerum Novarum,* states: "The fact that God has given the earth for the use and enjoyment of the whole human race can in no way be a bar to the owning of private property. For God has granted the earth to mankind in general, not in the sense that all without distinction can deal with it as they like, but rather that no part of it was assigned to anyone in particular, and that the limits of private possession have been left to be fixed by one man's own industry, and by the laws of individual races." Each man, it continues, "makes his own that portion of nature's field which he cultivates—that portion on which he leaves, as it were, the impress of his individuality; and it cannot but be just that he should possess that portion as his very own, and have a right to hold it without anyone being justified in violating that right. . . . Hence it is clear that the main tenet of socialism, community of goods, must be utterly rejected, since it . . . is directly contrary to the natural rights of mankind. . . . Men always work harder and more readily when they work on that which belongs to them; nay, they learn to love the very soil that yields in response to the labor of their hands, not only food to eat but an abundance of good things for themselves and those that are dear to them." "It is surely undeniable that, when a man engages in remunerative work, the impelling reason and motive of his work is to obtain property, and thereafter to hold it as his very own. If one man hires out to another his strength or skill, he does so for the purpose of receiving in return what is necessary for the satisfaction of his needs; he therefore expressly intends to acquire a right full and real, not only to the remuneration, but also to the disposal of such remuneration, just as he pleases."

Against this background, great practical acknowledgements of property occurred in the nineteenth century. These acknowledgements are present in most of the countries of the West. However, the following discussion shall be confined mainly to three nations which reflect the major systems of law, namely, France as an example of a civil law country; Germany as an example of a nation with a combination of customary and codified law; and the United States as an example of a common law country.

PROTECTION THROUGH LEGISLATION AND ADJUDICATION

In France, Germany and the United States, property was granted far-reaching protection by legislation and adjudication.

The French Revolution emancipated man from the bondage of the *ancien régime*. It considered private property as an inviolable and sacred right.[25] In spite of tendencies toward a more equal distribution of property and in spite of the attacks on the vested rights of institutions believed to be representative of the *ancien régime,* this fundamental attitude remained unchanged throughout the revolutionary period. Tendencies of the workers to bring about an equal distribution of property were not supported to any great extent. The rising of the egalitarians, headed by Babeuf, foundered. It merely made people aware of the dangers of egalitarianism and increased their desire for a firm government which could protect property. It aided the ascent of Napoleon Bonaparte to power.[26]

Napoleon did not disappoint the proprietors. At the turn of the century, he established a commission to draft a civil code, and presided over the majority of its meetings. In 1804, the code was promulgated. Due to the part the emperor had played in its formulation, it received the name *Code Napoléon*. This code was created by men who believed that private property is so sacred that it should be respected even by the sovereign. It was framed in order to secure the protection of free property.[27]

The Civil Code deserves its description as "code of property."[28] Provisions covering property constitute the largest part of the law. They occur everywhere, and not merely in the parts which are expressly concerned with property. "For its framers, the right of property was the cornerstone of the social system. All rights, *in rem* as well as *in personam*, the manner of acquiring them and of losing them, the rules of inheritance, contracts, including prenuptial agreements,—all these topics are organized in relation to the rights of property, although this is often poor logic."[29] Even logic, the most characteristic feature of French codification, was sacrificed to property.

The Civil Code freed property from the shackles of the *ancien régime*. Under the old law, for instance, the ownership of real property was divided into that held by the lord who kept the eminent domain and the rights following therefrom, and that held by the tenant, who had the right to enjoy the property. Also, the rights of ownership, of lords as well as of alodial owners, were greatly restricted by family rights. A certain portion of land could not be given away, either among living persons or by will; estates in the nature of fee tail were generalized; powers of pre-emption were vested in the family, even for conveyances for consideration. Generally, the power of alienation of the owner was limited by numerous restrictions. Similarly, property controlled by the church was governed by special rules of ownership which removed them from the channels of commerce. The Civil Code eliminated these restrictions to a great extent. By a truly "revolutionary approach," it rid the French law of property of all the previous complications inherent in feudalism.[30]

In line with the abolition of feudal restrictions, the Civil Code grants property broad protection. Security from the public power is guaranteed by article 545, which reads quite similarly to article seventeen of the Declaration of the Rights of Man and Citizen. It states that "property implies the right to enjoy and dispose of things in the most absolute manner, provided one does not use it in a way that is prohibited by laws and regulations." The proprietor possesses not only the right to use and to draw fruit but also the right to abuse.

The code's validity did not remain confined to France. It was introduced into states that were dominated by France, such as Belgium, the Netherlands, Luxembourg, Monaco, and Germany.[31] In all these nations, the code survived the defeat of Napoleon. Even where new civil laws were adopted, like in Belgium and the Netherlands, the influence of the Civil Code remained. The code's ideas were adopted also by states which were independent of France. They can be seen in the civil codes of Louisiana (1825) and Quebec (1866), in the Italian *Codice Civile* of 1865 as well as in the Spanish *Codigo Civil* of 1889. The influence of the masterpiece of Napoleonic legislation can be noticed also in the Balkans, in Egypt, Latin America, and Japan.[32] Napoleon could very well state on St. Helena: "My true glory is not to have won forty battles. .... What nothing will efface, what will live forever, is my *Code Civil*."[33] His importance as a legislator has been likened to that of Justinian, and the reception of the Napoleonic Code to that of the Roman law.[34] This appeal of the Civil Code has been due mainly to the same reason as that of the Roman law: it provides for a widespread protection of free property.[35]

Such protection also became a keynote of German legislation. After some steps had been taken by the Bavarian Maximilian Code of 1756, the trend to emancipate and protect property continued throughout the nineteenth century.

The high evaluation of property found expression in the first major codification, the General Land Law for the Prussian States of 1794. That law was conceived by Frederick the Great.[36] This monarch, who had said that the king was the first servant of the state and that it was the citizen's first obligation to serve his country,[37] who was a symbol of the fulfillment of one's duty toward the state, whose way of life strongly inspired German idealistic philosophy—had great respect for property.

The introduction to the Prussian code proclaims that "the general rights of man are based upon his natural freedom to further his own well-being so long as he does not interfere with the rights of someone else." Private property is considered in accordance with this principle. Even the state—and we must keep in mind that this was the "absolute" Prussian state—found its limits at property rights. The law provides that the state can restrict the property of its citizens only if it serves to prevent great damage to others and the state, or to gain them considerable advantage, and if it does not result in any disadvantage to the proprietor. Private property could also be restricted if the advantages to the state or other citizens were out of proportion to the disadvantages suffered by the proprietor. However, a full and prior indemnity for losses always had to be paid. The restriction of any right connected with property was considered a restriction of property and had to be specified. In the absence of such specification, each use of property was legal. The proprietor could dispose of the substance of an object or a right irrespective of others. He could possess, use, or give up property.[38] A few restrictions upon certain types of property are exceptions which do not question the law's capacity to protect property rights.

Like the Prussian code, the General Civil Law Code of Austria stressed the idea of the freedom of the individual. Following Kant, its drafter Franz von Zeiller stated that the freedom to act constituted the law in the subjective sense and that restrictions of freedom are permissible only if they served to enable others to pursue their aims as free citizens.[39]

The comprehensive protection of freedom is evident in the provisions concerning property. They establish the principle of the owner's absolute power over his property. He may arbitrarily dispose of the substance and fruits of a thing, and exclude others from it. He may use his property arbitrarily, or not at all, or destroy, transfer, or desert it.[40] Although section 364 stipulates that the right to use one's property is limited by the rights of third persons and by the laws providing for the public weal, the Austrian code in section 358 provides that restrictions on property by the owner or the law, resulting from a division of property, shall not do away with the completeness of property. In distinction to Prussian law, the Austrian code does not even prohibit the use of property to the detriment of others. No duties to cultivate the soil are stipulated. No restrictions are imposed to assure that the use of property would be conducive to the public good. "Although many changes of property, brought about by the owner," commented von Zeiller, "can be a great nuisance, a great disadvantage, and really very unfair, as long as the owner keeps within the bounds of his own territory and does not interfere with the person or natural freedom of others, or encroach upon others' property or threaten their rights, he cannot be accused of illegal actions and not be restricted in the disposal of his property, even if he acted out of sheer pleasure to do harm to others. Such a reproach is to be adjudged by conscience. Thus the proprietor may build on his ground as he desires. He may heighten the building even if this deprives his neighbor of a view and of light, or he may change it or let it deteriorate."[41] Aside from eminent domain, "the owner's arbitrary use of his property finds its bounds only by the sphere in which someone else could act arbitrarily"—by the property rights of others.[42]

Certain feudal institutions, involving mainly real estate, were not regulated by the Prussian and Austrian codes. In these cases, property was still restricted in as much as some people could not acquire it. However, the ideas of the French Revolution were not unnoticed east of the Rhine. People felt a need to emancipate property from feudal restrictions. Consequently, during the first decades of the nineteenth century, laws were passed that made the acquisition of any kind of property possible for all men.

Prussian legislation was characteristic of that trend. The first important law was the Edict Concerning the Facilitated Possession and Free Use of Real Estate as well as the Personal Conditions of the Rural Population of 1807. Its introduction stressed that justice and the principles of a well-ordered political economy required the abolition of all obstacles which until then had prevented the individual from acquiring as much property as he could through freely using his abilities. Section one provides that every inhabitant has the right to own all kinds of real property, that the nobleman may possess not only noble, but also unnoble, bourgeois and peasants' property, just as peasants may possess not only bourgeois, peasants' and other unnoble grounds, but also noble estate. Now everyone could own any kind of real estate. Similar to the situation in France,[43] real property became liberated. The owner could dispose of such property with less difficulty and others could acquire it more freely. Moreover, the Edict provided for the abolition of other restrictions.[44]

Hardenberg's Edict for the Improvement of Land Culture of 1811 emancipated property to an even greater extent. It eliminated some of the remaining restrictions on real estate. Every owner could dispose of his grounds freely as long as he did not interfere with the rights of third persons. He was permitted to increase or decrease his property through unrestricted buying or selling or other legal means. Appurtenances could be left to one or more heirs, exchanged, given away or disposed of in some other manner. It was felt that an unlimited right to dispose of property was the safest way to prevent an owner from falling into debt. In case an owner needed money, he could sell as much property as he desired. Moreover, it was argued that the parents would have the desirable and blessed liberty of distributing their land among their children as they wished. People trusted that an unrestricted freedom to dispose of one's property was a safe way of instilling in the owners a desire to improve their estates. As bad as the forced sale by an impoverished peasant was, it was felt that in such a case the property would be cared for better by the new proprietor, whereas it would have deteriorated under the former, careless, owner. The liberty to sell and buy was matched by the right to use real property freely. Provisions concerning the cultivation of land were abolished. The Edict stated that forests can be treated as the proprietor saw fit. They can be divided or transformed into farm land. Farm land can be transformed into forest or subjected to other changes.[45]

Besides these two major pieces of legislation, other laws for the emancipation of property were passed to complete what significantly was called *Befreiungsgesetzgebung*—"liberation-legislation."[46] This legislation provides a good example of the way in which property was freed from the restrictions of the feudal order. Other German states followed suit.[47] The idea of the inviolability of private property was maintained not only in civil codes, but as will be shown later, also in constitutions. Thus, although Germany was not a political entity, the Germans were united in a liberalism which was expressed to a great extent in a belief in free property. The idea of freedom was ingrained more deeply in the German mind than that of unification.[48] For whereas the problem of unification constituted the "German Question" of the century, the belief in free property, having been recognized by the main contenders for the political leadership of Germany as well as by smaller states, never posed any "question." Most Germans, no matter where they lived, knew that freedom required the expansion of property rights. Consequently, it was natural that once the country had become united and the need for a German civil code recognized, the new codification was as emphatic about the protection of private property as the legislation of the *Länder* had been. The Civil Law Code of the Empire (BGB.) became another code of property.

The desire to make the new codification such a code was evident from the beginning. The commission that was set up to draft the code was directed "to examine the private law in Germany for its expediency, inner truth and consistency, to find out, especially in the case of major existing legislation, whether deviations from the principles of Roman law that would meet the requirements of modern juridical science are justified."[49] Thus the main purposes of the commission were to maintain the principles of the property-conscious Roman law and to draft a bill that met the requirements of a juridical science that believed in those very principles. Although the suggestion of the first draft, to permit the proprietor to dispose of his property arbitrarily, was changed to read that he could dispose of it as he desired, the representative of the government, Planck, who later edited an outstanding commentary to the BGB., emphasized that the right to freely dispose of one's property was inherent in the very idea of property.[50] The strong position property enjoyed in the final draft is so evident that Rudolf Sohm, a romanist who represented the government at the first reading before the Reichstag in 1896, could state: "Freedom of property—absolutely necessary for all of us. Of this freedom, we live. Our whole public and moral liberty, which we possess as individuals, the most precious legal good we have, is made possible by private property, by free private property, alone! . . . Free property! We have finally achieved it. The nineteenth century has given it to us in all respects. It will be the basis for all future development."[51]

In accord with the professed purposes of the commission, the final draft secured a comprehensive protection of property. Section 903 provides that "the proprietor can do with his property as he wishes and exclude others from exercising any influence upon it, as long as his actions do not interfere with the law and the rights of others." The latter qualification was not intended to state that property could be subjected to restrictions, but, rather, to emphasize that "the exclusive power of the proprietor is unrestricted as long as it cannot be proved that it is restricted."[52] As a matter of fact, the importance of the qualifying clause was seen in the presumption of the principle of an absolute protection of property. It was argued also that the clause expressed the elasticity of property in so far as property rights would increase automatically if existing restrictions were abolished.[53] Section 903 reveals the attitude of the entire code toward property. Apparently clauses providing for restrictions of property rights were adopted reluctantly as concessions to the principles of Germanic law. They have a marginal character and present exceptions to the general rule that favors an absolute protection of property.[54] Like the Austrian code, adopted in the beginning of the nineteenth century, the German BGB., framed at its close, expresses the individualism of the Roman law as well as the prevailing desire for individual freedom.

The representative German codifications of the nineteenth century had an impact beyond the territory for which they were devised. An influence of the Austrian law is visible in the Serbian civil code of 1844, and in some of the Swiss cantons. When Lombardy and Venetia were under Austrian rule, their civil law was mainly that provided by the Austrian code.[55] The German BGB. influenced codification in Japan, the Balkans, and Latin America.[56]

The protection of property, which was accomplished in France and Germany mainly through legislation, was effected in America by means of adjudication. The American Constitution, adopted partly for the protection of private property, was interpreted as an instrument for such protection during the nineteenth century. The major vehicles for that interpretation were its contract and due process clauses.

In the first half of the century, property rights usually received protection under the contract clause. As early as 1787 John Marshall wrote to Joseph Story, his future colleague on the bench, that he considered the clause that no state shall pass any law impairing the obligation of contracts to be of "high value."[57] As Chief Justice, "by employing a far broader conception of contract than had been prevalent in 1787, and by combining this conception with the principles of eighteenth-century natural law, he was able to make of the contract clause a mighty instrument for the protection of the rights of private property."[58] It has been suggested that he did so in order to promote national power. It is probably more correct that the great disciple of Hamilton believed that the protection of property was of primary concern. Like Hamilton, Marshall considered a more perfect Union as a means for securing the rights of the individual, among which those of property figured prominently.[59] He never altered his opinion. Toward the end of his career, Marshall was a "supreme conservative" rather than a nationalist, a man who wanted protection of property more than anything else.[60]

Several opinions reveal Marshall's desire to protect property. In Fletcher v. Peck, he proclaimed the doctrine that a state may not rescind its grants. This case involved problems as to whether a law could be a contract; whether such a contract, in view of the fact that a state was a party to it, would fall under the contract clause; and whether that clause would apply to executed contracts as well as to executory ones. Desiring to protect property rights, Marshall answered all these questions in the affirmative.[61] In particular, his answers to the last two questions show his broad interpretation. The framers of the Constitution had not suggested that the clause would cover contracts to which a state was a party. Marshall knew that their apprehensions that state legislation would be inimical to property were concerned only with legislative interference in private contracts.[62] Moreover, the Federalist Papers did not state that the contract clause would cover public contracts.[63] Nevertheless Marshall, asserting that the words of the Constitution "are general and are applicable to contracts of every description,"[64] maintained that public contracts are ruled by the contract clause. He even supported his idea by asserting that the framers were concerned about legislative infringements upon private property prior to the meeting of the Federal Convention! Marshall's dictum that an executed contract is subsumed under the contract clause amounts to a similar *coup de force*. The usual interpretation of the obligation of contract had been that it implied an obligation to fulfill the terms of an executory contract only.[65] As if he wanted to make sure that property would be protected, Marshall was not content with relying merely on the contract clause. He had recourse also to more general principles of justice, saying that "it may well be doubted whether the nature of society and of government does not prescribe some limits to the legislative power; and, if any be prescribed, where are they to be found, if the property of an individual, fairly and honestly acquired, may be seized without compensation?"[66]

In New Jersey v. Wilson,[67] Marshall, once again motivated by the desire to protect property, extended the application of the contract clause further, going beyond the scope which Hamilton, whose opinion[68] had served as a guide to the decision of Fletcher v. Peck, had allowed it. The question raised in New Jersey v. Wilson was as to whether a legislative act, providing for perpetual exemption from taxation of a tract of land granted to the Indians in colonial times, could be revoked after the Indians had sold the tract. In spite of the fact that the power of taxation is indispensible and vital for every state, "Marshall was so desirous of placing limitations upon state legislatures to the end of protecting the vested rights of property"[69] that he held that the land was immune from taxation.

In Terrett v. Taylor, decided in 1815, the Marshall court protected property rights by denying that the state of Virginia could appropriate lands of the Episcopal Church. Although the court did not expressly base its decision on the contract clause, it did so by implication.[70] Once again the protection of property was bolstered by the principles of natural justice. The court stated: "But that the legislature can repeal statutes creating private corporations, or confirming to them property already acquired under the faith of previous laws, and by such repeal can vest the property of such corporations exclusively in the state, or dispose of the same to such purposes as they may please, without the consent or default of the corporators, we are not prepared to admit; and we think ourselves standing upon the principles of natural justice, upon the fundamental laws of every free government, upon the spirit and letter of the constitution of the United States, and upon the decisions of the most respectable tribunals, in resisting such a doctrine."[71]

The contract clause was expanded further in the Dartmouth College case. In Fletcher v. Peck there had been a contract, although an executed one. Also, in New Jersey v. Wilson, a contract could be discerned to exist between the Indians and the colonial government. Although in these cases the application of the contract clause was not possible without an extensive interpretation of that clause, nevertheless it could be done without great difficulty. However, a different situation arose in the Dartmouth case, where the question was as to whether a charter granted by the crown was a contract. Certainly, the framers of the Constitution had not considered that possibility. However, in order to give property and vested rights protection, Marshall stated that the charter is a contract: "It can require no argument to prove that the circumstances of this case constitute a contract. An application is made to the crown for a charter to incorporate a religious and literary institution. In the application it is stated that large contributions have been made for the object, which will be conferred on the corporation as soon as it shall be created. The charter is granted, and on its faith the property is conveyed. Surely, in this transaction, every ingredient of a complete and legitimate contract is made."[72]

The work of Marshall was continued by his successor, Roger B. Taney. It has been argued that the transition from the Marshall to the Taney court can be compared to that from the Federalists to the Republicans a generation earlier. But just as it is dubious whether Jefferson was less interested in the protection of private property than John Adams, it can be said that Taney was scarcely a weaker defender of property than his predecessor had been. One can criticize the statement that "Jacksonian judges from agrarian states broke the historic safeguards thrown around property rights by the letter of the Constitution and the jurisprudence of John Marshall."[73] Due to Taney's continued application of the contract clause in favor of property, "the contract clause was a more secure and a broader base for the defense of property rights in 1864 than it had been in 1835."[74] Taney usually followed Marshall's interpretation of the clause. In as much as he was not the originator of its sweeping interpretations, he was not likely to become as appreciated as a defender of property as his predecessor had been. The Taney period is "one of consolidation and application" of the principles developed by Marshall.[75] However, as such, it is no less important for the protection of property than the Marshall period had been. The Charles River case is usually assumed to mark a radical departure from Marshall's property-friendly interpretation of the contract clause. But, besides the fact that this is the only decision that "represents anything approaching a major break with the Marshall tradition,"[76] it is doubtful whether a major break was really achieved here. One should not forget that the often cited dictum, "while the rights of private property are sacredly guarded, we must not forget that the community also have rights, and that the happiness and well-being of every citizen depends on their faithful preservation,"[77] is mere truism. In society, no right, including that of property, is absolutely protected. Still, Taney believed that property rights are "sacredly guarded." Infringements upon those rights were considered to be exceptional. This attitude remained unchanged throughout his tenure. Taney cherished property as much as Marshall had before him. Under the Taney court, the contract clause was applied more frequently and to a wider variety of subject matter than had been the case in the Marshall period. The number of cases in which the unconstitutionality of statutes was based upon the contract clause is almost exactly the same in the two periods.[78]

Under the contract clause, private property received a greater protection than the Founding Fathers had conceived. However, the protection of property by the judges did not cease here. Extended as the application of the contract clause was, it was not unlimited. As is inevitable in the judicial process, Marshall and Taney had established definite rules regarding the applicability of the clause. State legislatures had passed reservation clauses reserving the right to repeal charters of incorporation, and to levy taxes.[79] Although originally these restrictions to no small extent were due to a belief in the sacrosanctity of vested rights, they later were used to restrain the court's doctrines within desirable limits[80] and thus became restrictions on property. Therefore, since the urge for the protection of property continued to exist, the judges felt a need to base that protection on a basis that was broader than that provided by the contract clause. Consequently, the Supreme Court turned to the clause according to which no person could be deprived of his life, liberty and property without due process of law. And just as Marshall, desiring to protect private property, had given the contract clause a more comprehensive interpretation than that conceived by its framers, now the Court, motivated by the same desire, interpreted the due process clause in a truly novel manner. It shifted from procedural to substantive due process. This shift went beyond the orthodox common law concept of due process. It went beyond the Founders' idea of due process of law. It marked a departure from the Court's own traditional conception of due process.

In 1856, the newly established New York Court of Appeals declared invalid a prohibition law because it entailed, in regard to liquors in existence at the time of its enactment, an act of destruction of property that was not within the power of the government to perform "even by the form of due process of law."[81] A few months later, Taney rendered his famous Dred Scott decision in which he used the due process clause of the Constitution to protect property in slaves.[82] Thus the man who had rendered the decision in the Charles River case, through his substantive interpretation of due process, built a bridge from the protection of property under the contract clause to that under the due process clause! And just as one may say that Marshall laid the foundation for Taney's protection of property under the contract clause, so Taney's Dred Scott decision now provided the basis for the future protection of property under the due process clause.

The Supreme Court continued to provide property with broad protection and used substantive due process to a great extent. Confronted with governmental regulations of private business, it stated that the power of the government to regulate is not without limits and that it is not a power to destroy.[83] It declared that "there are, of necessity, limits beyond which legislation cannot rightfully go. . . . If, therefore, a statute purporting to have been enacted to protect the public health, the public morals, or the public safety, has no real or substantial relation to those objects, or is a palpable invasion of rights secured by the fundamental law, it is the duty of the courts to so adjudge, and thereby give effect to the Constitution."[84] In 1894, the Court declared that rates fixed by a commission are invalid, and claimed the power "to inquire whether a body of rates prescribed by a legislature or a commission is unjust and unreasonable, and such as to work a practical destruction to rights of property, and if found so to be, to restrain its operation."[85] In all these cases, and in many more which concerned the regulation of business, the Court based its control of the public power upon substantive due process.

However, the Supreme Court did not apply the due process clause only for the protection of existing property. Originally, the term "property" implied an ownership that was "exercised in its primary and fullest sense over physical objects only."[86] In due time, however, it was applied to other elements of ownership. It tended to merge more and more with the indefinite rights of "liberty." Following the urging of influential members of the American bar and the lead given by some of the state courts, the Court adopted the view that the word "liberty" as used in the fifth and fourteenth amendments was intended to protect freedom of contract.[87] Towards the end of the century, Justice Peckham stated that "liberty" in the due process clause "means not only the right of the citizen to be free from the mere physical restraint of his person, as by incarceration, but the term is deemed to embrace the right of the citizen to be free in the enjoyment of all his faculties; to be free to use them in all lawful ways; to live and work where he will; to earn his livelihood by any lawful calling; to pursue any livelihood or avocation, and for that purpose to enter into all contracts which may be proper, necessary and essential to his carrying out to a successful conclusion the purposes above mentioned."[88] By means of this extended concept of liberty, a greater defense of property was allowed under the doctrine of substantive due process.[89] From the application of the contract clause in the first half of the century to the adoption, toward the end of the century, of the idea that freedom of contract is an essential part of liberty, the basis for the protection of property had been strengthened to an extraordinary degree.[90]

The increased protection of property under the due process clause does not mean that no other constitutional provisions were applied toward that purpose. In the Sugar Trust case, for instance, the Court temporarily shelved the Sherman Anti-Trust Act of 1890 by invoking the commerce clause.[91] In the same year, it set aside the Income Tax Act of 1894 by stating that a tax on income derived from property was a direct tax that Congress could impose only by the rule of apportionment according to population.[92]

Throughout the nineteenth century, the Court's devices were many.

Its desire to protect property, on the other hand, was constant. By the turn of the century, American judges had rendered justice to the hopes of the Founding Fathers that private property, an unalienable right and an important part of freedom, would be protected.

PROTECTION THROUGH JURISPRUDENCE

The protection of property through legislation and adjudication was supported by jurisprudence.

In the United States the Supreme Court was not the only advocate of free property. Although it was probably the most decisive factor for promoting the protection of property, other forces also worked toward the same goal. Outstanding among them were the great writers in the field of jurisprudence.

James Kent is a case in point. The man who in 1799 had exhorted his younger brother to "be an enlightened and intrepid guardian of true old English and common law liberty and constitutional security,"[93] was rather partial to the Roman law because of its strong protection of private rights.[94] Above all, he was interested in the protection of property. "To this intricate subject he devoted the greater part of his treatise,"[95] the *Commentaries on American Law* (1826-30). Although Kent admitted that slavery was evil,[96] he, believing that "time, self-interest and reflection will gradually undermine domestic slavery," felt that the property of the slave owners should not be molested.[97] In view of this defense of property in human beings, his antagonism against an equal distribution of property in things is scarcely surprising. He took issue with modern theorists "who have considered separate and exclusive property and inequalities of property as the cause of injustice," and felt that "human society would be in a most unnatural and miserable condition if it were possible to be instituted or reorganized upon the basis of such speculations." "The sense of property," he stated, "is graciously bestowed on mankind for the purpose of rousing them from sloth, and stimulating them to action; and so long as the right of acquisition is exercised in conformity to the social relations and the moral obligations which spring from them, it ought to be sacredly protected. The natural and active sense of property pervades the foundations of social improvement. It leads to the cultivation of the earth, the institution of government, the establishment of justice, the acquisition of the comforts of life, the growth of the useful arts, the spirit of commerce, the productions of taste, the erections of charity and the display of the benevolent affections."[98] To insure that property would not be abridged too much for the public welfare, Kent carefully prescribed narrow limits for governmental regulation of the use of private property.[99] He opposed tax discrimination against the lands of the absentee proprietors, as well as unequal taxation, saying that "every person is entitled to be protected . . . from all unequal and undue assessments on the part of government."[100] He condemned as pernicious the regulation of wages by the government, relegating it to the same category as sumptuary measures which in his opinion "are calculated to destroy the stimulus to exertion."[101] "A state of equality as to property is impossible to be maintained," he wrote, "for it is against the laws of our nature; and if it could be reduced to practice, it would place the human race in a state of tasteless enjoyment and stupid activity, which would degrade the mind and destroy the happiness of social life."[102] Liberty, he maintained, "has very little concern with equality of property."[103] Kent's ideas on property were realized in decisions he rendered as a judge.[104]

Kent's defense of private property was matched by the other great commentator of his time, Joseph Story. In the Supreme Court, Story had been a staunch supporter of John Marshall, and made statements that were as good as any that were made in defense of property.[105] In 1821, he wrote Marshall on the situation in his home state Massachusetts: "Considering the popular cant and popular prejudices, I have some fears that we shall not have wisdom enough to maintain ourselves upon the present decided basis that protects property."[106] He voiced concern about Taney's decision in the Charles River case, feeling that it did not protect property as much as it should have. His disposition in favor of property also found expression in his *Commentaries*. In his remarks on the contract clause, Story quotes with approval the forty-fourth essay of the Federalist Papers with its strong denunciation of legislative activities that are inimical to property rights, and gives a broad interpretation of the clause.[107] Having praised the provision that no person shall be deprived of his property without due process of law, he writes on the concluding clause of the fifth amendment which provides that private property shall not be taken for public use without due process of law: "This is an affirmance of a great doctrine established by the common law for the protection of private property. It is founded in natural equity, and is laid down by jurists as a principle of universal law. Indeed, in a free government, almost all other rights would become utterly worthless, if the government possessed an uncontrollable power over the private fortune of every citizen. One of the fundamental objects of every good government must be the due administration of justice; and how vain it would be to speak of such an administration, when all property is subject to the will or caprice of the legislature, and the rulers."[108]

Thomas M. Cooley was as staunch a protagonist of private property and vested rights as were Kent and Story. However, unlike these jurists who were inclined to protect the rights of the individual under natural law, Cooley, revealing himself as an adherent of the historical school, felt that limitations upon governments were derived from prescriptive rather than from natural law. Although his doctrine resulted from a reaction to the natural rights school, he could not free himself from the values of that school. For its principles, having been transmuted by the Founding Fathers and the judges into positive law, had become part of the historically sanctioned law when Cooley wrote. Maintaining that "the right to private property is a sacred right,"[109] Cooley placed "emphasis upon property as opposed to personal rights."[110] This fact is evident in his *Constitutional Limitations*.[111] As a judge, feeling that the taxpayer's property should not be burdened for the support of certain private institutions, he had denied the power of the legislature to authorize municipalities to raise money in aid of railroads through taxation.[112] Furthermore, Cooley deplored the growing tendency toward government regulation and control of private business.[113] "To him, the granting of exclusive privileges to corporations and the denying to the individual of the right to pursue the ordinary avocations of life, except as the licensee of some board or organization, were generally objectionable on constitutional grounds, and as against the best interest of society. It is easy to understand how a man, who had, of necessity, lived a life of self-reliance, dependent only on individual effort, should guard jealously the rights of private property and personal liberty."[114] He considered the rights of property and freedom of contract to be equal to such unalienable rights as the rights to life, liberty and the right to form the marital relation. He "deplored the advent of a paternalistic government, which he believed despotic and intolerable in America."[115]

From Gersterding in the beginning of the nineteenth century to Windscheid-Kipp at its end,[116] the German representatives of *Pandektenwis-*

senschaft held fundamentally identical concepts of property. Adherents of the Roman law, they considered property unrestricted and exclusive by definition. Property rights were to be "complete" and "general," and to confer absolute power over a thing. It was maintained that property afforded any power possible from nature and law, that it included all rights that conceivably could exist over a thing, that it constituted the full legal subordination of a thing under the will of a person—that it was "the fulfillment of the law."[117] The proprietor was granted extraordinary powers. He was permitted to use his property arbitrarily for his egoistic purposes, to dispose of it according to his free arbitrary decision, and so on. The idea of the free will of the proprietor and his right to exercise it in an arbitrary manner, was always emphasized. It was stressed that the owner possessed the right to destroy his property.[118] Whereas some writers endeavored to enumerate the various rights of the proprietor for the sake of demonstrating his comprehensive power, others felt that, in view of the totality of property rights, it would not be possible to have a complete enumeration.[119] The idea of a total protection of property even led some authors to believe that the status of an owned thing was equal to that of a person and that, contrary to other rights, property rights were physical since their object was tangible. Moreover, it was asserted that property in land included ownership of what lay underground as well as complete jurisdiction over an infinite air column above the ground.[120]

Although the Romanists admitted that property could be restricted, they emphasized that restrictions did not alter the inherent principle of the freedom of property. A limitation was considered as something unnatural and contrary to the rule, as an artificial exception.[121] Windscheid defined property as the "negation of the restriction."[122] In cases of doubt, free property was always assumed. Its curtailments were to be interpreted narrowly. They were "temporary arrestments" which did not detract from the conceptual totality of property rights, a totality that would re-emerge as soon as the arrestments no longer existed. The "elasticity" of property was emphasized. In order to make it clear that the principle of the absolute protection of property was not abolished in spite of existing limitations, authors created new terms for their definitions of property.[123]

In accordance with this somewhat absolutistic concept of property, the assertion that the possession of property implied duties was denied. Property could be used even if it caused damage to others.[124] Savigny admitted that the moral law prescribed that the rich should regard their riches as a trust. However, he quickly added that the legal order was free from moral considerations. "As far as property relations are concerned," he wrote, "the rule of law is carried out well even if no consideration is given to the question whether a right is exercised morally or immorally. . . . Property rights being dealt with by private law, have nothing to do with morals. By maintaining this proposition, we do not deny the unqualified rule of moral laws; however, neither do we expose the nature of private law to ambiguities."[125]

Due to their belief in the unrestricted and exclusive use of property, the Romanists rejected institutions like that of divided property or of rights of several persons over one thing. "What really belongs to one," one of them said, "cannot at the same time belong to someone else. One thing can, therefore, always belong to one person only. It is inconceivable that each of several persons could be the owner of the whole thing. Similarly, property in one thing cannot be divided among several people."[126] Divided property and common ownership were considered contradictions in terms.

For the sake of securing the protection of private property, German jurists, in spite of all the nationalism and patriotism that existed during and after unification, did not hesitate to give a Romanistic interpretation to those institutions of Germanic law that had survived the reception of the Roman law, institutions which favored a restriction of private property for the public good. One author, writing during the Third Reich, believed that this individualistic attitude was disliked by the people, and complained that life and social conditions were adjusted to theoretical concepts of law rather than vice versa.[127] Be this as it may, it shows that the German jurists of the nineteenth century endeavored to protect the property of the individual.[128]

A similar situation existed in France. In 1910, it was stated that "the Napoleonic Code was the code of property."[129] Indeed such was the case throughout the nineteenth century.[130] No matter what commentator we consider, no matter what was his approach and school of thought, we will find that he was an advocate of private property. "Liberty is inextricably linked with property; the latter shares the fate of the former," said Troplong, one of the most influential jurists of the century.[131] Demolombe, an admirer, complimented him by saying, "individual property means work; it means liberty itself!"[132] Free property was considered as an essential part of freedom not only by the French Revolution and the authors of the Civil Code, but also by great commentators on the law. Already de Malville's work had given property an emphatic vindication. He states that Portalis "has perfectly proved . . . that property and the division of the soil, far from having been detrimental to the human race and a germ of evil, were, on the contrary, creative of order in society and the best guaranty for the stability of government. . . . Without property, there would be no agriculture, and without agriculture, nothing but savages would be running around on the surface of the globe; the causes of war would not be reduced among them; they would fight for the hunt in the forest and for the untilled soil, just as civilized people fight for the ownership of fields and cities. . . . It is wrong to admit that sovereigns should co-own the goods situated on their territory. Co-ownership . . . is by definition incompatible with property, which is something exclusive and has no other limits than those set by the laws; it would degrade the citizen's appreciation of property, for which his most intense attachment should be sought; for he cannot love his property, unless he loves the laws that protect it. . . . Nations prosper less because of the fertility of their soil than the stability of property and the liberty which each citizen possesses to use it to his greatest advantage. . . . Property has enlivened, spread and enlarged our very existence; through property, man's industry, that spirit of mobility and life that animates everything, has been carried over the seas and, under different climates, has given birth to all the germs of richness and might."[133] Similar remarks on the ethics of property were made throughout the century.[134]

In view of this fact, it is not surprising that French jurists favored a highly individualistic concept of property. De Malville referred to article 544 of the Civil Code, which granted extended powers to the proprietor, as "the translation of property."[135] The principle of the absolute rule of the owner was generally recognized. In the middle of the century, Marcadé wrote that property rights make the proprietor the master and lord over his belongings, giving him omnipotence, or despotic power.[136] Boileux felt that property rights are unlimited, inviolable, and exclusive.[137] Aubry and Rau stated that property by its very nature is an absolute right, that the proprietor is free to alter his belongings, even to degrade or destroy them.[138] Demolombe stressed that the right of property has two essential characteristics: it is absolute and exclusive.[139] The owner was said to have the *plena in re potestas*.[140]

Laurent wrote that article 544 contains a definition of the characteristic feature of property, and mentioned the proprietor's right to destroy and abuse his property. "The proprietor," he wrote, "can, from the moral standpoint, make foolish, sinful and wasteful use of property; still, from the juristic point of view, he is in his right. . . ."[141] Planiol, writing at the turn of the century, stressed again the right of the proprietor to use and abuse his property.[142] Moreover, it was maintained that property rights constitute the most perfect of all rights in realty (*droits réels*),[143] and that they are perpetual.[144]

As far as the evaluation of property is concerned, it can be said that French jurists were in general agreement with their German colleagues. This fact is not surprising. In the nineteenth century, there was a mutual give-and-take between the jurists of the two nations. French legislation and, in particular, its "code of property," exercised a strong influence in Germany. In turn, the German historical school and the pandectists, with their emphasis upon the absoluteness and exclusiveness of property, had an impact upon France.[145] In the nineteenth century, one could easily speak of a European *Rechtswissenschaft*. And the assertion that its supra-national character was facilitated by the general atmosphere of liberalism, [146] as well as by the desire for freedom and free property, is probably not an exaggeration.

CONCLUSION

In the preceding pages, an attempt was made to show how property rights received far-reaching protection through legislation, adjudication and juridical science during the nineteenth century. The omission of remarks on adjudication in the discussion of France and Germany, and on legislation in the discussion of the United States, should not lead to the conclusion that in the civil law countries adjudication was not relevant for the consolidation of property rights, or that in the United States no legislative forces were at work for that consolidation.

In both France and Germany, legislation in favor of property was supplemented by the courts.[147] It could not have been otherwise, since in civil law countries judges are permitted no leeway in interpreting laws. In contrast to common law countries, they apply only the legislative will. In the absence of judicial review, they cannot test laws for their validity or for their compatibility with constitutional or higher law.[148] Generally speaking, it can be said that the judges in these countries interpreted the law in the way in which this was done by the law professors. Judicial decisions were emphatic with regard to the protection of property.

Similarly, in the United States the work of the courts was complementary to legislation. For instance, although there was some unfavorable reaction to the Supreme Court's interpretation of the contract clause,[149] it can hardly be doubted that the majority of the people approved of the Court's attitude. This was a period in which not only the general feeling that everyone was free to become a proprietor existed, but in which also the sacrosanctity of property was favored. It should not be forgotten that a contract clause was adopted not only by the Philadelphia Convention. Before Marshall was made Chief Justice, the constitutions of Pennsylvania, Kentucky and Tennessee contained contract clauses in their bills of rights.[150] By the end of Marshall's term, such clauses could be found in the constitutions of Ohio, Indiana, Mississippi, Illinois, Alabama, Maine, Missouri, Virginia and Michigan.[151] It is interesting to note that even those states which were formed out of the old Northwest Territory did not adopt the type of contract clause which could be found in the Northwest Ordinance of 1787 and which prohibited merely the legislature from passing laws that would interfere with or affect private contracts, or engagements, *bona fide,* and without fraud previously formed. To the contrary, they used the more inclusive formulation of the federal Constitution. The same applies to state constitutions which were adopted during the Taney period.[152] The constitutional conventions that drafted these constitutions were dominated no longer by the rich and well-born, but mainly by the representatives of the common man. Also, these constitutions were usually ratified by popular vote, by people imbued with the democratic spirit of the frontier.

The supposition that the combined and intertwined forces of legislation, adjudication and juridical science, important as they were, were the only factors that contributed toward the protection of property, would be erroneous. They are merely a few, although major, reflections of the creative forces of the law.[153] In the nineteenth century, as in previous times, the institution of private property was defended on many grounds by numerous social forces and academic disciplines.

Property was defended also on various levels. American history exemplifies the fact that it was protected from the public power. As demonstrated prior, France and Germany provide examples that private property was protected within the framework of private law. Also the appreciation of property under private law in America and under public law in Europe, could easily be shown. Everywhere, the status of the proprietor increased. He gained a strong position not only over his property, but also vis-a-vis his fellow citizens and the public power. It is difficult to ascertain to what degree property was protected under public and private law in the various countries, since in the nineteenth century, these two aspects of the law were not as distinct as they are today. All positive law constituted more or less a unity. It was perhaps distinguished from natural or higher law,[154] but not divided within itself. Likewise, it is difficult to classify and to describe the different aspects of property rights, or to enumerate them. Property defies definition as much as does liberty,[155] and the aspects of property defy enumeration as much as do the aspects of liberty. Therefore, the examples furnished are mere indications of the protection of property. No matter, however, in what sphere of the law these indications might be present, and how different they might be, it is clear that individualism was favored over collectivism.

In the nineteenth century, private property enjoyed greater protection than ever before. The natural rights philosophy, having brought the appreciation of property to a climax in the previous century, was complemented by the historical school even though the latter was conceived as a reaction against *Naturrecht*. That school, founded by the civilist Savigny, largely believed in a law that was known for its individualism and for its protection of private property, namely, the Roman law. Considering that the schools of idealism and *laissez-faire,* as well as clerical thought, also favored private property as an inherent part of freedom, one probably is justified in maintaining that the century of liberalism was a century of free property.

IV

THE FALL OF PROPERTY IN THE TWENTIETH CENTURY

INTRODUCTION

CIVILIZATION might be defined as a state in which men are emancipated and able to enjoy freedom. It is not identical with progress. Although normally freedom results in progress, this need not be so. History is filled with examples of material and technical progress under conditions of oppression and exploitation. The transformation of Russia from an agricultural into an industrial society and the rise of German power under Hitler are only two of the many cases in point.

The higher a civilization develops, the nearer it moves to its decline. Western civilization with its high degree of individual freedom probably reached its climax at the turn of the century. So great was the freedom enjoyed then that people sensed that only a decline could follow. One spoke of the *fin de siècle*. Never before had one looked toward an "end of the century" with so much pessimism. More freedom could scarcely be expected. People feared not only that freedom would end; they feared more. Western civilization having reached its climax, the *fin de siècle* came to mean something beyond the literal meaning of the term. It meant the end of Western civilization.[1]

The twentieth century, undergoing unforeseen scientific and technical advancements, witnessed, in spite of a broadening of suffrage, a decline of freedom. The nineteenth century brought a qualitative and quantitative improvement of constitutional government. The twentieth century, with the arrival of communism, fascism, socialism and the welfare state,

93

experienced a decline of constitutionalism. In spite of the collectivism which some saw in the doctrines of Rousseau, the idealists and the romantics, the nineteenth century was a century of individualism. By contrast, the twentieth became one of the masses.[2] In the nineteenth century, freedom was the rule and infringements upon liberty, the exception. In the twentieth, although lip service is still paid to the inviolability of freedom, regulations of the individual's rights are so numerous that they seem to have become the rule, and freedom, the exception.

This is especially true of private property. The protection it enjoyed has waned. The increase of its protection during the nineteenth century, an increase that, no matter what forms it may have taken in the various countries and how far it may have gone, was so great that one could speak of the century of free property, was followed by a sharp decline. The former intensity of appreciation now was matched by one of disparagement. The exceptional qualifications of free property that had been permitted in the nineteenth century, increased until there were so many of them that restriction of property became the rule, and free property, the exception. Of all the liberties of the individual, that of property fared the worst. Its individualistic concept was replaced by a social one to a greater and greater extent. Not only was static property attacked, but also, the free use of property was restricted. To make things complete, even the freedom to acquire property was curtailed.[3] Property gained in the past, property existing at present, property to be acquired in the future—every kind of property was questioned.

This development became increasingly absurd. Originally, restrictions upon private property were justified on grounds of "social justice." Debatable as such a justification is in view of the vagueness of that term and the fact that people possessed equal rights to acquire and use property, restrictions were defended if they facilitated the acquisition of property by those who were underprivileged or handicapped. However, soon afterwards restrictions were made not for the sake of creating greater opportunities, but for that of giving property to those who did not take advantage of opportunities. Property, one of man's great incentives throughout history, became restricted for the sake of laziness. Restrictions for the sake of "social justice" degenerated, inevitably, it seems, into restrictions for the sake of the welfare state and socialism.

The curtailment of property did not occur suddenly. While private property was on its victorious march, there were forces at work that questioned its institution. In time, these forces gained the upper hand.

Once concessions had been made to them, they could not be halted. They are present in various schools of thought and are reflected in that mirror of thought—the law.[4]

ATTACKS BY NON-JURISTS

Private property was attacked by various schools of thought, ranging from communism to more lenient types of social thinking.

The nineteenth century, witnessing the climax in human striving for freedom and free property, also gave birth to what became the major challenge to these values—socialism. The year 1848, symbolic of the rising tide of liberalism, the year in which people all over Europe shed their blood in attempts to throw off the last vestiges of the *ancien régime,* also saw the distribution of the Communist Manifesto. In that work, Marx not only attacked the righteousness of existing possessions, but also denounced the bourgeois's use of property and the freedom to acquire property. He exhorted the "have-nots" to rise against the "haves," to expropriate and eliminate them. It has been asserted that Marx stood Hegel on its head. It can also be maintained that his denunciation of property stood civilization on its head. Never had a greater challenge to private property been advanced. While there had been plans of communism, they were considered utopian and did not have much opportunity to be realized. Marx' seemingly scientific approach became the opium of the intellectuals. Mainly by virtue of their acceptance of the new doctrine, his dogma became the credo of idealists, "have-nots," and the lazy. It became a ferment of societies.

Although the failure of the Paris Commune convinced socialists that revolutionary uprisings were likely to be doomed and that it would be better to gain power through the ballot, such revisionist thought did not decrease the threat to free property. In Europe and America alike, socialism, no matter how it might be acclimatized in the different nations, continued to challenge the existing liberal order and free property. There appeared to be two alternatives for those who were interested in saving property. One was to fight socialism through an unequivocal reassertion of free property; the other, to take the wind out of the socialists' sails by making concessions to social demands that were, so one believed, compatible with a free society. And while the former method prevailed for a while, the concessionist policy gradually became the leading doctrine.

More and more the individualistic concept of property was deserted in favor of a social one. More and more the free use of property and free competition came under attack. It is difficult to determine which was attacked first, the static or the more dynamic aspect of property. Since these variations of property rights are interdependent, this issue is not too important. Furthermore, it is hard to tell in what country, and from what side, free property was first challenged. It happened everywhere. Three groups of concessionists, however, seem to stand out: theologians and moralists, economists, and jurists.

Although property was defended throughout the nineteenth century by Catholic and Protestant thinkers, there also existed tendencies toward a rejection of the individualistic concept of property and the acceptance of a more social one. These tendencies grew stronger with time.

The year the Communist Manifesto was completed was important for Christian socialism. In England, Charles Kingsley and John Malcolm Ludlow witnessed the fiasco of the Monster Petition meeting organized by the Chartists. It prompted them to spend the night drafting placards which they posted the next day on the walls of London, proclaiming to the "Workmen of England" that "the Almighty God, and Jesus Christ, the poor man who died for poor men, will bring freedom for you, though all the Mammonites on earth were against you."[5] In Germany, J. H. Wichern, presumably an "opponent of Karl Marx," spoke of the failure of the church to recognize social needs in an address to a Protestant congress at Wittenberg. "There is a Christian socialism," he said, and added that "there is . . . no other salvation from social misery, but through Christianity."[6] In the following years, Christian socialism became an important force. A counterpoise to Marxism, it denounced the latter's atheism and materialism.

Influenced by Thomas Carlyle who had stated that the liberty to starve was not worth very much,[7] and by the protests of Southey and Coleridge against the *laissez-faire* of the Manchester school and the utilitarianism of Bentham, as well as by French experiments that had been the result of Fourierism, British Christian socialism was little influenced by the type of socialism that was proposed by the Communist Manifesto. Under the leadership of Ludlow and Maurice, the movement achieved legal reforms in the fifties and helped to keep the social conscience alive until new vitality was given to Christian socialism by the Anglo-Catholic movement toward the end of the century.

In Germany, Wichern was supported by Stoecker, court preacher at Berlin. A conservative, Stoecker founded the conservative Christian Social Workers' Party in 1878, aiming at aligning the workers with Christianity and the monarchy.[8] Friedrich Naumann, a minister of less conservative beliefs, having published his first works on the social program of the Evangelical Church, and on the workers' catechism,[9] founded the weekly *Die Hilfe* in which he attacked the materialism of the social democrats. In 1890, the Evangelic Social Church Congress met for the first time, and held regular meetings during the following years. As was the case in England, Protestant socialism also was matched by that of the Catholics. In 1845, the priest Kolping had organized Catholic apprentices' societies in an attempt to keep craftsmen from turning socialist. Twenty years later, the bishop of Mayence, Wilhelm Ketteler, published a book on the *Labor Question and Christianity*.[10] In 1870 the first Catholic christian-social workers' association was established. By the end of the century, Catholic socialism, like its Protestant counterpart, had become an important force.

In the United States, clergymen increasingly stressed the social duties of private property. "From the disorders and discontents that plagued America in the seventies, eighties, and nineties arose a stream of dissenting opinion on the merits of the free competitive order. Many Protestant clergymen now criticized industrialism. . . . While they sympathized with trade unions, especially as defensive organizations, they were troubled by the potentialities of industrial violence. They were learning about the doctrines and methods of European socialism, and feared, at the outset at least, their spread in the United States. They sought, therefore, for a compromise between the harsh individualism of the competitive order and the possible dangers of socialism."[11] Among the representatives of the social gospel were Francis G. Peabody, a professor of Christian ethics at Harvard, who felt that God was the "central cosmic energy" and responsible for all social reform; the Reverend A. J. F. Behrends, "who hoped to persuade Christians to forestall the menace of socialism by anticipating its more acceptable proposals;"[12] Lyman Abbott, editor of *The Christian Union;*[13] and Washington Gladden, who served for a time on the editorial staff of the *Independent*. Although attacking the exclusiveness of property and free competition,[14] Gladden felt that the rich should give to the poor only if it served "to stimulate the manhood and arouse the self-respect of the recipient."[15] He opposed an equal distribution of goods, and was here in agreement with the great majority of the advocates of the social gospel. For these advocates were not radicals. They hoped that a greater social appreciation of property could be achieved within the framework of the existing system. "The so-called Social Gospel, as represented by many of its leading advocates, denied the major concept implicit in its title."[16]

The new appreciation of property by moralists and clergymen was equal to that of political economists. In Germany, "Socialism of the Chair" was an attempt to halt Marxian socialism by creating a more social-minded attitude toward property among the *bourgeoisie*.[17] Adolph Wagner's tenure at the University of Berlin, lasting from 1870 to 1917, can be considered a symbol for the decline of the individualistic concept of property among the socialists of the chair. A respected economist, Wagner helped the formulation of the new approach toward property. His *General or Theoretical Political Economy,* first published in 1876, contested those who believed in an abstract, absolute concept of freedom and property. He maintained that this concept, under which the proprietor possessed unrestricted power, had to conflict with the historically developed law and the requirements of social relations. Wagner reproached the Manchester school for demanding an adjustment of existing conditions to that artificial concept rather than attempting to have the converse. He argued that *laissez-faire* economists, believing that the individualistic concept of property alone is compatible with the interests of the individual, wrongly identified these interests with those of the community, just as jurists wrongly believed that the principles of Roman law are ideally suited to present conditions. Usually it was forgotten, he argued, that private property is a "social-legal institution," based upon the life of the community as the source of law; that it is not an absolute concept, but a historical one, subject to change according to social conditions. Stressing the value of a "social-legal formulation of private property" for the economy, Wagner rejected the Roman idea on property. He advocated regulation by the government, and felt that it was desirable to introduce into private law a definition of property that would do greater justice to the idea that property could be restricted for the public good.[18]

Wagner's theories found many followers. One of the most important was Gustav Schmoller, his later colleague on the Berlin faculty and editor of an important annual.[19] In an answer to an article by Treitschke, Schmoller defended himself against the reproach that he was a socialist.

The growth of population and the crowded living conditions in the cities, he argued, made a greater restriction of private property imperative. He accused Treitschke and others, who opposed such restrictions, of ignoring new conditions, saying that their opposition resulted from "old inveterate *errors of a one-sided romanistic jurisprudence* and of an individualistic philosophy." Schmoller denied that those who profited from the individualistic concept of property have a claim to "the continuation of the existing legal order and distribution of property," if it is incompatible with the interests of society. He emphasized that property is not entitled to absolute protection, that it implies duties and that it can be restricted for the sake of the community.[20]

In spite of the desire of the socialists of the chair, among whom were also Brentano, Held and Roscher, to achieve a social appreciation of property, they did not want to abolish the existing order. Radical socialists and revisionist social democrats referred to them derisively as "sweet water socialists."

The socialists of the chair taught at a time when young Americans went to Germany to study. Among them were Richard T. Ely and Simon Patten who were influenced by the historical school and by the socialists of the chair in Halle and Heidelberg. Upon their return to the United States, they became prominent among those who, in the middle eighties, took issue with *laissez-faire*. In 1884, Ely published his essay on *The Past and the Present of Political Economy*, which challenged the classical economists' belief in *laissez-faire*. He questioned that only self-interest could serve as an explanation of human conduct, and emphasized that the interests of the individuals were not necessarily those of the community. For the sake of society, property rights could be restricted. In spite of his new orientation, Ely in principle respected the institution of private property, just as he was far from being a drastic opponent of the principle of free competition.[21] The same can be said of Patten. He questioned the social utility of free competition and expressed dissatisfaction with the theories of Malthus and Ricardo. However, he did not favor an absolute abolition of free competition but merely proposed certain alleviations of that system.[22]

Many younger economists agreed with these ideas. Under Ely's leadership, they founded the American Economic Association in 1885. Its program favored a mitigation of *laissez-faire* and an adjustment of property rights to new social conditions: "We regard the state as an agency whose positive assistance is one of the indispensable conditions of human progress. We believe that political economy as a science is still in an early stage of its development. While we appreciate the work of former economists, we look not so much to speculation as to the historical and statistical study of actual conditions of economic life for the satisfactory accomplishment of that development." *Laissez-faire*, probably the greatest progress in political economy since mercantilist days because of its emancipation of property from the restrictions of former economic systems, was said to be a rudimentary stage of political economy. Indeed, this was a challenge of free property. Nevertheless, it would be incorrect to describe the aims of the Association socialistic. Ely was not a socialist, and most of the Association's members were much less critical of the prevalent economic beliefs than was Ely.[23]

Moralists, clergymen and economists did not work in isolation from one another. They collaborated. For example, Stoecker's Christian social activities were supported by Adolph Wagner, a devout Protestant who became the president of the first Evangelical-Social Congress. Friedrich Naumann had strong ties with the *Kathedersozialisten*. The Protestant social congresses were composed of clergymen as well as economists. In the United States, economists of the new school, like Ely, John R. Commons and Edward Bemis, were influenced by the social gospel. Many ministers, desiring a new attitude toward property and *laissez-faire*, were interested in political economy. At one time, the American Economic Association listed more than sixty clergymen among its members.

The movement toward a new appreciation of property was not restricted to clergymen and economists. The shift in public policy toward property would not have been possible without the support of jurists.

ATTACKS BY JURISTS

The jurists' attacks upon the individualistic concept of property could be recognized first in the Germans' refutation of the Roman theory of property, in Duguit's ideas of the social function of property, and in American sociological jurisprudence.

Curiously enough, in Germany the primary assault upon the individualistic concept of property was launched by a Romanist. After engaging in studies on the dogmatics of Roman law, Rudolf von Jhering stated that "there is *no absolute property,* i.e., property that is freed from taking into consideration the interests of the community, and history has taken care to inculcate this truth into all peoples.[24] His *Law as a Means to an End* elaborates that idea. Believing that law is the "realized *partnership of individual and society*" and that it has the purpose of securing the living conditions of the community, Jhering maintained that constantly changing conditions make it impossible to define the interests of society and to determine exactly the scope of the individual's rights.[25] Thus property rights were considered to be relative. Jhering rejected the idea that the proprietor has unlimited power over his property. Society cannot permit a wrong use of property: "The principle of the *inviolability of property* amounts to the handing over of society to the stupidity, egoism and obstinacy, to the most contemptible, the most malicious egoism of the individual—everything may perish as long as I keep my house, land, and cattle! But do you really keep them, you shortsighted? The dangers that threaten all also threaten you: The sea, the fire, the disease, the enemy will overtake you, and you will even be buried in the general ruin—the *interests of society* are in truth *your own,* and whenever society restricts your property, it does so for your sake as well as for its own."[26] Even Roman law, which "has so clearly and conscientiously conceived and so energetically carried out the principle of individualism,"[27] provides no basis for the individualistic concept of property. For it left no doubt that private law exists in the interest of the community.[28] Jhering stated that if society has thus far refrained from interfering with free property, it was due to the hope that individuals, realizing that whatever was good for society was also good for themselves, would use their property in the interest of the community. However, these hopes proved to have been in vain. The existing individualistic conception of property, under the pretense of protecting the "sacrosanctity of property," has actually fostered "insatiability, voracity of egoism."[29] This led to an unjust distribution of wealth, which could be alleviated by taxation. Looking to the future, the Frisian prophesied: "One need not be a prophet to know that the social conception of property will replace the individualistic one to a greater and greater extent. The time will come when *property* will have a *different meaning than today,* when society will refuse to recognize the so-called right of the individual to scrape together as many of the goods of the earth as possible."[30]

Jhering's criticism of the Roman concept of property was complemented by the "Germanists," a group of jurists that had grown considerably with the unification of Germany. It favored a stronger reliance upon Germanic law which has a rather social conception of property. The Germanists' arguments were prominent especially after 1888, when the draft for the German civil code was published. Their most important spokesman was Otto von Gierke. His lecture before the Viennese Legal Society on the social function of private law, as well as his study on the draft of the German civil code, contain strong attacks upon the individualistic conception of property.[31] Gierke criticized the adoption of an "exclusive and absolute dominion" over property. Such a concept of private property is a fiction that is "dangerous to the commonwealth" because "it creates an assumption that property rights are unlimited and that restrictions upon them are few and exceptional."[32] In truth, the "living law" provides for numerous restrictions. Criticizing the draft for not prohibiting the misuse of property, Gierke asserted that every right implies a duty and has an inherent moral boundary. The moral duty to make the right use of property should be elevated to a legal duty. The draft is denounced for adopting the Roman concept of property and for not taking account of restrictions required by ethics and public law. Gierke called for "a drop of socialist oil" into private law. Property without duty has "no future."[33] He noticed with satisfaction the restrictions which have been increasingly imposed upon private property —"promising beginnings of a new social order of property." "If not all signs are deceiving," he proclaimed triumphantly, "we are in the midst of a renaissance of the Germanic legal idea of social harmony."[34]

The most conspicuous, systematic and profound attack upon the individualist concept of private property in France can be found in the works of Léon Duguit.[35] Duguit denounced the existing legal order as individualistic, subjective and metaphysical, and suggested that it be replaced by a more realistic, objectivistic, and social one. He argued that man had wrongly been conceived to be isolated from his fellow creatures. Unjustly he had been granted subjective rights irrespective of the consequences for society. Such an outlook upon the law was "metaphysical," because it was based upon abstractions and did not take into account the realities of life. Duguit suggested a "realistic" system of law. Under such a system, no subjective rights could be claimed. Man was not considered to be isolated from his surroundings, but rather a social being. As such, he has to fulfill certain functions, depending on his position.[36]

"All society being a discipline, man, just as he cannot live without society, also cannot live but under discipline." Such a discipline, or "rule of social conduct," is imperative in view of the increasing interdependence of social forces. All men, since they are members of society, are subject to this rule of social conduct which constitutes the objective law (la règle de droit). This law is not ideal and unchangeable, but the law which exists in reality, a continually changing, positive law.[37] It prescribes the fulfillment of definite functions by the individual. It is social because such fulfillment exists for the sake of the community.[38]

Duguit's new conception of law gave a new aspect to legal institutions. Among these, property was particularly affected. Duguit denounced the Civil Code and other individualistic codifications for having adopted the Roman concept of property. He regretted that under that concept the proprietor, just as he can use and dispose of his property as he sees fit, is also free not to use or dispose of it. He may leave his land uncultivated, his houses empty and falling to ruins, and hoard capital in an unproductive fashion. Such absolute rights of the proprietor are no longer feasible. The individual is not an end in itself, but exists for the realization of social purposes. "Social solidarity" and "social interdependence" require the proprietor "to employ his goods for the maintenance and improvement of social coherence." Individuals have the duty to serve society to the best of their ability. The owner (le détenteur de la richesse) has, due to the fact that he owns, the opportunity and duty of increasing the general wealth through the use of his goods. Society will grant him protection only if he does so. "Property is no longer the subjective right of the proprietor, but the social function of the holder of wealth."[39] Positive law does not protect a so-called subjective right of the proprietor, but rather his freedom to fulfill his social function. This is Duguit's "socialization" of property.

In the United States, a new appreciation of property was introduced by sociological jurisprudence. Until the end of the nineteenth century, judicial thinking, like that in Germany and France, was strongly influenced by enlightened ideas. Law was considered in a rather abstract manner. Although that tendency was mitigated by the common law tradition, Americans conceived of law as an absolute truth which ought to be followed unequivocally. Natural and common law were believed to establish absolute norms. Legislation, becoming more prevalent as the century wore on, had to conform to these norms, which were believed to have been transmuted into the Constitution.[40] The characteristic feature of American constitutionalism, judicial review, is based upon such reasoning. Property, being considered an absolute value, was treated as a sacrosanct institution throughout the nineteenth century. Its evaluation by common law jurists differed very little from that by the pandectists in Germany or by the expositors of the Napoleonic Code in France.

However, since the latter decades of the century, the traditional conception of law was attacked. There occurred a re-evaluation of private property. The feeling of its sacrosanctity waned. The general atmosphere in the decades prior to World War I, characterized by popular demands for social legislation, did not fail to have its impact upon jurists. Although Dean Pound's influence in the creation of sociological jurisprudence was probably as great as any,[41] the following discussion will be restricted to Oliver Wendell Holmes, Jr., and Louis D. Brandeis. As members of the Supreme Court, they had not only a theoretical, but also a practical impact upon the formulation of a new policy toward property rights.

In his famous dissent in Lochner v. New York, a case in which a New York statute restricting the working hours for bakers was held unconstitutional, Holmes attacked the Court's position on freedom of contract, i.e., the freedom of acquiring property. "This case is decided upon an economic theory which a large part of the country does not entertain," he remarked, attacking *laissez-faire* liberalism. Then he made a case for state regulation of freedom. Taking advantage of the fact that there existed some regulation of the acquisition of property, he used the time-honored method of saying that such regulation has been common practice. He stated: "It is settled by various decisions of this court that state laws may regulate life in many ways which we as legislators might think as injudicious or if you like as tyrannical as this, and which equally with this interfere with the liberty of contract. Sunday laws and usury laws are ancient examples. A more modern one is the prohibition of lotteries. The liberty of the citizen to do as he likes so long as he does not interfere with the liberty of others to do the same, which has been a shibboleth for some well-known writers, is interfered with by school laws, by the Post Office, by every state or municipal institution, which takes his money for purposes thought desirable, whether he likes it or not." Holmes continued: "The Fourteenth amendment does not enact Mr. Herbert Spencer's Social Statics . . . . Some of these laws embody convictions or prejudices which judges are likely to share. Some may not. But a constitution is not intended to embody a particular economic

theory, whether of paternalism and the organic relation of the citizen
to the State or of *laissez-faire*. It is made for people of fundamentally
differing views, and the accident of our finding certain opinions natural
and familiar or novel and even shocking ought not to conclude our judgment upon the question whether statutes embodying them conflict with
the Constitution of the United States."[42]

Here was, although in dissent, a fundamental shift in constitutional
interpretation. When John Marshall had asserted, "we must never forget, that it is a *constitution* we are expounding . . . . a constitution, intended to endure for ages to come, and, consequently, to be adopted
to the various *crises* of human affairs," he merely implied some flexibility
with respect to the machinery of government.[43] He did not consider challenging the rigidity of the Constitution as an instrument for the protection of the rights of the individual, among which those of property
figured prominently.[44] By contrast, Holmes, doubting the individual's
freedom to work under whatever conditions he desired, challenged that
principle. He advocated a relativistic appreciation of property rights
which was equivalent to a depreciation of these rights.

Brandeis aided him in this task. "I don't want money or property
most. I want to be free," Brandeis stated prior to World War I, strangely
discriminating between property and freedom, with property coming
out at the shorter end of the scale.[45] Later, he not only gave freedom
preference over property, but even part of freedom: "The fact that
speech is likely to result in some violence or in destruction of property
is not enough to justify its suppression. There must be the probability
of serious injury to the state."[46] In view of these statements depreciative
of static property, it is not surprising that Brandeis should attack more
dynamic aspects of property. He indicated the close connection between
static and dynamic property when he blamed the courts for having
ignored "newly arisen social needs." The courts, he stated with respect
to static property, "applied complacently eighteenth-century conceptions of the liberty of the individual and of the sacredness of private
property." And, in a polemic against dynamic property, he added immediately: "Early nineteenth-century scientific half-truths, like 'the
survival of the fittest,' which translated into practice meant 'the devil
take the hindmost,' were erected by judicial sanction into a moral law."[47]
While Holmes was dissenting in the Lochner case, Brandeis denounced
"the excesses of capital," and "the excesses of our financial magnates."[48]
He praised labor unions for being bulwarks against "the accumulation

of great fortunes."[49] He denied that there was absolute freedom of contract under the Constitution, maintaining that such a freedom has never existed.[50]

Like the Christian socialists and the socialists of the chair, the advocates of sociological jurisprudence were not socialists. Everywhere, they emphasized that they neither held any radical ideas nor favored socialism as it was desired by the socialist parties. They opposed expropriation. Considering socialism as a threat to free society, they stood for a social attitude toward private property only in order to detract from the appeal of socialism.

In the beginning of his career, Jhering believed in idealistic liberalism. After Germany had become unified, he was an admirer of Bismarck and William I. In spite of his earlier republican leanings, he wrote the former that he was a monarchist. Although he helped to inaugurate the social orientation of legal thought, and although many of his ideas seemed to agree with the demands of the social democrats, Marx does not appear to have influenced him. He was neither a theoretical nor a practical socialist.[51] He even ridiculed some socialist plans.[52] The situation is quite similar in the case of Gierke. In spite of his leanings toward a social concept of property, he never became a member of a socialist party. As a matter of fact, Gierke was rather conservative in many respects. Although he opposed liberalism for being destructive of the organic and social tradition of Germanic law, he was very much aware of the dangers of socialism.[53] Just as he had said that the "destatization" *(Entstaatlichung)* of the law, as conceived by individualism, amounts to the dissolution and death of national unity, in a like manner he emphasized that the nationalization of all law, as conceived by socialism, would be tantamount to serfdom and barbarism.[54]

Duguit's plan of "socialization" differed greatly from the socialists' program. He did not want to change ownership of the means of production, let alone other kinds of ownership. Private property was to remain protected; only the legal concept upon which its protection was based would be changed. Duguit stressed that the proprietor, besides his duty and power to use his property for the good of society, also had the duty and power to use it for the satisfaction of individual needs.[55] By doing so, the owner fulfills a social task, since any activity on his part increases the intensity of the social division of labor, and improves social coherence.

A proof of Holmes' professed antagonism toward socialism is provided by no less an authority than Harold Laski, theorist of the British Labour Party and one of Holmes's best known partners of correspondence. The conservatives, Laski wrote, "are, indeed, hopelessly wrong in attributing to Mr. Justice Holmes any corpus of radical beliefs; all he has is a willingness to experiment with novelty in fundamentals." Whereas socialists insist that change is necessary and urgent, Laski continued, Holmes "simply urges that since change is inevitable, we must provide for its coming and see to it only that the game is played in terms of the rules. Much of what passes to-day for radical doctrine he would, I think, privately regard as politically unsound and economically unwise. For him Marx is completely unscientific, the Webbs, the spinners of ethereal Utopias, socialists, a party seeking merely to transfer the burden from the strong to the weak."[56] Like Holmes, Brandeis opposed socialism. As his biographer notes, "Brandeis would not have paid *any* price to avoid socialism; but he would have paid a good price."[57] Again and again, Brandeis emphasized that his appreciation of property was nothing but a means for warding off the socialist threat. He advocated collective bargaining because it was essential to the survival of capitalism, and advised labor that socialism offered no solution to its problems.[58] He lauded the trade unions as "a strong bulwark against the great wave of socialism," and praised them for standing "for individualism as against the great uprising of socialism."[59] He denounced concentration of wealth because it was conducive to socialism.[60]

Although sociological jurists were opposed to socialism, their rejection of the individualistic concept of property was more beneficial to socialism than they had probably imagined. This fact is not surprising. Moralists and economists, although advocating the necessity of a new evaluation of property, did not agree on the scope of such re-evaluation.[61] The same can be said of the jurists. No limits of the permissibility of infringements upon the property of the individual for the sake of the community were established. In short, although the jurists were professedly opposed to socialism, some of them were less opposed than others. The difference between Holmes and Brandeis is an example. The latter appears to have been more willing to permit infringements upon property.[62] Once, when he was disappointed that a bill favoring big business had been enacted, he exclaimed, "I am rapidly becoming a socialist."[63] We would search in vain for such a remark from Holmes. In view of these differences of opinion, property rights, which thus far constituted an absolute value, were relativized. The attack upon these rights by the new evaluators would have been sufficiently bad if they had decided upon definite limits for restrictions; it was worse because no agreement was reached. If property was devaluated by Holmes to some extent and by Brandeis even more, there was no reason why others would not have devaluated it further. Brandeis was Holmes's junior by age as well as by seniority on the Supreme Court. In a sense, this is symbolic for the increasing lack of appreciation of property from generation to generation.

We turn now to this lack. Everywhere, the appreciation of property declined.[64] It did not occur suddenly. In view of the conservative character of the law, this could not be expected. But its gradualness did not detract from the seriousness of the process, although it might have veiled it. Rather, it signifies the inevitability of that decline once cracks in the bastion of property had appeared. Like the sea, having broken a hole in a dam, will break away piece after piece until the dam is destroyed and civilization inundated, an attack on property, as soon as it has succeeded in restricting its protection, will remove more and more protection until finally none is left. Attempts for an abolition of freedom usually know no bounds, and neither does the desire for social reform, involving restrictions of free property. Inevitably, it seems, individualistic property was doomed once the basic principle of its absolute protection had been abandoned. And just as, in the last decades of the nineteenth and the first decades of the twentieth century, the individualistic concept of property was attacked and replaced by a social one, subsequent decades witnessed the substitution of the latter concept by one which was more radically socialistic.

RESTRICTION THROUGH INTERPRETATION

At first, attacks on private property were based on seemingly ethical grounds. More and more, the individual's property became restricted, although he was hardly aware of it in most cases.

Property, considered an ethical institution until the end of the nineteenth century, was not apt to be subjected to a frontal attack. The idea that it was something good and desirable was too deeply ingrained in the people. Therefore, first it was assaulted by arguments which were likely to be palatable even to its defenders. One of these arguments was that property, while it should be used comprehensively, should not be used to the detriment of others. Restrictions to that effect were said to be negligible. It was argued that the advantages accruing from them to other individuals and society were out of proportion to the disadvantages suffered by the proprietor. Another argument maintained that civilists in France, pandectists in Germany as well as American jurists, had believed in the highly individualistic, absolute and exclusive concept of property not so much because they were in favor of it, but rather because they had been slaves of the abstract law as sanctioned by the French and American revolutions, or deduced from the Roman law. The more modern approach to the law, characterized by greater realism and the inductive method, led to a different, more social evaluation of property. The ideas of sociological jurists became realized through legislation and adjudication. The individualistic concept of property slowly disappeared.

First the proprietor's right to use his property to the detriment of others will be considered. In every country, this right was curbed to a greater and greater extent. In France, the classic case was decided as early as the middle of the nineteenth century, when a court ruled that a proprietor who had built a giant fake chimney merely in order to annoy his neighbor, had to tear it down.[65] This decision "deprived the Shylocks of the benefit of an apparent law and initiated for the European continent the beginning of a general theory of the abuse of legal rights."[66] In France, the jurists developed the idea of *abus de droit*.[67] Until today, it has been maintained that property deserved the protection of the courts only if used in a way that does not conflict with the interests of other individuals.

The development was similar in Germany. Generally speaking, the jurists of the nineteenth century agreed that the proprietor's malicious conduct was permissible.[68] The opinion of Windscheid and other representatives of *Pandektistik* that the exercise of a right which exclusively served the purpose of hurting others was not permitted, had not much practical value since it was difficult to prove that the proprietor had no interest other than that of hurting others.[69] However, the German Civil Code, although its drafters were motivated largely by the desire to give property as absolute a protection as possible, gave effective sanction to the prohibition of chicanery. The second commission was still ardently opposed to such a prohibition, feeling that it would be more conducive to malicious conduct of third parties by their maliciously asserting a chicanery of the proprietor, than in preventing the chicanery of the proprietor. However, the final draft recognized the prohibition of chicanery.[70]

In the United States, the common law tradition of permitting malicious use was more and more abandoned. A decision of 1889, dealing with spite fences, still maintained that "at common law, a man has a right to build a fence on his own land as high as he pleases, however much it may obstruct his neighbor's light and air."[71] Ten years later, when a proprietor built a forty-foot-high wall about three feet from his neighbor's building, "thereby cutting off the latter's light, air, and view," and without doubt doing this "wrongfully and maliciously and unnecessarily and for the purpose of injuring the plaintiff and the plaintiff's property," the court held that the considerations of the defendant were irrelevant, as long as she built on her own property.[72] However, soon American statutes and court decisions took a less lenient attitude. They declared "structures put up in a spirit of malice for the sole purpose of injuring the adjoining neighbor" to be a "legal wrong."[73] Justice Holmes stated in 1889: "It is plain that the right to use one's property for the sole purpose of injuring others is not one of the immediate rights of ownership. It is not a right for the sake of which property is recognized by the law. . . . We are of the opinion that the statute, thus concerned, is within the limits of the police power, and is constitutional. . . . It simply restrains a noxious use of owner's premises, and although the use is not directly injurious to the public at large, there is a public interest to restrain this kind of aggressive annoyance of one neighbor by another, and to mark a definite limit beyond which it is not lawful to go."[74] More and more American states passed laws against spite fences and spite walls. Where there were no such laws, the courts have tended to consider the construction of buildings "with no other purpose than the vindictive one of shutting off the plaintiff's view, or his light, and air," as a nuisance and as inadmissible.[75]

Although the prohibition of malicious conduct amounts to a restriction of property, it was not likely to provoke much protest. The element of chicanery was too obvious. Also, in most cases prohibitions of malicious use of property were beneficial to another person's property. Individual property stood against individual property. All that happened was that some form of the active exercise of property rights, the right to use property harmfully, was restricted in favor of the passive

side of property rights, or of the right to have one's property unmolested. Even the most ardent advocates of free property could scarcely
object to this. For what today they might consider an infringement upon
their right to use their property, tomorrow might be a protection for
that very property.

The situation was not likely to differ greatly when property was used
to the disadvantage of others in the absence of the element of chicanery.
The protection of neighbors' rights provides a good example.

In France, where articles 1382 ff. of the Civil Code prohibit only a
use of property that is incompatible with the laws, one would expect that
in the absence of restrictive laws, the owners would be free to do with
their property whatever they wanted. However, this is not so. French
jurisprudence restricted the proprietor. Just as in the case of malicious
conduct it had developed the doctrine of "abuse of right" *(abus de droit)*,
it now prohibited an "anormal" use of property, even though such
use was technically within the bounds of the letter of the law. After the
middle of the nineteenth century, proprietory rights were increasingly
restricted for the sake of neighbors.[76] It may be asked today whether
restriction has not become the rule, and freedom, the exception.[77]

In Germany, the *gemeine Recht* had maintained that the proprietor
need not respect the interests of his neighbors. It was debated, but not
decided, whether such nuisances as noise and odor had to be kept from
neighboring territory.[78] However, the German Civil Code, in spite of
its general tendency to protect the proprietor's rights, provided for a
protection of neighbors. As if moved by the desire to subordinate property rights to the requirements of good neighborhood, German jurisprudence gave this provision a wide scope.[79] It was not only applied to
real property, but also to personal property. Furthermore, it was said
to protect not only the owners, but also persons who had merely obligatory claims.[80] A general view of German jurisprudence on the rights
of neighbors reveals that the individualistic concept of property was
more and more abandoned for a communal one. Property increasingly
implied the duty of not using it to the detriment of others.[81]

It is dubious whether the restrictions imposed upon property were
greatly resented in the cases just mentioned. Although the element of
chicanery, facilitating an acquiescence in restrictions, was absent, individual property was still pitted against individual property. To the
degree to which the active proprietary rights of one person were cur-

tailed, to that degree the passive proprietary rights of another were preserved. No actual restriction of the rights of the individual for the sake
of that anonymous body, society, had yet taken place.

The situation differs when the proprietor is prohibited to use his property to the detriment of society. Now restrictions can be said to amount
to a "socialization" of private property, to use the term in the mild sense
in which it was employed by Duguit. The proprietor's abuse of his
property, his wasting or destroying it, are cases in point. Examination
of the development in the various countries reveals a continuous and
increasing restriction of the rights of the proprietor for the sake of
the community. This occurred with respect to specific kinds of property,
in normal times as well as in periods of emergency.

By 1936, Georges Ripert had good reason to complain about the
socialization of the law, and the law on property, in France.[82]
Duguit's example set a bad precedent. His followers went further and
further toward the left. Edouard Lambert, a pioneer of the study of
comparative law, invited jurists to consider the Soviet Civil Code as the
kind of civil code that could be realized by Western nations if they chose
the way to progress.[83] Emmanuel Lévy advocated "juridical socialism."[84]
In Germany also, the right to abuse one's property was more and more
restricted. Justus Wilhelm Hedemann took issue with the belief that the
proprietor could destroy his property irrespective of the interest of the
community.[85] Other jurists shared his opinion. The advocates of Germanic law came to the fore.[86] Legislation and adjudication in the twenties
were not uninfluenced by the social revolution that had taken place at
the end of World War I, a revolution that had held that property did
not only confer rights, but also involved duties. The situation is not much
different in the United States. "The riper a people, the more can be done
to develop the social side of private property and to prevent its waste
and misuse," an author stated shortly before World War I.[87] At the beginning of the New Deal, he was complemented by another writer who
wrote that "under the conditions of crowded life the reckless and un-
conscionable use of one's property is becoming more and more dangerous."[88] Legislation and adjudication have been consistent with these
ideas.[89]

Aside from general restrictions of the free use of property there were
restrictions of a more particular character. Covering personal as well
as real property, these restrictions varied, although they were concerned mainly with the conservation of goods. Specific types of property

were curbed. Such curbs were motivated by different considerations, ranging from those of an aesthetic to those of an ethical, and from those of a more ideal to those of a more material nature. Private property was restricted for the beautification of town and country; for the planning of housing; for securing food supplies; in the interest of good working conditions; in the interest of traffic, to name only some major instances.[90] There was a veritable deluge of regulations.

In view of the restrictions of private property in normal times, it is not surprising that property became even more curbed in times of emergency. It is not necessary to go into detail here. All of us have seen the many controls that were exercised over property in such times. Even the land of plenty, the United States, adopted drastic measures in World War I, more drastic ones during the Depression, and still more drastic ones during World War II. In the great majority of emergency measures, it was not only the right to abuse one's property that was curbed. Restrictions were more comprehensive. Quite normal—and not at all abusive—uses of property came under control.

But even though in all these cases property was restricted not for the sake of a specific individual, but for that of an anonymous society or an impersonal state; despite the fact that the restriction of one's property was not matched by the preservation of another person's property, restrictions of property for the sake of the community were not greatly resented. The reason seems obvious. In normal times, such restrictions, being mostly directed against the right to abuse one's property, against the right to waste and destroy, were curbs on aspects of property that were considered to be of a rather dubious character. They were quite acceptable if the community could profit by the individual's mere abstinence from wasting and destroying his property. It was felt that laws imposing such abstentions could be defended on ethical grounds, since only the least ethical part of property—the right to waste and destroy —was curbed. Also, restrictions of property in times of emergency were not overly resented. It was recognized that emergencies require abnormal emergency measures. People believed that once the emergency ceased to exist, the restrictions would be removed and free property would re-emerge. Because of their temporary character, such restrictions did not seem to challenge the sanctity of property.

However, the restrictions mentioned in the preceding pages were not as harmless as they appeared. Restrictions of the right to abuse one's property are problematic in spite of the presumption that they restrict only the less desirable "excesses" of property rights. For whereas in the case of malicious use of property or a use to the detriment of another person's property, the "excesses" were in proportion to the degree to which another individual's property remained unmolested, the situation is different when the individual's property is restricted for the sake of the community. The argument that such restrictions are justified because the benefit accruing to the community outweighs the damage suffered by the proprietor can be countered easily by the argument that the restriction of the proprietor is often all out of proportion to the benefit accruing to each *individual* member of society. The aesthetic appreciation by merely one member of the community of beautiful landscaping will not necessarily be equal to the damage suffered by the owner because he could not put the land to a more profitable use. The advantage accruing to only one member of society from the fact that corn is grown on a piece of land does not necessarily match the disadvantage the owner suffered because he could not leave the land a meadow or wasteland. If I am prohibited to tear down an old building because of its historic value and to build a new one in its place for more profitable use, the damage I suffer is likely to be out of proportion to the benefit reaped by each particular visitor with historical interests. These examples demonstrate that restrictions of private property for the sake of the community, even if they apply only to such "excesses" as the right to abuse, waste and destroy, are a risky undertaking. It is difficult to determine precisely what an "excessive" use of property actually is. Someone who does not cultivate a fertile vineyard could, of course, be considered a "waster." But is not the person who throws away a bottle filled with wine also a waster? Or even the person who throws away an empty bottle? Is not the poor man who wastes a bottle, from his own point of view, possibly wasting more than the rich man who wastes a whole vineyard? Is it not the use of land for grazing wasteful as compared with its use for growing corn? Does the razing of an intact building constitute waste if the new building erected in its place is likely to be more profitable to the owner? In short, where can the line be drawn between waste and non-waste? Who is to decide this question? The people, society, or the government? Is not the owner better qualified? These considerations show some of the problems involved in restricting even the right to waste or to destroy property. Once such restrictions are permitted, an element of relativity is introduced which is likely to expose free property to the will of the government. This relativity contains potential restrictions which not only prevent the abusive, but also the useful use of property.

As the examples in the preceding pages show, restrictions of so-called "excessive," "unethical" uses of property for the sake of the community are dangerous. All too frequently the lines between the *ius abutendi* and the *ius utendi* are blurred and, under the cover of preventing merely "unethical excesses," restrictions will occur that curtail the normal use of property. This leads to a consideration of a similar development, where, again under the cloak of ethics, private property became restricted for the sake of others. This process occurred in such a gradual manner that once again people were hardly aware of the dangers involved for free property.

RESTRICTION THROUGH LEGISLATION

Social legislation, first characterized by its supposedly humanitarian character, became increasingly based upon pseudo-humanitarian considerations, and finally appeared as overtly discriminatory toward property rights.

Restrictive as interpretations of the law may have been of property rights, they could hardly do away with the individualistic features of existing law and free property. While under common law judges would not be eager to overrule precedents, a change of legislation through interpretation was well nigh out of the question in civil law countries. The depreciation of property was thus more or less harmless not only from the substantive point of view, but also from that of procedure.

However, even in the more "harmless" stages of the disparagement of property, described in the preceding pages, legislation inimical to property had already made its appearance. And more of it was still to come.[91] It cannot be seriously doubted that legislation attacking property constitutes a greater danger to property than interpretation. The social or socialist interpreter of a liberal law, while he might dangerously approach an elimination of the law's values, is still prevented from complete success in this undertaking. He is, after all, bound by the law. By contrast, the legislator is not. Under the principle that later law supercedes previous law (*lex posterior derogat priori*), he may undo the values of previous law. He may abolish law that grants a rather comprehensive protection to individualistic concepts of private property by passing laws that favor more social concepts.

The smaller procedural safeguard that is implied in increasing legislation augured ill for the protection of property rights. As might be expected, these rights declined further. The legislation most characteristic of modern times, social legislation,[92] while as restrictive of property rights as the curtailments so far considered, is more dangerous. It restricts private property not only for the sake of other individuals; it limits the right to abuse one's property not merely for the sake of the community; it curtails the right to use one's property not just in order that the capable may profit. Rather, it restricts property for the sake of the weak, the unable and the unfortunate. Also, whereas under the restrictions previously mentioned nothing would actually be taken from the proprietor but a right to do something—be it the right to chicanery, to molest the neighbor, the right to use or abuse one's property—property would now be taken in order to be distributed to others. Thus social legislation goes beyond the "socialization" Duguit had in mind, or the social appreciation of property Jhering and Gierke, Holmes and Brandeis conceived. It does not merely prescribe that the owner use his property in the interest of the community. It takes from A in order to give to B. Because of the gradual development of social legislation, people recognized this at a late stage only, after this legislation had been well under way.

Social legislation began in a manner that apparently did not offend many defenders of property. In the beginning, it was stressed that only the "excesses" of liberalism and free property were to be curtailed. And just as the prohibition of chicanery and nuisance had been defended on ethical grounds, social legislation was defended on humanitarian grounds.

It started out with labor legislation.[93] The industrial revolution had certain features which were considered objectionable.[94] Child and woman labor were probably the most conspicuous ones. They were soon attacked. In the United States, Massachusetts, at that time the most industrialized of the American states, was the pioneer in legislation protecting children. In 1842, it passed a ten-hour law for children under twelve. By 1853, six other states had similar laws. Although the remaining states lagged behind Massachusetts, depending upon the degree of industrialization, there was enacted a considerable amount of legislation restricting child labor. Whereas early legislation was usually concerned only with work in factories, soon more comprehensive laws were passed. By the turn of the century, practically every American state had some kind of legislation on the subject. Even national legislation became concerned with child labor. Although the federal child labor laws of 1916 and 1919 were declared unconstitutional[95] and although the child labor amendment to the Constitution was not adopted, the general legislative trend appears clearly. The situation was similar in Germany and France. In the former country, Prussia led the way with a Children's Protective Act in 1839. In the sixties, the North German League adopted an industrial code that regulated child labor. Upon unification, that code became Reich law. In France, an act of 1841 limited the working hours of children to eight hours for those under twelve and to twelve hours for those under sixteen. Further legislation was passed later.[96]

With respect to the employment of women, Massachusetts again led the way in America. A law of 1874 established a ten-hour day. Other states followed suit. By the time of World War I, all the states had some type of legislation regulating the work of women. Soon, the federal government was concerned with the problem. Legislation protecting women also became qualitatively more intensive. In Germany, the industrial code also provided protection for women. In time, that protection became more comprehensive. The same can be said of France. In 1913, a law was passed that prohibited women to work in the weeks following childbirth. Four years later, a law provided that mothers could take one hour a day off during working hours to attend their children.[97] In later years, women were more protected.

Aside from restricting working hours for women and children, the legislator proceeded to limit such hours for adult males. Again, this was done on supposedly humanitarian grounds. It was asserted that such restrictions were conducive to the health of the workers. As in the case of child and woman labor, this process was gradual. In the beginning, maximum hours were prescribed for only a few occupations that were considered especially hazardous. Soon, however, the list of hazardous professions was extended. In the end, distinctions between dangerous and non-dangerous professions were no longer made. Maximum hours were established for most occupations. But this was not enough. Once maximum hours had been granted, the maximum was steadily decreased. Aspirations for an eight-hour day were followed by those for a forty-hour week.

On the whole, it is characteristic of the legislation just discussed that it was not a take-care legislation in the narrower sense of the word. Rather, individuals were restrained from working as hard as they wanted and from acquiring wages. On the other hand, usually they were not paid for not working. It was believed that they were prevented, at least in the case of children and women and males working under unhealthy conditions, from ruining their health. And although the cherished principle that consent precludes injury *(volenti non fit iniuria)* was flagrantly disregarded in these instances, the humanitarian aspect was considered to be so out of proportion to the loss of the freedom to acquire property that the latter was not overly resented by many people.

However, the examples given here indicate that labor legislation was not as unproblematic as it might have appeared. Restrictions of labor by children under twelve is one thing; restrictions of the work by those under sixteen is already another thing; restrictions of the employment of adult women is still another matter. In all these instances, the infringement upon the liberty of the individual to work and acquire property was increased under the questionable guise of humanity, while the humanitarian motive actually decreased. This is even more obvious in the case of maximum working hours for men. Such hours might perhaps be defended in professions that are greatly detrimental to health, although we doubt the justification of such a defense due to the interference with the freedom to work. They can be defended to a lesser extent in less hazardous occupations. The general establishment of maximum hours, irrespective of whether the worker is in danger or not, can scarcely be defended. The humanitarian factor of preserving the health of the worker is too small to justify interference with the individual's right to work and to acquire property.[98] Legislation restricting free work and free property, felt to be defensible as long as the humanitarian advantage was out of proportion to the liberal disadvantage, became less defensible as soon as this disadvantage increased. Liberty, originally restricted by "humanitarian" considerations, gradually became curtailed under pseudo-humanitarian motives.

But even such pseudo-humanitarian legislation was not greatly resented. Although it involved undesirable restrictions of freedom, they were not opposed by the majority of the people, who were interested in shorter working hours rather than in the freedom to work longer.[99] Employers, on the other hand, were not substantially hurt; they had to pay less in wages for shorter working hours. Nor was the general public hurt.

Their taxes were not used to compensate for losses suffered by labor or management.

The situation differs whenever social legislation implies take-care legislation,[100] i.e., where those protected are being taken care of by society and thus indirectly by the taxpayer, or by specific individuals. In these cases, property is taken from A and given to B. Social insurance and relief are examples.

There are good reasons to favor private insurance.[101] However, public social insurance has spread. It is argued that for the sake of the protection of the taxpayer's money, society has a right to prevent its members from becoming public charges. If the individuals neglect to make some provision for old age and inability—and the chances are that they will—they are likely to become public charges. Then, it is felt, the government might prescribe compulsory social insurance to prevent this. It is argued that such insurance is hardly incompatible with the protection of property. What the individual is forced to save, he is likely to get back when in need. Enforced savings provide a certain guaranty that in case of sickness or old age, the individual himself, and not the taxpayer, will pay for his security.[102] Be this as it may, the argument avoids a problem that arises in connection with social insurance, namely, whether the employer or the government should also contribute to the insurance. Obviously, the latter contributions are infringements upon the property of the taxpayer and upon that of the employer. And while the insurance payment by the government has been defended on the grounds that, in the absence of social insurance, society would have to take care of the sick and old anyway, the employer's contribution could not be defended on such grounds. It has been argued that the employer, due to the fiduciary relationship that binds him to his employee, has a certain obligation to help his employee when in distress. But, in our time of rapid migration of labor and of powerful labor unions, this argument frequently will not be cogent.[103]

In the case of unemployment, the situation is fundamentally different. The merely unemployed hardly deserves the pity which the sick and the old merit. Therefore, humanitarian obligations on the part of others to contribute to his insurance are less binding. Curtailments of the taxpayer's and the employer's property for the sake of unemployment insurance are objectionable from still another point of view. A fit person, knowing that he will be taken care of in case of unemployment, may be less eager to keep his job. He is likely to be less conscientious about his work. Once unemployed and receiving support, often he will not be anxious to work again. What applies to unemployment insurance, applies, *a fortiori,* to unemployment relief. Usually the unemployed are the less valuable members of society, people who either do not work well or do not like to work. Helping them would be due to false pity. To spend other people's money on them would be an indefensible infringement upon property. It is admitted that there are instances in which people are unemployed due to no fault of their own. Although even in cases of major disaster the better individuals will often be more likely to keep their position than those who are not so good,[104] many of the unemployed will be eager to work and deserving of help. But whether compulsory contributions to unemployment insurance and relief can be expected from taxpayers and employers on these grounds is a different question.

If social welfare has a dubious character, this is even more the case with legislation that goes beyond social welfare, by relieving individuals of obligations they have contracted toward others. Such legislation is clearly directed against property rights. Like social legislation, it has been defended on humanitarian grounds. Like that legislation, it has increased greatly. As in the case of social legislation, the motives for relieving debtors have steadily become more pseudo-humanitarian.[105]

Today no one would believe in the Roman practice of turning the insolvent debtor over to the creditor who could detain him in a cage and sell him on the slave market or, as was permitted under the Twelve Tables, have him torn to pieces.[106] Most of us would even be reluctant to send the insolvent debtor to a public jail, a practice which marked the outstanding improvement of the debtor's lot in Rome, and prevailed down to the nineteenth century. And although one may wonder whether such treatment was not often justified, for instance, in the case of the dishonest borrower, people are inclined to agree with the enlightened idea that the dignity of men prohibits incarceration for debts.[107]

However, recent improvements of the debtor's lot are so devoid of humanitarian motives that they appear to be indefensible. Having obtained the security of his person in the nineteenth century, the debtor achieved the security of his belongings in the twentieth century. Whereas in former times the creditor could satisfy his claims by taking the goods of the debtor, and the debtor was permitted to retain only things that were essential for living, the number of such "essentials" was continually increased. Real estate that could not be taken away from the debtor was enlarged. Salary became immune from confiscation. Procedures enabled the debtor to evade the creditor.[108]

Furthermore, debtors, one of the greatest of which has been the state itself, were favored more indirectly by means of inflation, especially during the past decades. The injustice of infringements upon property rights due to inflation has been evident in most nations, even though they were spared the experience of Germany after World War I, when the absurd principle *"Mark equals Mark"* was maintained despite the fact that the value of the mark had been reduced to less than one millionth of its original value.[109]

In view of the degeneration of humanitarianism into a mere cover for helping the weak, whether they might deserve help or not, it is not surprising that also laws were passed that explicitly interfered with free property without any humanitarian excuse. Infringements upon property under pseudo-ethical motives became accepted to such an extent that no such excuse was considered necessary. In the following, merely one example of such legislation will be discussed, namely, progressive taxation. It demonstrates how policy toward property has moved toward arbitrariness.

Attempts to introduce that kind of taxation were not unknown in the beginning of the liberal era. But at that time they were not crowned with success. During the French Revolution, Turgot suggested indignantly that one ought to execute the author of progressive taxation rather than that type of taxation itself.[110] Later, when progressive taxation was advocated prior to the revolutions of 1848, it was on the whole opposed. "The moment you abandon the cardinal principle of exacting from all individuals the *same proportion of their income* or *of their property,* you are at sea without rudder or compass, and there is no amount of injustice and folly you may not commit," wrote J. R. McCulloch in the 1830's.[111] Adolphe Thiers referred to progressive taxation as "hateful arbitrariness."[112] John Stuart Mill called it "a mild form of robbery."[113]

But the social reformers did not give in. Disavowing any desire to alter the distribution of incomes, they contended that the tax burden should be distributed according to the ability to pay in order to secure an equality of sacrifice. Progressive taxation seemed to be the ideal solution. When a progressive taxation bill was finally introduced in Prussia, it was on such a moderate scale—the income tax rise was from 0.67 to

4 percent—that it was enacted without much difficulty. The great proponent of the *Rechtsstaat,* Rudolf von Gneist, opposed it in vain as an abandonment of the principle of equality before the law.[114] Once the ice had been broken, not only was progressive taxation introduced in country after country, but also the rates were considerably increased. In the United States, for instance, where progressive taxation was adopted in 1913 rising to the then spectacular figure of 7 per cent, that figure rose to as much as 91 per cent within one generation. In view of this enormous change in the absolute rates, the proponents of progressive taxation no longer attempted to justify it on the basis of the capacity to pay, but "reverted to the original, but long avoided, justification of progression as a means of bringing about a more just distribution of income."[115] Irrespective of whether a person might deserve a large income, property was taken from him. Merely for the sake of a more equal distribution of property, without any further pretense that this was ethical or humanitarian, honest ownership and the work from which it usually derived were punished.

In view of these ever increasing inroads upon property through legislation, the question arises whether such legislation was valid. Did not constitutionalism imply the guaranty of the individual's property? Was not the legislature restricted by constitutional law from encroaching upon property rights? These questions have to be answered in the affirmative. The American Constitution expressly provided for the protection of property. French constitutions, if they made no specific provision for such protection, made it by implication because the Declaration of the Rights of Man and Citizen was considered part of every constitution. In Germany, even if constitutions made no express provision for the protection of property (most of them did), the *Rechtsstaat* implied the safety of "well earned rights."[116] And yet, in spite of their professed devotion to constitutional government, all countries permitted inroads upon property by the legislative power. A strange phenomenon took place. Laws discriminating against property superseded constitutions that protected property!

The first constitution that sanctioned a social concept of property was that of Weimar, adopted in 1919. Characteristically, it has been lauded as the most democratic constitution of the world. Although it does not proclaim a "social" republic in so many words, it contains provisions which indicate a strong turn to the left. The provision on property is one of them. While that provision "contains old liberal ideas," these ideas have become "enriched by a more social conception of property which has more and more come to the fore during the past years and which differs from the rigidly individualistic conception of earlier epochs."[117] This change can be seen in the formulation of article 153. So far, German state constitutions had followed, with insignificant variations, the unequivocal formulation of article nine of the Prussian constitution of 1850, "property is inviolable." The Weimar constitution broke with that tradition. It merely states that "property is guaranteed by the constitution." The new formulation was likely to support the belief that property rights were not beyond the reach of the human lawmaker. Even Anschütz, while holding that the change of terminology was legally not relevant, admitted that under the republic property was more at the mercy of the government than in Imperial Germany, and that the new state encroached upon it in a more inconsiderate fashion than the old state.[118] The social conception of property is also evident in the last paragraph of article 153, which reads: "Property implies duties. Its use shall be determined by what is best for the community." Although the majority of jurists maintained that this provision constituted nothing but a principle by which the legislator should let himself be guided, there were commentators who maintained that it created direct legal duties for proprietors.[119]

Under the Basic Law of Bonn, adopted thirty years later, the development toward a more social conception of property continued.[120] The idea of the social character of property was more strongly recognized by the Parliamentary Council than by the National Assembly of Weimar. If that idea is not clearly evident in article 14, which is more or less an adoption of article 153 of the Weimar constitution, this was due merely to the inability of the drafters to give this idea "a more cogent formulation." The provision, "property implies duties, its use shall serve the public weal," is no longer believed to imply direct duties for the proprietor by merely a handful of jurists, but by the great majority of commentators.[121] This more social interpretation is scarcely surprising. In contrast to the Weimar constitution, the Basic Law expressly proclaims the Federal Republic to be a "social" state.[122]

In France also, there has been a trend toward sanctioning social ideas under constitutional law. As early as 1848, the insertion of the word "social" in the preamble of the constitution had been planned. However, as Lamartine remarked, the word was finally omitted as a result of "the days of May and June, when the term 'social' was compromised by the violence against the Assembly and by revolutionary outbreaks."[123] The constitution of the Third Republic was "in conformity with the essential principles of economic liberalism, i.e., the respect of private property and free enterprise." Although these principles were never revoked, they have been replaced more and more by interventionism after World War I. "Interventionism manifested itself in three ways: social laws, the development of public administration, and a customs and fiscal policy that favored certain great masses of the electorate or certain interests that were politically influential. During the war of 1914-1918 and the years after, state intervention in the directions mentioned developed further. But this movement was especially promoted by the arrival of the great economic crisis of the thirties and by the popular front government of 1936. 1936 is both an echo and a repetition of 1848: the appeal to an economic and social democracy which should complement and invigorate political democracy."[124]

The anti-liberalism that had shown itself during the last years of the Third Republic found confirmation after World War II. The preamble to the constitution of the Fourth Republic, while recognizing the liberal rights of the Declaration of the Rights of Man and Citizen in a rather general statement, introduced a whole catalogue of "social" rights. Since these rights were specifically enumerated, one can gain the impression that they were considered more important than the old liberal rights. Also, the word "social" was now adopted to characterize the French republic, "social" being "a common denominator of the various social tendencies that became part of the constitution, be they of the catholic socialist, solidarist, or socialist, brand," the word indicating "clearly the aim of making the Republic democratic not only in the political domain, but also in the economic and social spheres."[125] The constitution of the Fifth Republic did not effect a change. In its preamble, it pays respect to the rights of man as they are defined in the Declaration of 1789, as "complemented by the preamble of the Constitution of 1946." In article two France is declared a "social" state.

In the United States, no formal recognition of social ideas by the constitution-maker took place. The American Constitution, being conceived by its framers as a constitution of property, was not formally discarded in favor of a more social one. And neither was it formally amended to that effect. This does not mean, however, that social concepts would not have found recognition. A constitutional change of a more indirect, and, therefore, probably more serious, nature took place, a transformation that was effected through interpretation rather than legislation.[126] In the Dred Scott decision, Chief Justice Taney, a man who, in spite of the egalitarianism of the Jacksonian revolution, recognized the Constitution's quality as an instrument for the protection of property, said of the supreme law: "It speaks not only in the same words, but with the same meaning and intent with which it spoke when it came from the hands of its framers, and was voted on and adopted by the people of the United States. Any other rule of construction would abrogate the judicial character of this court and make it the mere reflex of the popular opinion or passion of the day."[127] Today, it may be said that the Constitution is no longer a constitution of property. The Supreme Court, having become a tool of the social and socialist passions of the day, has deprived the Constitution of that character. Due to political pressures resulting from the Great Depression, the Court has interpreted the Constitution in a social manner and transformed it into an instrument for the fulfillment of social needs rather than for the protection of the freedom of the individual and of private property.[128]

CONCLUSION

The advocacy of free property in the nineteenth century was honest and straightforward. Nothing was hidden in the fight for the emancipation of property from the last fetters of the *ancien régime*. Nothing had to be hidden, since that emancipation was an essential part of freedom, and freedom then occupied first rank. By contrast, attacks on property were, for the most part, less straightforward. Probably the most honest attack came from Karl Marx. He was clear and uncompromising. But all those "defenders" of private property who deviated from an uncompromising defense of the liberal concept of property in order to check socialism were, looking at it from an objective point of view, dishonest. It should not be understood that the sincerity of the social gospel movement, the social-minded economists and jurists is doubted. Holmes and Brandeis, Jhering and Gierke, Duguit—they all were perhaps as much friends of property as they were of liberty. There is no reason not to give them the benefit of the doubt. On the other hand, in consideration of the increasing depreciation of private property that took place in the wake of their ideas, it cannot be denied that they sowed a seed for the decline of property.

It is significant that the re-evaluation of property began by a mere interpretation of existing law, and that it started with a reinterpretation of private law, a law that deals with the relations among individuals. Mere reinterpretation of the concept of property, especially if confined to the sphere of private law, was not likely to arouse suspicion. In private law, where individual is pitted against individual, the restriction of one individual's property is likely to benefit the rights of another individual. That was accepted. The prohibition of malicious use of property, of a use that was detrimental to the neighbor, are a few examples of a seemingly harmless social interpretation of property rights. But once the liberal or individualistic concept of property had been questioned, then it was only a small step to restrict individual property for the sake of the community. The social interpretation of private property, originally kept within the realm of private law, intruded into the field of public law. The individual was no longer confronted with the rights of fellow individuals, who were his equals, but with the demands of society. His property was subjected not only to social interpretation, but also to social legislation.

Also in this more dangerous stage, legislators were not straightforward. Restrictions of property were achieved gradually. Labor legislation, originally attacking free property on humanitarian grounds, came to restrict property on pseudo-humanitarian grounds. The same can be said of other social legislation. In the end, legislation interfering with private property was passed without any pretense of ethical motives. Even constitutional law was not immune from the new trend. Progressively, with many people unaware of this progression, private property declined. First interpreted away in private law, then legislated away by public law, then given up by constitutions, the individualistic concept of property was replaced by a social one. Private property entered the road leading to its destruction.

This development implied the negation of the progress of civilization, a progress which had achieved its height in the nineteenth century. Private property, which has been one of the major incentives to human action throughout history, was deprived of that quality. The sick have conquered the healthy: social security, with benefits that are often out of proportion to needs, makes it less and less likely that the sick are eager to get healthy again and that they want to stay healthy for work. The lazy have conquered the diligent: unemployment compensation, having become more and more generous, makes it less and less likely that the unemployed are eager to get back to work, and that they do their best to stay in their jobs. The debtors have conquered the creditors: legislation having come to favor the debtor out of proportion to what is justifiable on humanitarian grounds, the debtor can take it easy in repaying his debt. To top it all, even work is being punished today: due to progressive taxation, the hard working individual will have a tax cut that is out of proportion to the amount he would pay if he did not work so hard. These examples are only a few demonstrations of the fall of property in the twentieth century.

V

PROPERTY AND DEMOCRACY

INTRODUCTION

THE FALL of private property, an event so far-reaching that it is probably the outstanding social feature of our time, provokes questions about the reasons for that fall. How could free property, having finally been established after centuries of struggle, having become transmuted from a natural right into positive law, and solemnly been confirmed by constitutions, decline as much as it did within the short span of a few decades? We witnessed in this century how the material achievements of generations were destroyed within seconds. We have lamented the values that were thus lost. But these earthly things, precious as they may have been, are usually replaceable. The situation is more serious when ideas are being destroyed. And, although it has hardly been as much noticed as the destruction of more tangible goods, the destruction of the idea of free property is probably the greatest loss we have suffered during this century.

As could be expected in the case of such an important institution, many reasons have been advanced for that destruction. The reason most frequently and least discriminately given is that of the "failure of liberalism." Communists, fascists, socialists and the adherents of the welfare state emphasize that their ideas on property will remedy the "failures" of liberalism. This is not surprising. Liberalism having been the way of life of the last century, anything occurring thereafter is likely to be, in some way, a consequence of liberalism. Liberalism, however, has too many aspects to justify putting the blame for the fall of property simply upon the movement as a whole. This is done only by communists and fascists, who reject all aspects of liberalism. Less totalitarian movements, though hardly less dangerous to the protection of private property, contented themselves with mainly attacking the "economic aspects" of liberalism, i.e., Manchester liberalism, or *laissez-faire*. Others still attributed the decline of property to the "excesses" of *laissez-faire* and its "super-individualism." But whether liberalism as a whole, or *laissez-faire,* or the "excesses" of the latter, were responsible for the decline of property is a question that has to be answered with caution. As far as the jurists are concerned, unrestricted property was often claimed merely from the point of view of legal logic, complementary as this may have been to their social convictions.[1] It was admitted that the owner was not free to use his property irrespective of moral and ethical considerations which were taken into account even under the "individualistic" Roman law.[2] The practice was, on the whole, in conformity with these considerations. Property was not used as ruthlessly as it was asserted by the advocates of more social concepts of property.[3] Even if "ruthless" use was made, the proprietors usually kept within the limits of the law. On reading the literature of the later nineteenth century, one gains the impression that reports on individualistic "abuses" of property are exaggerated, obviously with a view of bringing about the transmutation of moral and ethical standards favoring a social use of property into legal norms.[4] Although this undertaking was crowned with success, and the position of property was weakened, liberal "excesses" only do not account for the decline of property. Such "excesses" could have been prevented through interpretation of existing laws. While these excesses may have motivated some legislation introducing a more social conception of private property, they did not require the great bulk of welfare and take-care legislation that has been enacted.

The decline of the individualistic concept of property, as well as that of individualism as such, has been attributed to the emergence of nationalism with its emphasis upon community-feeling. This assertion seems fairly plausible. It appears to be most obvious in the case of Germany. The revival of Germanic law with its emphasis upon the social function of property was probably strongly aided by the movement for unification.[5] Once unification had been achieved, the vogue for that law did not subside. The German civil code of 1900, although mainly influenced by Roman law, was not as "Roman" as the *gemeine Recht* had been; it contained quite a few Germanic features.[6] With regard to France, it could be argued that during the nineteenth century, individualism became more and more submerged in nationalism. The Second Empire was based upon an organic rather than a contractual concept of the state. The chauvinism characteristic of its last years continued during the Third Republic. How little the individual was worth became evident in the Dreyfus affair. French nationalism hardly ever had more ardent exponents than Poincaré and Clemenceau. In the United States, the Civil War brought in its wake an increase of nationalistic feeling. By the beginning of the twentieth century, when the nation emerged as a world power, that feeling was enhanced, reaching a climax during World War I. It was during that period that Holmes and Brandeis tried to convince their countrymen of the value of sociological jurisprudence.[7] On the whole, it could probably be maintained that by the beginning of the twentieth century, the organic theory of the state had found increasing —though often unconscious—acceptance not only in Germany, but also in France and the United States. Naturally, if this affected the position of the individual in society, it was likely to affect also his property. Still, one ought to refrain from overestimating the influence of the new community-consciousness upon the decline of private property. While that influence became marked in the super-nationalism of unfree societies like fascist Italy and national-socialist Germany, it was not so great in societies that remained relatively free. It cannot be denied that nationalism had made inroads upon individualism by the end of the nineteenth century, and that it probably aided the re-emergence of paternalism.[8] However, it would be wrong to assume that the "nationalists" did not recognize the value of the protection of private property for the sake of the nation. Legislation passed merely in order to protect the health of the people might have been influenced by nationalistic considerations because health was considered an asset to the nation. This kind of legislation, however, barely infringed upon property rights. On the other hand, legislation that was detrimental to property, i.e., pseudo-ethical and pseudo-humanitarian legislation, legislation that was conducive to idleness, was not good for the nation. It would be strange indeed if nationalists had favored it.

It is absurd to look to nationalism and liberalism for the causes of the decline of property. That decline occurred because it was desired by the forces which had been latent throughout the liberal era, namely, the forces of egalitarianism. In spite of the emancipation of men and the opening of opportunities to all, human nature remained the same. Liberalism, securing to men the right and opportunity to become rich, also permitted them to remain poor. It was not only an incentive to hard work, but also a license to laziness. Owing to social conditions, but probably more as a result of their inclinations toward idleness, many people remained poor and did not come to share the enormous wealth that was produced as a result of the emancipation of property. Since the later nineteenth century, these poorer segments of society came increasingly to the fore. Aided by the march of democracy, they came to constitute a powerful majority. As such, they were able to impose their will upon the property-owning minority.

PROPERTY AND NEW LIBERAL RIGHTS

The decline of property stands in contrast to the protection of other liberal rights.

The decline of property rights during the twentieth century does not imply a general decline of the rights of man. It is *sui generis*. To whatever country one looks, and whatever right one may consider, one will, on the whole, notice an ever-increasing protection of rights that had been recognized since the eighteenth century. Furthermore, the recognition of new rights can be found.

Freedom of assembly and freedom of association are cases in point. They actually constitute different though closely related rights. The former was generally recognized earlier than the latter, largely because it constituted less of a threat to the government. It is not necessary here to make a strict distinction. The discussion will concentrate upon freedom of association rather than that of assembly, because the former marks a more relevant enlargement of the rights of man.

Rousseau was as strongly opposed to the formation of associations as Hobbes had been.[9] "Since for him the state embodied the general will which is by definition infallible, any lesser will must necessarily be inferior in quality and hurtful in action. He therefore urged the undesirability of associations on the ground that they interfere with the duty of the individual to give himself wholeheartedly to that general will which as embodied in the actions of the state represents his best interest." In France, therefore, "save for brief moments of revolutionary temper, as in 1789-91 and 1848-49, freedom of association has been rigorously controlled."[10] No mention is made of it in the Declaration of the Rights of Man and Citizen. Since, however, associations were founded in the wake of the Revolution, the Law of Chapelier of 1791 prohibited them. The Napoleonic autocracy, resulting from the Revolution but desirous of re-establishing, for its own gain, the absolutism of the time of Louis XIV, adopted the same ideas. According to Napoleon's Penal Code, association without permission constituted a severe offense. The prohibition of associations was further emphasized by the law of April 10, 1834. Although the monarchy of July applied the prohibitory provisions of criminal law with measure, and although, after the revolution of 1848, laws were passed that permitted the formation of associations, legislation adopted in 1849 and the years after abrogated the tolerant revolutionary laws and reinstituted the state of affairs as it had existed previously. But the fight for the right of association continued. Slowly, the hostility against collective organizations subsided. In 1875, associations for the distribution of information and higher education were permitted; nine years later, professional syndicates; shortly before the end of the century, mutual security enterprises. At the beginning of this century, general freedom of association was recognized.[11] Though it was not guaranteed in as comprehensive a manner as in England, Germany, Switzerland and the United States,[12] the ice was now broken. After World War II, freedom of association received constitutional sanction. It is considered a right of man under the constitutions of both the Fourth and Fifth Republics.[13]

In Germany, the Prussian General Land Law had provided that associations could be prohibited. In 1798, the Prussian government went a step further. It prohibited all political and secret organizations. This measure was reaffirmed in 1816 and extended to the territories Prussia had newly acquired. The constitutions of the southern German states, adopted after the Congress of Vienna, did not guarantee freedom of association, and neither did the all-German Federal Act. The Carlsbad Decrees of 1819 prohibited students' associations, and the Confederate Decree of 1832, all popular assemblies and all political associations. Against these measures the liberal forces fought for what they considered to be an unalienable right of man. After the revolutions of 1848, freedom of association was, next to freedom of assembly, included in the bill of rights of the Frankfurt constitution. Although this constitution was not adopted, its liberal spirit influenced state legislation.[14] Once Germany had become united, attempts were made to bring about freedom of association under Reich law. As in France, however, there was first passed legislation with respect to the association of specific people. It was not until 1907 that the government introduced a bill providing for a more general freedom of association, which was adopted as the Association Law in 1908. Ten years later, a proclamation of the Council of the People's Representatives dispensed with most of the qualifications that had still existed under that law. Freedom of association was finally guaranteed by the Weimar constitution and the Basic Law.[15]

In the United States, voluntary associations of individuals originally obtained legal recognition merely under the common law right of contract. But this recognition did not amount to much protection. By ordinary law or administrative decrees, the right of association was restricted whenever associations were felt to have "unlawful purposes," and the definitions of what constituted such purposes were rather arbitrary. Like most of the state constitutions that preceded it, the Constitution of the United States, while expressly guaranteeing freedom of assembly, did not mention freedom of association.[16] The only right of association that was elevated to constitutional status was that for religious purposes.[17] "But this position was a unique one, and other types of associations had only general due process provisions of constitutions or statutory safeguards to protect their right to exist and grow." The interpreters of the first amendment for a long time rejected the idea that the right of association was "logically . . . clearly a right cognate to the right of assembly."[18] Rather, they applied the principle *inclusio unius est exclusio alterius*: since the right of religious association was specifically mentioned in that amendment, other rights of association, not being mentioned, were not guaranteed. In the course of time, the general right of association was protected under the fifth and fourteenth amendments.[19] It was not until 1937, however, that the Supreme Court indicated that freedom of assembly might include freedom of association, though it did not specifically mention the latter right.[20] And only during the past decade did the open recognition that freedom of association was protected under the first amendment occur.[21]

The addition of such rights as freedom of assembly and association to the bills of rights is a significant phenomenon. It demonstrates not only an extension of the scope of these bills, but also a shift in the meaning of liberal rights. Freedom of religion, of speech, of the press, freedom from imprisonment, protection from double jeopardy, the right to a trial by jury—they all have, no matter what specific aspect of freedom they may cover and how their exercise may be regulated under different legal systems at various times, one feature in common. They all are concerned with the individual, and with him only. He has the right to certain aspects of freedom and he alone will profit from that right. The person who speaks exercises his freedom to speak individually. His speech remains identified with him only, even if it was one of many speeches made for a common cause. The person who commits a crime claims his rights to a fair trial individually, irrespective of whether he is an accomplice and is accused with others, or whether he is the only person accused. He alone will always remain identified with his own trial, no matter whether or not he was tried with others, even if his degree of participation in a specific crime was the same as that of others and even if his punishment has been the same as that meted out to others. In the future, he alone can claim the protection from double jeopardy. He will always enjoy that protection, irrespective of how many accomplices, having not been brought to trial before, will, owing to new evidence, be given harsher sentences than he was given. More examples of cases in which a right of an individual, invoked individually, remains identified with that individual and with him only could be mentioned.

The situation differs with regard to such rights as freedom of assembly or freedom of association. Although these rights possess some features in common with the rights just described, they fundamentally differ from them in many respects. They have in common the individualistic character of invoking the right. The person who goes to an assembly acts by virtue of his own individual right, irrespective of how many other people might also go. The same can be said of the person who joins an association. His joining is individualistic in character, no matter how many other people may also join. However, as soon as the individual is part of an assembly or association, his individuality begins to disappear. His actions became so-to-speak de-individualized and anonymized. He becomes a participant; a member. Whatever he does in that capacity, is more or less part of assembly or association action. It becomes identified with the group rather than the individual. Freedom of assembly and of association are less individualistic than such rights as freedom of speech or trial by jury. The latter are independent of other individuals. Freedom of assembly and association, by contrast, presuppose such individuals. An assembly or association requires the participation of at least two men. It is admitted that the member of the group does not lose his individual status altogether. He retains the right to leave the group, dubious as this right may be in many cases.[22] During his membership, however, his individuality more or less disappears.[23]

The introduction of such rights as freedom of assembly and association, resulting in group dependence rather than in individual independence, constitutes an expansion of the original concept of liberal rights. In their original meaning, these rights were purely individualistic. The individual was confronted only by society as a whole. His freedom was not challenged by any other group. With the recognition of such rights as freedom of assembly and association, however, the individual's freedom became challenged by groups within society. He no longer confronted society as a free and identifiable individual only, but also as a somewhat dependent and anonymous member of the group. Liberal rights, originally meant to secure freedom, became adulterated through the inclusion of rights that entitled the individual to surrender part of his freedom to some group.

The effects of this expansion of liberal rights upon freedom are obvious. People created groups to further their aims. But this undertaking was a Trojan horse. While the individual was likely to get greater concessions for himself through group action, he was also likely to receive just the same as his fellow members and no more. He was more apt to be secure, but also more likely to receive nothing but average rewards. His position vis-a-vis the state was not strengthened for the state is as superior to the group as it is to the individual. On the contrary, this position was probably weakened. Governments have generally obligated themselves to respect such rights as freedom of religion and freedom of speech, etc. On the other hand, while they may have guaranteed the right to join groups, they have been reluctant in guaranteeing the protection of groups themselves. Thus, the individual may be hurt by a government action against the group in a way in which he could not be hurt if he were outside the group. Also, it should not be overlooked that the government has in the group an instrument with which it can regulate the life and actions of the members of the group.[24] By such indirect interference, the government can probably direct the behavior of group members more easily than that of unattached individuals.

It may have been for these reasons that the right to form groups was not included in certain early bills of rights. This omission did not occur by mere default. Associations were expressly prohibited. Too much had one been aware, under the *ancien régime,* of the dependence of the members upon their respective associations and guilds. Freedom of association reminded people of feudalism and paternalism. They had had enough of that. It has been argued that associations were resented mainly because membership in them had been compulsory. This argument is not without foundation. However, it does not explain why also voluntary associations were prohibited. There is reason to believe that it was feared that such associations would be detrimental to freedom.

We know today that this scepticism was justified. The admission of the right of association entailed serious consequences. Inevitably, it seems, though such was probably not intended, it worked toward the elimination of individualism.[25] Once associations were permitted, they became like vortices that pulled everyone within their orbits. People joined associations because they believed they would secure the protection of their interests. Associations increased in numbers, and became more powerful in getting concessions for their members. To become still more powerful, they turned against those individuals who had not yet joined, often applying pressure to induce them to become members. In the end, nearly all persons doing a certain type of work became members of the association, or "union." More and more associations were established. In time, nearly all workers became associated, or, to use a term that expresses the loss of freedom more clearly, "organized." The organization of workers was matched by that of employers. To workers' and employers' associations were added associations of so-called "free professions." Today, few free, unorganized, individuals are left. The community of free men has degenerated into an "organization man."[26]

Freedom of association, compromising the individualism of liberal rights, was not without effect upon that highly individualistic liberal right—the right of private property. The right of association made private property less immune from attacks. Its admission led to the foundation of more and more associations and to the "organization" of more and more people. This situation, while it results from a liberal right—though an adulterated one—actually amounts to a step back from the liberal era, a step back to the *ancien régime.* In a way, it constitutes a realization of Gierke's concept of the corporate society, which is composed of groups rather than individuals.[27] Corporation or association, implying a loss of individuality, also implies a depreciation of private property. It was not just by chance that Gierke, the author of the *Genossenschaftsrecht*, was also an advocate of a social appreciation of property.

The decrease of the immunity of private property is due to a variety of causes that are the result of association. In general, members of a group feel a certain restraint in promoting their individual and egoistic aims toward fellow members. The greater the degree of group coherence, the greater the compulsion for self-restraint is likely to be. This applies also to the use of private property. A member of an association feels a certain reluctance to use his property to the detriment of another member. It is probable that this self-restraint toward fellow associates brings about a self-restraint toward all fellow men. Since this feeling is more or less common to the members of most associations, ultimately property will be considered to fulfill a group function rather than an individualistic function. Property will become "socialized."

But association does not only tend to "socialize" property. It does not only prompt the owner to a less individualistic use of his property. It also makes the proprietor less appreciative of his property, because through association, property can become, and has very much become, anonymized. The joint stock company is an example. Ever since the admission of free associations, that specific brand has grown by leaps and bounds. More and more joint stock companies have been formed,[28] more and more has their membership expanded, more and more has property been transformed into shares. Today, the percentage of property invested in shares is much greater than it was in the nineteenth century. The owner has become separated from his property. Of course, he owns a share as much as he owns a car or a house, and can dispose of the one as much as of the other. However, there is a different degree of attachment to and thus a different degree of appreciation of the various kinds of property. Most legal systems recognize this fact by giving credit to things with "sentimental value." As a rule, a person feels more attached to a house than to a car and more to a car than to a share. A house, as a permanent abode, is more likely to have the owner's affection than a car. He may have been born and raised in the same house in which his parents may have lived and his children been born. Usually an attachment to a car is less strong, though also here some sentimental value may exist. By contrast, the ownership of a share has no sentimental value. A share is something that most proprietors often will not see. With an easy heart, they will swap it for another share, or sell it.

It may be argued that attachment to property has nothing to do with the existence of property rights and that the formal right to a share is as restricted or unrestricted as the formal right to a house. This is, on the whole, correct. However, it can scarcely be denied that the feeling of attachment enhances the appreciation of property. Appreciation, in turn, increases the willingness to fight for what is one's own. The Struggle for Law is, as Jhering pointed out in his well known study, largely based upon the individual's attachment to his goods. It is, therefore, not surprising that of all people, the farmers, whose property consists chiefly of land, put up the most unequivocal fight for their rights.[29] On the other hand, with the number of shares having continually increased and with more and more people owning them, the likelihood for an appreciation of property and the willingness for its defense was decreased.

It may be argued that the "anonymization" of property, i.e., the distribution of shares, has helped to bridge the gap that existed between the rich entrepreneur and the many poor and thus weakened the latters' desire to destroy large accumulations of wealth. But, again, it appears doubtful whether this is conducive to the protection of property. It should not be overlooked that the creation of the joint stock company opened up the possibility of the many poor shareholders to control the few rich.[30]

With its position weakened and its immunity decreased, property invited attacks, and these attacks came quickly. The willingness of owners to make a more "social" use of their property was likely only to be taken as an admission that "individualistic" uses of property were bad. It could hardly fail to give incentive to the foes of private property. Community feeling does not merely prompt the owner to refrain from "unsocial" uses of property. It also induces the community to impose restrictions upon private property. And just as property became weakened by its anonymization, it became attacked by that powerful anonymous body, that dubious representative of the interests of the people— the popular majority.[31]

It is not surprising that property should be attacked by the majority. The majority is the representative of the masses. Since the masses have not only advanced, as Hegel envisaged,[32] but also become organized, the majority today is representative of the militant masses. And these masses "can destroy everything and have the tendency not to suffer greatness and independence."[33] Small wonder that they turned against that distinctive feature of society, property.[34] It has been asserted that the organized masses "are without brains and inhuman,"[35] and that "majority is nonsense" and that "brains were always only with the few."[36] Be this as it may, it must be admitted that the majority always has had enough brains to know how to restrict private property.

Majority rule, the outstanding feature of democratic government, has become increasingly identified with democracy. Therefore, it could be maintained that property, having come under attack by the majority, has come under attack by democracy. As a matter of fact, many attacks upon property have been made in the name of democracy. It has become fashionable to separate the protection of property from democracy. Democracy, it is argued, can exist without that protection. Here is a change of attitude of truly fundamental dimensions! Whereas originally free property was an end one hoped to achieve through self-government, democracy has now become an end in itself, irrespective of how property fares. More and more, the rights of the individual have been appraised merely under the criterion of whether they are conducive to democracy. Not being considered to be so conducive, property rights became neglected and discredited. A favorite among liberal rights during the democratic revolutions, they became the stepchild of modern democracy. Today, property rights are not only considered to be unnecessary for democratic government, but even to be incompatible with democracy. This development is due to fundamental changes that have come about in the nature of democracy.

DEMOCRACY, ABSOLUTE DEMOCRACY AND PROPERTY: THE THEORY

Owing to the growth of egalitarianism, democracy has become authoritarian and a threat to private property.

Modern democracy came about as a reaction against the *ancien régime*. That regime, no matter how it may have appeared in the different countries, was, on the whole, characterized by feudalism and absolute monarchy. The individuals were unequal, and, as mere subjects, unfree. Since feudalism and absolute government, or legal inequality and the absence of freedom, go well together, their concomitance did not present a problem for the *ancien régime*. This may be one of the reasons why that regime lasted as long as it did.

Modern democracy, having come about as a reaction against the *ancien régime*, has for its *raison d'être* the rejection of the major features of that regime. It was established as a polemic against feudalism and absolute government. Its purpose was to institute equality among men and to make them free. If it fails to secure these ends, it is no longer justified.

It is likely that that event will happen. Striving for both equality and freedom, democracy is confronted with a dilemma. Equality poses a problem for the existence of freedom, just as freedom poses a problem for equality. Unlimited freedom is likely to result in inequality, just as unqualified equality will have a restriction of freedom in its wake. This problem has been generally recognized and does not require further elaboration. Here only the question of how those who abolished the *ancien régime* for the sake of equality and freedom felt the problem should be solved is of concern. They solved it by giving freedom priority over equality.

The two outstanding proclamations of the democratic revolutions, the American Declaration of Independence and the French Declaration of the Rights of Man and Citizen, pay high tribute to the idea of equality. However, this does not mean that they subordinate freedom to equality. Quite to the contrary! Jefferson's exclamation that all men are created equal before his statement that they are endowed with unalienable rights does not imply that for him equality comes first, and freedom, second. Rather, he believed that all men are equally entitled to freedom, possibly thinking that the American colonists were as much entitled to it as the English.[37] For him, all men have an equal claim to the rights recognized by natural or positive law, i.e., men are equal before the law.[38] If people have an equal claim to unalienable rights, these rights are an end to which they aspire. Equality is nothing but a means to insure the equal enjoyment of these rights.

Since the slogan of the French Revolution, "Liberty, Equality, Fraternity," put liberty before equality, it is not surprising to find the same sequence of values in the Declaration of the Rights of Man and Citizen. Article one says that "men are born and remain free and equal in rights." The words "equal in rights" have no other meaning than "equal" in the Declaration of Independence. They mean equality before the law. This is confirmed by the most egalitarian provision of the French document, article six. This article states that the law "must be the same for all" and that "all citizens are equal in the eyes of the law." As if it wants to emphasize that equality means nothing but equality before the law, it also states that "all citizens are equally admissible to all honors, places and public employment *according to their capacity and without any other distinction but that of virtue and talent.*"[39] Furthermore, the superiority of freedom over equality follows from the fact that liberty is rated among the "natural and imprescriptible rights of man," whereas equality is not.

The denial of a superiority of equality over freedom can also be seen in the actual rejection of egalitarian movements at the time of the democratic revolutions. In England, the Diggers formed a mere minority among the revolutionaries. In the United States, Shays's Rebellion, attempting to bring about a more equal distribution of property, hastened action against egalitarian tendencies that manifested themselves in various states. In France, the people fought the egalitarianism of Babeuf. His Manifest of the Equals (1796) was generally rejected. The uprising of the egalitarians was put down. Babeuf was guillotined.

The forms of democratic government that emerged from the revolutions indicate a desire not to permit equality to gain the upper hand over freedom. In the English revolutions, the one which was staged by Cromwell as well as the Glorious Revolution, men were careful not to extend the democratic right to participate in government to all people, because they feared that such an extension would result in an equality through rather than before the law, and restrict freedom. A similar caution can be noticed in the United States, where the Founding Fathers excluded potentially egalitarian segments of the population from participating in government. Even the French Revolution, the most egalitarian of them all, did not produce equal suffrage.

Although the superiority of freedom over equality was more or less secured by the restriction of suffrage, some were not content with that precaution. Further safeguards were adopted. The branches of government which were likely to tend toward egalitarianism were checked. The House of Lords was not abolished. It remained a check upon the Commons.[40] In the United States, a system of checks and balances, notably the institution of judicial review, was established.[41] In France, the government by assembly, under which majority rule was omnipotent, was soon followed by a government that detracted from the power of the most democratic branch of government.[42]

The legal documents that resulted from the democratic revolutions confirm the liberal balance between equality and freedom. Equality, while recognized as an important means to the enjoyment of freedom, was considered inferior to its end. In the English Bill of Rights, freedom has priority before equality. (The words "equal" and "equality" are not mentioned in that document.) The same can be said of the American Constitution with its bill of rights.[43] The situation does not differ in the case of France. Constitutions adopted during the revolutionary era gave freedom priority over equality.

In view of the strong position freedom enjoyed vis-a-vis equality, it is scarcely necessary to mention that private property, being considered an essential part of freedom, was safe during the democratic revolutions. In spite of all emphasis upon equality—an emphasis that was due to the absence of equality before the law under the *ancien régime*—the institution of private property, having enjoyed protection under that regime, survived the revolutions quite comfortably and emerged in its old, if not greater, splendor.

The democratic revolutions had solved the problem arising from the concomitance of freedom and equality by establishing a constitutional, limited, or classic democracy.[44] Under that form of government, the majority of those enjoying full citizenship, i.e., of a privileged group, ruled. However, for the sake of freedom or for that of the protection of the capacities of naturally unequal individuals, the majority was restricted under a constitution or higher law. Equality meant merely equality before the law both with respect to the individual's participation in government and to the protection of his rights. Unequal talents were unequivocally protected. Accordingly, equality was restricted.

The different degree of the restriction of equality in the various countries indicates that there is no firm rule regarding the scope of that restriction. The same is true if we consider the situation in merely one country. Since "there is no retrograde step in the rear of democracy,"[45] the questions arise as to how far constitutional democracy has changed and how that change affected that feature of constitutionalism—the subordination of equality under freedom. Montesquieu wrote that "the love of democracy is that of equality."[46] Was that love strong enough to elevate equality over freedom? This question can be answered in the affirmative. With the march of democracy, a reduction of the restriction of equality occurred. The result was a decline of freedom.

It should not be understood that freedom did not advance with democracy. Under democratic government, the protection of the rights of the individual increased quantitatively as well as qualitatively. Not only were new liberties guaranteed, but also, liberties that had already

H. A. IRONSIDE
MEMORIAL LIBRARY

been recognized were given greater and greater scope. However, at the same time, there existed an ever increasing quest for more equality. Babeuf, in his Manifest of the Equals, had mocked equality before the law as a "beautiful and sterile fiction."[47] It has been remarked that Babeuf foresaw, in spite of the rejection of social equality in the Declaration of the Rights of Man and Citizen, that, in the end, such equality would result from the Declaration.[48] Indeed, in the governments established by the democratic revolutions, the desire for more and more freedom was matched by the quest for greater and greater equality. In view of the competitive character of these values, it was not unlikely that a readjustment of the relative importance of freedom and equality would occur. That adjustment favored the growth of equality.

One important reason for the victory of equality is that equality is a mass right. By contrast, freedom is an individualistic right. That is why absolute freedom is anarchy. It is the essence of freedom that it entitles an individual to be outside the crowd and independent of others. A person caring for freedom cares for being able to do things in his own way. He prays the way he wants to and joins the associations he wants to, irrespective of what others think or do. Equality, on the other hand, is not characterized by individualism. It is a collective right, a right that is dependent upon other people and presupposes the existence of such people. It is the essence of equality that it entitles an individual to be equal to others, i.e., to be one among many rather than to be outside and independent of them. A person caring for equality, while he may care for being able to do things his own way, does so mainly because others have the right to do these things. He wants to be—or at least to appear—as free as the Joneses. He wants freedom of religion because they have it. He wants freedom of contract because they have it. He wants the right to join an association because they can do so. Furthermore, he might want all these rights merely in order to go to the same church as the Joneses do, to buy the same things, to join the same clubs. Of course he wants his freedom. But he does not want it so much in order to be free, but in order to be equal. Inadvertently, equality has become an end in itself. Freedom has been reduced to a mere means to that end. Unlike freedom, equality has the existence of the masses for a *conditio sine qua non*. Unlike freedom, which is individual-centered, equality is mass-centered. Small wonder that at a time that witnessed not only the advancement but a veritable revolt of the masses,[49] equality progressed until it was superior to freedom.

The expansion of equality is not surprising in view of the fact that, as compared with freedom, equality, having been more restricted than freedom, had more room to expand. Like freedom, equality tends to be absolute. However, the equality that was established in the democratic revolutions was nothing but a qualified equality, namely, an equality before the law. And that law was made not by all people, but only by a select group. There was no equality in the law-making process. Clearly, here was a vacuum to be filled. And, unsuspecting as they were, the freedom-loving forces helped to fill that vacuum. Having experienced the blessings of popular government for liberty, they admitted the expansion of the popular basis for government. Before, people had been equal before the law, a law that was not made by all, because not everyone had equal rights to participate in the democratic process. Now it was believed that for the sake of freedom, all men should possess equal rights to participate in that process.

The broadening of suffrage is a demonstration of egalitarian tendencies in the march of democracy. It is a universal phenomenon and can be found in all democratic nations.[50] In his *Spirit of the Laws,* Montesquieu wrote that "all the inhabitants . . . ought to have a right of voting at the election of a representative, except such as are in so mean a situation as to be deemed to have no will of their own."[51] It can be said that democratic governments have acted in accord with this statement. However, whereas in the beginning they were cautious about giving people in "mean" situations the right to vote, that caution disappeared later. The abolition of property qualifications is a case in point.[52]

The French Declaration of the Rights of Man and Citizen had proclaimed universal suffrage as a natural right of man. Thomas Paine "contrasted this principle with the practice in England, where the basis of representation consists in royal patents and embodies a grant or boon."[53] Robespierre, supported by other revolutionaries of the left, in a speech of October 22, 1789, took a strong stand against property qualifications. Nevertheless, the electoral law of December 22 excluded from voting persons who did not pay a certain amount of taxes, and those who were bankrupt and insolvent. The constitution of 1791 provided for similar requirements. The electoral law of 1792 and the constitution of the following year recognized universal suffrage in the abstract, though servants and persons on relief were not yet permitted to vote. Although the Restoration restored property qualifications, they were essentially reduced during the following decades. In 1848, they were abolished altogether.[54] "The right to vote belongs to all without exception," the proclamation of March 16th stated, continuing, "there are no longer any proletarians in France. Every Frenchman of age is a political citizen. Every citizen is a voter. Every voter is sovereign. The law is equal and absolute for all. There is not one citizen who could say to another: 'You are more sovereign than I am!' " An attempt to reinstitute a disguised form of property qualification by the law of May 31, 1850 was short-lived. One of the first acts of Louis Napoleon was to abolish that law. Ever since, suffrage in France has not been restricted through property qualifications.[55]

In Germany, no universal suffrage existed prior to 1848. The legislatures of the states were usually composed of representatives of the various estates, such as nobility, cities and universities. On the whole, the right to vote was dependent upon the ownership of real or personal estate, or the payment of taxes. Under the influence of the movement of 1848, however, a trend toward the abolition of property qualifications can be noted.[56] Some states relaxed these requirements, others outrightly proclaimed universal and equal suffrage. An all-German electoral law merely excluded from voting bankrupt persons and public charges. Although during the years following the abortive revolutionary movement most states readopted property qualifications, their attempt to curb universal suffrage was short-lived. From the 1860's on, the ideas of 1848-49 were more and more realized. Article twenty of the constitution of the North German League, which became that of the empire, proclaimed the principle of universal suffrage. The example of the Reich was followed by the *Länder*. Property requirements for voting were lessened or abolished altogether. Even Prussia, having retained its three-class system after other states had introduced universal suffrage, followed suit.[57] The Weimar constitution brought the development to a conclusion. Not content with providing universal suffrage merely for the Reich, as had the Imperial constitution, it prescribed that type of suffrage also for the *Länder*.

In spite of the statement of the American Declaration of Independence that all men are created equal and that government exists by the consent of the governed, the new independent American states did not establish equal suffrage for all.[58] The ownership of real estate, or personal property, or the payment of taxes were prerequisites for the right to vote. Before the end of the eighteenth century, however, more liberal trends can be noted in the original thirteen states. New Hampshire, which in 1784 had shifted from property holding to tax paying, removed the latter requirement in 1792. In the same year, Delaware shifted from ownership of personal property to the payment of taxes. Vermont, the first state admitted to the new union in 1791, had full manhood suffrage. In the course of the nineteenth century, suffrage without property qualifications can be found in Maryland (1809), Indiana (1816), Connecticut and Illinois (1818), Maine (1819), Missouri (1820), New York and Massachusetts (1821), Mississippi (1832), New Jersey (1844), Louisiana (1845), Virginia (1850), Ohio (1851), North Carolina (1856). Other states eased their property qualifications. When Lord Bryce wrote his *American Commonwealth*, he noted that a few states had merely tax requirements.[59] The twentieth century saw a further abolition of these requirements.

The introduction of universal suffrage was extremely important for the development of democracy. Democratic government acquired a broader basis. With the abolition of property qualifications, that basis consisted no longer of the well-to-do, but also of the not so well-to-do. The more property qualifications were eased, the more government became based upon the vote of the poor. Democracy, originally based on virtue and talent, became increasingly based upon numbers. Gradually the poor came to rule the rich. Moreover, with the increasing abolition of property qualifications poorer and poorer elements were admitted to the ruling majority. More and more, the moderately poor were outnumbered by the very poor. The ruling majority became poorer and poorer.

Combined with the "pauperization" of the majority was an increase of its power. This changed the character of democracy. In an enlightened democracy, the power of the majority under a system with property qualifications is limited by the existence of those who cannot vote. The fight for the abolition of these qualifications renders proof of that fact. Those who could not vote were alert and aware of the discrimination against them. They constituted a part of the population which the government could not ignore. Aside from this external limitation upon the "majority," there were self-imposed restraints. Being composed of representatives of the more distinguished members of society, the government was likely to respect the rights of the individual as they were protected by older law. By contrast, such limitations do not exist in the absence of property qualifications. The numerical majority of all the inhabitants is not externally constrained. It is a real majority, not just one artificially created by law, one that may actually be a numerical minority. Also, self-imposed constraints are not likely to exist. Being representative of the less distinguished members of society, the government is not apt to show much respect for the very values that make the poor look undistinguished. Quite to the contrary. If under older law the poor were riff-raff, it was necessary to destroy that law in order to obliterate that blemish. Consequently, older standards were destroyed as ruthlessly as possible. The majority became authoritarian.

The quest for equality—inevitable in a democracy[60]—largely aided by the introduction of universal suffrage, thus resulted in the replacement of limited popular government by authoritarian democracy. The latter, although it is the result of the quest for more equality, proves the hypocrisy of egalitarianism. The government of property owners had been attacked because of its disrespect for social equality. It was said that the owners oppressed the non-owners. Unfounded as this accusation is on the whole, things did not improve after the government of the proprietors had been abolished. The new government, based on universal suffrage, unrestricted as it was, could and did suppress the minority. And now, although only the minority was suppressed and not the majority, the amount of suppression was scarcely reduced. It was simply shifted from a qualitatively probably smaller "suppression" of the many to a qualitatively probably greater suppression of the few.

Absolute democracy, being an unlimited or authoritarian form of government, cannot be a government under which the individual is free. Freedom is assured, as it was recognized by those who originally replaced the *ancien régime* through popular government, only if equality is restricted to mean nothing but equality before the law. As soon as it means more, freedom is endangered. Under unlimited democracy, equality has come to mean more than merely equality before the law. The equality of all to make the law, brought about by universal suffrage, has tended to become an equality through the law. Although this development has not yet reached its final conclusion, the general trend appears to be clear. Freedom is about to be replaced by unlimited equality.

Under authoritarian democracy, the evaluation of the rights of the individual gives property a low ranking. Absolute democracy thrives on equality. Universal suffrage is its very lifeblood. The more people there are who participate in the democratic process, the better. The rights to participate in government rank the highest. Rights that were considered nothing but a means for the achievement of freedom under limited democracy, have become an end in themselves. More, they have become identified with freedom.[61] Needless to say, that kind of freedom is something different from traditional freedom as the sum total of liberal rights. It is a "new freedom." Under this new freedom, the individual is no longer free from constraint. Rather, he is free to constrain. He is free to make laws by which his fellow men are restricted for the sake of the community.

Authoritarian democracy not only elevates democratic rights over liberal rights, but it also causes a democratic distinction among the latter. Liberal rights that are supposedly conducive to participation in government are protected more than rights that do not appear to be so. Rights that are considered a prerequisite for democracy enjoy a "preferred position." Freedom of speech, of the press, of assembly, of association, often referred to as "civil" rights because civility is believed to imply participation in government, have come to be ranked higher than rights which are not considered to be prerequisite for democracy.

The right that is least compatible with egalitarianism is that of private property. Consequently, that right has become the stepchild of authoritarian democracy. Of all rights, it ranks the lowest and enjoys the least protection. Taking into account the probability that people who own real property have the greatest appreciation of property; that people who own personal property have a high, though already smaller, appreciation; that people who have nothing but the money they earn appreciate property still less; that those who have nothing at all hardly appreciate property at all, it may be said that the gradual abolition of property qualifications for voting had a definite relation to the gradual depreciation of property. The abolition of real property requirements decreased the power of those who were the most appreciative of property. The abolition of personal property requirements decreased the power of those who had a high, though already smaller, appreciation of property. The abolition of tax requirements decreased the power of those who had some appreciation of property. Finally, the admission of those who had no property, and no income, and perhaps even debts, to the democratic process, increased the power of those who had either no appreciation of, or even displayed a negative attitude toward, property rights.

Thus the expansion of the suffrage as the democratic means to bring about greater equality results in the progressive limitation of elements that favor a protection of property, and the increasing power of those who do not care about property rights. The outcome is a decrease in the appreciation of private property. Equality, as soon as it is more than an equality before the law, is incompatible with the protection of freedom and its most unegalitarian aspect—the right of private property. Democracy, having become egalitarian, is unlikely to protect property. How it lived up to that expectation will be considered in the following.

DEMOCRACY, ABSOLUTE DEMOCRACY AND PROPERTY:
THE PRACTICE

The transformation from a limited to an absolute democracy brought with it a qualitatively as well as a quantitatively unrestricted lawmaker, and resulted in a decline of the law and of property rights.

Unlimited democracy means unlimited majority rule. Since ruling amounts largely to lawmaking, unlimited democracy means an unlimited legislative power of the majority. This non-limitation expresses itself mainly in the non-recognition of norms that bind the lawmaker. It is one of the characteristic features of limited democracy that the ruling majority recognizes such norms. The degeneration of limited democracy into absolute democracy is demonstrated mainly by the absence of such a recognition.

The evolution in France is an example. The *ancien régime* was attacked on the grounds of higher law. The rights of the citizen were considered to be identical to the rights of man, rights that were supposed to have existed prior to human law.[62] The belief in natural law did not disappear once the Revolution had been completed. When Cambacérès presented his draft of a civil code to the Convention, he emphasized that it was based upon nature and reason.[63] In 1803, the project of the Civil Code still affirmed in its first article the existence of natural law which, as natural reason, was the source of all positive law.[64] The omission of a similar statement in the final product was not due to the fact that natural law was no longer recognized, but rather to the fact that the existence of natural law was taken for granted. "In the year XII, everybody believed in natural law."[65]

But this admission through omission was not without problems. The antagonists of higher law could argue that reference to natural law had been omitted because that law's superiority was no longer taken for granted. Also, the admission of natural law through omission implied the dangerous supposition that the legislator, whenever he acted, could act only in conformity with natural law; that positive law, since it supposedly consisted of a transmutation of natural law, had to be good and beyond reproach. Although lip service was paid to natural law,[66] people felt more and more that while an appeal to natural law was justified against absolute monarchy, it was out of place under popular government. It was felt that if the law was made by the people, it could not be contrary to natural law and bad. Thus the democratic legislator was freed from taking into consideration higher law. He became an absolute ruler.

The situation was not different on the other side of the Rhine, where the degeneration of a limited democracy into an absolute one is symbolized by the replacement of the *Rechtsstaat* through the *Gesetzesstaat*. *Recht* means "right," and *Gesetz* is positive law. However, *Recht* can also mean positive law, and has come more and more to have that meaning. The interchangeability of these terms demonstrates the dilemma of the law. It shows, on the one hand, how identical man-made law and what is right can be, and, on the other hand, how people can win the impression that man-made law must necessarily be right and just. In the first half of the nineteenth century, the term *Rechtsstaat* was applied to a government bound by a constitution that was oriented toward natural law and guaranteed the rights of the individual. The two great exponents of the *Rechtsstaat* during that time, Robert von Mohl, a student of American constitutionalism, and J. F. Stahl,[67] employ the term in that sense. Laws made by the monarch or the legislative assembly had to conform to the principles of justice and natural law.[68] However, later in the century, it was increasingly stressed that *Rechtsstaat* meant the rule of the laws as they were made by the legislative body, i.e., of the *Gesetze*. One gains the impression that those who employed the term *Rechtsstaat* at that time did not really feel that *Gesetze* ought to be right, but rather that they necessarily *were* right and just. In later years the idea of right disappeared and the term *Rechtsstaat* was used simply in the sense of *Gesetzesstaat*.[69] Under the democratic

Weimar Republic, juridical positivism finally freed the legislator of all restrictions of natural law.[70] The legislator had become omnipotent.

In the United States, the process in which the legislator became omnipotent took longer, but was not less complete. Due to the fact that Americans had experienced the oppressions of legislative omnipotence and had guarded themselves against democratic despotism during their formative period, it was more difficult for the legislator to reassert his power. The belief that legislative acts were inferior to the Constitution and natural law was too strong. All too frequently the lawmaker was reminded of this belief. Although the first half of the nineteenth century was characterized by the "great debates" in Congress, it was by no means a time during which the legislature could be called supreme. Rather, it was a period when such outstanding jurists as Marshall, Kent and Story confirmed the doctrine that the lawmaker was under the Constitution and under older law. The situation scarcely changed in the following decades. Only sociological jurisprudence, asserting that the will of the majority should not be tested for its compatibility with the Constitution and natural law, launched the lawmaker on a successful march toward omnipotence. As was the case in France and Germany, people became more and more convinced that the laws made by their representatives were necessarily right and good and just. In this atmosphere, the democratic lawmaker in America as well as in France and Germany, was apt to feel himself less and less restricted by considerations of justice and higher law. It is probably not exaggerated to maintain that there has come into existence in the United States as much of an omnipotent legislator as in the European nations.

Although power has been called evil,[71] it must not necessarily be evil. It depends on whoever is exercising it and how it is being exercised.[72] On the whole, popular government has been considered superior to other forms of government because it is felt that the people are the best guardians of their liberties. This supposition is justified, as long as people are sufficiently wise and educated to appreciate their liberties and to know how to protect them. Also, it is generally believed that majority rule is superior to minority rule as far as the protection of the rights of the individual is concerned. Again, this is true as long as the majority cares sufficiently for the rights of the individual, irrespective of whether he belongs to the majority or not. On the other hand, as soon as the majority cares only for its members and not for other individuals, it becomes dangerous. The opinion, cherished in France, Germany and the

United States alike, that the majority will necessarily make good laws, is fraught with danger. It paved the way for the belief that the democratic lawmaker could do no wrong, *vox populi, vox dei*. It made restrictions upon the legislator appear unnecessary. It gave him *carte blanche*. Intoxicated with so much power, he was likely to lose judgment of what was right and wrong.

The intoxication of the democratic lawmaker was not only dangerous from a qualitative point of view, but also, from a quantitative one. The people, finally having been given the right to make their own laws, made generous use of that right.[73] The first half of the nineteenth century saw so much legislative activity that already toward the middle of the century one realized that the laws were becoming all too numerous. But the number of laws which were passed during that period were few as compared with the number of those that were passed later. In the second half of the century, legislation grew by leaps and bounds. It became still worse in the twentieth century, when a rapidly increasing number of legislative enactments became matched, if not outnumbered, by a veritable bulk of administrative decrees.[74] One has spoken of the motorized lawmaker.[75] It may be asked whether the jet lawmaker is not around the corner.

As early as 1788, Madison had warned of the danger of too many laws. In the sixty-second essay of the Federalist Papers, he wrote: "The internal effects of a mutable policy are . . . calamitous. It poisons the blessings of liberty itself. It will be of little avail to the people, that the laws are made by men of their own choice, if the laws be so voluminous that they cannot be read, or so incoherent that they cannot be understood; if they be repealed or revised before they are promulgated, or undergo such incessant changes that no man, who knows what the law is to-day, can guess what it will be to-morrow."[76] Savigny, confronted with the problem of legislation in Germany, had similar misgivings.[77] A generation later, Jacob Burckhardt saw one of the most disastrous consequences of the French Revolution in the fact that it granted an "authorization for perpetual revision." He felt that "the decisively new thing that was introduced by the French Revolution . . . is the possibility of and the desire for changes."[78] Maurice Hauriou complained in the beginning of this century that the French Revolution "resulted in a perpetual state of revolution, because the mobility of the written law was no longer neutralized by certain customary institutions, and because the forces of change were stronger than those of stability."[79] All these men realized that of which Madison had been so aware during the critical period of American history, namely, the danger of the democratic legislator's running amok and showering the world with laws and thus creating a state of legal insecurity.

Legislation that came about as a result of democracy, and, especially, of absolute democracy, had a revolutionary impact upon existing law. The unlimited democratic lawmaker passed laws of a truly revolutionary nature. He replaced the law that previously had been made for the benefit of the individual by one that was made for the sake of the majority of "society."[80] The fact that not only a few laws were passed, but a veritable deluge, resulted in a comprehensive replacement of the old law. The impact of democratic legislation was so great that it ensued in a "decline of the law."[81]

The growth of absolute democracy is reflected not only in a socialization of private law, but also in the gradual elimination of that law. In the course of time, private law—assuring free relations among individuals—was replaced by public law, a law restricting such relations. Montesquieu, having freedom very much at heart, stated in the *Spirit of the Laws* that it makes no sense to regulate by public law matters that fall within the sphere of civil law.[82] The great advocate of free government recognized clearly the dangers ensuing from the public regulation of private matters. However, only two generations later, Portalis wrote: "All Revolution is conquest. One cannot think of anything except making laws when an old government is replaced by a new one. No longer is one occupied with private relations among men. One sees only the political general object. In times of Revolution, everything becomes public law, because of the exalted desire to sacrifice all rights to the political end and not to admit other considerations than those of the mysterious and variable interest of the state."[83] This statement is generally valid for the democratic development under which everything became public law. The democratic lawmaker made greater and greater inroads into private law, the excuse for which has always been the same. Portalis called it the "mysterious and variable interest of the state." Today we speak of the "public interest."

In his attempts to further the public interest, the democratic lawgiver has been ingenious in devising a great variety of ways and means, ranging from prohibition to nationalization. A simple method is that of prohibition. Of course, prohibitions of certain actions have always been provided for by civil codes. Still, they were exceptions. But in time, such prohibitions increased for the sake of the public interest, the *öffentliche Wohl*, or the *ordre public*. They have become so numerous that one wonders whether they are still the exception, or rather, the rule. This development can be noted in Germany. In France, the situation does not differ: "The number of prohibitions has multiplied. . . The famous *verboten* has moved into French customs," one author complained.[84] Similar trends can be observed in the "land of the free," the United States. Everywhere, the public power has encroached upon the freedom of the individual as existing under private law. Everywhere, public law has replaced private law.

Another method of replacing private law has been that of authorization. Private actions have to be specifically "authorized" in order to be legal. Also, this method is not new. The institution of authorization by public authority has always existed. But whereas during the nineteenth century the trend had been toward decreasing the number of required authorizations, the modern tendency has been toward the reverse. It has been generally admitted that certain establishments or the exercise of certain professions should be subject to authorizations because of the health problems involved. But such authorizations were the exception and not the rule. In the twentieth century, this has changed. Today, so many actions of the individual require special authorization that one may wonder whether specifically authorized action has not become the rule rather than the exception. This development is as universal as that in the case of prohibition. Everywhere, the requirements to have individual actions authorized mark serious inroads upon the fundamentally unrestricted nature of private law. Increasingly, private law has become replaced by public law.

Private law was also challenged by the imposition of obligations upon more and more legal transactions and institutions. Again, such obligations are nothing new. They can be found in all civil codes. But again, they are exceptional features of these codes. As a rule, civil codes do not impose conditions upon the transactions of individuals. In the twentieth century, however, more and more laws have been passed which impose more and more obligations upon more and more individuals. Types of contract have been prescribed. The freedom of contracting became replaced by the more or less compulsory "public" contract.

To assure compliance with its orders, the state proceeded to appoint

functionaries for the control of private activities. Such control or intervention exists mainly for the protection of labor and for the securing
of income to the national treasury. The execution of labor contracts
has increasingly come under the surveillance of government officials.
Incessantly, the jurisdiction of these officials has been enlarged. To make
sure that the public treasury is being filled, government officials super-
vise the income of enterprises. Often, these enterprises are permitted to
operate only under the condition of state supervision. The state sees
to it that the enterprises are conducted in the public interest. The degree
of state supervision in many instances is so extreme that formally private
enterprises have received such names as "societies in the public interest,"
or "national societies." The control of private establishments by the government may not yet have reached a high degree in some countries. The
general trend toward increasing state control is beyond doubt.

From the control of private enterprises through the government it is
but one step to the final stage in the replacement of private law through
public law, a stage that can be said to deliver the death blow to private
law—nationalization. Like other means working toward a destruction
of private law, that of nationalization has grown considerably. First
undertaken by a few countries with respect to certain "key industries,"
it was adopted by more and more nations and applied to an increasing
number of enterprises.[85] It is true that some nations have been more
reluctant than others in nationalizing. But this does not change the general picture. Even in countries that thus far have not undertaken nationalization, more and more people favor it.

The democratic legislator, unrestricted as he has become, has had
no qualms of conscience about doing away with that law the strength
of which has been a major guaranty of the freedom of the individual—
private law. The more powerful he became, the more he came to disregard
those whom he did not represent. Motivated by the desire to please the
majority rather than to protect the individual, he saw to it, as Portalis
had envisaged, that the individual's rights were subordinated to the public interest. The process did not occur suddenly. With the gradualness
that seems to be characteristic of democratic development, it was accomplished step by step. But the steps got bigger and faster all the time,
being propelled by the ever increasing force of democracy. Legal security diminished by leaps and bounds. Majoritarian law was imposed
upon individuals in an inconsiderate fashion. There was no *noblesse*.
There hardly could have been. The masses are unlikely to have *no-*

blesse.[86] This absence of *noblesse* with its disregard for the rights of the minority and the individual was a natural corollary to the increasing rejection of older law. As might well be expected, this rejection contributed to the decline of the law. The rule of law has as a premise the recognition of an ethical guide for the human lawmaker. For man-made law is, as was pointed out by a great positivist, nothing but an ethical minimum.[87] Also, the recognition of older law is a guaranty for the constancy of the law and the legal security that goes with it, features that are characteristic of the rule of law.

The decline of the law proceeded more smoothly than many would have expected. Inexhaustible as democratic power appears to be, it is not necessarily successful in the elimination of traditional forces. The victory of democracy over the law probably would not have been so fast and complete if it had not been for the fact that it was aided by those whose natural function it is to protect the law, namely, the jurists. For the decline of the law "we must, above all, blame the jurists. It was they who for half a century undermined the conception of individual rights without being aware that they thereby delivered these rights to the omnipotence of the political state. Some of them wished to prove themselves progressive, while others believed that they were discovering traditional doctrine which the liberal individualism of the nineteenth century had obliterated."[88] It could be added that the omnipotence of the political state was that of the democratic state. The jurists were the captives of democracy, which, "like a force of nature," exercised "a profound, mysterious, irresistible, powerful and fatal attraction."[89] This attraction made them reject higher law and deify legislation.

Although the doctrine of natural law became "official" in nineteenth century France,[90] soon afterwards it was mere window-dressing. It is true that the great commentators of that century stated that natural law is superior to positive law and should be the guide for human lawmakers.[91] But, after that short "salute," these jurists never mention natural law again "because they are convinced that the positive law they expound corresponds to the principles of natural law." However, statements like that of Bugnet, "I do not know civil law. I only teach the Napoleonic Code," or that of Demolombe, "my principle, my belief is this: the texts before everything!"[92] make one wonder how firmly the belief that codified law is a transmutation of natural law was actually entrenched, and whether this belief would survive its major exponent, the School of Exegesis.[93] As a matter of fact, it did not. Although people spoke of a renaissance of natural law before World War I;[94] although after that war a revival of natural law occurred as a reaction against certain German jurists; although "the brutal materialism of the economic crisis maintained the assertion of natural law since 1919," natural law was no longer important.[95] Legal positivists came to the fore. Wherever natural law survived, it did so in an adulterated form, as a natural law that had become adjusted to the progress of democracy. Saleilles helped to bring about that adjustment.[96] He had many followers.[97] His attempt to reconcile natural law with the historical school[98] introduced a rather relativistic concept of natural law. Natural law could be adjusted to historical conditions. Within the framework of the march of democracy, this meant that natural law became what the people, or the majority, wanted it to be. The relativization of natural law weakened its importance. There is not much difference between a natural law oriented toward social aims and a positive law realizing such aims. Jurists not only acquiesced in social legislation, but even recommended "social progress" to the legislator.[99]

German jurists acted in a similar manner. They promoted the replacement of older law through legislation. Even the founder of the historical school, Savigny, capitulated before legislation! In 1814 he had sounded a warning on the dangers of legislation in his famous answer to Thibaut's plea for a codification of German law.[100] Ironically enough, in 1842 he accepted an appointment as Minister for Law Revision, and, five years later, as President of the Prussian state council. While the historical school was still in its bloom, Hermann von Kirchmann mocked the jurists' impotence toward and their dependence upon legislation.[101] "A stroke of the pen by the legislator," it was said, "and whole volumes of learned commentaries become obsolete."[102] Not only the members of the historical school were ridiculed, but also the jurists who believed in natural law. With the growth of democracy, that law fared no better than historical law. "The dream of natural law is over," said Windscheid in an address at Greifswald in 1854.[103] In order to secure the survival of natural law before the onslaught of positivism, Stammler expounded the idea of a natural law with a variable content. He introduced a relativistic concept of natural law.[104] But, as in France, this adjustment to democratic legislation failed to save natural law. On the contrary, it weakened its position vis-a-vis legal positivism. Advanced at the end of the last century mainly by Bergbohm who endeavored "to eradicate the weed of natural law stock and barrel,"[105] legal positivism was given its most consistent philosophical basis a generation later by Kelsen's pure theory of law.[106] According to Kelsen, "a wrong of the state must under all circumstances be a contradiction in terms."[107] At the end of the 1920's, legal positivism was so prevalent that "to be found guilty of adherence to natural law theories [was] a kind of intellectual disgrace."[108] Democratic legislation assumed an omnipotence which was no longer challenged.

The same situation occurred in the nation which has always claimed to possess a "government of law, not of men"—the United States. As Stammler in Germany and Saleilles in France, Holmes rejected the belief in a constant invariable older law that was a guaranty for legal security and free government. He did not care whether such law had demonstrated its value over generations.[109] "The first requirement of a sound body of law" was for him that law correspond "with the actual feelings and demands of the community," and that it help in "reaching a social end which the governing power of the community has made up its mind it wants." It did not matter to Holmes whether the demands of the community are "right or wrong."[110] As long as the community has its way, one can rest satisfied. In the following years, similar ideas were expressed by other jurists. The 1920's and the early 1930's saw "a flood of antirule-of-law literature which had considerable influence on later developments."[111] Charles G. Haines, for instance, resented the traditional rule of law and thought it an illusion. Taking issue with the concept that American government is one of law and not of men, he pleaded that "the American people should establish governments on a theory of trust in men . . ."[112] Jerome Frank launched a violent attack upon the whole idea of the certainty of the law.[113] These works paved the way for a re-orientation of legal thought in favor of unrestricted majority rule. They exercised great influence upon the generation of the New Deal.[114] By a not unexpected paradox, that generation, believing with Frank that the certainty of the law, resulting from the traditional rule of law, was the product of "a childish need for an authoritative father,"[115] did not object to the paternalism of the New Deal legislator.

Although the decline of the law evidenced similarities in the various nations, some differences may be noted. In the continental countries, that decline occurred more gradually, in a process which began during the early part of the nineteenth century. Legislative power continually increased to the degree older law declined. The structure of government was scarcely changed during that process. In the United States, the situation differed. The decline of the law was more rapid, and took place within the short span of one generation. As could be expected, it had a more conspicuous impact. It was combined with a fundamental change in the American form of government, since it resulted in the decline of the outstanding feature of American constitutionalism—judicial review.

Unlike continental countries where the legislator appeared as the great liberator from the *ancien régime* and where it was felt that he could do no wrong, the Americans, having experienced legislative despotism, were wary of legislative omnipotence from the time they became a nation.[116] Accordingly, they established judicial review. Based upon the idea that statutes, in order to be valid, have to conform to the Constitution and older law,[117] that institution was conceived as a check upon democratic majoritarianism. Hamilton desired that the judiciary be a "citadel of public justice," which would serve as an "excellent barrier to the encroachments and oppressions of the representative body,"[118] and Jefferson thought that it was a "stronghold and . . . battery" from which "all the works" of egalitarian democracy would "be beaten down and erased."[119] During the nineteenth century and the first decades of the twentieth, the judges fulfilled these expectations. Honoring older law and the Constitution they invalidated legislation which did not conform to superior law. They were neither intimidated by the march of democracy, nor by the flood of democratic legislation that was showered upon them. The more laws there were passed, the more would be declared unconstitutional.[120] Judicial review, exercised for the sake of freedom from democratic action, became such an outstanding feature of American government that Edouard Lambert of France spoke of a "government by judges," and Jerome Frank, of a "cult of the Robe."[121]

However, soon the cult of the robe was replaced by that of the democratic vogue. It is scarcely surprising that the institution which was the most instrumental in preserving the government of law against the government of men, judicial review, was challenged with the decline of the rule of law. Holmes had stated that the United States would not come to an end if the judges lost their power to declare an act of Congress void.[122] Both Charles G. Haines and Jerome Frank were opponents of judicial review.[123] After the arrival of the New Deal and its majoritarian pressure, the Supreme Court put up a last fight for the preservation of the traditional rule of law. It was in vain. Weakened internally through the addition of Stone to the Holmes-Brandeis minority and threatened with annihilation by the court-packing plan, the Robe capitulated before the popular vogue in 1937. The individual was abandoned to the majority.

Democratic despotism did not equally affect all the rights of the individual. Restrictions of these rights depended upon their utility for absolute democracy. Thus the rights to participate in government did not suffer under the replacement of limited popular government by absolute democracy. On the contrary, they were expanded. Similarly, liberal rights that were conducive to absolute democracy, such as freedom of speech, of the press, of assembly and association, were enlarged rather than curtailed. On the other hand, property rights were restricted. This is not surprising. It merely reflects the decline of private law, a law that had been a bastion of private property. Also, since property rights are probably the most individualistic of all rights, they were most likely to be attacked in a democracy that had become social and egalitarian.

The decline of property rights can be noticed in all countries. Values of older law, putting emphasis upon the necessity of protecting private property, were ignored by the democratic legislator. For that legislator was interested primarily in serving the majority, a majority that was no longer property-conscious and appreciated social ideas more than liberal ones. However, the decline of property by virtue of democratic government was due not only to the new ideological attitude. Like the decline of the law itself, it was brought about also by the quantitative expansion of legislation. Already the *Federalist* had pointed out that too much legislation was detrimental not only to legal security in general but particularly to the security of property.[124] The sheer quantity of laws concerning property was harmful to that institution.

Inroads upon property were made not only through new restrictions. Existing restrictions were expanded and more frequently applied. A good example is that of eminent domain. More and more causes were admitted to justify its exercise. Procedural safeguards for the protection of the individual were relaxed. "Full" and "prior" indemnification was replaced by an "adequate" and "later" one.[125]

The forces that traditionally had been the guardians of property failed to halt this development just as they failed to prevent the decline of the law. The United States Supreme Court had been a bulwark for the protection of property ever since its inception. It ceased to be so when it capitulated before the democratic forces in 1937. Although it launched an ambitious program of protecting civil rights because these rights were considered necessary for the functioning of democracy, it sanctioned legislation that interfered with free property.[126] In France and Germany, where judicial review did not exist, democratic actions against private property could not be halted by the courts. Still, the judges could have sounded warning that the disregard for property was dangerous. They did not do so. They betrayed one of the law's greatest traditional values—property. Neither did the law professors act in behalf of property. Like their brethren of the bench, they actually aided its decline.[127]

CONCLUSION

Thus the very institution that was originally considered a *conditio sine qua non* for the protection of property came to play a substantial role in the destruction of property rights—democracy. This was due to the march of democracy, which brought about fundamental changes in democratic government and the law.

The idea that freedom would be best protected by popular government, which can be considered the gist of the philosophy of the democratic revolutions, remained the core of democratic thought during the following generations. It could hardly have been otherwise under the definition of democracy as a government by the people. As a result, the popular basis of government was continually broadened. More and more people were given the right to participate in the democratic process. People, throughout centuries nothing but subjects, became citizens. More than that. Having been ruled since time immemorial, they now became rulers. Although initial limitations upon voting made the right of all to rule appear rather theoretical, that right became realized with the broadening of suffrage. The idea of the democratic revolutions, that the individual as an individual is something divine, was replaced by the belief that the individual is divine only as an insignificant part of the crowd. This, in turn, resulted in the belief that the crowd is divine. The people became deified. The dubious idea *vox populi, vox dei* became enthroned.

The realization of that idea had inescapable consequences. Deities tend to be exclusive. What is declared divine is not likely to endure challenges. This applied to the divine right of kings. It applies, *a fortiori*, it seems, to the divine right of the people. If the voice of the people is the voice of God, it necessarily has to be right. The acceptance of this maxim indeed amounted to a revolution. No longer did the people have to respect the deity of the law of nature and of God. They had to recognize only the law made by themselves. Older law, existing prior to that law, was re-evaluated and discarded. During the French Revolution "the law, put on the throne . . . received royal honors."[128] The position of the law was similar in the democratic revolutions in England and the United States. But in these initial stages of democratic government the law was still oriented toward older law, toward divine, natural, and historic law. Democracy was limited accordingly. During the course of time, this situation changed. The law still remained on the throne, but that throne, not hallowed by tradition, became rather shaky. For the law was just made by the people whenever they deemed lawmaking convenient. This does not mean that natural law was flatly rejected. Any ruler, including the democratic one, would be reluctant to do so because it would deprive him of a valuable means to prove his legitimacy. Still, the characteristic of older law as being superior to democratic rule was challenged more and more. It has been said that Grotius secularized divine law. The democratic ruler went even further. He secularized deistic natural law. Only law made by the people was recognized as natural law, be it made through the transmutation of higher law into positive norms or, what happened more frequently, through the creation of such norms irrespective of higher law. Positive law became the equivalent of the law of God. Indeed, here was a revolution in the law. It was fraught with danger. For, as one writer sarcastically pointed out, "as soon as one has come to know those who make the laws a little better, it becomes difficult to discover in them a divine power."[129] Many of the laws made by the "divine" democratic legislator under the principle that right is what is good for the people,[130] became terrible demonstrations of the word, *summum ius, summa iniuria.*

Democratic lawmaking has had a disastrous impact upon property rights. The march of democracy was also a march toward egalitarianism. Equality before the law was complemented by the equal right of all to make the law. But this was not enough. The equal right of all to make the law resulted in the tendency to make all equal by the law. Since other privileges had been abolished in the democratic revolutions, the surviving privilege of wealth was likely to receive increased attention as an anomaly in a democracy. A thorn in the eyes of a few at the beginning of the democratic era, it became a beam in the eyes of many once egalitarian democracy had advanced. Having become absolute, democratic government, the mouthpiece for the underprivileged masses, endeavored to gain a more equal distribution of property. Of course, this could be done only by impairing the property rights of the individual. Justice degenerated into "social justice." The love of equality, which appeared to Montesquieu as the characteristic feature of democracy,[131] had reached its final conclusion. The "holy dogma of equality," of which Volney had spoken,[132] had become a hard fact.

VI

THE DECLINE OF PROPERTY: SCOPE, CONSEQUENCES AND PROSPECTS

INTRODUCTION

IN THE preceding pages, an attempt was made to show how infringements upon private property were brought about by the growth of democracy. It remains to make a few comments on the tragic aspects of this development and to suggest ways and means for improvement.

Of first concern is the extent of the disregard for property. Clearly, the development described here was not confined to the United States, France, and Germany. The very fact that property lost its protection in all of these nations indicates a universal trend, for these nations are not only representative of different legal systems. They are also representative of different forms of democracy. If we consider the development of other democracies, we can make the same observation: Everywhere, the protection of private property has declined. It could scarcely be otherwise, because the decline of property rights is not a national, but a democratic phenomenon. The communists' denial of these rights is perhaps nothing but a derivation from that phenomenon.

Still, no matter what the other issues between Western democracy and communism are today, the key problem concerns private property. Most people agree that Western democracies still grant property a higher degree of protection than do communist nations, and that the former profess to favor such a protection to a greater extent than the latter. This provokes the question whether Western democracies, although unable to preserve the protection of property within their own boundaries, were able to preserve it in the international field.

164

Discussion of this question will be followed by an examination of the consequences of the decline of property rights. After some remarks on the paradoxical nature of that decline, further discussion will demonstrate how restrictions on private property resulted in its general disparagement, and how the latter, in turn, had ill effects upon morals.

The chapter will conclude with suggestions for a reinstitution of the protection of property rights as a way of revitalizing Western democracy and of preventing the total collapse of our freedom.

THE DECLINE OF PROPERTY IN INTERNATIONAL LAW

The rise and fall of property which occurred in various nations can be seen also in the field of international law.

It cannot be denied that the protection of private property under international law had made some progress prior to the end of the eighteenth century. It was advanced particularly during the Enlightenment. Montesquieu, whom we encountered as a staunch defender of property within society, also wanted protection of property in the international sphere. By the end of the eighteenth century, even the property of enemy aliens, as well as that of the inhabitants of occupied territory, had become relatively secure.[1] Rousseau had stressed that "war is not a relation of man to man, but of state to state, in which individuals are enemies only accidentally, not as men nor even as citizens but as soldiers, not as members of their country but as its defenders."[2] This passage reflects the idea that belligerents should attack state property rather than private property, an idea that came to be one of the principles of modern war. The governments emerging from the French Revolution adhered to this new humanitarianism, as all civilized nations did throughout the nineteenth century. International custom and convention increasingly provided for the protection of foreign private property in times of war. Needless to say, such property enjoyed protection also in times of peace.[3] On the whole, international law secured a greater protection of private property during the nineteenth century than it ever did before.

In the twentieth century, the situation was altered. The protection of private property under international law declined. That century witnessed not only confiscations of foreign private property by Western governments, but also a general signing away of property rights in international agreements by these governments. We need not be concerned here in particular with unilateral confiscations of private property. Regrettable as these confiscations are because they mark the rejection of civilized features of international law, they are too well known to merit further comment.[4] What is less obvious, and thus warrants elaboration, is the giving up of the protection of private property by international legislation. This process has taken place in such an inconspicuous and seemingly harmless manner that it reminds one of the beginnings of social legislation in national law. There has been initialled, during the past decades, the socialization of international law by international legislation just as, around the turn of the century, the socialization of national law by national legislation was begun.

We can confine our considerations to an examination of recent international legislation. The Atlantic Charter contained the Four Freedoms proclaimed by President Roosevelt in his Annual Message to Congress on January 6, 1941: freedom of speech and expression, freedom of worship, freedom from want and freedom from fear, "everywhere in the world."[5] These four freedoms were subsequently endorsed by a resolution of an Inter-Allied Meeting in London,[6] by the United Nations Declaration of Twenty-Six Nations in Washington,[7] as well as by the Ministers of Foreign Affairs of the American Republics in Rio de Janeiro.[8] No one seems to have thought of the necessity of guaranteeing what Herbert Hoover called the Fifth Freedom, which in essence amounts to a protection of free property.[9]

The situation did not change after the war. The Moscow Declaration Regarding Italy stated that "freedom of speech, of religious worship, of political belief, of the press and public meetings shall be restored in full measure to the Italian people who shall be entitled to form antifascist political groups."[10] In a similar vein, the Potsdam Conference declared that freedom of speech, press and religion shall be permitted, that religious institutions shall be respected and that the formation of free trade unions shall be guaranteed.[11]

When at that time the International Labor Organization held its twenty-sixth meeting, it adopted a declaration affirming the principle that "freedom of expression and association are essential to sustained progress," and stressing that "all human beings, irrespective of trade, creed or sex, have the right to pursue both their material well-being and their spiritual development in conditions of freedom and dignity, of economic security and equal opportunity."[12]

The Latin American nations in Chapultepec adhered, by their resolution forty, to "principles established by international law for safeguarding the essential rights of man," but in resolution forty-one confined themselves to stressing such rights as racial equality and freedom of religion.[13] Other resolutions dealt with freedom of information and the rights of women. Again, as in the Moscow Declaration Regarding Italy, the Potsdam statement and the declaration of the International Labor Organization, the protection of private property was neglected. As a matter of fact, when such things as the right to the formation of trade unions, the right to "material well-being" and to "economic security and equal opportunity" are specifically stressed, it appears as if one was interested mainly in the protection of rights that are detrimental rather than complementary to the protection of private property.

The same may be said about the San Francisco Conference. In the opening session, President Truman spoke of building a new world, "in which the eternal dignity of man is respected."[14] Mr. Stettinius of the United States expressed hope that all nations would achieve freedom from fear and want, maintaining that the cooperation of nations in the promotion of human rights was one of the prerequisites for peace.[15] The Deputy Minister of Australia stressed that a stable peace could be maintained only by an organization which would "assure the peoples of the world a full opportunity of living in freedom from want as well as in freedom from fear of external aggression."[16] All these statements, which are characteristic of the then prevalent conception of human rights, show how the San Francisco Conference was prepossessed by the four freedoms and neglected the safeguarding of private property.

This is also evident in the United Nations Charter itself. The preamble reaffirms a "faith in fundamental human rights, in the dignity and worth of the human person, in the equal rights of men and women" and speaks of the promotion of "social progress and better standards of life in larger freedom." Human rights are coupled with social progress. The protection of private property is not mentioned in so many words. The next reference to human rights can be found in article one, which says that the purposes of the United Nations are "to achieve international cooperation in solving international problems of an economic, social, cultural and humanitarian character, and in promoting and encouraging respect for human rights and for fundamental freedoms for all without distinction as to race, sex, language, or religion." Again, social ideas, as well as the idea of equality, stand in the foreground. No mention is made of private property. The situation is similar in the wording of article thirteen. Chapter nine, dealing with international economic and social cooperation, contains a number of references to human rights and fundamental freedoms, but again, they are mentioned in connection with such things as higher standards of living, full employment, conditions of economic and social progress and development, and the solutions of international economic, social, health and related problems.[17] A reference to property is also omitted in other articles concerned with human rights. Article sixty-two empowers the Economic and Social Council to make recommendations for the purpose of promoting respect for, and observance of, human rights and fundamental freedoms for all. Similarly, article sixty-eight provides that the Economic and Social Council shall set up commissions in economic and social fields and for the promotion of human rights. Finally, article seventy-six states that one of the basic purposes of the trusteeship system is "to encourage respect for human rights and for fundamental freedoms for all without distinction as to race, sex, language, or religion."

Thus the United Nations Charter makes definite concessions to those who wanted world government for the protection not only of international peace, but also for the sake of the rights of the individual.[18] There can be no doubt that the Charter constitutes a progress toward the affirmation of human rights in international legislation. Still, the omission of a statement concerning the protection of property appears to be a serious gap and creates a rather one-sided concept of human freedom.

The question therefore arises whether this gap was filled by subsequent legislation. Quite a few delegates at San Francisco felt that the manner in which human rights were mentioned in the Charter was not sufficient. They desired the inclusion of a regular declaration of human rights. Smuts, the Prime Minister of South Africa, pleaded: "Let us, in this new Charter of humanity, give expression to this faith in us, and thus proclaim to the world and to posterity, that this was not a mere brute struggle of force between the nations but for us, behind the mortal struggle, was the vision of the ideal, the faith in justice and the resolve to vindicate the fundamental rights of man, and on that basis to found a better, freer world for the future."[19] President Truman remarked when the Charter was signed: "Under this document we have good

reason to expect the framing of an international bill of rights acceptable
to all the nations involved. That bill of rights will be as much a part
of international life as our own Bill of Rights is a part of our Constitution."[20]

Truman's hope was only partially fulfilled. A Commission on Human
Rights was set up in 1946 and authorized to prepare an international
bill of rights.[21] Its draft declaration was adopted by the General Assembly as the Universal Declaration of Human Rights.[22] But whereas
the United States Bill of Rights, while providing for the protection of
other rights, is also a bulwark for private property, it appears doubtful
whether this can be said of the Universal Declaration of Human Rights.

That Declaration mainly specifies the idea of human rights as it can
be seen in the United Nations Charter. Article one states that all human
beings are free and equal in dignity and rights, that they are endowed
with reason and conscience and should act toward one another in a spirit
of brotherhood. Thus the ideas of the French Revolution, liberty,
equality and fraternity, stand out as the *leitmotif*, which means that the
Declaration is burdened with a conflict between equality and liberty.
That conflict is resolved in favor of equality. True, the Declaration provides for a far-reaching protection of many parts of human freedom.
However, it does not provide for the protection of that part of freedom
which appears to be most likely to secure the primacy of freedom over
equality, namely, the right of private property. That right is relegated
to a status of second order, since it is not as absolutely protected as other
rights.

The Declaration guarantees, on the one hand, an absolute protection
of certain rights. For instance, article four provides that "no one shall
be held in slavery or servitude; slavery and the slave trade shall be prohibited in all their forms." Article five says that "no one shall be subjected to torture or to cruel, inhuman or degrading treatment or punishment." Article thirteen prescribes that "everyone has the right to freedom of movement and residence within the borders of each state" and
"everyone has the right to leave any country, including his own, and
to return to his country." Freedom of thought, conscience and religion,
of opinion and expression, and of assembly are among other rights that
appear to be absolutely protected by the Declaration. In contrast, the
provision of article seventeen, concerning property, reads: "Everyone
has the right to own property alone as well as in association with others."
So far, so good. But then comes the second sentence: "No one shall be

arbitrarily deprived of his property." In other words, whereas the individual may not be deprived at all of his freedom of thought, religion, opinion or expression, he may not *arbitrarily* be deprived of his property. However, he may be deprived of his property if such deprivation is not an arbitrary one. We know what "arbitrary" means. It means in most countries "without the basis of a law." In a word, the lawmaker —whoever he may be in a specific country—has the right to deprive the individual of his property. This is, indeed, a far-reaching restriction of private property.

The degrading of the right of property to second order becomes even more obvious in view of the fact that "social" rights appear to enjoy absolute protection. Article twenty-two guarantees to everyone the right to social security, and to the economic, social and cultural rights indispensable for his dignity and the free development of his personality. In a similar vein, the following article states: "Everyone has the right to work, to free choice of employment, to just and favorable conditions of work and to protection against unemployment. Everyone, without any discrimination, has the right to equal pay for equal work. Everyone who works has the right to just and favorable remuneration insuring for himself and his family an existence worthy of human dignity, and supplemented, if necessary, by other means of social protection. Everyone has the right to form and to join trade unions for the protection of his interests." Article twenty-four guarantees to everyone the right to rest and leisure, including reasonable limitation of working hours and periodic holidays with pay, and article twenty-five provides for such things as a right to an adequate standard of living, including food, clothing, housing and medical care and necessary social services, as well as the right to social security in the event of unemployment.

Thus it appears that private property does not only occupy a position that is inferior to such liberal rights as freedom of religion, expression and assembly, but is also inferior to the so-called "social rights." As one author, writing in 1948, pointed out, the provision of the Declaration on private property "sanctions a capitalistic system of private property in the United States, a socialist system in Great Britain and France, and a communist system in the Soviet Union."[23] Clearly, if human rights are so formulated as to be acceptable to communist and socialist societies as much as to capitalistic ones, the protection of private property cannot be very strong. The Declaration of Human Rights thus by no means fills the gap that was left open, as far as the protection of private property is concerned, by the Charter of the United Nations. On the contrary, it confirms the idea that among human rights, those of property are of a secondary order.

The disregard for property in modern international law is not surprising. For that law is no longer made chiefly by nations that have regard for property rights. It is also made by communist nations and other states in which the appreciation of private property is rather negligible.

The "socialization" of international law, however, was due not only to the need for a *modus vivendi* between free and communist nations. It was due also to the fact that Western democracies had become sympathetic to a social appreciation of property, whether they openly professed such a sympathy in international negotiations or not. No matter how gradually and imperceptibly it may have happened, a social conception of property has become so generally accepted by the so-called free societies that it constitutes a veritable *ius gentium*.[24] Inevitably this new outlook had to become reflected in international law. For it would indeed be absurd if national governments, while denying the protection of property to their own citizens, would grant such protection to foreigners.

On the whole, the process of restricting property rights has taken hold of international law as it has of national law. The process is likely to be as complete and comprehensive. Also, the growing disregard for property in international law was largely due to the march of democracy in the society of nations. Until recently, international law was made chiefly by nations of some wealth and power. There existed, in a sense, property qualifications for the participation in international lawmaking. These qualifications have now become largely abolished. Poor and insignificant nations have been increasingly accepted as equal partners in the making of international law. The result was an "equalization" of international law. Property rights became less protected. As it did within nations, the march of egalitarian democracy has contributed to their decline among nations.

But this discourse on the spreading of the disregard for property to the field of international law, showing the enormous quantitative extension of the new ideas, takes us to a final discussion of some consequences of the decline of the protection of private property.

CONSEQUENCES OF THE DECLINE OF PROPERTY RIGHTS

The consequences of the decline of property can be seen in national societies as well as in the society of nations. In both cases, they have been so serious that they might well have been responsible for the dilemma in which the West finds itself today.

The decline of property rights within society poses a dilemma. That dilemma evolves around fundamental values such as human dignity, freedom, and the government supposedly most conducive to these values —democracy. It reflects many paradoxes of our democratic situation.

We have usually thought of democracy as the best guaranty for the freedom of the individual. Indeed, popular government was established for that purpose in the great democratic revolutions. Many of us still believe that democracy has continued to fulfill this function. But is not such a belief an illusion? Has not popular government, originally adopted to end despotism, itself become despotic in the degenerated form of sheer majority rule?

Whereas the rights of man steadily advanced throughout the nineteenth century, the situation changed thereafter. No longer were these rights protected. Freedom, previously constituting a unity which defied attack, has become so disintegrated that it invites assaults. Its component parts, formerly considered to be of about equal importance, have been re-evaluted. And this new evaluation—undertaken by the uncontrolled numerical majority—decided that property rights did not deserve as much protection as other rights. The rights which reflect individualism to the greatest extent were relegated to a secondary order. Rights we are merely born with—important as they may be—were considered more essential than rights that have the further distinction of having labor mixed with them. Rights we happen to possess by mere chance were preferred over rights with which effort has been mingled.

The new evaluation was not only harmful to property rights, and did not only entail many disadvantages resulting from the insecurity of those rights, but was also detrimental to freedom as a whole. Freedom was harmed not only because free property is essential to it, but because the discrimination against property was bound to destroy the notion of the unalienability of the rights of man: If property rights could be curtailed, there was no reason why other rights could not be restricted. This relativism showed that democratic government had lost its rationale. For it was no longer the protector, but the arbiter, of the rights of man. A democracy that permitted curtailments of property while, at the same time, assuring its love for freedom, was likely to appear hypocritical.

Also, infringements upon property are detrimental to the survival of democracy. They quell individual effort, the very prerequisite for progress. This deprives man of his dignity. In the welfare state, the individual is not only induced to be lazy, but he is also considered to be unable to take care of himself. The healthy are treated as if they were sick, the mature as if they were children. The physically fit are made psychologically ill, and the naturally independent are made artificially dependent. Individuals become spoiled and lose self-confidence. This must be suicidal if it occurs at a time when Western society is engaged in a struggle for survival.

The welfare state not only treats the healthy and mature in an undignified manner. In a complementary process, it abets the less desirable elements of society. The bad results of legislation favoring debtors has been noted. What has not been mentioned is something worse, namely, that such legislation does not only in a dubious manner help people in their plight, but that it even induces them to get into a plight. Since the end of the last century, more and more people have become debtors for buying more and more goods on installment.[25] Western society has become largely a society composed of perennial debtors for whom credit accounts have become more cherished than savings accounts. Neurotically, people worry a lifetime over paying their debts. An increasing number even acquire luxuries without bothering about the obligations they contract, trusting that their irresponsible attitude will be matched by their government through further legislation in favor of debtors, complemented by inflation. *Après nous, le déluge!*

The consequences of the decline of property rights are as disastrous in the international field. Again, we are faced by a dilemma. Today's struggle between East and West, no matter what the many other values involved may be, is fundamentally a struggle turning around the appreciation of private property. The West professes to believe in a protection of that institution, the East does not. The Western nations maintain that their attitude is conducive to freedom and justice, and the communists assert the same of their position. It is obvious that the communists' sanction of the trend toward a lesser appreciation of property in international law is quite natural and not in contradiction with professed communist aims. The same cannot be said of the sanction by Western nations of that trend. The Western attitude is inconsistent with the values the West professes to stand for. It is both paradoxical and suicidal.

The Western nations, when not insisting on a protection of property in international law, cut their own throats. While their professed aim in view of the communist challenge requires them to maintain that the protection of private property is a prerequisite of international justice, they have, through their participation in the making of recent international law, admitted that infringements upon property are justified. Specific infringements upon private property are bad enough. Although they might appear as being of an exceptional nature, they can, if not objected to, easily become general practice. Even more dangerous is the approval of international agreements that discriminate against property, such as, for instance, the Charter of the United Nations or the Universal Declaration of Human Rights. For here the principle of the protection of property is not disregarded in a specific instance only, and not just exceptionally ignored. It is given up altogether; literally signed away. There can be only one effect of such an attitude: a distrust of the West. Clearly, if the West contributes to curtailments of property under international law while professing to stand for a protection of property rights, it must appear as hypocritical, unreliable and untrustworthy.

A world-wide welfare state, achieved largely through foreign aid, in all probability will have the same drawbacks as its national counterpart. Perhaps it ought to be stressed first that this author, who as a believer in free property is also a believer in progress, wants progress as much as free property for all. He sincerely hopes that the day may not be far when the standard of living will be high in nations that, for the time being, are not materially well off. He also feels that the citizens of the more prosperous nations should sympathize with the genuine efforts of their less fortunate brethren in other parts of the world and be willing to help them to help themselves. There are many ways in which such help can be rendered. For instance, Western institutions of learning could be opened for students from the developing countries, just as previously European schools were open to Americans; teachers, doctors and technicians from economically more advanced nations could be encouraged to work in less advanced countries; private investment could be made attractive to aid the development of these countries; free trade could be encouraged through a lowering of tariffs. Methods such as these both guarantee the voluntary character of giving aid and prevent infringements upon the property of the citizens of the more prosperous nations. At the same time, they give due respect to the dignity of the developing nations.

However, it will hardly be expected from an author who condemns a national welfare state on account of its incompatibility with free property, to condone such an enterprise on an even broader scale at the international level. And since this author believes that the continuation by the Western governments of their present form of foreign aid might well result in a welfare state of world-wide dimensions, he wants to advance some arguments against such aid. For that aid does not seem to have any of the advantages mentioned in the preceding paragraph.

To begin with, foreign aid is not based upon voluntary actions of the citizens of the donor nations. Rather, it has for its basis infringements by the governments of these nations upon the property of their subjects: It is largely the taxpayer's money that is used to defray the expenses of foreign aid. This act of injustice is matched by one of unfairness toward the receiving nations. For foreign aid is scarcely a sign of respect for the dignity of those nations. It indicates a belief that their inhabitants are unable to take care of themselves, that they are immature and sick—"underdeveloped." It was not without justification that the people concerned protested against this label as if they had been insulted. By the same token, they should consider it beneath their dignity to request and accept foreign aid. But these considerations do not exhaust the arguments against that institution.

The relationship between donor and donee has always been a problematic one. It has been so even if it existed between two individuals. But in such a relationship, a feeling of personal gratitude throughout the lifetime of the donee could perhaps reasonably be expected. In politics the situation is different. Politics knows no lasting gratitude. We all have had opportunity to make this observation in internal politics. Here the partners are usually individuals representing groups. And groups, anonymous as they are, do not have the sense of ethics that characterizes most individuals. What one group receives today is not necessarily acknowledged by it tomorrow, because that group is likely to be composed of different individuals. The same applies to the international scene. It could perhaps be maintained that it applies *a fortiori*, since the relation between nations will as a rule be characterized by a greater indifference toward one another than that between groups within one nation. Experience proves that the giving of aid so far has made the donor nations more popular with the receiving nations only in exceptional cases. For instance, today there can hardly be found a nation which likes Americans better than she did before the United States launched a program of foreign aid, the generosity of which is unequalled in the history of mankind.[26]

For the time being, foreign aid might be desirable to the receiving country, although cogent arguments have been advanced that deny even this proposition.[27] In the long run, however, foreign aid is hardly conducive to the well-being of the receiving nations. It makes them rely on aid, and deprives them of the incentive that is the very prerequisite for progress. Nations that grow through foreign aid are not likely to enjoy the respect of other nations. Everywhere, the self-made man is more respected than the person who achieved something through the help of others. It is not different with nations. All contemporary great nations, the United States being an outstanding example, were, in a sense, once "underdeveloped." Yet they were developing and achieving prosperity and greatness largely by means of their own efforts. We even venture to say that their rise might not have been possible had they received much aid!

It may be argued that foreign aid should not be viewed merely from the point of view of the receiving nations, but also from that of the donor nations; that, while it might not be in the long-range interest of the former, it is in the present interest of the latter, since it is likely to prevent the spreading of communism. The weakness of that argument is, however, already indicated by the fact that in spite of all aid given to the developing countries, most of them have so far refused to actively support a policy of anti-communism. More often than not they seem to side with the communist bloc rather than with the West.[28] Indeed, this attitude raises the question whether the giving of foreign aid might not actually be dangerous for us. It was already mentioned that foreign aid is not possible without infringements upon the property of the inhabitants of the donor state, or, for that matter, without a diminution of the latter's assets. However, if such infringements served the purpose of preventing world communism, they might be worth the sacrifice. Unfortunately, it is more probable that foreign aid will facilitate an international socialist movement that desires to expropriate the donor nations. Since foreign aid is often given in the form of loans, it helps to create debtor nations. It is an old truth that debtors don't like their creditors. Debtor nations probably will have all the proclivities of their counterparts within a nation. They will advocate measures that mitigate or abolish their debtor status. They will combine against the creditor nations. It is true that such a combination might also exist among nations that are poor and unaided. A threat from those nations might thus exist *without* foreign aid. But this possibility does not refute our thesis that such a threat will also come from nations to whom foreign aid has been granted. Besides, the latter threat, aside from involving a greater disappointment for us, is likely to be more dangerous. For the donor nations are weakened by foreign aid, whereas the challenging nations have been strengthened—if only temporarily—by such aid.

Foreign aid probably will have still another bad result. The receiving nations will want more and more. They will first want aid in order to have the necessities of life. But they will not be content with that. They will desire aid for luxuries. And if they do not get all they want, they will, not appreciating how much they already received, turn against us. They will begin with blackmail. They will threaten to align themselves with the communist bloc.[29] The sums demanded will become bigger and bigger. In the end, when we finally refuse to pay because we are being bled white, they will join the hostile camp. We, their benefactors, will become their victims. Aided nations will not merely forget to show their appreciation. They will openly display that want of appreciation and not shy away from attacking us.[30]

National and international welfare states thus have similar disadvantages. And these disadvantages have resulted in the disparagement of property throughout the world.

Now there have always been restrictions of free property, especially before the ideas of the Enlightenment were realized. But these restrictions as a rule did not result in a general decline of the appreciation of property. As a matter of fact, it seems that they enhanced that appreciation. The history of property provides ample proof of this. And just as there were restrictions of free property, there existed welfare states. But again, it seems doubtful whether these states brought about the high degree of disappreciation of property that is characteristic of our time.

The want of an appreciation of property is more serious today simply because it is more prevalent. Previously, welfare states occurred now and then. They were not general phenomena. They were challenged and influenced by societies that were not of the welfare type. Today the situation differs. Not only has there been a tendency in more developed nations to become welfare states, but also in less developed ones. Whereas formerly the welfare state was the exception, today it is more or less the rule. Whereas formerly only a certain degree of the appreciation of property was missing in merely a few welfare states, today there exists a general disappreciation of property in the many welfare states that form the major part of the free world.

The absence of this appreciation is more serious than it might appear at first sight. For it implies more than just a want of appreciation of material goods, bad as that is. It means the lack of appreciation of all we have been able to accumulate through hard work during the course of our civilization. It implies disregard for our cultural achievements. It amounts to a rejection of our heritage. It involves the negation of ourselves as spiritual beings. We have become uprooted and exist in a vacuum.

Possibly here lies the hard core of our plight. No longer are we proud of our achievements and our civilization and our heritage. No more do we consider them values worth defending. We are not willing to sacrifice for them. We have come to like the easy life. We have become easytakers and easygoers. The revolution of the masses of which Ortega complained a generation ago, detrimental as it was for property, still did not amount to a disregard for property rights. It did not induce men to be easygoing and careless. Quite to the contrary! Ortega's masses were a militant group. They affirmed their right to share the life that thus far had been enjoyed by only a few. They had the desire to advance. But only a generation later, the revolution of the masses degenerated into a revolution of the failures. And that revolution is characterized by passivity rather than activity. Its "revolutionaries" are evolutionaries, meek people that defy comparison with the evolutionaries which Darwin and Spencer had in mind a few generations ago. Their main characteristic is mediocrity. They do not fight for a better life. They are content with whatever is allotted to them. They want to have what others have, but seldom for the price of an effort. They are hardly interested in sharing the great achievements of our civilization for they have largely become detached from the property of that civilization. All that they want is to exist. They detest the idea of the survival of the fittest. All they desire is survival.

So often today we read that the West has no direction, no aim. But we cannot very well have direction and aim if the individual citizen is not encouraged to aim at something that he can be sure will be his permanently. And this cannot be realized as long as private property is not safe. As was stated, John Adams once said that "the moment the idea is admitted into society that property is not as sacred as the laws of God, and that there is not a force of law and public justice to protect it, anarchy and tyranny commence." Today, many of us are experiencing the tyranny and anarchy he dreaded. It is the tyranny of the great regulator and distributor, of the New Leviathan of majoritarian democracy, over its gluttonous yet timid citizens. It is the anarchy of a society whose members are at a loss where to go because they feel there is no property to strive for, a society that has come to acknowledge the dogma of the impropriety of property, with all its bad consequences.

Our life has become fraudulent, our interests thin. Even academe does not offer much consolation. Often, mediocrity rides the waves.[31] The charlatan, the fraud is evident everywhere. The gregarious type is often the best paid "professor," and the detached professor is condemned. People accept prizes for books for which they have not done the research, a work that was performed by those intellectual coolies of our time, the research assistants.[32] Research is now often based on mere hearsay. Interviews of people "who do not want to be named" serve as the basis for statements. No longer can we check the truth of these statements nor, for that matter, whether the persons credited with them were actually interviewed. Students, often with the connivance and even support of their teachers, receive money from foundations under false pretenses.[33] No more are we interested in reading the complete works of great authors. We are content with reading so-called "representative excerpts" that are handed to us on a platter in that peculiar product of our time, the book of readings. And these excerpts are usually anything but representative; they are distortions. Most students desire only the knowledge required for examinations. Few care whether it is the truth.

People have become neurotic. This is the era of chain-smoking, coffee breaks, sleeping pills and psychoanalysis. The cocktail party where people float and drift from standing group to standing group to chat about "interesting" trivialities has replaced the more intimate sittings where more substantial matters were discussed. Ours is the time of the flirt and the divorce. Few things have enduring quality. Even our belongings have become more or less temporary. Deeper affection for a few owned things has been superseded by a shallow interest in merely being acquainted with many things. Formerly, people owned a few books that were life-long companions. Today, many books are borrowed, read quickly, and never looked at again.[34] "Rental galleries" supply pictures that satisfy our temporary tastes for a few weeks and are then exchanged for other temporary sights. We appreciate that we perceive only on a temporary, superficial basis. Perhaps that is the reason why the impressionist painters are so fashionable. They depict fleeting appearances, and their message can be grasped in a short, relaxing look.[35] Many of us are even afraid of owning and of possessing. Even those who still have some appreciation of property have become panicky. Seeing the swelling tide of curtailments upon property, they live just for the day, spending, while they still have something to spend, as much as they can. The man who saves is considered a fool.

In our neurotic state, we have become jittery and afraid of death. We know that we are finite, and yet we avoid admitting it. This cruel awareness of our existence derives from something more than the mere fact that we must die. It derives from the feeling that we will die not only physically, but also as spiritual beings. As long as people faced only physical death they could face it with the calmness that comes with the confidence in a hereafter, in the perpetuity of the material and spiritual values they lived for, in the perpetuity of their property.[36] Today we no longer have that confidence.

This lack of confidence is more than justified. If our present attitude of carelessness continues—and there is no reason to believe that it will not—the future will be dark indeed. There is not much hope for the survival of the West. Mr. Khrushchev's prophesy that the world will be red in another twenty years is probably a modest estimate. An estimate of half the time might be closer to the mark.

This raises the question of whether anything can be done to secure the survival of free society. And although this author feels that it is rather late to halt the swelling tide that has been drowning freedom, he still wants to propose some suggestions, even though he is almost certain that these suggestions will not be followed and decried as undemocratic, reactionary, and what not. But feeling that there is too much concern about democracy today and too little about freedom, he considers the following remarks worthwhile.

The term "reaction" has a bad connotation today. But, having experienced the denunciation of the "reaction" by the Nazis for twelve long years,[37] the author feels that this is unfair. Let it be stated first that there is nothing inherently wrong with reaction in politics. Politics is nothing but a chain of reactions. Reaction need not retard progress. Indeed it can be a great blessing if it is conducive to freedom. No one would doubt that this was the case with the popular reaction against absolute monarchy. How then can it be denied that a reaction against the despotic features of majoritarian democracy will not also be a blessing? Perhaps the friends of freedom and progress could denounce the "reaction" when it aimed at a re-establishment of the *ancien régime*. Today, however, a denunciation of the "reaction" must be as bad as it was under the Hitler regime. For today, the reaction hardly advocates a reinstitution of absolute monarchy. It largely stands for the preservation of the very regime that, for the sake of freedom and progress, was devised to replace absolute monarchy, namely, limited or constitutional democracy.

SUGGESTIONS FOR IMPROVEMENT

Improvement of our plight can come only from a reaction to the excesses of democracy. This reaction can take two major forms: a rather passive one that tries to stop the further decline of property rights, and an active one that attempts to restore those rights to their original eminence.

It is obvious that the first method must be less satisfactory than the latter because it cannot reinstitute property rights to their old importance. However, if we consider that the trend to curtail these rights seems to be a continuing one, its mere cession must amount to an improvement of our situation. Besides, it is likely to pave the way for more complete measures, which, in view of the prevailing opinion that "the clock cannot be turned back," do not appear to be feasible without some preparatory steps.

It was shown how the new, more social appreciation of property, beginning in the latter part of the nineteenth century, occurred rather gradually. Rousseau's political philosophy, no matter how much it might have stressed the importance of the rights of the individual, was fraught with danger. If the individual could achieve freedom only as a member of the group, and if the general will was elevated to be something sublime, it was inevitable that the rights of the individual would, in the end, be defined by, and thus be at the mercy of, the group. The Rousseauistic philosophy, important as it was for the emancipation of man, bore within itself the roots of a new enslavement of the individual. Too great was the probability that people would overlook what he had said about the old idea of the need for protecting the rights of the individual, because they were overwhelmed by what was new in his philosophy—the idea of the sublimity of the general will. And no matter how much the importance of private property was emphasized, property rights were open to social interpretation. They were to become more and more "socialized" as the general will became constituted by the masses rather than by the property-owning *élite*. For the masses would all too willingly forget what lay buried in a few pages of Rousseau's work on the value of private property, while they would eagerly emphasize Rousseau's glorification of themselves. And whereas radical movements in favor of a more social interpretation of property were consistently rejected in the Western nations, gradual efforts to the same end were, inconsistently enough, not.

It is possible that the gradualist social appreciators of property of the late nineteenth and early twentieth centuries, the Holmeses and Brandeises and their European counterparts, did not expect that collectivism would emerge from their attitude toward property and that this attitude would bring about a general disregard for property. Obviously, they were given the benefit of the doubt by many who dreaded collectivism and loved freedom. Otherwise, their social ideas could scarcely have been accepted as quickly as they were. But considering the fact that already the followers of these first advocates of a social interpretation of property became more radical and that some of them did not even deny that they were Marxists; considering how radical the results of gradualism actually were, it is hard to discern a substantial difference between a radical and a gradualist movement in favor of a social evaluation of property. The radical end was attained merely more slowly by the gradualist approach. This scarcely detracts from the radicalness of the final result. As a matter of fact, it may be asked whether gradualism is not actually more dangerous than radicalism, since the latter frightens people in time, whereas the former allows the acceptance of ideas that ultimately will incur disaster.

Therefore, we should be more wary of a gradualist socialism that is often disguised as "liberalism."[38] We must be on our guard against wolves in sheeps' clothing. Unfortunately, human beings are not immune from the influences of others. The decline of property proves this sufficiently. Therefore, if guarding against gradualist doctrines is to prevent a further deterioration of property, it must stop the evil at its source. It must limit the advocacy of ideas endangering property.

As was shown, the various liberties of the individual are essential to freedom, and thus deserving of equal protection. It will, of course, not always be possible to insure an absolutely equal protection. Certain limitations of certain liberties seem to be inevitable under certain conditions.[39] And, as long as such limitations do not assume proportions that seriously endanger the original balance of the degrees of protection enjoyed by the various liberties, there is no cause for alarm. However, there is cause for alarm if one liberty becomes so much restricted that it is relegated to a right of secondary order, or if one right is used so that it destroys another right, i.e., if it is abused. The fair balance among the various liberties would then be jeopardized. It is irrelevant whether that balance is destroyed radically or gradually. Thus if freedom of speech is used in a manner that might radically or gradually destroy free property, it ought to be tempered.

It has been said that infringements on free speech would make our society as unfree as Soviet society. By the same token, it could be argued that existing curtailments of property actually *have made* our society similar to Soviet society. Those who complain about the *potential* degeneration of a free society into an unfree one by means of a limitation of free speech would do well not to close their eyes to the *actual* serfdom to which we have been subjected owing to restrictions upon free property.

Considering the enormity of existing infringements upon property, certain limitations of free speech would be defensible if they could prevent a further decline of property and thus restore the fair balance among the various parts of freedom. It is admitted that this suggestion is made with reluctance. Too much has the author suffered from curtailments of free speech under the national-socialists. But this reluctance was partly overcome by the belief that some limitations of free speech would not be really detrimental to the original conception of the rights of man under which free speech was merely on a par with free property. Such limitations would mean only the diminution of the "preferred" position of free speech and thus only destroy an artificial concept that resulted from the rather perverted glorification of unlimited democracy.

Today we face problems similar to those that were encountered by our grandparents. The problems, however, have grown. The total decline of freedom is much more imminent because property rights are no longer as firmly entrenched as they were a few generations ago. Just as radical doctrines of socialism were then generally rejected and gradualist ideas approved, so today many of us, while still rejecting an outright plunge into communism, feel that a gradual transition to communism would be acceptable. Needless to say, such a gradual transition would result as much in the end of free institutions as would a sudden and violent establishment of a communist state. Consequently, there is no apparent reason for granting gradualist advocates of socialism greater protection than the proponents of violent subversion. For although a violent overthrow of free institutions might appear more illegal, it is for this very reason also less likely to succeed than a gradual abolition of such institutions. It is, ultimately, less dangerous.

This raises the question of whether the freedom to advocate political change in a non-violent manner should be limited. Cogent arguments could be advanced against such an action. On the other hand, it should be asked whether freedom deserves protection if it is used to destroy freedom. While it is admitted that many defenders of freedom are honest, it should not be overlooked that there are people who pose as defenders of freedom only in order to be unmolested in attempts to destroy freedom. Goebbels, Hitler's propaganda chief of ill-fame, was quite frank about it. He boasted that the aim of the Nazis was to liquidate the Weimar Republic and in the same breath mocked that republic for being foolish enough to enable them to do so. We should draw our lesson from this. We should not permit our liberties to degenerate into a license to destroy them.[40] We should guard ourselves as much against being fooled by those who use freedom to further the socialism of the Marxist brand, as the Weimar Republic should have prevented, by means of the necessary restrictions of freedom, the assumption of power by the socialists of the Nazi brand. Oliver Wendell Holmes, whose social interpretation of property we criticized, was right when he stated in World War I that free speech could be curtailed if there was a clear and present danger.[41]

Few people will doubt that today the danger to the free world is as clear and present as it ever was. It may even be maintained that although there is no war today, the cold war threatens the free world much more than World War I threatened the United States. Consequently, there is no apparent reason why restrictions of freedom more stringent than those permitted by Holmes would not be justifiable.

Our continual connivance at gradualist socialism has led us far astray. Two generations ago, when orthodox and even revisionist Marxism were rejected for their radicalism, more gradualistic movements were accepted. Only a generation later, while the communism of the Third International was still objected to, socialism of milder types had already advanced sufficiently to permit social democratic and labor parties to govern Western nations. Our generation has turned still further toward the left. Today's sympathy for communism is rather genuine, though many are afraid of admitting it. Whereas Stalinism is still generally rejected, Khrushchevism has become fairly acceptable. And although many still fear that a war might suddenly and violently plunge them into communism, they do not seem to mind being peacefully and gradually "co-existed" into communism. Again, the question arises whether gradualist world communism is less dangerous than a radical one. We are inclined to answer this question in the negative. The contrary is probably true. A gradual communization of the world, although perhaps more legal than a radical one, probably is more dangerous because it is more likely to succeed. Past experience supports this thesis, and Mr. Khrushchev, proposing world communism through coexistence, obviously agrees with it. Consequently, it is advisable to exercise as much, if not greater, caution and scepticism toward the soft line of Soviet policy as toward the hard line and to rebuke Western friends of Russia's soft line as much as sympathizers of her hard line.

Owing to the world-wide proportions of the movement against property, our attention cannot be confined to our own countries. Although, as a matter of principle, it does not seem advisable to interfere in the internal affairs of foreign nations, we should, if we do so, not support the wrong side in these nations. We should not support movements that are likely to degenerate into socialism and communism. Latin America is a case in point. Ever since I have been teaching, I have maintained that the United States should not meddle in the internal affairs of Latin American nations. I have especially emphasized that we should abstain from imposing democracy upon Latin America. Simon Bolívar, the Liberator, although in favor of democracy, recognized the impossibility of making it work in the Latin America of his time.[42] And despite the fact that the chances of popular government have increased ever since, it is probably not yet feasible in many parts of that continent. I particularly warned that one should not be deceived by movements that propose social and political reform under the banner of "liberalism" and democracy. I was sceptical toward such reforms, feeling that once they started, there would be no halting them and that Latin America would sooner or later become socialistic and communistic. Cuba demonstrated that this will happen sooner rather than later. When Castro was still fighting in the Sierra Maestre, I warned that his professed liberalism might be fraudulent. My students thought that I was too sceptical. When he expropriated land and industry, I suspected that he was a communist, although he asserted the contrary. My students tended to believe him rather than myself. After he had consolidated his regime, Castro confessed that he had been a Marxist-Leninist all along. Whether this was actually the case or whether he was overwhelmed by the radical elements in his movement does not really matter. In both instances the proposal to be wary of so-called liberal and democratic movements gains support.

The further deterioration of private property can also be prevented by guarding against socialist gradualism in international organization. For better or for worse, the Western nations became members of the United Nations, an organization that is, as was shown, not too enthusiastic about the protection of property. The West should here try to halt socialist trends. This could be done in the field of international legislation. Admission of nations that favor a social orientation toward property should be opposed. For an admission of nations so inclined (and many of the poor new nations admitted in recent years are so inclined), will, since the natural affinity of these nations is with the communist rather than the Western bloc, have detrimental results for the nations that cherish private property. Sooner or later, the latter will find themselves opposed by a strong socialist grouping and will be outvoted.

Since the deterioration of property was due largely to the march of democracy, a containment of trends toward a further deterioration must amount essentially to a containment of democracy, i.e., to the prevention of a further degeneration of popular government into egalitarian majoritarianism. It is not difficult to perceive that the suggestions made in the preceding pages are tantamount to proposals to prevent democracy from

becoming more egalitarian and thus potentially more socialist and communistic.

The situation can scarcely differ with respect to suggestions which
propose not only to prevent a further deterioration of property, but also
to bring about a reinstitution of its old eminent status.

Given the present political situation, this does not appear to be feasible in international organization, where socialist powers are strongly
represented. Whereas we may keep pro-socialist nations out of the United
Nations, we cannot very well emit those which are members. Thus we
cannot restore the voting balance in favor of the more property-conscious
nations. Moreover, we are probably in no position to revoke international
legislation that is detrimental to private property. One resort seems to
lie in leaving the United Nations. Such a step could perhaps enable us
to bar the application of international social legislation at least in our
own countries.

We cannot very well influence the developing nations to undo their
measures unfavorable to private property. On the other hand, there is
no reason why we should not be more sympathetic to the forces in such
nations that favor a reinstitution of property to its old status. We seem
to have been doing exactly the reverse by lending support to groups that,
like communists and fascists, are pressing for "social reform."[43]

The best prospects for a reinstitution of property appear to be in the
Western countries themselves. However, this author is pessimistic about
the possibility of their realization. For such reinstitution would involve
undoing all the harm that has been done to private property ever since
the end of the last century. It would entail revoking such things as progressive taxation, legislation in favor of debtors, and other social legislation. It would involve "turning the clock back" to the nineteenth century. This idea at first sight appears to be retrogressive. Whether it
actually is, is a different question. There is, to begin with, nothing inherently wrong with conserving old values. It all depends upon what these
values are and whether they deserve preservation. They often do, and
are truly enduring and classic. Considering that social legislation passed
under the banner of "progressivism" was anything but progressive and
indeed rather retarding, the reinvigoration of nineteenth century liberalism must be desirable. After all, that liberalism with its free property
was symbolic of what was probably the highest degree of freedom men

ever achieved. If one also takes account of the fact that the crux of free property, free enterprise, is a progressive feature of free society, a reluctance to revive the values of the nineteenth century is likely to disappear.

One way of bringing about such a revival would be through education. The public must be made aware of the pitfalls of the welfare state and the ill-effects of curtailments of private property. Fundamentally, this amounts to re-educating that vital center, the middle class, and to make labor realize that its fortunes lie with a free rather than a regulated society. It is, however, especially important to raise a new generation that once again believes in the liberal tradition and firmly rejects infringements upon free property. That task necessitates teachers who are devoted to that tradition.

Unfortunately, the chances of revitalizing our aims through education are slim. The young are taken care of to a greater extent than ever before, and they like it. Teachers have become enthusiastic adherents of the welfare state, and seem to be more to the left than most other groups of the middle class. And neither can that class be considered any more as the class that sustains states. It is no longer the state's vital center.[44] Under the spell of the welfare state, it has become more and more devitalized. Nor is labor apt to favor the reinstitution of private property, since it has reaped the greatest benefits from social legislation. In a word, the great majority are not likely to be sympathetic to our proposals. This means that our present kind of democracy, majoritarian as it is, cannot bring about the needed reforms. Only its curtailment can offer some hope for the re-establishment of an individualistic concept of property, just as only the containment of democracy could prevent the further deterioration of property rights.

A reintroduction of property qualifications for voting does not seem feasible. Although these qualifications, as well as educational ones, are probably as little detrimental to a working democracy as they are a blessing to the freedom of the individual, egalitarian democracy probably has progressed too far to consider that their adoption is possible. We must look for more subtle, though perhaps less effective, means to regenerate absolute popular government into limited democracy and to bring about a recognition of a more individualistic concept of property. We must seek devices that, in spite of general participation in the democratic process, are likely to prevent democratic power from becoming despotic. The two most obvious ways to achieve that end are probably the following: rendering the elected government fairly independent of the whims and passions of public opinion, and dividing governmental power. The first suggestion is based on the consideration that, whatever the disadvantages of democracy may be, it is probable that under that form of government the rulers will be of a higher caliber than the ruled, and will tend to be more favorably disposed toward property than those who elected them.[45] In regard to the division of governmental power, it should exist on both territorial and institutional levels. In view of the enormous centralization that has occurred in various countries, territorial power division will largely amount to giving more power to the local units, be they states, counties, or municipalities. Institutional power division must involve, owing to the enormous increase of the power of the political departments, a decrease of that power and a corresponding increase of the power of the non-political branch of government—the judiciary.

The institution of judicial review is suggested here as a major means for the control of democratic excesses and for the reinstitution of a more individualistic conception of property. Judicial review could check popular vogues and passions not only as they are expressed in the legislature and executive, but also, as they are evident in national and local governments. Being the only democratic institution that has retained some aristocratic features, judicial review could help to regenerate absolute democracy into a limited one, and to achieve the desired protection of property.[46]

Inevitably, the question arises whether a more limited democracy can be established at a time when everyone seems to be concerned only with making the world more democratic than it already is. Is it possible to bring it about in a legal manner? If not, could it be realized illegally?

We shall answer the latter question first. Often, illegal acts are permitted for reasons of state.[47] *A fortiori,* since under democratic theory the primary reason of state is the protection of the rights of the individual,[48] illegal acts must be permitted if they serve to protect those rights. Positive democratic law here coincides with the principles of natural law which admit a right of revolution. Supposedly "illegal" acts of curbing democracy, performed for the sake of freedom, are legitimate. If democracy, by virtue of "legal" infringements upon rights it was supposed to protect, loses its legitimacy, "illegal" reforms leading to an abolition of such infringements by means of a restriction of democracy must be permissible. For they only curb the illegitimacy of democracy and thus reinstitute its legitimacy. Although steps against an existing order should not be made for insubstantial reasons, there is no reason why such steps should not be taken if that order has evidenced its illegitimacy by consistent and severe infringements upon the rights of the individual.

The question of whether a legal transformation of an absolute into a limited democracy is possible of course can be answered in the affirmative. History furnishes many examples, and more were supplied by recent developments in Europe. But this takes us to a consideration of the prospects of private property in the old and new worlds.

THE PROSPECTS OF PRIVATE PROPERTY IN EUROPE AND AMERICA

In recent years, there has been a trend in Europe to strengthen the individualistic concept of private property. This trend cannot be observed in the United States.

Since World War II, steps have been taken in European nations toward a more limited form of democracy under which the rights of the individual, including those of property, would be better protected. While the desire toward a greater protection of property is often only slightly expressed, the Europeans show an interest not only in halting a further deterioration of private property, but also in reinstituting property rights to their former status. The following description shall, again, be confined to France and Germany.

In both countries there occurred a definite reaction not only to the authoritarianism of the Vichy regime and the Third Reich, but also to that of the democracies under the Fourth and Weimar republics. While one of the major tasks after the war was to reinstitute popular forms of government, a reassessment of democracy took place. In Germany, that reassessment can be seen in the Bonn Basic Law. In France, it is evident in the constitution of the Fifth Republic. In both countries, devices for limiting democracy were adopted. We can confine the discussion to enumerating a few key features. The government, once elected, was better guarded against being influenced by or dependent upon temporary popular whims and passions.[49] Governmental power became more divided. Germany, highly centralized under Hitler, not only condemned that centralization, but even rejected the less centralized system of Weimar, and adopted a federal form of government. France, such a classic example of centralization that this aspect survived the *ancien régime,* took steps toward decentralization.[50] Both nations also adopted a more genuine institutional division of powers. The Germans, in spite of their historical disposition in favor of a strong head of state, made the president of the republic less powerful. France, the classic country of government by assembly, elevated the president of the republic to a position that was at least on a par with that of the legislature. To make further improvements, both nations, having traditionally rejected judicial review as undemocratic, took steps toward its establishment.[51]

These institutional devices, designed to secure a limited rather than an absolute democracy, were complemented by provisions concerning the rights of the individual. Here again, fear of democratic license is evident. This applies especially to Germany, where the pitfalls of democracy led to the national-socialist dictatorship.[52] Government became more restricted. Whereas previously the legislature could restrict the rights of the individual, the new constitutions limited the exercise of that power. Freedom was also granted greater protection from individuals and groups. Bills of rights no longer were a license to destroy free government. It was made plain that those who abused the liberties guaranteed by the state could not claim their protection.[53]

Under the new constitutions freedom (believed to have existed before its component parts were defined and before all government, including the democratic form of government), was preserved in its entirety. That entirety was to the framers of these constitutions a symbol of the dignity of man.[54] None of the particular liberties was given preference over others, for they were all considered to be equally essential to freedom. Small wonder, then, that the protection of private property was given fairer consideration than in preceding decades. References to "social rights" do not alter the picture as constitutional interpretation has demonstrated.[55] In Germany, a reaction against the social interpretation of property, which had reached a climax under Hitler, took place. The "end of subjective rights" that had taken place under the Third Reich was followed by a "restitution of private law."[56] The individualistic concept of free property was reinstituted. Similar trends can be observed elsewhere in Europe.[57]

The European reaffirmation of the dignity of man, largely aided by a revival of and a new look at natural law,[58] was accomplished in a fairly comprehensive manner. Ample precautions to secure its survival were taken. Popular government was precluded from degenerating again into despotism. Provisions securing free government could no longer be the subject of constitutional amendment.[59] Thus by the middle of the twentieth century, the Europeans, having finally become aware of the pitfalls of democracy, adopted, for the sake of freedom, an undemocratic device that had been conceived for the first time in the Philadelphia Convention.[60] But this must raise the question whether the recent promising developments in Europe found their counterpart in the United States. Encouraging as the situation in Europe may be, it alone can, given the present world situation, hardly ensure the victory of freedom. Although the United States will always be smaller than the West, a survival of the West without American support is as unlikely today as it was during and after World War II. But that support is not likely to be very effective if in the United States the ideas of collectivism rather than those of individualism continue to prevail.

Unfortunately, this appears to be the case. America was spared the shock of World War II, an experience that made Europeans aware of the road to disaster they had been traveling upon. A rather blind belief in democratic values was permitted to persist. It was not recognized how much democracy could gradually degenerate into a rather absolutist type of government. Unlike other nations, America profited from the last war. She was the sole victor in it. She was the only nation that was capable of achieving victory without too great a sacrifice. There was no devastation, no occupation of the country; there was no remarkable decrease in the standard of living; nor was there a great loss in manpower. The war weakened all of the other participants, be they winners or losers. It strengthened the United States. She emerged as the most powerful nation in the world. In view of this, a reaction against the form of government under which victory was achieved could scarcely be expected. Democracy, as it had existed under the New Deal, continued. It existed during the Eisenhower administration. It is present now. There were no major and effective steps toward restoring free government against majoritarianism.

The institutions of government are cases in point. Federalism, separation of powers, judicial review—they all, once having become the victims of democratic majoritarianism, remained exactly that. They were not revived and restored to their original role as a means for the protection of the individual. Ever since the founding of the American republic, there has been a growing tendency toward increasing national power at the cost of states' rights . However, largely due to the guardianship exercised by the courts, the federal character of the Union remained unchallenged for a long time.[61] Since the New Deal, the situation has changed. Doubts as to whether this is still a genuine federal form of government are now justified.[62] The situation does not differ greatly with respect to the separation of powers. Although the balance between the three branches of government was never stable and rigid, it also was not seriously challenged for a long time. American government became known as the outstanding example of the separation of powers. But in recent decades, this situation changed. Executive power became stronger than ever before, even in the field of legislation.[63] In the 'thirties, severe blows were dealt to the institution of judicial review. Today, the freedom of the individual is more or less at the mercy of the political branches of the national government, of the representatives of the national majority —Congress and the President. The courts no longer seem to dare to challenge that majority on important issues.[64] There are no indications that these conditions will change.

In view of the fact that national majoritarianism has decimated the classic American institution of limited government, it is not surprising that today the government is more the captive of public opinion than ever before. Its independence from temporary popular passions and proclivities, once considered a distinctive feature of American government, has largely disappeared. There are no signs that it will re-emerge.

With the institutional devices securing limited government greatly reduced and with government having more and more degenerated into a mere mouthpiece of the unrestricted majority, the prospects for the rights of the individual and especially those of property, are dim indeed. During the past decades the idea that freedom is an entity and that all its parts are essential to the dignity of man has suffered severe blows. No longer is the value of the rights of man judged in terms of their conduciveness to the fulfillment of the individual's desires, but rather in terms of their serving collective aims. Free property has been discriminated against for being too individualistic. And there are not many indications of a strong desire to take stock of the disadvantages and injustices inherent in a collectivistic appreciation of private property and to put an end to the discriminations against property rights.

Previously, the disadvantages of restricted property were mentioned. Thus we can forego a discussion of the manner in which they occur in the United States. One point, however, which at present appears to be of special importance for the well-being of the nation, shall be dwelt upon—the absence of incentive. In the 'twenties, an outstanding French observer of the United States wrote that America had come of age.[65] He was impressed by what he saw in a nation that had emerged as one of the great powers from World War I, a nation that had progressed ever since it was created. Today, many of us no longer are so enthusiastic. Rather, we feel inclined to ask whether America has not already come of old age, a nation inhabited by people for whom progress largely consists in being taken care of. We are no longer impressed by her vigor. We are disturbed by her apathy.[66]

If we ask for the reason behind the fast transition from coming of age to growing old, a transition that implies a rather sudden absence of the desire for progress, we are led to ask whether the belief in progress, characteristic of young and vigorous America, has disappeared or changed. The answer is that to a great degree it has. This is largely due to an ominous alliance that has come about in America. That is the alliance between a few rich and many poor. Of course, such an alliance is not necessarily detrimental to progress. As long as the rich appreciate private property, progress is likely to be ensured. However, the situation changes as soon as the rich have lost their appreciation of property. And in America there are indications that some of them have. The few rich that are allied with the many poor in what could be called the New Alliance usually are not self-made men. They were born rich. They were born so rich that they never had to bother to work for a living. With no effort of their own, they lived in splendor and luxury, being taken care of by their parents' wealth. That wealth even helped them to win election to highest public office. They profited from their property and the fact that they could use it the way they wanted. *Honi soit qui mal y pense!*

It should not be assumed by the reader that we feel there is something wrong with being born rich, with living in luxury and even with being able to get elected to public office by means of inherited wealth. Although this author is aware that many among those who inherit property are not worthy of it and although he has often been perturbed by the extravagance, loose morals, and stupidity of those people, he feels that the right to leave one's wealth to whomever one wants, provides too valuable a stimulus for human effort to be discarded. Consequently, the protection of property advocated here extends beyond a mere protection of property that has been acquired through the owner's own efforts. On the other hand, it is felt that those who have been fortunate enough to profit from a far-reaching protection of property and thus have enjoyed life without much effort, should at least support the immunity of property that has been acquired through effort. It seems to be the limit of frivolity if people who get elected to public office by means of inherited rather than worked-for wealth advocate social measures in order to further their political ambitions and thus deny to those who were not born rich, those who have to struggle for a living and perhaps a few luxuries, to keep what they earned through honest efforts. If rich politicians are sincere in their desire to aid the poor, they are free to distribute their own wealth, down to the last coat, as St. Martin had done. Their magnanimity will be admired. But to advocate the disappropriation of others who in most cases acquired their property through diligence and deprivation, and, at the same time, to keep enough of their merely inherited wealth to enable them to live in luxury and splendour, is utterly hypocritical.

Unfortunately, some rich Americans who chose to enter the New Alliance do not seem to have felt that way. To promote their own ambitions, they catered to the masses. By means of promises of social legislation, they assured themselves the support of the poor. Once elected, they supported measures that essentially deprive those who work of part of their wages, and those who work hard of an even greater part of their earnings. Such behavior is not only dubious on grounds of justice. It is also to be condemned for reasons of state. For those who work hard form the backbone of society. They are the ones that insure progress. If they are deprived of their well-earned property, they will lose incentive. The progress of society will be stifled.

The New Alliance has largely abolished the old American concept of progress, a concept that had been based upon free property. Its way of achieving this was rather hypocritical. One did not dare to discard the word "progress." That word had come to mean too much to Americans. The word was kept as a facade, but its meaning was changed. The old, genuine progress was replaced by a new, rather fraudulent one. Nurtured by the ideology of the "progressives," the New Alliance proclaimed that progress could be found in the welfare state.

The hypocrisy of progressivism as it appeared in the New Deal has been discussed too often to justify further comment. However, it might be worth-while to point out the hypocrisy of the present successor of the New Deal—the New Frontier. Its campaign platform was not only hypocritical; it was self-contradictory. While it lamented the apathy of the nation, it advocated additional welfare legislation. In a word, while

Americans were urged to "get moving again," measures were proposed that are likely to deprive them of the incentive to get moving! The very thing that probably had the lion's share in the decline of national progress—social legislation—was hailed as a means for bringing about greater progress!

Frontiers exist to defend and spread the values that have made a nation great. They are not there for the advancement of ideas that are likely to weaken that nation. Thus the American Frontier of old fame was a genuine frontier. The New Frontier is not. It is as much a fake frontier as the New Freedom was a fake freedom. Much to the dismay of his (mainly academic) audience, this author suggested this idea as early as 1957, when no one had yet heard of the New Frontier. He felt then, as he does today, that America's new frontiers were not where people wanted to be taken care of according to their needs—on the welfare "front"—but, rather, where the individual's freedom to develop his abilities was threatened. He said that America's new frontiers are far away from her shores, wherever freedom and free property were in jeopardy. He emphasized that it made no difference whether freedom was threatened by fascism or by the "despotism of the communist brand."[67]

The New Frontier is all the more questionable because it supports a fraudulent progressivism not only in the United States, but also abroad. Latin America may again serve as an example. In its "Alliance for Progress" program, the New Frontier ties American aid to the condition of social reform.[68] Recognizing a "social revolution" in Latin America, the New Frontier does nothing to support the forces that favor a protection of vested rights and private property. On the contrary, believing (or wishfully thinking?) that a social revolution is inevitable (the parallel of the communist belief that the world revolution is inevitable inevitably comes to mind!), it jumps on the social or socialist bandwagon. It does so in spite of the fact that the "progressive" forces of Latin America, wherever they have gained the upper hand, have proposed or carried out large-scale expropriations of private property.[69]

Still worse, the New Frontier supports outright communist governments. It supports Tito. It gives aid to communist Poland. The loss of face (or faith?) that results from this is said to be compensated for by the encouragement of a split in the communist camp. However, there are scarcely indications that this expectation is justified. In crises, both Poland and Yugoslavia were found in the communist camp.[70] The New

Frontier has aided world communism in still another respect. By default (or defeatism?), it has supported the Soviet Union in her attempts of aggrandizement. It has permitted her to confront the West with accomplished facts. It has appeased her again and again, letting down and estranging America's allies. It has thus promoted a major aim of Soviet policy, namely, the splitting up of the Western camp. In Cuba, it permitted the establishment of a Soviet satellite.[71]

To be fair, this attitude characterizes not only the present administration. Mistakes were made before. But it is not surprising that what happened was permitted to occur. The assertion that the attitude of recent American governments has sprung from a malicious intent to aid communism might be an exaggeration, although in a free society the right to levy such accusations should not be denied.[72] The question does not seem to be whether American governments wanted all these things to happen, but whether they really could have prevented them from happening. In asking the latter question, we do not have in mind the pressure public opinion may have brought to bear upon governmental decisions. We think of a deeper, more inherent compulsion. We ask whether a strong will to halt communist aggression could have existed in view of existing innate sympathies for leftist movements. No one can jump over his own shadow. Since the United States has increasingly become a nation in which socialist ideas enjoy popularity, it is not surprising that her governments should have become the captive of the new "progressivism." As such, they could hardly be expected to pursue a foreign policy that would be opposed to the new American credo. American policy makers, being sympathetic to a social appreciation of property at home, could and can scarcely help favoring similar movements abroad. If they confess no open sympathy for these movements, their "resistance" to them must be lukewarm. For deep down in their hearts, they are bound to harbor sympathy for what they often profess to fight.

This, of course, cannot be an apology for what has been permitted to happen. And if one is inclined to give those responsible for what has occurred the benefit of the doubt by believing that they acted as naive captives of the new "progressivism" rather than as malicious agents of communism, there is no reason why no doubts should be raised as to whether they deserve such benefit. It cannot be seen why the question should not be asked as to whether those who have ruled America in recent years have really tried to extricate themselves from socialist entanglements, whether they really have done everything possible to bolster the cause of freedom. It is easy to denounce and ridicule individuals and groups who criticize governmental policy as conservatives, reactionaries, right-wing radicals and what not, especially so since these groups are a definite minority.[73] But this way out appears to be too simple. After all, it should be recognized that radicalism does not occur without some reason. It usually develops only if people are troubled about things. If, of all people, Americans, known for their optimism, show signs of apprehension, there is reason to believe that there is substantial cause for alarm. It can also be said that the more people are worried, the more radical their actions are likely to be. The degree of disturbance is thus a barometer of the degree things have gone off track. If Americans today are disturbed to the point of radicalism, the situation is likely to be very serious indeed. Therefore, rather than merely denouncing those who criticize the government in a radical manner, one should query as to whether things have not radically gone off course, painful as this examination, like any self-examination, might be. It should be examined as to whether we have not radically departed—evolutionary as the process may have been—from the traditional American way of life, a way of life that was based upon free property and the progress that resulted from it. It ought to be asked whether there are not valid reasons why those responsible for the change should be called to account for their omissions and actions by those who have suffered in the past, who suffer at present, and will suffer in the future. It should be examined whether a denunciation of the latter's misgivings would not amount to prohibiting attempts to restore constitutionalism and to permitting the degeneration of constitutional government to continue. It should be asked whether such denunciation would not mean to condemn those who try a change for the better for the sake of those who have brought about a change for the worse.

The right to resist oppression has been a cherished American right. It has become part of the American political credo. When Americans realized it for the first time, they did so in a large measure for the protection of property. At that time, the colonists were not suddenly deprived of their property. Their rights were infringed upon by acts of Parliament step by step, in an evolutionary manner. The colonists endured the situation for some time. But when they saw no end to oppression, they resisted. Once the thirteen colonies had won independence, a similar development took place. Private property was attacked by the popular majorities in the states. Once again, this happened gradually, by way of legislation. Again, Americans suffered it for some time. But then again, when infringements upon private property did not cease, the point of resistance was reached. By a veritable *coup d'état,* the Articles of Confederation were discarded and replaced by the Constitution.

The right of revolution being an important feature of American thought, there must, *a fortiori,* be a right of non-violent criticism, radical as it may appear. Instead of flatly denouncing it as "radicalism," it is advisable to examine how radical it actually is and what its ends and aims really are. One ought to ask whether those denounced as right wing radicals, a group that consists largely of conservatives and true liberals, want a radical overthrow of the government or rather a reform of a government that has, by the original standard of American constitutionalism, become radically defective. In the opinion of this writer, most of them merely want to restore government to its original and only legitimate function—the protection of freedom, including free property. They advocate no revolution, although such advocacy, if made for the protection of freedom, would be in the American tradition. Their aim is more moderate. They only denounce majoritarianism and bewail its devastating consequences. They thus fundamentally repeat what was done by the Founding Fathers when they adopted the Constitution. Their hopes are similar to those of the Founders, namely, that a restriction of majoritarianism facilitates the protection of private property and is conducive of progress, order and justice.

Will their attempts be crowned by success? We do not think so. The forces favoring a restoration of free government are too weak, and the forces opposing it, too strong. Too powerful is the "progressivism" of the New Alliance, as it was adopted by the New Freedom and institutionalized by the New Deal and the New Frontier, three products of the twentieth century that are as new as they are not true, as appealing to the masses as they are inimical to freedom. And too strong is the general sympathy for a social rather than individualistic conception of property that came with them.

CONCLUDING REMARK

THE PRECEDING pages contained criticisms of contemporary America. For a long time, I have wondered whether I should make them. I wondered not so much because I am aware that, although Americans can stand much self-criticism, they are very sensitive to criticisms made by people from abroad;[1] rather, my doubts were due to fears lest my criticisms might be considered a sign of ingratitude. For indeed I owe a great deal to America. I am not exaggerating when I confess that these doubts have literally tormented me. Frequently they almost impelled me to omit criticism in order to make absolutely sure that nobody could question my gratitude toward this country. When finally I decided to risk being called unappreciative, it was largely due to the consideration that the consequences which my criticisms might have for myself did not really matter very much, and that it was better to think in broader and more altruistic terms. Omission of my critical remarks would have amounted to not telling the truth as I saw it. This would have been unfair not only to the American institution with which I am associated and its motto, *veritas vos liberabit,* but also to the general public, the more so since that motto is, in the biblical passage from which it is taken, preceded by the words, "Ye shall know the truth."[2] Often patients do not like to hear how sick they are. And if the truth cannot help them, there is no impelling reason why they should know it. Aside from being incapable of freeing them, it would only spoil their last days. However, the situation differs if the truth can be beneficial, if it can make people free and able to survive. For no matter how pessimistic the preceding evaluation of America may have been, some hope still remains.

Consequently, America may be rendered a service by criticism. Criticisms are, of course, unpleasant to hear. On the other hand, it should be realized that what is presently American is not necessarily good, just as what is good is not necessarily American. America can be God's own country only if God permits Americans to make it so and, what is just as important, if Americans use their opportunities accordingly. No matter how great the American potential is—and it is enormous indeed—America will always be just what her people make her to be. This is true of any nation, no matter how superior it might be considered to be. Germany was hell under Hitler in spite of all the assertions that she was greater and better than ever before. Compared to Hitler's Germany, the United States is like heaven even today. However, it may be questioned whether she is, if measured by more reasonable standards. Indeed, she is not by the standards set up by her founders—standards that existed throughout the period of her growth to the most powerful nation on earth.

I made the criticisms of contemporary America not merely as a person who spent the better part of his adult life in the United States, but also as a European who is deeply concerned with the fate of the old world. The survival of Europe today depends largely upon a free and strong America. America should not desert Europe. For America could scarcely have attained her present condition without the help of Europe. Europeans discovered her, and only the transplantation of European population and civilization has made possible the America as we know it today.

That transplantation occurred in a manner which was extremely fortunate for America. The immigrants brought many good things with them and left many bad things behind. If the idea that America is God's own country can be justified at all, it is only by virtue of the fact that her inhabitants were free to use what the new world offered. And this freedom existed mainly because the immigrants left behind them the vestiges of feudalism.[3] The American colonists can well be called the first people with a Western civilization that enjoyed property freed from these vestiges. This was a gift from God. But like all such gifts, it implies obligations.

The colonists fulfilled that obligation when they decided to become independent. The timing of this important event was likely to make the United States a symbol of free property. For in the very year in which Americans took the decisive step for securing free property in the new world by declaring independence, there was published, in the very country that represented to them the fetters of feudalism, the treatise that marks the beginning of the abolition of these fetters in the old world— Adam Smith's *Wealth of Nations*. Thus America, while fighting England to secure free property, received into her cradle a gift that exonerated property. When feudalistic America broke her formal link to feudalistic Europe, a Scotsman gave her the book to live by. Whatever may have been the relations between Adam Smith and the United States during that eventful year; whoever may have influenced whom, no other nation had the privilege of being born the very year the classic work on free property saw the light of day.[4]

The title of that work, referring to nations rather than one nation, seems to suggest that America's task was not confined to keeping property free only within her own boundaries, but to keep it free on a much broader scale—in other nations as well as among nations. Was America destined to become the protector of free property throughout the world and thus a true *defensor pacis*?[5] We believe that the constellation at her birth justifies such speculation, and that the ideological content of the *Pax Americana* is, above all, the protection of free property. If America was so blessed and privileged, she was assigned a formidable task indeed. For that task implies that her duty to protect free property must be greater than that of any other nation; that her failure to protect free property must be more sacrilegious than similar failures of other nations; and that, consequently, she could be more reproached for such failures than could other nations.

Here is another reason why an omission of a criticism of the United States is not permissible. One may even venture to say that here is a reason why higher standards could be applied to the United States than to other countries in criticisms of national actions detrimental to free property. It can be argued that social legislation, measured in absolute terms, goes further in other Western nations than it does in the United States. But absolute standards do not really matter so much here, important as they are for the future. Considering America's tradition of and mission for free property, her infringements upon property are as dangerous as those that occurred in Europe, especially if one takes into account that the European tradition has much less been one of free property, and that there is no such thing as a traditional European mission for free property. By the same token, recent European trends toward a reaffirmation of free property must be hailed, whereas the absence of such trends in the United States must be deeply regretted.

A leader always has greater obligations than those whom he leads. The assumption of such obligations is probably the essence of his charisma.[6] If today America wants to lead the free world in a crusade for freedom, her program must be exemplary.[7] A *Pax Americana* can be accepted only if it stands for freedom and the progress that results from it, a progress that has given us our high degree of civilization. As mentioned prior, both freedom and progress are inconceivable without free property. Consequently, a *Pax Americana* can be acceptable only if America fulfills her manifest destiny in defending free property.[8]

America had not only the fortune of being the first nation to enjoy free property. She was also the first nation to solve the problem of democracy, a problem that is bound to arise from the concomitance of the ideas of free property and popular government. That problem centers around the question to what degree the popular will, while ruling, should be restricted for the sake of the rights of the individual. It was solved by giving the liberal principle of the protection of the individual, considered as an end, primacy before the democratic principle of popular government, taken as a mere means.

Unfortunately, the United States during the past decades has been unable to project that solution to the rest of the world. She has failed not only in protecting free property, but she has failed also in seeing to it that popular government is of the limited rather than the absolute type. This failure seems to be due to her enthusiasm for self-determination all over the world.

That enthusiasm results from the third great fortune with which America was blessed at an early stage, freedom from colonialism. Evident when the Spanish American colonies fought for their independence, it has been very strong after World War II when, often to the disappointment of her allies, the United States posed as the champion of anti-colonialism.[9] Her sincerity in doing so is not doubted. Although it has been maintained that whenever the colonial powers left their colonies, American influence in these territories increased,[10] it is believed that in her support of anti-colonialism, the United States was motivated largely by the feeling that like the American colonists, all other people have a right to liberate themselves from colonial rule. However, this author, while he considers himself fortunate to have lived only in nations which possessed no colonies, and while he is opposed to the principle of colonialism, still wonders whether this attitude of the United States has been a blessing to the freedom of the individual in these groups, and whether it has fostered the cause of Western civilization.

It seems to have been overlooked that there are important differences between America's struggle for independence and that of modern nations. American independence was a blessing to Western civilization because it propagated the major value of that civilization—freedom.[11] By contrast, the attainment of independence by many modern nations cannot likewise be called a blessing. For a protection of the rights of the individual has not always resulted from the end of colonial rule. Often, the departure of the colonial power was followed by the establishment of authoritarian governments, democratic as they may have been, that encroach upon the freedom of the individual and, especially, upon his property.[12] Although it is possible that the indigenous population enjoys more democratic rights in India today than it did under British rule, or in Indonesia than it did under Dutch rule, or in Goa than it did under the Portuguese, or in North Vietnam than it did under the French, or in the Congo than it did under the Belgians (these examples show the whole questionability of the glorification of democratic rights), doubts can be raised whether today people in these nations enjoy liberal rights, including those of property, as much as they did before. It seems that self-determination often has not yet resulted in a protection of the individual from governmental control. Considering the indigenous mores and the fundamentally non-individualistic tradition of these nations, it is unlikely that this situation will change.

This development is hardly a blessing. For it has reduced the territory in which a belief in the humanistic value of freedom prevails. American support of self-determination, idealistic as it may be, has thus been destructive of Western values. It could perhaps even be asked whether it has not actually resulted in selling out the West to the rest of the world. Clearly, this question imposes itself if we regard the new United Nations, where now the West can be outvoted.[13] Toynbee's prognosis that the Western minority will be faced by a non-Western majority has been proven here.[14] The hope that this will not lead eventually to an elimination of the West is merely a faint one. In all probability the West, for centuries considered the natural aristocracy of the human race, will become a victim of the world-wide march of egalitarian democracy just as previously national aristocracies, including the "natural" ones of which Jefferson spoke, became victims of the march of democracy in the various nations. The egalitarian pitfalls of the French Revolution, which originally existed on a national level, will occur on a world-wide scale. Equality before the law will be replaced everywhere by equality through the law. And that law will be made by an anti-Western majority that will decree the decapitation—perhaps physical—of the West and the distribution of its property.

It is not easy to be a leader, and the responsibility with which the United States is blessed today is a burdensome one indeed. But it is doubtful whether any other nation could carry that burden better. As stated in the foregoing, America has some unique qualifications that seem to designate her to leadership in the free world: For the freedom of the individual, she was first in rejecting colonialism, in solving the problem of democracy by limiting popular government, and in propagating free property as an essential part of freedom. Thus destined to leadership, the United States should not carry that leadership lightly. She should not abuse the trust given to her by lending support to forces that are detrimental to freedom and free property. If she does, she forfeits not only her leadership, but also her manifest destiny.

That destiny is to promote free property and the freedom of which such property constitutes an essential part. Advocacy of popular government can be justified only as long as it serves that end. However, America's advocacy of self-determination and popular government in other countries for the sake of free property and freedom can hardly be convincing if her own government no longer exists for that purpose. Therefore, if America wants to be an effective leader of the free world, first she must reform popular government at home.

That reform would essentially amount to something that is as American as could be, namely, a reaffirmation of the Jeffersonian concept of natural aristocracy. And this, in turn, amounts to a reaffirmation of property rights.[15] The American government must cease persecuting the American aristocracy, the more educated and more wealthy, by depriving them of a relatively large part of their property. It must stop taking away what has been gained by effort. It must refrain from punishing honest work. Only in this way can it fulfill America's manifest destiny at home. And only if America lives up to that destiny at home, can she prevent the decline of the West, which still, for the most part, is considered the natural aristocracy of the earth.

With these suggestions I conclude. Planned as a study of property, this treatise turned out to be an essay on the decline of freedom. Conceived at the University of Virginia, it was written in Washington, the capital of the nation that claims the leadership of the free world. Scarcely could there have been a better location. Also, the time in which it was written was a fitting one. It was written in the year that saw the arrival, with much fanfare, of the New.Frontier.

Between the conception and completion of the work, the situation about which I was worried when I began this study has not improved. No indications were given in the last months of the Eisenhower administration that property would be reinstituted to its eminent position in the United States. As to American foreign policy, world communism received greater official sanction than it ever had before. Khrushchev was welcomed at the White House, only to humiliate his host a few months later by shouting at him that he was not welcome in the Kremlin. The arrival of the New Frontier did not meliorate the situation. It hardly could have. For the New Frontier is by its own admission more in agreement with the social ideas of the New Deal than was Eisenhower republicanism. So far, the New Frontier has given all indications that property will be further infringed upon through social legislation. As to foreign affairs, Khrushchev's hope that the Kennedy administration would be more desirable than one under Nixon has not been refuted.[16] Communism was permitted to rapidly gain further ground. In its first year, the new administration suffered one defeat after the other everywhere in the world, in Asia, Latin America and Europe. And the defeats increased in magnitude. First came the backdown on Laos, resulting in a feeling among SEATO allies that an alliance with the United States was not really worth very much. Then came the Cuban debacle, giving everyone the impressions that if the United States would not risk anything to stop communism only ninety miles from her shore, she would hardly be willing to run a risk for the defense of freedom somewhere else.[17] Berlin proved that this supposition was not without foundation. The building of the Wall eliminated that city as a haven of liberty, because no one can any longer flee to that haven.[18] Looking into the future, there is no reason to believe that the sellout to the communists will not continue.

While in Washington, I paid frequent visits to the Jefferson Memorial. Because of its simple beauty, I have always liked it best of the capital's monuments. Its architectural style reminded me of Jefferson's as I had admired it in Charlottesville. Its setting is beautiful; its position—significant: The memorial is situated on the prolongation of the axis of the White House. The statue of Jefferson thus faces the office of the President of the United States, as if it was supposed to be an admonition to him. This perhaps was the reason for choosing the memorial's site. But, I wondered, was this the only reason? And if it was, was the memorial really a reminder of the principles Jefferson stood for? As to the first question, the date of the memorial's erection made me wonder. It was built during the New Deal, when the new "progressivism" was being realized in a way that was felt by many to be incompatible with American constitutional government.[19] Significantly, the memorial quotes Jefferson's statement that "laws and institutions must go hand in hand with the progress of the human mind." Was the monument perhaps built to serve as an excuse for Roosevelt's new social ideas? Were quotations put in that could conceivably serve as an apology for the "progressivism" of the New Deal? Be this as it may, doubts arose in my mind whether for an incumbent President the memorial could actually serve as a reminder of Jefferson's true thoughts. And the view the President has of the memorial from the White House seems to substantiate that question. Usually it is not a clear view. The mists emerging from the Potomac makes the memorial appear a little hazy. The picture is reminiscent of an impressionist painting. It is easy and relaxing to look at. It makes the spectator aware of the pleasures of life rather than its duties. Did some genial stroke of nature create a symbol here of how vaguely and carelessly Jefferson is seen from the White House? Or was the apparent stroke of nature perhaps the work of man? Had the creator of the New Deal erected a monument whose sight permitted him to interpret Jefferson the way he saw fit? For the haziness in which the memorial is usually shrouded lets it appear somewhat mystical. But that mysticism hardly suggests the idea of the individual's inalienable rights. For the round cupola and the Ionic columns of the memorial do not lead one's eyes toward heaven. Its mystical aura appears earthly, as earthly as the democratic dogma that the voice of the people is the voice of God.

But a mystical Jefferson, convenient as he may be to serve as an apologist for what is done by the representatives of the people, is not necessarily the real Jefferson. And even the inscriptions inside the memorial, irrespective of how their selection might have been motivated by the desire to make the apostle of the Democratic party appear as the prophet and apologist of the New Deal, hardly fulfill the hopes put in them by their selectors. From among the two that were conceivably selected with such a purpose, none actually implies a disregard of private property. That the Declaration of Independence, excerpts of which are engraved into the memorial, is a defense of property rights, has been demonstrated above. The situation does not differ with regard to the following statement of the old Jefferson, which, of all the other statements engraved, is most likely to favor the New Progressivism: "I am not an advocate for frequent changes in laws and constitutions. But laws and institutions must go hand in hand with the progress of the human mind. As that becomes more developed, more enlightened, as new discoveries are made, new truths discovered and manners and opinions change, with the change of circumstances, institutions must advance also to keep pace with the times. We might as well require a man to wear still the coat which fitted him when a boy as civilized society to remain ever under the regimen of their barbarous ancestors."[20] At first sight, this statement seems to amount to a green light for new "progressive" movements. But on close scrutiny, we arrive at the belief that Jefferson could have thought only of the genuine progressivism that results from free property. To the author of the Declaration of Independence and the *Notes on Virginia*, an important distinction between the regimes of our barbarous ancestors and civilized society was that under the former, freedom, including property rights, had been restricted whereas under the latter, man had become emancipated and property had become free. It was this very emancipation of freedom and property that was the result of the human mind's becoming "more developed" and "more enlightened"—a result of "the progress of the human mind."[21]

The progress of the human race, while it may be aided by broadening the democratic basis of government, is unthinkable without a natural aristocracy, an aristocracy that exists by virtue of its striving and its achievements, i.e., by the propriety of property. Such an aristocracy is thus inconceivable without the acceptance of the idea that property is something proper. Restrictions of property necessarily question its propriety and result in its disparagement. They discourage achievement and incentive. They also prevent a natural aristocracy and hinder the progress of mankind.

A natural aristocracy, based, as Jefferson put it, upon virtue and talents, is not incompatible with democracy. As a matter of fact, democratic government can serve the important function of emancipating men and of giving the virtuous and talented an opportunity to become natural aristocrats. Thus democracy can be conducive to progress. Obviously, this was the original *ratio* behind the establishment of popular government. By the same token, democracy must lose its rationale if it precludes a natural aristocracy, if it transforms the equality of opportunity into an egalitarianism that gives to each not according to his ability, but according to his need. The moment that happens, progress is hindered. Incentive and effort are punished because property and achievement are made to appear improper.

Here lies a major problem of Western democracy. We lost the sense for the propriety of property. Ever since free property, having been achieved in a long struggle which was propelled by the conviction that property is something proper, has become restricted, our appreciation of property has declined. Since this curtailment of property has been effected by modern democratic government, the question arises as to whether that type of government has not lost its legitimacy. For it has destroyed one of the main factors in the growth and progress of our civilization, namely, the belief in the propriety of property.

NOTES

INTRODUCTORY REMARK

1. See Heinrich O. Meisner, ed., DENKWÜRDIGKEITEN DES GENERAL-FELDMARSCHALLS ALFRED GRAFEN VON WALDERSEE (1923), II, 233.

2. Shortly before Jefferson retired from the presidency, he stated in his Eighth Annual Message of Nov. 8, 1808: "I carry with me the consolation of a firm persuasion that Heaven has in store for our beloved country long ages to come of prosperity and happiness." THE WRITINGS OF THOMAS JEFFERSON (Memorial ed., 1903), III, 485 f. He also wrote: "I do believe we shall continue to grow, to multiply and prosper until we exhibit an association, powerful, wise and happy beyond what has yet been seen by men." *(Id.,* XIII, 123); "Not in our day, but at no distant one, we may shake a rod over the heads of all [European nations], which may make the stoutest of them tremble." (To Thomas Leiper on June 12, 1815. *Id.,* XIV, 308); "We are destined to be a barrier against the returns of ignorance and barbarism. Old Europe will have to lean on our shoulders, and to hobble along by our side, under the monkish trammels of priests and kings, as she can. What a Colossus shall we be when the southern continent comes up to our mark! What a stand will it secure as a ralliance for the reason and freedom of our globe." (To John Adams on Aug. 1, 1816. *Id.,* XV, 58 f.)—For opinions of Jefferson's contemporaries, see Hezekiah Niles, ed., PRINCIPLES AND ACTS OF THE REVOLUTION (1822), 52 ff., 59, 64-72, 85; Washington's First Inaugural Address and his proposed address to Congress of 1789, as well as his Farewell Address (John C. Fitzpatrick, ed., THE WRITINGS OF GEORGE WASHINGTON [1939], XXX, 294 f., 306 f.; XXXV, 217 f., 234); David Humphrey, "A Poem, on the Happiness of America," in A POEM, ADDRESSED TO THE ARMIES OF THE UNITED STATES OF AMERICA (1785); Joel Barlow, THE VISION OF COLUMBUS (1787); John Adams' letter to Jefferson of Nov. 15, 1813 (THE WRITINGS OF THOMAS JEFFERSON, XIV, 6): "Our pure, virtuous, public-spirited, federative republic will last forever, govern the globe, and introduce the perfection of man; his perfectability being already proved by Price, Priestley, Condorcet, Rousseau, Diderot, and Godwin." Alexander Hamilton's optimism is expressed in "A Full Vindication" and "The Continentalist." THE WORKS OF ALEXANDER HAMILTON (Fed. ed., 1904), I, 19; 286 f. It can also be seen in THE FEDERALIST (Modern Library ed., 1937), 69.

3. Comp. Benjamin Rush's statements in a letter to Richard Price of May 25, 1786 (Lyman H. Butterfield, ed., LETTERS OF BENJAMIN RUSH [1951], 388), and in his address to the American people in January, 1787. (Niles, *op. cit.,* 402). On July 4, 1787, the same position was taken by Joel Barlow *(Id.,* 386). Similar views were advanced by Richard Price

and Condorcet. (Comp. Merle Curti, THE GROWTH OF AMERICAN THOUGHT [1943], 154).
For a modern view of the idea, see the book by the editors of *Fortune Magazine*, U.S.A.
THE PERMANENT REVOLUTION (1951).

4. The dissertation was later published: ÜBER FORMULIERUNG DER MENSCHENRECHTE
(1956).

5.   *Den Vereinigten Staaten*

        Amerika, du hast es besser
        Als unser Kontinent, das alte,
        Hast keine verfallene Schlösser
        Und keine Basalte.

        Dich stört nicht im Innern,
        Zu lebendiger Zeit,
        Unnützes Erinnern
        Und vergeblicher Streit.

        Benutzt die Gegenwart mit Glück!
        Und wenn nun eure Kinder dichten,
        Bewahre sie ein gut Geschick
        Vor Ritter—, Räuber— und Gespenstergeschichten!

SÄMTLICHE WERKE (Jubiläumsausgabe, 1912), IV, 127. See also Goethe's statement to Eckermann of Feb. 21, 1827, in Johann Peter Eckermann, GESPRÄCHE MIT GOETHE IN DEN LETZTEN
JAHREN SEINES LEBENS (6th ed., 1885), III, 83 f.

6. "La mayor cosa después de la creación del mundo, sacando la encarnación y muerte
del que lo crio, es el descubrimiento de las Indias, y por eso las llaman Nuevo Mundo."
(López de Gómara).

7. Leo L. Matthias, DIE ENTDECKUNG AMERIKAS ANNO 1953 (1953), appears to be a product
of the cold war. A reviewer, Ludwig Freund, characterized that book as "ein Zerrbild der
Vereinigten Staaten" in POLITISCHE LITERATUR (1954), I, 59.

8. Harry L. Golden, ONLY IN AMERICA (1958); ENJOY! ENJOY! (1960).

9. Comp. Ernst Fraenkel, AMERIKA IM SPIEGEL DES DEUTSCHEN POLITISCHEN DENKENS
(1959), 29. When Goethe sent Harvard University his collected works, he wrote the following dedication: "Möge mir hierdurch das Vergnügen und der Vorteil werden, immer näher
mit dem wundervollen Land bekannt zu werden, welches die Augen aller Welt auf sich
zieht, durch einen feierlichen gesetzlichen Zustand, der ein Wachstum befördert, welchem
keine Grenzen gesetzt sind." Quoted *id.*, 24.

10. See Benjamin Franklin's "Information to Those Who Would Remove to America"
of 1782. Albert H. Smith, ed., THE WRITINGS OF BENJAMIN FRANKLIN (1905-7), VIII, 603.
The theme of that work is that America is a desirable habitat only for those who work
hard. At the same time, Franklin held that America was an asylum for liberty: "Tyranny
is so generally established in the rest of the world, that the prospects of an asylum in
America for those who love liberty gives general joy. . . . We are fighting for the dignity
and happiness of human nature. Glorious it is for the Americans to be called by Providence
to this post of honor." Claude H. Van Tyne, THE AMERICAN REVOLUTION 1776-1783 (1905),
333.

11. Alpheus T. Mason, FREE GOVERNMENT IN THE MAKING (1949), vii.

12. Henry A. Wallace, NEW FRONTIERS (1934).

13. Woodrow Wilson, THE NEW FREEDOM (1913). The New Freedom remained at first
confined to the ideological sphere. Wilson, having conservative inhibitions, did not press
for the institutionalization of his new ideas. On the other hand, Franklin D. Roosevelt,
free from such inhibitions, pressed for the realization of his social ideas. He did not even
care for a noble catchword, and offered a mere "deal." Wilson, who was accepted by many
contemporary conservatives, was not accused of breaking the Constitution. Roosevelt, on

the other hand, was. Under him, the seed sown by Wilson bore fruit, and it was only during his administration that most people became aware of the importance of the ideology of the New Freedom.

14. Carroll D. Murphy and Herbert V. Prochnow, THE NEXT CENTURY IS AMERICA'S (1938).

15. See Dietze, THE FEDERALIST—A CLASSIC ON FEDERALISM AND FREE GOVERNMENT (1960), 65, 335. The Founders' emphasis upon the importance of property rights was due merely to the fact that these rights were, at their time, more infringed upon than other aspects of freedom. Their freedom, they felt, was especially jeopardized through encroachments upon their property. (For the thesis that the guaranty of specific aspects of freedom is nothing but a consequence of oppressions of these specific aspects, see Georg Jellinek, DIE ERKLÄRUNG DER MENSCHEN—UND BÜRGERRECHTE [1895]).

16. In these notes, published in 1782, Jefferson complains of the "elective despotism" that existed in his home state due to a concentration of power in the legislature. He expresses apprehension lest money and liberty might not be safe if they are at the disposition of the unchecked representatives of the people. Paul L. Ford, ed., THE WRITINGS OF THOMAS JEFFERSON (1892-99), III, 223 ff.

17. Comp. infra, pp. 205, 208 f.

18. As a matter of fact, it could perhaps be asserted that the probability that property owners are an elite is greater than that of a racial group constituting an elite. From this point of view, persecutions of property owners would be worse than persecutions of racial groups.

19. Carl J. Friedrich, CONSTITUTIONAL GOVERNMENT AND DEMOCRACY (Rev. ed., 1950), 15.

20. Law was called an "ethical minimum" by the great positivist Georg Jellinek in DIE SOZIALETHISCHE BEDEUTUNG VON RECHT, UNRECHT UND STRAFE (2nd ed., 1908), 45.

21. Charles H. McIlwain, CONSTITUTIONALISM, ANCIENT AND MODERN (1940), 39, uses the term "older law" for "higher law." In the following, these terms will be used interchangeably. Both comprise natural as well as common and customary law.

CHAPTER I

1. The line between the idealistic and materialistic is hard to draw. While it is believed that there is too much materialism in the world, we are also aware of the pitfalls idealism offers and of the hypocritical use that is made of it. The "idealistic" may thus actually be something materialistic. On the other hand, the "materialistic" may well turn out to be something idealistic. As far as property is concerned, it is often assumed that its connotations are materialistic rather than idealistic. But what about the person whose property helps others and advances civilization, even if, at the time of acquisition, he had no such aims? Is the lazy dreamer necessarily an idealist, and the hard worker, out for money, a materialist? Is the utilitarian argument in defense of property less ethical than the claim that property is sanctioned by God? These are only a few questions that demonstrate the difficulty of distinguishing between "idealistic" and "materialistic" ethics.

2. LEVIATHAN (1651, reprinted 1929), 98; TWO TREATISES OF GOVERNMENT (1690), 245. For the meaning of the word "propriety" in the seventeenth century, see Richard B. Schlatter, THE SOCIAL IDEAS OF RELIGIOUS LEADERS 1660-1688 (1940), 87.

3. Quoted in Pierre Larousse, GRAND DICTIONNAIRE UNIVERSEL DU XIXᵉ SIÈCLE, XIII, 265.

4. A. J. Carlyle, A HISTORY OF MEDIEVAL POLITICAL THEORY IN THE WEST (2nd ed., 1927), I, 8 f.

5. Plato's communism was a qualified one. It was restricted to the guardian class, and did not apply to such people as workers, artisans and farmers.

6. POLITICS, Book II, secs. 1262a-1264b.

7. Comp. id., Book II, sec. 1263a.

8. Id., Book II, sec. 1261b. (Jowett transl., reprinted 1945).

9. *Id.*, Book II, secs. 1261b-1263b.

10. *Id.*, Book II, sec. 1266b. Comp. Hastings Rashdall, "The Philosophical Theory of Property," PROPERTY, ITS DUTIES AND RIGHTS (3rd ed., 1922), 35.

11. LAWS, Book I, sec. 10; REPUBLIC, Book I, sec. 17.

12. REPUBLIC, Book IV, sec. 5.

13. Secs. 21, 22.

14. REPUBLIC, Book I, sec. 45.

15. Fritz Schulz, CLASSICAL ROMAN LAW (1951), 335 f.

16. Richard Schlatter, PRIVATE PROPERTY (1951), 35.

17. A. J. Carlyle, "The Theory of Property in Mediaeval Theology," PROPERTY, ITS DUTIES AND RIGHTS (3rd ed., 1922), 128. For another argument that property was recognized by the church fathers, see Otto Schilling, DIE CHRISTLICHEN SOZIALLEHREN (1926), 62 ff.

18. Heinrich Singer, ed., DIE SUMMA DECRETORUM DES MAGISTER RUFINUS (1902), 6 f.

19. SUMMA UNIVERSAE THEOLOGIAE (1482 ed.), Book III, question 27, division (membrum) 3, arts. 2 and 3.

20. See O. Lottin, LE DROIT NATUREL CHEZ SAINT THOMAS ET SES PRÉDÉCESSEURS (1926), 38.

21. SUMMA THEOLOGICA, Book II, Pt. II, question 66, art. 2.

22. DE REGIMINE PRINCIPUM, Book II, Pt. III, chs. 5-6; Book III, Pt. I, chs. 9, 11, 16-18; Pt. II, ch. 31. See Schlatter, PRIVATE PROPERTY, 57 f.; Richard Scholz, DIE PUBLIZISTIK ZUR ZEIT PHILIPPS DES SCHÖNEN UND BONIFAZ VIII (1903), 32 ff.; Jean Rivière, LE PROBLÈME DE L'ÉGLISE ET DE L'ÉTAT AU TEMPS DE PHILIPPE LE BEL (1926), esp. 204 ff.

23. DE JUSTITIA ET JURE (1593-1609), 2° d. 20, no. 5.

24. DE JUSTITIA ET JURE CATERISQUE VIRTUTIBUS CARDINALIBUS (1606), ch. 5, no. 3.

25. Comp. Suarez, DE LEGIBUS, Book II, ch. 14, no. 13 ff. Suarez also pointed out that private property was necessary.

26. Wycliffe's theory on property is described by R. L. Poole in an article on Wycliffe in the ENCYCLOPAEDIA BRITANNICA (11th ed.), and in that author's preface to his edition of Wycliffe's DE CIVILE DOMINIO (1885).

27. WERKE (Erlangen ed., 1826-57), XXII, 20, XLIII, 144 ff.; WERKE (Braunschweig ed.), VII, 348, 525; WERKE (Walch ed., 1739-50), XIII, 2460 ff.; WERKE (Weimar ed.), XI, 251 f.; Henry Wace and C. A. Buchheim, ed., FIRST PRINCIPLES OF THE REFORMATION (1883), 71. For Luther's impact on capitalism, see Ernst Troeltsch, DIE BEDEUTUNG DES PROTESTANTISMUS FÜR DIE ENTSTEHUNG DER MODERNEN WELT (3rd ed., 1924); Max Weber, "Die protestantische Ethik und der 'Geist' des Kapitalismus," ARCHIV FÜR SOZIALWISSEN-SCHAFT UND SOZIALPOLITIK (1905, reprinted 1934), XX I, XXI, I; R. H. Tawney, RELIGION AND THE RISE OF CAPITALISM (1926); H. G. Wood, "The Influence of the Reformation on Ideas concerning Wealth and Property," in PROPERTY, ITS DUTIES AND RIGHTS, 141. Luther's ideas on property were systematically elaborated by Melanchthon, who accepted the arguments on the value of property that had been used by Aristotle. Men living in a communistic society, he felt, had no longer the will to acquire, to use, and to share things. Communism did not work "because some men contributed nothing to the common stock and took more than their share from it," thus destroying the original equality and depleting the common stock. There was nothing better and more perfect for man to work, to acquire property and to respect the property of others. LOCI COMMUNES (Hill transl., 1944), 122-128, *passim*. See also OPERA (1555 ed.), XXII, 283-97. Schlatter, PRIVATE PROPERTY, 93 ff.

28. Arthur Dakin, CALVINISM (1946), 205. This does not mean, however, that Calvinism considered the acquisition of property as an end in itself. Rather, wealth was a means for the fulfillment of the Christian life. Its accumulation and use was to take place within the framework of Christian ethics. See *infra*, note 36; Georgia Harkness, JOHN CALVIN—THE MAN AND HIS ETHICS (1931), 216 ff. See André Bieler, L'HUMANISME SOCIAL DE CALVIN (1961).

29. OPERA OMNIA QUAE SUPERSUNT (1863-90), V, 171, VII, 45. INSTITUTES OF THE CHRIS-TIAN RELIGION, Book II, ch. 8, secs. 45-46; Book IV, ch. 20, secs. 3, 8, 13, 20, 24.

30. Baxter was convinced that men were not capable of holding ownership in common. See "Mr. Baxter's Dying Thoughts" and his "Treatise of Self-Denial," WORKS (1683), XVIII, 387; XI, 309 f.

31. Similarly, the early reformers had disavowed the Anabaptist doctrine in the Eliza-

bethan Articles of Religion, of which Art. 38 asserts that "the Riches and Goods of Christians are not common as touching the right, title, and possession of the same, as certain Anabaptists do falsely boast."

32. See Richard Schlatter, THE SOCIAL IDEAS OF RELIGIOUS LEADERS 1660-1688 (1940), esp. 87-186.

33. Id., 86, 90-95. See Richard Cumberland, A TREATISE OF THE LAWS OF NATURE (English ed., 1727), 32, 34 f., 65 ff., 321 ff.; Richard Baxter, "Reasons of the Christian Religion," and "Mr. Baxter's Dying Thoughts," WORKS (1683), XX, 462 f., and XVIII, 387; Gabriel Towerson, EXPLICATION OF THE DECALOGUE, EIGHTH COMMANDMENT (n.d.); Thomas Sprat, HISTORY OF THE ROYAL SOCIETY (1667), 379 ff; "The Irenicum" and "Ecclesiastical Cases," WORKS (1659), II, 175, and WORKS (1750), III, 614.

34. CHRISTIAN DIRECTORY (1673), pt. IV, ch. 21. In part I, ch. 3, grand direction 10, Baxter writes: "Especially be sure that you live not out of a calling, that is, such a stated course of employment in which you may be best serviceable to God. Disability is indeed an irresistible impediment. Otherwise man must either live idly or content himself with doing some littel charres as a recreation or on the by; but every one that is able, must be statedly and ordinarily employed in such work as is serviceable to God and the common good."

35. Sermon 50, "On the Use of Money," (Quoted by Wood, op. cit., 160 f.).

36. For the fact that the Puritan could afford himself moderate pleasures, see H. G. Wood, op. cit., 161 f. For the idea that property serves as a means for charity, see Calvin's INSTITUTES OF THE CHRISTIAN RELIGION, Book III, ch. 7, sec. 2; Book IV, ch. 20, sec. 21. Baxter writes that "the denial of propriety would destroy all exercise of charity." "Treatise of Self-Denial," loc. cit., XI, 309. Similar Gouge, "Sermon XI," in MORNING EXERCISES (n.d.), I, 229; Tillotson's sermon of April 14, 1691, in THE WORKS OF THE MOST REVEREND DR. JOHN TILLOTSON (1752), I, 673; Thomas Manton's "Sermon IX" in A FOURTH VOLUME (1681-1701), 84; John Conant, "Sermon V," in SERMONS PREACHED ON SEVERAL OCCASIONS (1693-1722), I, 237; Isaac Barrow, "The Duty and Reward of Bounty to the Poor," in THE WORKS OF THE LEARNED ISAAC BARROW (1700), I, 54 f. For the importance of a protection of property to justice, see Richard Baxter, "Reasons of the Christian Religion," THE PRACTICAL WORKS OF THE LATE REVEREND AND PIOUS MR. RICHARD BAXTER (1830), XX, 462 f. For John Tillotson, justice meant the execution of good laws, "which are the guard of private property, the security of publick peace, and of religions and good manners." "Sermon XLVII," in WORKS, I, 335. Thomas Manton said that without property there would be no justice, "because justice consists largely in giving every man his own." "Sermon II on Titus ii, 12," A FOURTH VOLUME OF SERMONS (n.d.), 84. Richard Cumberland wrote in his A TREATISE OF THE LAWS OF NATURE (English ed. 1727), 316, that property rights are consistent with the Justinian principle that "justice is the constant and perpetual will to give every one his own right." See Schlatter, THE SOCIAL IDEAS OF RELIGIOUS LEADERS 1660-1688, esp. 87 ff., 124 ff.

37. THE SIX BOOKS OF COMMONWEALE (Richard Knolles ed., 1606), Book I, ch. 1.

38. Id., Book I, chs. 2, 6; Book VI, ch. 4; METHOD FOR THE EASY COMPREHENSION OF HISTORY (Beatrice Reynolds transl., 1945), 296 ff.

39. THE SIX BOOKS OF COMMONWEALE, Book II, ch. 2.

40. Id., Book I, ch. 8; Book VI, ch. 2.

41. W. F. Church, CONSTITUTIONAL THOUGHT IN SIXTEENTH-CENTURY FRANCE (1941), 257.

42. DE L'AUTORITÉ DU ROI (1587), leaf 17. Quoted by Schlatter, PRIVATE PROPERTY, 118.

43. DE REGNO ET REGALI POTESTATE (1600).

44. See Henri Sée, LES IDÉES POLITIQUES EN FRANCE AU XVIIᵉ SIÈCLE (1923); for Louis XIV's concept of his duties, see 138 ff.

45. TREW LAW OF FREE MONARCHIES, written 1598, in C. H. McIlwain, ed., POLITICAL WORKS OF JAMES I (1918), 62 f.; comp. also Charles' speech before Parliament in 1609. Id., 308.

46. Speech of 1609, loc. cit., 309 f.

47. Schlatter, PRIVATE PROPERTY, 117.

48. ELEMENTA PHILOSOPHICA DE CIVE (1647), 89 f.

49. LEVIATHAN (1929 ed.), 98 f.
50. ELEMENTS OF LAW (Ferdinand Tönnies, ed., 1928), 55 f.
51. Comp. Schlatter, PRIVATE PROPERTY, 141.
52. ELEMENTS OF LAW, 144.
53. LEVIATHAN, 163; ELEMENTS OF LAW, 143.
54. LEVIATHAN, 258.
55. Schlatter, PRIVATE PROPERTY, 142.
56. John Cooke, UNUM NECESSARIUM (1648). Quoted by David W. Petegorsky, LEFT WING DEMOCRACY IN THE ENGLISH CIVIL WAR (1940), 111 f.
57. Thus art. 7. cl. 8 of the Agreement of the People, presented to Parliament on Jan. 20, 1649, reads "That no Representative shall in any wise render up, or give, or take away any of the foundations of common right, liberty or safety contained in this Agreement, nor shall level men's estates, destroy propriety, or make all things common." The following items were suggested for insertion in the Agreement, but, as the most eminent grievances, judged fit to be redressed by the next representatives: "It shall not be in their power to make or continue any law whereby men's estates, or any part thereof, shall be exempted from payment of their debts"; " . . . men's lives, limbs, liberties, and estates may not as hitherto be liable to be taken away upon trivial or slight occasion"; "they shall not continue or make a law for any other ways of judgment or conviction of life, liberty, or estate, but only by twelve sworn men of the neighborhood." Arthur S. P. Woodhouse. ed., PURITANISM AND LIBERTY (1938), 365. See also "Certain Articles for the Good of the Commonwealth, Presented to the Consideration of his Excellency Sir Thomas Fairfax, and to the Officers and Soldiers under his command," articles 19-21. Id., 337. The Levellers' "Petition to the House of Commons" of Sept. 11, 1648, states that they would have expected from Parliament "that you would have bound yourselves and all future Parliaments from abolishing propriety, levelling men's estates. or making all things common." Id., 340. William Walwyn, one of the Levellers, stated in "A Manifestation": "We profess . . . that we never had it in our thoughts to Level men's estates, it being the utmost of our aime that the Commonwealth be reduced to such a passe that every man may with as much security as may be enjoy his propriety." William Haller and Godfrey Davies, ed., LEVELLER TRACTS (1944), 279.
58. Rousseau's opinion on property can be found in the second part of the DISCOURSE. That part starts out with the words: "Le premier qui ayant enclos un terrain s'avisa de dire, Ceci est à moi, et trouva des gens assez simples pour le croire, fut le vrai fondateur de la société civile." In the last paragraph of the DISCOURSE. Rousseau writes: "Il suit de cet exposé que l'inégalité, étant presque nulle dans l'état de nature, tiré sa force et son acroissement du développement de nos facultés et des progrès de l'esprit humain, et devient enfin stable et légitime par l'établissement de la propriété et des lois." C. E. Vaughan, ed., THE POLITICAL WRITINGS OF JEAN JACQUES ROUSSEAU (1951), I, 169, 196.
59. Everyman's Library ed., 271.
60. Book I, esp. chs. 6-9.
61. DER STREIT DER FAKULTÄTEN IN DREI ABSCHNITTEN (1798), 400.
62. REFLECTIONS ON THE REVOLUTION IN FRANCE (1790).
63. Arts. 5, 11, 12, 17. The draft is printed in the RÉIMPRESSION DE L'ANCIEN MONITEUR, I, 339 f.
64. Comp. arts. 2-6, 22. Id., I, 362 f.
65. Speech of Sept. 21, 1792. H. M. Stephens, ed., ORATORS OF THE FRENCH REVOLUTION (1892), II, 171 f.
66. See J. M. Thompson, THE FRENCH REVOLUTION (1945), 388 ff.
67. Quoted by Harold Laski, THE RISE OF EUROPEAN LIBERALISM (1936), 230.
68. Schlatter, PRIVATE PROPERTY, 231.
69. Comp. André Lichtenberger, LE SOCIALISME ET LA RÉVOLUTION FRANÇAISE (1899), 23 f. It was feared that once the property of a certain group or institution was attacked, this would be but the first step toward an attack on all property. Comp. the arguments of M. Camus and the bishop of Uzés in defense of church property. ARCHIVES PARLEMENTAIRES, IX, 416-18, 487 ff. Significantly, the National Assembly shied away from directly ex-

propriating the Church, and preferred to state that it would merely take over the admin istration of church estates, thus leaving undecided who would own these estates. The decree of Nov. 2, 1789, read: "All the ecclesiastical estates are at the disposal of the nation, on condition of providing in a suitable manner for the expenses of worship, the maintenance of its ministers, and the relief of the poor." Comp. also the debates in the National Assembly on the ownership of mines and on the right of testators (1791), reported in ARCHIVES PARLE-MENTAIRES, XXIV. See also Henri Hayem, ESSAI SUR LE DROIT DE PROPRIÉTÉ (1910), 198 f.

70. Léon Duguit, TRAITÉ DE DROIT CONSTITUTIONNEL (1921-25), III, 610. Ch. Giraud, PRÉCIS DE L'ANCIEN DROIT COUTUMIER FRANÇAIS (2nd ed. 1875), v, calls the Code a "véritable Constitution politique de la France."

71. DE JURE BELLI AC PACIS (F. W. Kelsey et al., transl., 1925), 14, 40, 189 ff., 206 ff., 297 ff., 807.

72. Schlatter, PRIVATE PROPERTY, 144 ff.

73. William S. Carpenter, ed. (1924), 129 ff., 136, 138 f., 141, 179 f., 228 ff. Locke writes that men should make use of the world "to the best advantage of life and convenience"; that "the earth and all that is therein is given to men for the support and comfort of their being"; that "the measure of property Nature well set, by the extent of men's labour and the conveniency of life." He is happy about "the conveniences we enjoy," saying that what man "applied to the support or comfort of his being, when invention and arts had improved the conveniences of life, was perfectly his own, and did not belong in common to others." Id., 129, 132, 136, 138. The importance of the good life is also evident when Locke connects "right and convenience," id., 141. Man was commanded by God and reason to improve the earth for the benefit of life. God did not want that the world "should always remain common and uncultivated." It should be "improved." Id., 132. God wanted man to subdue and cultivate the earth and to have dominium, i.e., private property: "God, commanding to subdue, gave authority so far to appropriate. And the condition of human life, which requires labour and materials to work on, necessarily introduces private possessions." Id., 133. See also p. 136, where Locke says that through improvements by labor people are able to enjoy more conveniences. (Comp. also id. 134, 138). For Locke, the individual could acquire as much property as he wanted to, provided nothing was spoiled. See id. 139, 141.

74. COMMENTARIES (12th ed., 1794), II, 3-9; I, 299; II, 11, 411; IV, 9; I, 138; II, 400. For a description of Blackstone's ideas on property, see D. J. Boorstin, THE MYSTERIOUS SCIENCE OF THE LAW (1941).

75. COMMENTARIES, I, 41.

76. Id., I, 139; II, 288. Blackstone also mentions cases where "the law of the land has postponed even public necessity to the sacred and inviolable rights of private property." Id., I, 140. See Schlatter, PRIVATE PROPERTY, 169, 171.

77. ESSAYS, MORAL, POLITICAL, AND LITERARY (T. H. Green and T. H. Grose, ed., 1875), II, 274 f.

78. Id., II, 183, 188 f.

79. Id., II, 189.

80. Comp. Schlatter, PRIVATE PROPERTY, 206.

81. THE SPIRIT OF THE LAWS (Thomas Nugent transl., 1878), II, 160 f.

82. Bradford, HISTORY OF PLIMOTH PLANTATION (1901 ed.), 162, 167.

83. John Dickinson, LETTERS FROM A FARMER IN PENNSYLVANIA TO THE INHABITANTS OF THE BRITISH COLONIES (1768). In letter XII, Dickinson writes: "Let these truths be indelibly impressed on our minds—that we cannot be happy without being free—that we cannot be free without being secure in our property—that we cannot be secure in our property if without our consent others may as by right take it away."

84. Printed in Henry S. Commager, ed., DOCUMENTS OF AMERICAN HISTORY (3rd ed., 1947), 66 f.

85. Comp. Dietze, THE FEDERALIST (1960), 58 ff.

86. "Declaration and Resolves of the First Continental Congress," in Worthington C. Ford, ed., JOURNALS OF THE CONTINENTAL CONGRESS (1904-37), I, 63 ff.

87. See Ford, op. cit., and Edmund C. Burnett, ed., LETTERS TO THE MEMBERS OF THE CONTINENTAL CONGRESS (1921-36).

88. Carl L. Becker, THE DECLARATION OF INDEPENDENCE (1922), 27. A contemporary of Jefferson, Henry Lee, observed that the Declaration was "copied from Locke's treatise on *Civil Government*." John Foley, ed., THE JEFFERSONIAN CYCLOPEDIA (1900), 244.

89. Becker, *op. cit.*, 25.

90. To Richard Henry Lee on May 8, 1825. WRITINGS (Mem. ed.), XVI, 118.

91. Paschal Larkin, PROPERTY IN THE EIGHTEENTH CENTURY (1930), 148, referring to a statement by Jefferson in Foley, ed., *op. cit.*, 727, writes: "The theory that property is the reward of industry appealed so much to Jefferson that he was prepared to tolerate any inequality in the distribution of property arising from a man's personal effort, or that of his father."

92. The constitution of Maryland of 1776 states in its bill of rights that "every freeman, for any injury done him in his person or property, ought to have a remedy," that "the trial of facts where they arise, is one of the greatest securities of the lives, liberties and estates of the people," and that "no freeman ought to be taken, or imprisoned, or disseized of his freehold, liberties and privileges, . . . or deprived of his life, liberty, or property, but by the judgment of his peers, or by the law of the land." (Arts. 17, 18, 21). The idea of the protection of property is evident in articles 14 and 17 of the constitution of New Jersey of 1776. The constitution of North Carolina of 1776 prescribes in art. 10 "that no freeman ought to be taken, imprisoned, or disseized of his freehold, liberties, and privileges, or outlawed, or exiled, or in any manner deprived of his life, liberty, or property, but by the law of the land," in art. 14, "that in all controversies at law, respecting property, the ancient modes of trial, by jury, is one of the best securities of the rights of the people, and ought to remain sacred and inviolable," and in art. 25, that "the property of the soil, in a free government, being one of the essential rights of the collective body of the people, it is necessary, in order to avoid future disputes, that the limits of the State should be ascertained with precision." The constitution of North Carolina of 1776 states in its preamble that there should be no taxation without representation, and that of 1778 provides for the protection of property in art. 41. The constitution of Georgia of 1777 complains at the very beginning of taxation without representation. The constitution of Vermont of 1777 states in its bill of rights: "I. That all men are born equally free and independent, and have certain natural, inherent and unalienable rights, amongst which are the enjoying and defending life and liberty; acquiring, possessing and protecting property, and pursuing and obtaining happiness and safety. . . . II. That private property ought to be subservient to public uses, when necessity requires it; nevertheless, whenever any particular man's property is taken for the use of the public, the owner ought to receive an equivalent in money."

93. Benjamin Rush, "Observations on the Government of Pennsylvania" (1777), in Dagobert D. Runes, ed., THE SELECTED WRITINGS OF BENJAMIN RUSH (1947), 70.

94. A great part of the Shaysite agitation was directed against the high taxes the state was levying on behalf of the public debt. Comp. Richard Hildreth, THE HISTORY OF THE UNITED STATES OF AMERICA (1880), III, 472 f.; Richard Hofstadter, William Miller, Daniel Aaron, THE AMERICAN REPUBLIC (1959), I, 222 f.

95. Letter of Henry Knox to George Washington of Oct. 23, 1786. F. S. Drake, LIFE AND CORRESPONDENCE OF HENRY KNOX (1873), 91 f.

96. John Adams, "Defense of the Constitutions of Government of the United States of America," in Charles F. Adams, ed., THE WORKS OF JOHN ADAMS (1850-56), VI, 8 f.

97. Charles A. Beard's AN ECONOMIC INTERPRETATION OF THE CONSTITUTION (1913), which was a product of the "progressive" era, has been refuted by Robert E. Brown, CHARLES BEARD AND THE CONSTITUTION (1956), and Forrest McDonald, WE, THE PEOPLE (1958).

98. See the author's THE FEDERALIST.

99. This does not imply, however, that a protection of property was desired mainly from materialistic and egoistic motives. That protection was as much desired from an idealistic and altruistic point of view, since the protection of property meant to the Founders a prerequisite for individual freedom, peace and order.

100. *Quicquid bene dictum est ab ullo, meum est.* EPISTOLAE, XVI, 7.

101. For a short summary of that influence, see R. W. Lee, THE ELEMENTS OF ROMAN

LAW (2nd ed., 1949), 19 ff. Paul Koschaker, EUROPA UND DAS RÖMISCHE RECHT (2nd ed., 1953), gives a comprehensive evaluation of the influence of the Roman law.

102. Koschaker, *op cit.,* 55.

103. The *Lex Romana Visigothorum,* issued by Alarich II in 506, shows strong elements of Roman law. Lee, *op. cit.,* 19. Likewise, the *Lex Romana Burgundiorum,* issued at about the same time by Gundobad, as well as the Ostrogothic Edict by Theodoric, reveal traces of Roman law. Koschaker, *op. cit.,* 58, remarks that in drafting the *leges romana* use was made of the Imperial constitutions, and to a smaller degree also of Roman jurisprudence.

104. Koschaker, *id.,* 57.

105. See Charles H. Haskins, THE RENAISSANCE OF THE 12TH CENTURY (1927); Paré-Brunet-Tremblay, LA RENAISSANCE DU XIIe SIÈCLE (1933).

106. For the impact of Roman law upon Spain, see Charles P. Sherman, ROMAN LAW IN THE MODERN WORLD (1937), I, 268 ff.; Rafael Altamira, "Das römische Recht in Spanien," in R. Leonhard, ed., STIMMEN DES AUSLANDS ÜBER DIE ZUKUNFT DER RECHTSWISSENSCHAFT (1906), 42 ff.

107. See Emile Chénon, HISTOIRE GÉNÉRAL DU DROIT FRANÇAIS PUBLIC ET PRIVÉ DES ORIGINES À 1815 (1926-29), I, 510 ff.; Martin, PRÉCIS DE L'HISTOIRE DU DROIT FRANÇAIS (2nd ed., 1934), note 245; Sherman, *op. cit.,* 224 ff., 344 ff.; James Mackintosh, ROMAN LAW IN MODERN PRACTICE (1934).

108. For the adoption of Roman law in the Netherlands, see Sherman, *op. cit.,* I, 254 ff.

109. "It was the Roman pagan conception of absolute property that triumphed at the close of the Middle Ages. This idea, which is the foundation of modern capitalism, led at the same time to further attempts to depress the peasants into slavery. It has been fraught with a thousand evils, from which even now the world is slowly and with many struggles trying to recover. The 'reception', as it is called, of the Roman law in 1495 in Germany may be taken as the date when the Middle Ages came to an end and the Roman ideas of property had conquered the West." J. N. Figgis, THE POLITICAL ASPECT OF SAINT AUGUSTINE'S CITY OF GOD (1921), 99.

110. Koschaker, *op. cit.,* 139. Roman law, as developed by the German jurists by the latter half of the 19th century, strongly influenced the drafting of the *Bürgerliche Gesetzbuch* (BGB), in spite of the then prevalent trends to replace Roman law by Germanic law. The BGB., in turn, influenced civil law in Austria, Switzerland, Greece, China, Japan, and several Latin American states. See Andreas B. Schwarz, "Einflüsse deutscher Zivilistik im Auslande," in SYMBOLAE FRIBURGENSIS IN HONOREM OTTONIS LENEL (1931), 425, esp. 470 ff.

111. See Sherman, *op. cit.,* I, 290, 305; R. W. Lee, AN INTRODUCTION TO ROMAN-DUTCH LAW (1931); "Roman law in the British Empire, particularly in the Union of South Africa," ATTI CONGRESSO BOLOGNA (n.d.), II, 253; Kerr-Wylie, "The Present Crisis of Roman Law and its Bearing on the Legal Situation in South Africa," SOUTH AFRICAN LAW JOURNAL (1939), LVI, 208; Leopold Wenger, "Römisches Recht in Amerika," in STUDI DI STORIA E DIRITTO IN ONORE DI ENRICO BESTA (1937-39), I, 153; Sherman, *op. cit.,* I, 407.

112. See Carl Schmitt, DIE LAGE DER EUROPÄISCHEN RECHTSWISSENSCHAFT (1950).

113. Schulz, *op. cit.,* 337.

114. See Max Weber, *op. cit.*

115. "Whenever you have active Calvinism in the past, wherever you have the air of Calvinism surviving today, there you have mercantile order, mercantile adventure, mercantile foresight, mercantile success; and such order and foresight and the rest are even more developed on the side of finance than on the side of commerce. It is the story of New England, it is the story of Scotland, it is the story of Geneva, it is the story of the French Huguenots." Hilaire Belloc, MONARCHY (1938), 310. See also Troeltsch, PROTESTANTISM AND PROGRESS (1958), 137.

116. See Max Weber, *op. cit.,* 28 f., 135 ff., 150 ff., 163 ff.; Ernst Troeltsch, DIE SOZIAL-LEHREN DER CHRISTLICHEN KIRCHEN UND GRUPPEN (1912), 427 ff., esp. 794 ff.

117. Our emphasis upon the alternative, private property vs. common ownership, does not imply that private property can only be challenged by communal ownership. We emphasized that alternative because in the last analysis, infringements upon private property are likely to result in common ownership. For in a democratic society such infringements

—insignificant as they may appear—will usually serve some common good. Consequently, increasing infringements must result in the increasing achievement of a communistic society. Needless to say, the defenders of private property often recognized not only the threat of a total abolition of private property, but also, that of seemingly minor infringements upon that institution.

CHAPTER II

1. See the author's ÜBER FORMULIERUNG DER MENSCHENRECHTE (1956), 17 ff.

2. Georg Jellinek, ALLGEMEINE STAATSLEHRE (3rd ed., 1914), 419, writes: "Religionszwang und Zensur haben die Vorstellung der Religions- und Pressefreiheit entstehen lassen, durch polizeiliche Eingriffe und Verbote sind Hausrecht, Briefgeheimnis, Vereins—und Versammlungsfreiheit gefordert worden. Nähere Überlegung ergibt leicht, dass hier nicht *einzelne* Rechte vorliegen, sondern nur besonders anerkannte Richtungen der individuellen Freiheit, die aber in sich einheitlich ist und den vom Staatsgebot freien Zustand des Individuums bezeichnet." Léon Duguit, TRAITÉ DE DROIT CONSTITUTIONNEL (2nd ed., 1921-25), III, 594, defines "la liberté" as "le pouvoir qui appartient à tout individu d'exercer et de développer son activité physique, intellectuelle et morale."

3. *Magna Carta Libertorum* means "great charter of liberties." On hearing that term we know at once that it is a document of freedom, but we are not so sure about the specific liberties it secures. As a matter of fact, the meaning of its various clauses has been the subject of controversy. The same is true of the Bill of Rights of 1689. The man in the street will know that it secures him freedom, but he will have doubts as to what specific liberties are guaranteed by the Bill.

4. "Life, liberty and the pursuit of happiness" are considered to be "among" the "unalienable rights" of men. While it could be argued that the words "among these" indicate that "liberty" means just one specific part of freedom, such as, for instance, physical freedom (a view that gains support from the argument that also "life" and the "pursuit of happiness" are parts of freedom), we are inclined to believe that the word "liberty" is here used in a more comprehensive sense, as comprising various particular liberties. Should the assumption prove incorrect, the assertion that the Declaration of Independence distinguishes between general freedom and its various parts could still be supported by the argument that the vague term "certain unalienable rights" corresponds to general freedom which is then described in its parts through the enumeration of "life, liberty and the pursuit of happiness."

5. Comp. art. 4: "La liberté consiste à pouvoir faire tout ce qui ne nuit pas à autrui; ainsi, l'exercice des droits naturels de chaque homme n'a de bornes que celles qui assurent aux autres membres de la société la jouissance de ces mêmes droits." Art. 6 of the declaration of rights of 1793 reads: "La liberté est le pouvoir qui appartient à l'homme de faire tout ce qui ne nuit pas aux droits d'autrui: elle a pour principe la nature: pour règle la justice; pour sauvegarde la loi; sa limite morale est dans cette maxime: Ne fais pas à un autre ce que tu ne veux pas qu'il te soit fait." See also art. 2 of the declaration of rights of the year III.

6. As recent a constitution as the Bonn Basic Law, for instance, after generally stating in art. 2 that "everyone shall have the right to the free development of his personality," proceeds in the following articles to enumerate such specific rights as physical inviolability, freedom of faith, conscience and religion, of expression, speech and writing, and others. The constitution of the Fourth Republic reaffirms the Declaration of the Rights of Man and Citizen and thus accepts that document's distinction between general freedom and particular liberties. For the value and necessity of distinguishing between freedom and its parts, see Dietze, ÜBER FORMULIERUNG DER MENSCHENRECHTE, 17 ff., 38 ff., 42 ff., 49 ff.

7. The connection between "miser" and "misery" should not be overlooked. A miser was

originally not only an avaricious person, but one who lives miserably in order to hoard wealth. "Misery" was formerly used for "miserliness."

8. U.S. v. Carolene Products Co., 304 U.S. 144, 152 note 4 (1938); West Virginia School Board v. Barnette, 319 U.S. 624 (1943); Thomas v. Collins, 323 U.S. 516 (1944).

9. Georg Jellinek, DIE ERKLÄRUNG DER MENSCHEN- UND BÜRGERRECHTE. The uncertainty about what are the particular components of freedom and the admission that new components may always be discovered is evident in the ninth amendment to the United States Constitution which says that "the enumeration in the Constitution of certain rights shall not be construed to deny or disparage others retained by the people." Comp. Bennett B. Patterson, THE FORGOTTEN NINTH AMENDMENT (1955). A modern constitution, the Peronista constitution of Argentina of 1949, contains a similar provision in art. 36: "The declaration, rights and guaranties which the Constitution enumerates shall not be considered to be a denial of other rights and guaranties not enumerated, but which arise from the principle of sovereignty of the people and the republican form of government." On the fact that the English Petition of Right was concerned not with all, but only with a few, rights, a speaker commented in the Commons that only those rights were selected that were, for the time being, most severely threatened. Walther Rothschild, DER GEDANKE DER GESCHRIEBENEN VERFASSUNG IN DER ENGLISCHEN REVOLUTION (1903), 9.

10. This is evident in the case of suffrage. The right to vote appeared in the foreground whenever people felt they were disfranchised unjustly, be it because they did not meet certain property qualifications (as in the United States in the beginning of the 19th century), or because they did not belong to a certain class (as in Britain prior to the Reform bills), or to a certain race (as in the United States prior to the fifteenth amendment), or to a certain sex (as in the United States prior to the nineteenth amendment). As soon as the right to vote was guaranteed, it was increasingly taken for granted, and no longer emphasized. Similarly, the provision of the third amendment of the United States Constitution, that "no soldier shall, in time of peace, be quartered in any house without the consent of the owner, nor in time of war, but in a manner to be prescribed by law," while considered important when adopted due to grievances that helped to bring about the American Revolution, later dropped more and more into oblivion. Edward S. Corwin, THE CONSTITUTION AND WHAT IT MEANS TODAY (12th ed., 1958), 205, does not mention one case in which that amendment would have been relevant.

11. Religious intolerance in our time—the communist and nazi dictatorships are cases in point—is an example of the re-emergence of a right that since the nineteenth century had become so generally accepted that it was almost taken for granted.

12. Georg Jellinek, SYSTEM DER SUBJEKTIVEN ÖFFENTLICHEN RECHTE (2nd ed., 1905), 94, speaks of the "negative status" of the individual. The term "negative Rechte" has been used by German jurists for rights that secure the individual's freedom from coercion.

13. Jellinek, id., 94, characteristically identifies his "negative status" with "status libertatis."

14. The term "positive Rechte" has been used by German jurists. The French have used the term "droits politiques." "Political rights" has been used by Americans.

15. Unlike laws defining liberal rights, those regulating the rights of participation in government differ considerably. This is an indication of the fact that "positive rights" are the creation of positive law and, as rights granted by the government, can be rather restrictive. Restriction seems to be the rule, and non-regulation, the exception. In the case of liberal rights, restrictions appear as the exception, and liberty, as the rule. Comp. Carl Schmitt, VERFASSUNGSLEHRE (1928), 158. The different regulation of positive rights is not only evident in different nations, but also in the member states of a federal state. This, again, stands in contrast to the relatively uniform way in which these states acknowledge liberal rights.

16. See Georg Meyer, DAS PARLAMENTARISCHE WAHLRECHT (1901), 653 ff.; Austin F. Macdonald, GOVERNMENT OF THE ARGENTINE REPUBLIC (1942), 107 f. Even though abstaining from voting was not punished in Nazi Germany, pressure was exercized upon non-voters, who were blacklisted.

17. For the fears of the American founding fathers of democracy and its despotism, see

the author's THE FEDERALIST, esp. 60 ff. Jacob L. Talmon, THE ORIGINS OF TOTALITARIAN DEMOCRACY (1952), shows the democratic despotism that emerged from the French revolution. For a polemic against the New Deal, see Raoul E. Desvernine, DEMOCRATIC DESPOTISM (1936). For the problem faced by constitution-makers after World War II with respect to democratic excesses, see the author's "Natural Law in the Modern European Constitutions," NATURAL LAW FORUM (1956), I, 73. (Italian transl. in JUS, RIVISTA DI SCIENZE GIURIDICHE [1957], VIII [N.S.], 529). Comp. also Clinton Rossiter, CONSTITUTIONAL DICTATORSHIP (1948).

18. The Declaration of Independence, for instance, states that "to secure these rights [the unalienable rights of men], governments are instituted among men, deriving their just powers from the consent of the governed." The constitution of Maryland of 1776 states in art. 5 that "the right in the people to participate in the Legislature is the best security of liberty, and the foundation of all free government." This idea is also indicated in the French Declaration of the Rights of Man and Citizen, articles 3, 6, 14.

19. Duguit, op. cit., III, 581, writes that the majority of the members of the Assembly that framed the Declaration of the Rights of Man and Citizen did not consider the rights to participate in government as rights, but rather as functions.

20. Paradoxically, this distinction was made by the court that has probably the best reputation as a protector of liberal rights, namely, the United States Supreme Court. Comp. Earl Latham, "The Majoritarian Dilemma in the United States Supreme Court," CONFLUENCE (No. 4, 1953), 22. The distinction is out of tune with the traditional practice that considered civil rights as comprising all liberal rights, including those of property. Already Blackstone's COMMENTARIES (14th ed., 1803), I, 127, note, distinguished between "civil and political liberty." "Civil" rights were also distinguished from "political" rights, i.e., the rights to participate in government, in an early case, Amy v. Smith, 11 Kentucky 327, (1822), and also in Kent's COMMENTARIES (3rd ed., 1836), II, 257, note. In all these instances, "civil liberty" resp. "civil rights" comprise all liberal rights, including those of property. Blackstone, op. cit., I, 129, speaks of "civil privileges" that fall into "three principal or primary articles; the right of personal security, the right of personal liberty, and the right of private property." For the fact that property rights are "civil rights," see also Heirn v. Bridault, 37 Miss. 209 (1859), and the Civil Rights Acts of 1866 and 1870. As late as 1930, Robert E. Cushman wrote that "civil liberty is a concept, basic to modern political thought, which in its most general usage connotes the freedom of the individual with respect to personal action, the possession and use of property, religious belief and worship and the expression of opinion." "Civil Liberties," ENCYCLOPAEDIA OF THE SOCIAL SCIENCES (1930-35), III, 509. Characteristically, the same author's CIVIL LIBERTIES IN THE UNITED STATES, published in 1956, does no longer mention property rights! This is symbolic of the change in the meaning of "civil rights." The United States President's Committee on Civil Rights, established in 1946, lists among the rights it considers "essential" merely such rights as "the right to safety and security of the person," "the right to citizenship and its privilges," "the right to freedom of conscience and expression" and "the right to equality of opportunity." See its report, TO SECURE THESE RIGHTS (1947). Also the hearings of the Subcommittee on Constitutional Rights of the Committee on the Judiciary of the United States Senate, dealing with "civil rights," do not deal with property rights.

21. It is realized that social legislation usually is not part of criminal law and that, according to accepted doctrine, the principle nulla poena sine lege does not apply. On the other hand, it is felt that it should not be overlooked that fines, i.e., deprivations of property, are provided for by most criminal codes. It cannot be seen why it should be unfair to deprive a person who committed a misdemeanor or crime of his property by fining him, because the crime was not punishable when it was committed, while, on the other hand, it should be just to deprive an innocent person of his property through civil legislation. The principle nulla poena sine lege should apply here a fortiori, since otherwise the criminal would be better off than the innocent. For support of this position, comp. Marshall's statement in Fletcher v. Peck, 6 Cranch, 87, 138, 139 (1810); Chancellor Kent in Dash v. Van Kleeck, 7 Johns. (N.Y.), 477, 505 (1811); Justice Johnson in Satterlee v. Matthewson, 2 Pet. 380, 414, 415 (1829).

22. In the French Revolution, for instance, the original government was, after the purge of the Girondists, followed by a Jacobin anarchy which, in turn, was succeeded by the directorate and Napoleon. The democratic constitutions that were adopted by the Spanish American nations after independence, resulted in anarchy followed by caudilloism. See the author's "Der Peronismus," ZEITSCHRIFT FÜR POLITIK (1955), II (N.F.), 97. The Weimar Republic, with its very democratic constitution, witnessed fights among the delegates of the Reichstag and street fighting among the various parties. Its democratic features have been blamed for facilitating Hitler's rise to power.

23. This idea was one of the keynotes in the Philadelphia Convention as well as in the sessions of the *Parlamentarische Rat* in Bonn. It is obvious in the constitution of the Fifth Republic.

24. The tendency to degrade "civil" rights to democratic rights is indicated by John Dickinson when he writes that "the term 'civil rights' is sometimes used by the courts in the broad sense of rights enjoyed and protected under positive municipal law in contrast with so-called 'inherent rights' vesting in the individual by virtue of supposed 'natural law.'" "Civil Rights," ENCYCLOPAEDIA OF THE SOCIAL SCIENCES, III, 513. This confusion is due to the fact that the idea of "civil" is often connected with the idea of civil society and its man-made laws rather than with that of civilization as connoting the progress of the human race in freedom.

25. It may be argued that the Harringtonian principle that political power follows property has too often been realized to permit such a statement. But, for the reasons mentioned previously it appears doubtful whether we can, in case property is used for governing purposes, speak of a degeneration of property rights into democratic rights. While property may, of course, degenerate into a mere means of governing, it would be likely to be a means that is conducive to a working and stable democracy and thus, to freedom. Whereas emphasis on "civil" rights has proved to be oppressive of property rights and freedom, a rule by property owners will hardly result in the oppression of "civil" rights and thus not really prove to be oppressive of freedom.

26. See Raphael Petrucci, LES ORIGINES NATURELLES DE LA PROPRIÉTÉ (1905). On p. 220, Petrucci writes: "C'est ainsi qu'apparaît le fait de propriété comme une affirmation de la vie, comme le résultat d'une activité liée aux besoins de l'être vivant, liée, par conséquent, à la protection de l'individu et de l'espèce. Ce sont là, en effet, les activitées les plus essentielles. Par le fait même que la matière vivante existe, elle tend à se maintenir. Elle ne peut le faire qu'en empruntant les matériaux du monde extérieur, en l'exploitant, par conséquent, et en les modifiant de façon à les intégrer à sa propre structure. La cause première déterminante du fait de propriété apparaît donc comme liée au besoin de nutrition et au besoin de protection. Avant de prendre la forme collective, ces besoins sont individuels; c'est donc comme un reflet de la structure individuelle que se manifeste tout d'abord le phénomène de propriété. Etant lié dès l'origine aux relations de l'individu avec le milieu extérieur, il est l'expression d'une adaption. C'est comme une conséquence de ces adaptions qu'il prend la forme collective."

27. The immediate connection between shelter and life is most evident in the case of animals that have their shelter attached to them and where the deprivation of the shelter is tantamount to the death of the animal, as for instance, in the case of crustaceans.

28. Emile de Laveleye, DE LA PROPRIÉTÉ ET SES FORMES PRIMITIVES (1874); Henry James Sumner Maine, ANCIENT LAW (1861); Friedrich Engels, DER URSPRUNG DER FAMILIE, DES PRIVATEIGENTUMS UND DES STAATES (1884).

29. V. Lacombe, L'APPROPRIATION DU SOL (1912); V. L. Ségal, PRINCIPES D'ÉCONOMIE POLITIQUE (1936).

30. René Gonnard, LA PROPRIÉTÉ DANS LA DOCTRINE ET DANS L'HISTOIRE (1943), 5.

31. *Id.,* 7

32. For instance, Fustel de Coulanges, RECHERCHES SUR QUELQUES PROBLÈMES D'HISTOIRE (1891); Paul Guiraud, LA PROPRIÉTÉ FONCIÈRE EN GRÈCE JUSQU'À LA CONQUÊTE ROMAINE (1893); Henri Sée, LES CLASSES RURALES ET LE RÉGIME DOMANIAL EN FRANCE AU MOYEN AGE (1901); Jules François Toutain, L'ÉCONOMIE ANTIQUE (1927).

33. Guiraud, *op. cit.*, demonstrates the probability that collective and communal ownership were not the most ancient forms of ownership in ancient Greece. On the contrary, they were created out of the *res nullius* that existed between the lands owned by the individuals.

34. Gonnard, *op. cit.*, 9.

35. Camille Jullian, HISTOIRE DE LA GAULE (1908-26), II, 71 ff.; Fustel de Coulanges, L'INVASION GERMANIQUE ET LA FIN DE L'EMPIRE (3rd ed., 1911), 288. Following de Coulanges, more and more historians agreed that the famous example of public ownership, the *Mark*, came into existence only after private ownership had already been established, as the result of the sovereign's taking over the *res nullius* that existed between the private estates of individuals. For a recent study, see Robert Latouche, THE BIRTH OF WESTERN ECONOMY (Engl. transl., 1961).

36. Comp. Oliver Leroy, ESSAI D'INTRODUCTION CRITIQUE À L'ÉTUDE DE L'ÉCONOMIE PRIMITIVE (1925), 42: "Celui qui considère sans être préjugé les formes de la propriété dans les sociétés simples, s'aperçoit bientôt que la vie, plus riche que les théories, admet libéralement la propriété privée à côté de la propriété commune, ces formes extrêmes laissant place au moyen terme de la propriété familiale, et sans que rien nous suggère une séquence chronologique."

37. Other provisions, like the coveting of the neighbor's wife and servants and goods, and the prohibition of adultery, are closely related to the protection of what belongs to someone else. Comp. Otto Schilling, KATHOLISCHE WIRTSCHAFTSETHIK (1933), 78.

38. See James Paterson, THE LIBERTY OF THE PRESS, SPEECH, AND PUBLIC WORSHIP (1880), 516 f.; L. Scherger, THE EVOLUTION OF MODERN LIBERTY (1904), 2.

39. Guido de Ruggiero, "Religious Liberty," ENCYCLOPAEDIA OF THE SOCIAL SCIENCES, XIII, 241.

40. Johann Caspar Bluntschli, ALLGEMEINE STAATSLEHRE (5th ed., 1876), 381 ff.

41. Especially in his lectures in Salamanca, held about 1538-39, DE IURE BELLI HISPANORUM IN BARBAROS. See V. Beltram de Heredia, LOS MANUSCRITOS DEL MAESTRE FRANCISCO DE VITORIA (n.d.).

42. In his CONTRAT SOCIAL, he writes: "Il y a donc une profession de foi purement civile dont il appartient au souverain de fixer les articles, non pas précisément comme dogmes de religion, mais comme sentiments de sociabilité, sans lesquels il est impossible d'être bon citoyen ni sujet fidèle. Sans pouvoir obliger personne à les croire, il peut bannir de l'Etat quiconque ne les croit pas: il peut le bannir, non comme impie, mais comme insociable, comme incapable d'aimer sincèrement les lois, la justice, et d'immoler au besoin sa vie à son devoir. Que si quelqu'un, après avoir reconnu publiquement ces mêmes dogmes, se conduit comme ne les croyant pas, qu'il soit puni de mort; il a commis le plus grand des crimes: il a menti devant les lois." THE POLITICAL WRITINGS OF ROUSSEAU (C. E. Vaughan, ed., 1915), II, 132.

43. Articles 15, 35, 37.

44. See John B. Bury, A HISTORY OF FREEDOM OF THOUGHT (1913), 120 f.

45. Doris M. Stenton, "Magna Carta," ENCYCLOPAEDIA BRITANNICA (1958), XIV, 628. See also Faith Thompson, MAGNA CARTA (1948).

46. Clauses 9-11, 12, 28, 30, 31, 52.

47. Clauses 41 and 42.

48. Clauses 20, 36, 54.

49. The parallel of the French Revolution, where the revolutionary slogan, *Liberté, Egalité, Fraternité*, was followed by a detailed enumeration of the rights of man in the Declaration of the Rights of Man and Citizen, comes to mind. It is, of course, open to question whether a short, slogan-like command or a longer, more circumscribed provision is more conducive to the protection of a specific right. Comp. the author's ÜBER FORMULIERUNG DER MENSCHENRECHTE, esp. 58 ff.

50. In 1649, the assembly of Maryland issued the famous act of toleration, the first decree granting religious freedom to emanate from an assembly. For the history of religious freedom in America, see Sanford Cobb, THE RISE OF RELIGIOUS LIBERTY IN AMERICA (1902).

51. J. M. Landis, "Freedom of Speech and of the Press," ENCYCLOPAEDIA OF THE SOCIAL SCIENCES, VI, 456.

52. Articles 15, 35, 37.

53. The article reads: "That the Act and Ordinances of Parliament made for the sale or other disposition of the lands, rents and hereditaments of the late King, Queen, and Prince, of Archbishops and Bishops, etc., Deans and Chapters, the lands of delinquents and forest-lands, or any of them, or of any other lands, tenements, rents and hereditaments belonging to the Commonwealth, shall nowise be impeached or made invalid, but shall remain good and firm; and that the securities given by Act and Ordinance of Parliament for any sum or sums of money, by any of the said lands, the excise, or any other public revenue; and also the securities given by the public faith to the nation, and the engagement of the public faith for satisfaction of debts and damages, shall remain firm and good, and not be made void and invalid upon any pretence whatsoever."

54. For the fact that Jefferson did not intend to replace the then prevalent sentiment that it was necessary to protect "life, liberty and property" by the new concept of "pursuit of happiness," see *supra*, pp. 31 f. A German nobleman in American service spoke of America during the revolutionary period as a "beautiful and happy land, where every one is happy and where poverty is unknown," and thus closely connected happiness with protection of property. Scherger, *op. cit.*, 217.

55. Constitutions of Massachusetts (1780), art. 1; New Hampshire (1780), art. 2; Pennsylvania (1776), art. 1; Vermont (1777), chapter I, art. 1.

56. Constitutions of Massachusetts, art. 15; New Hampshire, art. 20; North Carolina (1776), art. 14; Pennsylvania, art. 11; Vermont (1777), art. 13.

57. Constitutions of Maryland (1776), art. 21; Massachusetts, art. 14; New Hampshire, arts. 15, 17; North Carolina, art. 12; South Carolina (1778), art. 41.

58. Constitutions of Maryland, art. 23; Massachusetts, art. 14; New Hampshire, art. 19; Pennsylvania, art. 10; Vermont, art. 11.

59. Constitutions of Massachusetts, art. 10; New Hampshire, art. 12; Pennsylvania, art. 8; Vermont, art. 9.

60. See Edward S. Corwin, "The Progress of Constitutional Theory between the Declaration of Independence and the Meeting of the Philadelphia Convention," AMERICAN HISTORICAL REVIEW (1924-25), XXX, 534 ff.

61. Amendments VI and VII.

62. Though the Declaration was originally drafted as a bill of rights for the new constitution and though it became an explicit part of later French constitutions (those of 1848, 1852 and 1946), French jurists are in agreement that the principles of the Declaration are valid for any French constitution. See A. Lebon, DAS VERFASSUNGSRECHT DER FRANZÖSISCHEN REPUBLIK (1909), 174; Adhémar Esmein, ÉLÉMENTS DE DROIT CONSTITUTIONNEL FRANÇAIS ET COMPARÉ (8th ed. by Henry Nézard, 1927), I, 561; Duguit, *op. cit.*, II, 159; III, 563. Comp. art. 16 of the Declaration: "Toute société dans laquelle la garantie des droits n'est pas assurée, ni la séparation des pouvoirs déterminée, n'a point de constitution."

63. Louis Philippe le Comte de Ségur, MÉMOIRES, SOUVENIRS ET ANECDOTES (Fs. Barrière, ed., 1859), I, 51, tells us how the news from Boston harbor was received in Spa, the fashionable resort of the European aristocracy: "Je me souviens qu'on appelait alors les Américains insurgés et *Bostoniens;* leurs courageuse audace électrisa tous les esprits, excita une admiration générale, surtout parmi la jeunesse, amie des nouveautées et avide des combats; et dans cette petite ville de Spa, où se trouvaient tant de voyageurs ou députés accidentels et volontaires de toutes les monarchies de l'Europe, je fus singulièrement frappé de voir éclater unaniment un si vif et si général intérêt pour la révolte d'un people contre un roi." He adds that the same agitation prevailed in Paris and that Americans like Sileas Deane and Arthur Lee were treated like the sage contemporaries of Plato or republicans of the time of Cato and Fabius. *Id.*, I, 53, 69. See also *id.*, I, 149, 165; Thomas Jefferson, MEMOIR, CORRESPONDENCE, AND MISCELLANIES (2nd ed., by T. J. Randolph, 1830), I, 56; Mme. Campan, MÉMOIRES SUR LA VIE PRIVÉE DE MARIE ANTOINETTE (4th ed., 1823), I, 233; Mme. de Staël, CONSIDÉRATIONS SUR LES PRINCIPAUX ÉVÉNEMENTS DE LA RÉVOLUTION FRANÇAISE (1818), I, 88.

64. For instance, Etienne Clavière and J.-B. Brissot, DE LA FRANCE ET DES ÉTATS-UNIS OU DE L'IMPORTANCE DE LA RÉVOLUTION DE L'AMÉRIQUE POUR LE BONHEUR DE LA FRANCE (1787); Abbé Raynal, RÉVOLUTION DE L'AMÉRIQUE (1781); Abbé de Mably, OBSERVATIONS SUR LE GOUVERNEMENT ET LES LOIS DES ÉTATS-UNIS D'AMÉRIQUE (1784); Mirabeau, CONSIDÉRATIONS SUR L'ORDRE DE CINCINNATUS (1784). See also Filippo Mazzei, RECHERCHES HISTORIQUES ET POLITIQUES SUR LES ÉTATS-UNIS DE L'AMÉRIQUE SEPTENTRIONALE (1788).

65. OEUVRES (1847-49), VI, 556. See also id., IX, 168.

66. This declaration was included in his pamphlet, "Address to the Batavians Concerning Stadtholdership" (1788).

67. MÉMOIRES, CORRESPONDENCE ET MANUSCRITS (1837), II, 303-5. See also ARCHIVES PARLEMENTAIRES, VIII, 221 f.

68. Id., VIII, 289 f.

69. Id., VIII, 256-61.

70. Id., VIII, 438 f.

71. See Félicien Challaye, HISTOIRE DE LA PROPRIÉTÉ (1958), 83.

CHAPTER III

1. Significantly, Adam Smith referred to colonialism as "a manifest violation of the most sacred rights of mankind." WEALTH OF NATIONS (Cannan ed., 1930), II, 83.

2. The classic economists of the early 19th century, esp. Ricardo and his followers, characteristically defended private property on utilitarian grounds as well as on principles of natural law.

3. For the role of Roman law in the 19th century, see Koschaker. op. cit.

4. Josiah Stamp, MOTIVE AND METHOD IN A CHRISTIAN ORDER (1936), 114, writes: "The immense economic advance of the nineteenth century was the joint product of Calvin and James Watt. Their departed spirits worked in unconscious partnership to make the greatest business concern the world has ever known."

5. John Browning, ed., THE WORKS OF JEREMY BENTHAM (1843), I, 303.

6. Id., I, 309 ff. See also "On the Levelling System," id., I, 358. For Bentham's arguments against levelling, see also his "Radicalism Not Dangerous," id., I, 599.

7. For instance, James Mill stated that "the greatest possible happiness of society is attained in insuring to every man the greatest possible quantity of the produce of his labor." "Government," printed in E. A. Burtt, ed., ENGLISH PHILOSOPHERS FROM BACON TO MILL (1939), 859. That article appeared first in a supplement to the fifth edition of the ENCYCLOPAEDIA BRITANNICA (1816-32). For deviations from absolute property rights, advocated and practiced by the Benthamites, see the writings of Jacob Viner. See also Lionel Robbins, THEORY OF ECONOMIC POLICY IN ENGLISH CLASSICAL POLITICAL ECONOMY (1952).

8. PRINCIPLES OF POLITICAL RIGHT (W. Hastie, transl., 1891), 38, 41, 44.

9. PHILOSOPHY OF RIGHT (S. W. Dyde, transl. 1896), 48 f., 52 f., 55 f., 65 ff.

10. REFLECTIONS ON THE REVOLUTION IN FRANCE (Everyman ed.), 35, 240 f.

11. Id., 35.

12. This is so evident in his praise of the English constitution and his denunciation of the French Revolution that the idea of the protection of property rights appears to be the keynote of his political writings. As Schlatter, PRIVATE PROPERTY, 178, remarks, Burke's "defense of the English political structure was a theory of property as well as a theory of politics."

13. When the Duke of Bedford showed radical inclinations, Burke reminded him that the House of Bedford's wealth, though largely based upon the spoils of Henry VIII's confiscations, was now legitimate and "guarded by the sacred rule of prescription." "The Duke of Bedford," he added, "will stand as long as prescriptive law endures—as long as the great stable laws of property, common to us with all civilized nations, are kept in their integrity." "Letter to a Noble Lord," THE WORKS OF THE RIGHT HONORABLE EDMUND BURKE

(1894-99), V, 209. Comp. also Burke's statement on the expropriation of French groups believed to represent the ancien regime: "With the National Assembly in France, possession is nothing. I see the National Assembly openly reprobate the doctrine of prescription, which, one of the greatest of their own lawyers tells us, with great truth, is a part of the law of nature. . . If prescription be once shaken, no species of property is secure. . . I see the confiscators begin with bishops, and chapters, and monasteries; but I do not see them end there. . . They have at length ventured to subvert all property of all descriptions throughout the extent of a great kingdom. . . We entertain a high opinion of the legislative authority; but we have never dreamt that parliaments had any right whatever to violate property, to overrule prescription." REFLECTIONS ON THE FRENCH REVOLUTION, 148 f.

14. "Speech on the Reform of Representation," (1782). WORKS, VII, 94.

15. REFLECTIONS ON THE REVOLUTION IN FRANCE, 102. See also his "A Letter to a Member of the National Assembly," (1791). WORKS, IV, 246.

16. See his VOM BERUF UNSERER ZEIT FÜR GESETZGEBUNG UND RECHTSWISSENSCHAFT (1814); "Stimmen für und wider neue Gesetzbücher," ZEITSCHRIFT FÜR GESCHICHTLICHE RECHTSWISSENSCHAFT (1816), III, No. 1.

17. VILLAGE COMMUNITIES (3rd ed., 1913), 230.

18. L'ORDRE NATUREL ET ESSENTIEL DES SOCIÉTÉS POLITIQUES (Daire ed. 1846), 444.

19. Comp. Schlatter, PRIVATE PROPERTY, 182 ff.

20. See Thomas C. Cochran and William Miller, THE AGE OF ENTERPRISE (1942), 124 ff.; Richard Hofstadter, SOCIAL DARWINISM IN AMERICAN THOUGHT (1944), 18 ff.

21. SOCIAL STATICS (Rev. ed., 1892), 62 f.

22. *Id.*, 66 f. Spencer writes: "If, as M. Proudhon asserts, 'all property is robbery'—if no one can equitably become the exclusive possessor of any article, or, as we say, obtain a right to it—then, among other consequences, it follows that a man can have no right to the things he consumes for food. And if these are not his before eating them, how can they become his at all? As Locke asks, 'when do they begin to be his? when he digests? or when he eats? or when he boils? or when he brings them home?' If no previous acts can make them his property, neither can any process of assimilation do it: not even absorption of them into the tissues. Wherefore, pursuing the idea, we arrive at the curious conclusion, that as the whole of his bones, muscles, skin &c., have been thus built up from nutriment not belonging to him, a man has no property in his own flesh and blood—has no more claim to his own limbs than he has to the limbs of another; and has as good a right to his neighbour's body as to his own! Did we exist after the same fashion as those compound polyps, in which a number of individuals are based upon a living trunk common to them all, such a theory would be rational enough. But until Communism can be carried to that extent, it will be best to stand by the old doctrine." Property is as strongly defended in the revised edition of the SOCIAL STATICS as in the original one of 1851. As far as property is concerned, the accusation that Spencer in the later edition appeared to be less of an individualist (see Jay Nock's introduction to THE MAN VERSUS THE STATE [1940], viii), does not seem to be justified. The revised edition merely omits chapters on "The Right of Property in Character," and "The Right of Exchange." It is interesting to note that in the first edition, Spencer deals with property rights before taking up such topics as "The Right of Free Speech," "Further Rights," "The Rights of Women," "The Rights of Children," and "Political Rights." In the revised edition, the order remains the same, but the chapters on free speech and further rights are omitted. Also, that edition does not contain the attacks on land ownership.

23. Hofstadter, *op. cit.*, 26.

24. See the essays published in the 1940 edition of THE MAN VERSUS THE STATE. For American restatements of laissez-faire, see Francis Wayland, THE ELEMENTS OF POLITICAL ECONOMY (1837, recast by Aaron L. Chapin, 1883), i, 4-6, 174; Francis Bowen, AMERICAN POLITICAL ECONOMY (New York ed., 1887), 18; Arthur L. Perry, INTRODUCTION TO POLITICAL ECONOMY (1880), 52, 60, 75, 100; J. Laurence Laughlin, THE ELEMENTS OF POLITICAL ECONOMY (1888), 349.

25. Art. 17 of the Declaration of the Rights of Man and Citizen; Art. 87 of the constitution of 1791.

26. Challaye, *op., cit.*, 82 f.

27. Comp. Napoleon's statement: "La propriété, c'est l'inviolabilité dans la personne de celui qui la possède: moi-même, avec les nombreuses armées qui sont à ma disposition, je ne pourrais m'emparer d'un champ, car violer le droit de propriété d'un seul, c'est le violer dans tous." Locré, LA LÉGISLATION CIVILE DE LA FRANCE (1836 ed.), IV, 235. See Challaye, *op. cit.*, 83.

28. Barthélemy Terrat, when writing on property in the Civil Code, gave his article the heading, "Du régime de la Propriété dans le Code Civil." LIVRE DU CENTENAIRE, published by La Société d'études législatives (1904), I, 327. Poithier, an eminent jurist of the ancien regime who played a major part in the drafting of the Code, was the author of DU DROIT DE PROPRIÉTÉ (1777) and an authority on property rights. The framers of the Code believed in natural law. Significantly, art. 1 of title one of the *livre préliminaire* of the Code reads: "Il existe un droit universel et immuable, source de toutes les lois positives: il n'est que la raison naturelle en tant qu'elle gouverne tous les hommes." See A. Boistel, "Le Code civil et la Philosophie du Droit," LIVRE DU CENTENAIRE, I, 45. Also, property was considered a natural right. In his *Discours préliminaire,* Portalis proclaimed that "le droit de propriété, en soi, est une institution de la nature," Locré, *op. cit.*, I, 181. See also *id.*, IV, 75 f.

29. Claude Léwy, "The Code and Property," in Bernard Schwartz, ed., THE CODE NAPOLEON AND THE COMMON LAW WORLD (1956), 164.

30. André Tunc, "The Grand Outlines of the Code," *id.*, 38 f.

31. For a general discussion of the influence of the Civil Code, see Jean Limpens, "Territorial Expansion of the Code," *id.*, 92. A more detailed discussion can be found in the second volume of the LIVRE DU CENTENAIRE. See also Uriah Rose, THE CODE NAPOLEON (1906); Semaine Internationale De Droit, L'INFLUENCE DU CODE CIVIL DANS LE MONDE (1950). For the Code's influence in various countries, see Hanssens, "Le Code civil en Belgique"; C. D. Asser, "Le Code civil dans les Pays-Bas"; P. Ruppert, "Modifications apportées au Code civil dans la Grand-Duché de Luxembourg"; Bon de Rolland, "Le Code civil de 1804 dans la Principauté de Monaco," LIVRE DU CENTENAIRE, II, 679, 791, 805, 815. For the influence of the Code in Germany, see Otto Stobbe, HANDBUCH DES DEUTSCHEN PRIVATRECHTS (3rd ed., 1893), 105 ff.

32. See G. Ireland, "La Louisiane, vue nouvelle de son système de droit," in RECUEIL LAMBERT, II, 94; P. B. Mignault, "Les rapports entre les lois civiles et le common law au Canada, spécialement dans la province de Quebec," *id.*, I, Introduction à l'étude du droit comparé; P.-B. Mignault, "Le Code civil au Canada," LIVRE DU CENTENAIRE, II, 723; G.-P. Chironi, "Le Code civil et son influence en Italie," *id.*, II, 761; C.-G. Dissescou, "L'influence du Code civil français en Roumanie, *id.*, II, 847; Pierre Arminjon, "Le Code civil et l'Egypte," *id.*, II, 733. In the Dominican Republic, the original code is still in effect. The Bolivian code of 1831 was largely a translation of the Civil Code. The Chilean code of 1865 was strongly influenced by the Civil Code, and was copied by Ecuador in 1861 and by Colombia in 1873. The Civil Code also influenced the codes of Uruguay of 1867 and Argentina of 1869. See Limpens, *op. cit.*, 99 ff. As to Japan, the French jurist Boissonade, following the Civil Code, had drafted the Code Boissonade of 1890 which, however, was resisted by Japanese legislators. The Japanese civil code of 1898, while showing features of the *Code Boissonade,* also shows the impact of drafts to the German *Bürgerliche Gesetzbuch.* See Goraï, "Influence du Code civil française sur le Japon," LIVRE DU CENTENAIRE, II, 779.

33. Quoted by Carl J. Friedrich, "The Ideological and Philosophical Background," in Schwartz, *op. cit.*, 7-8.

34. Koschaker, *op. cit.*, 135 f.

35. Terrat, *op. cit.*, 352, writes on the Codes' spirit on property: "Il s'est inspiré du droit romain qui avait été l'expression la plus énergique et la plus scientifique de la propriété individuelle. Il a fortement sanctionné ce droit individuel qui, malgré toutes les attaques dont il est l'objet, reste le pivot et le moteur de nos civilisations modernes."

36. While the influence of the enlightenment upon the *Allgemeine Landrecht für die Preussischen Staaten* (ALR.) cannot be denied, there is no reason to believe that it was influenced directly by the French Revolution. (Heinz Werner Schwender, WANDLUNGEN DES

EIGENTUMSBEGRIFFES IN DER DEUTSCHEN RECHTSAUFFASSUNG UND GESETZGEBUNG [1936], 33).
Carl J. Friedrich suggests that Napoleon's desire to be a lawgiver might have been prompted
by his reading the works of Frederick the Great, in which was mentioned that in 1788
Cocceji had edited the *code Frédéric.* "The Ideological and Philosophical Background,"
Schwartz, *op. cit.,* 13.

37. In his last will of Jan. 8, 1769, Frederick the Great had written: "Unser Leben führt
uns mit raschen Schritten von der Geburt bis zum Tode. In dieser kurzen Zeitspanne ist
es die Bestimmung des Menschen, für das Wohl der Gemeinschaft, deren Mitglied er ist,
zu arbeiten." AUSGEWÄHLTE WERKE FRIEDRICHS DES GROSSEN (G. B. Volz ed., 1916), II, 93.

38. Part I, title 8, secs. 9, 21, 23, 25, 29, 30, 31.

39. COMMENTAR ÜBER DAS ALLGEMEINE BÜRGERLICHE GESETZBUCH (1811-13), I, 102.

40. Sections 354, 362.

41. *Op. cit.,* II, 125.

42. Schwender, *op. cit.,* 36. Comp. also sections 297, 340-43, 413, 422, 425 ABGB; Zeiller,
op. cit., II, 126.

43. Here real estate was declared to be free from all restrictions, as free as the people
who lived on it. Code Rural of 1791; decree of the National Assembly of Aug. 25-28, 1792.

44. Under section 4, the division of real estate was facilitated. The *Verwandtenretrakt*
ceased to exist and only the *Lehnsretrakt* and other *Retrakte* were left intact.

45. Secs. 1, 4, 5.

46. The *Regulierungsedikt* of 1811 allowed the replacement of *Obereigentum.* The *Gemein-
heitsteilungsordnung* of 1821 sought to abolish common ownership of real property in favor
of individual ownership. The emancipation of property was concluded by the Law Concerning the Abolition of *Reallasten* of 1850, as well as by the constitution of that year.

47. See Otto Stobbe, GESCHICHTE DER DEUTSCHEN RECHTSQUELLEN (1860-64), II, 375 ff.

48. Characteristic is Rotteck's statement at a meeting of liberals in Badenweiler on
June 2, 1832: "Ich will lieber Freiheit ohne Einheit als Einheit ohne Freiheit." Quoted in
Heinrich von Treitschke, DEUTSCHE GESCHICHTE IM 19. JAHRHUNDERT (1879-95), IV, 265.

49. L. Enneccerus, LEHRBUCH DES BÜRGERLICHEN RECHTS, ALLGEMEINER TEIL (14th ed. by
H. C. Nipperdey, 1952), 32.

50. Comp. PROTOKOLLE DER KOMMISSION FÜR DIE ZWEITE LESUNG DES ENTWURFS DES BGB.,
3525, 3527. The words "nach Belieben" were primarily chosen because one was afraid that
the words "nach Willkür" could be interpreted to mean that the owner was not even bound
by the commands of morals. As far as legal transactions of the proprietor are concerned,
however, the substitution of "nach Belieben" for "nach Willkür" does not seem to have
had any relevance. Comp. F. Tönnies, DAS EIGENTUM (1926), 7.

51. 1., 2., UND 3. BERATUNG DES ENTWURFS EINES BGB. Stenographische Berichte, 102.
Quoted also by Justus Wilhelm Hedemann, SACHENRECHT DES BÜRGERLICHEN GESETZBUCHS
(2nd ed., 1950), 11.

52. MOTIVE ZU DEM ENTWURF DES BGB. FÜR DAS DEUTSCHE REICH, III, 262.

53. *Id.,* III, 262; Mugdan, *op. cit.,* III, 145.

54. Absalon, *op. cit.,* 29, points out that laws under which property was restricted and
which were still valid under articles 109 and 111 of the introductory law to the BGB
(EGBGB), such as provisions concerning trade and building police, or laws governing
forests, hunting and mining, were considered like "foreign matter" (*Fremdkörper*).

55. Otto Stobbe, HANDBUCH DES DEUTSCHEN PRIVATRECHTS (3rd ed., 1893), 108; Koschaker,
op. cit., 131 f.

56. *Id.,* 131 f. Comp. the Greek civil code of 1940, the Hungarian code, and the civil
codes of Brazil (1916), Mexico (1928), and Peru (1936).

57. "The questions which were perpetually recurring in the State legislatures and which
brought annually into doubt principles which I thought most sacred, which proved that
everything was afloat, and that we had no safe anchorage ground, gave a high value in
my estimation to that article of the Constitution which imposes restrictions on the States."
Quoted by Corwin, JOHN MARSHALL AND THE CONSTITUTION, 151, note. Comp. also that
author's "The Basic Doctrine of American Constitutional Law," MICHIGAN LAW REVIEW
(1914), XII, 247.

58. Benjamin F. Wright, THE CONTRACT CLAUSE OF THE CONSTITUTION (1938), 28.

59. For the thesis that national power was for Hamilton a means for the protection of property, see the author's "Hamilton's Concept of Free Government," NEW YORK HISTORY (1957), XXXVIII, 351. Marshall had reacted unfavorably toward Shays's Rebellion, a rebellion that aimed at a more equal distribution of property. (Corwin, JOHN MARSHALL AND THE CONSTITUTION, 35). The opening words of his first speech in the Virginia Convention were: "Mr. Chairman, I conceive that the object of the discussion now before us is whether democracy or despotism be most eligible. . . . The supporters of the Constitution claim the title of being firm friends of liberty and the rights of man. . . . We prefer this system because we think it a well-regulated democracy. . . . What are the favorite maxims of democracy? A strict observance of justice and public faith." Id., 36 f. "A strict observance of justice and public faith" meant for Marshall the same thing it meant for the authors of the Federalist Papers, namely, the honoring of contractual obligations and the protection of property rights.

60. Albert J. Beveridge, THE LIFE OF JOHN MARSHALL (1916-19), gives this title to the next to the last chapter of his four-volume biography. That chapter deals, among other things, with Marshall's role in the Virginia Constitutional Convention, a role that demonstrates Marshall's lasting interest in the protection of property. IV, esp. 470 ff.

61. For the fact that the injustice of the repudiation of contractual obligations by the legislature of Virginia had an influence upon Marshall, see id., III, 582; I, 224 ff.; see also I, 119, 196, II, 206.

62. See his opinion in Ogden v. Saunders, 12 Wheat. 213, 354, 355 (1827); comp. also John Marshall, THE LIFE OF GEORGE WASHINGTON (1804-9), V, 85 f.

63. Essays 7 and 44.

64. 6 Cranch 87, 137 (1810).

65. Wright, op. cit., 32.

66. 6 Cranch 87, 135 (1810). It is interesting to note that the words are preceded by the following statement: "When, then a law is in its nature a contract, when absolute rights have vested under that contract; a repeal of the law cannot divest those rights; and the act of annulling them, if legitimate, is rendered so by a power applicable to the case of every individual in the community." The protection of property under the contract clause and under more general principles of justice appear to be tied together.

67. 7 Cranch 164 (1812).

68. Printed in Robert C. Harper, THE CASE OF THE GEORGIA SALES ON THE MISSISSIPPI, CONSIDERED WITH REFERENCE TO LAW AUTHORITIES AND PUBLIC ACTS (1799), 88 f.

69. Wright, op. cit., 36.

70. The case has been cited by the Court as a contract case in Piqua Branch Bank v. Knoop, 16 How. 369, 389 (1853); Von Hoffman v. Quincy, 4 Wall. 535, 550 (1867); Pennsylvania College Cases, 13 Wall. 190, 213 (1872); Miller v. New York, 15 Wall. 478, 489 (1873).

71. 9 Cranch 43, 52 (1815).

72. 4 Wheat. 518, 627 (1819).

73. Charles A. Beard and Mary Beard, THE RISE OF AMERICAN CIVILIZATION (1927), I, 689.

74. Wright, op. cit., 62. Wright's book shows that there was no fundamental difference between Marshall's and Taney's interpretation of the contract clause. He takes the same position in his later work, THE GROWTH OF AMERICAN CONSTITUTIONAL LAW (1942).

75. Wright, THE CONTRACT CLAUSE OF THE CONSTITUTION, 63.

76. Id., 63.

77. 11 Pet. 420, 548 (1837).

78. Wright, THE CONTRACT CLAUSE OF THE CONSTITUTION, 63.

79. Early reservation clauses in acts of incorporation can be found in the Virginia Act to Incorporate the Virginia Marine Insurance Company of Jan. 31, 1805; the Massachusetts General Manufacturing Law of 1809; the Connecticut acts incorporating the Derby Fishing Company and the Ocean Insurance Company. For general reservation clauses, SEE REVISED STATUTES OF NEW YORK (1829), I, 600, and Furdon's DIGEST OF THE LAWS OF PENNSYLVANIA (6th ed., 1841), 187. Reservation clauses can be found in the constitutions

of Delaware (1831), art. 2, sec. 17; Pennsylvania (1838), art. 1, sec. 25; Louisiana (1845), title 4, art. 124; Texas (1845), art. 7, sec. 31; Iowa (1846), art. 8, sec. 12; New York (1846), art. 8, sec. 1.; Wisconsin (1848), art. 11, sec. 1; California (1849), art. 4, sec. 31; Michigan (1850), art. 15, sec. 1. Comp. Wright, THE CONTRACT CLAUSE OF THE CONSTITUTION, 58 ff., 84 ff. The first tax clauses can be found in the constitutions of Iowa (1846), art. 8, sec. 2; Kansas (1858), art. 14, sec. 3; Nevada (1864), art. 8, sec. 2. Comp. Wright, *id.*, 85 f.

80. See *id.*, 59, 255.

81. Wynehamer v. People, 13 N. Y. 378 (1856).

82. Scott v. Sanford, 19 How. 393 (1857).

83. Stone v. Farmer's Loan and Trust Company, 116 U.S. 307 (1886).

84. Mugler v. Kansas, 123 U.S. 623, 661 (1887); comp. also the previous decision Bartemeyer v. Iowa, 18 Wall. 129 (1874), where the Court makes a statement similar to that made in Wynehamer v. People, as quoted.

85. Reagan v. Farmers' Loan and Trust Co., 154 U.S. 362, 397 (1894).

86. T. E. Holland, ELEMENTS OF JURISPRUDENCE (13th ed., 1924), 211.

87. Edward S. Corwin, THE CONSTITUTION AND WHAT IT MEANS TODAY (12th ed., 1958), 218 f.

88. Allgeyer v. Louisiana, 165 U.S. 578, 589, 590 (1897). In an earlier case, the Court had announced that one has the right to "his enjoyment upon terms of equality with all others in similar circumstances of the privilege of pursuing an ordinary calling or trade, and of acquiring, holding, and selling property." Powell v. Pennsylvania, 127 U.S. 678, 684 (1888).

89. It is interesting to note that during the first ten years after the adoption of the fourteenth amendment, not a dozen cases came before the Court under the clauses of that amendment put together. However, in the following two decades, more than two hundred cases arose, most of them under the due process clause. During the ensuing twelve years, the number more than doubled. See Charles W. Collins, THE FOURTEENTH AMENDMENT AND THE STATES (1912), 188 ff.

90. See Benjamin R. Twiss, LAWYERS AND THE CONSTITUTION, HOW LAISSEZ FAIRE CAME TO THE SUPREME COURT (1942).

91. U.S. v. E.C. Knight Co., 156 U.S. 1 (1895).

92. Pollock v. Farmers' Loan and Trust Co., 157 U. S. 429 (1895); 158 U.S. 601 (1895).

93. To Moss Kent, Jr., on May 21, 1799. Quoted by John T. Horton, JAMES KENT, A STUDY IN CONSERVATISM (1939), 123.

94. COMMENTARIES (12th ed., edited by Oliver W. Holmes, Jr., 1873), I, 547 f.

95. Horton, *op. cit.*, 273 f.

96. COMMENTARIES II, 250.

97. *Id.*, II, 253 f. See also his letter of Oct. 7, 1833 to Moses Kent, Jr., in KENT PAPERS (Library of Congress), VII, and his letter to William E. Channing of Apr. 18, 1842. AMERICAN HISTORICAL REVIEW (1931-32), XXXVII, 520 f.

98. COMMENTARIES, II, 319.

99. See his letter to Joseph Story of June 23, 1837. STORY PAPERS (Massachusetts Historical Society); COMMENTARIES, II, 339 f.

100. *Id.*, II, 331.

101. *Id.*, II, 330 note.

102. *Id.*, II, 328.

103. *Id.*, II, 330.

104. See Gardner v. Newburgh, 2 Johns. Ch. 161; Croton Turnpike Road Co. v. Ryder, 1 Johns. Ch. 101; "Restrictions upon the State Power in Relation to Private Property," UNITED STATES LAW INTELLIGENCE AND REVIEW (1829), I, 94.

105. Comp. his opinion in Wilkinson v. Leland, 2 Pet. 657, 658 (1829): " . . . government can scarcely be deemed to be free where the rights of property are left solely dependent upon the will of a legislative body without any restraint. The fundamental maxims of a free government seem to require that the right of personal liberty and private property should be held sacred. At least no court of justice in this country would be warranted in assuming that the power to violate and disregard them—a power so repugnant to the com-

mon principles of justice and civil liberty—lurked under any general grant of legislative authority, or ought to be implied from any general expressions of the will of the people. The people ought not to be presumed to part with rights so vital to their security and well-being without very strong and direct expressions of such an intention. We know of no case in which a legislative act to transfer the property of A. to B. without his consent has been held a constitutional exercise of legislative power in any state of the Union. On the contrary, it has been constantly resisted as inconsistent with just principles by every judicial tribunal in which it has been attempted to be enforced."

106. "The truth is," he continued, "that we have yet much to learn as to the nature of free governments; and it will be matter of surprise if in our rage for experiments to ascertain with what weakness in its institutions the government may possibly go on and stop and go on—we should not shipwreck the cause of liberty. I endeavor to hope for the best —but there are many painful forebodings about us." Mortimer D. Schwartz and John Hogan, ed., JOSEPH STORY (1959), 135.

107. COMMENTARIES ON THE CONSTITUTION OF THE UNITED STATES (1833), III, 240 ff.

108. *Id.*, III, 661

109. A TREATISE ON THE CONSTITUTIONAL LIMITATIONS WHICH REST UPON THE LEGISLATIVE POWER OF THE STATES OF THE AMERICAN UNION (8th ed., 1927), 745.

110. William Seagle, "Cooley, Thomas McIntyre," ENCYCLOPAEDIA OF THE SOCIAL SCIENCES, IV, 357.

111. On p. 96, he mentions, quoting a Missouri case, property before personal freedom and political liberty. On p. 733 he mentions property on a par with life and liberty, omitting to mention other rights. His high appreciation of property also seems to follow from his arrangement of chapters. He takes up the discussion of property rights before that of liberty of speech, of the press, and of religion. For the fact that Cooley considered the right to vote as nothing but "a franchise, which the state might grant and withhold at will," and "did not regard it as a natural right in any sense," see Jerome C. Knowlton, "Thomas McIntyre Cooley," MICHIGAN LAW REVIEW (1907), V, 323.

112. People v. Salem, 20 Mich. 452 (1870).

113. "Limits to State Control of Private Business," PRINCETON REVIEW, March, 1878.

114. Knowlton, *op. cit.*, 323.

115. O. Douglass Weeks, "Some Political Ideas of Thomas McIntyre Cooley," SOUTHWESTERN POLITICAL AND SOCIAL SCIENCE QUARTERLY (1925-26), VI, 36.

116. F. C. Gersterding, AUSFÜHRLICHE DARSTELLUNG DER LEHRE VOM EIGENTUM UND SOLCHEN RECHTEN, DIE IHM NAHEKOMMEN (1817); B. Windscheid, LEHRBUCH DES PANDEKTENRECHTES (8th ed., by Th. Kipp, 1900).

117. See G. F. Puchta, PANDEKTEN (4th ed., 1848), 207; H. Dernburg, LEHRBUCH DES PREUSSISCHEN PRIVATERECHTS UND DER PRIVATRECHTSNORMEN DES REICHS (4th ed., 1884), 435; C. F. Sintenis, DAS PRACTISCHE GEMEINE CIVILRECHT (1844), I, 472 f.; Windscheid, *op. cit.*, 755 f. Windscheid used the expression "die Fülle des Rechts."

118. See A. J. F. Thibaut, SYSTEM DES PANDEKTENRECHTS (8th ed., 1834), II, 225; Sintenis, *op. cit.*, 472 f.; J. N. von Wening-Ingenheim, LEHRBUCH DES GEMEINEN CIVILRECHTS (1822), I, 204; J. F. L. Göschen, VORLESUNGEN ÜBER DAS GEMEINE CIVILRECHT (2nd ed., 1843), II, 19; Gersterding, *op. cit.*, 4; Windscheid, *op. cit.*, sec. 167; C. F. Mühlenbruch, LEHRBUCH DES PANDEKTEN-RECHTS (1836), II, sec. 245; F. Mackeldey, LEHRBUCH DES HEUTIGEN RÖMISCHEN RECHTS (1829), I, 68; L. Arndts Ritter von Arensberg, LEHRBUCH DER PANDEKTEN (8th ed., 1874), sec. 130.

119. See Göschen, *op. cit.*, 19; Sintenis, *op. cit.*, I, 472; Mackeldey, *op. cit.*, I, 68; A. Randa, DAS EIGENTUMSRECHT MIT BESONDERER RÜCKSICHT AUF DIE WERTPAPIERE DES HANDELSRECHTS NACH ÖSTERREICHISCHEM RECHTE (2nd ed., 1893), 6; Windscheid, *op. cit.*, 167.

120. See A. Brinz, LEHRBUCH DER PANDEKTEN (2nd ed., 1873), I, 471; E. Pagenstecher, DIE RÖMISCHE LEHRE VOM EIGENTUM IN IHRER MODERNEN ANWENDBARKEIT (1875), I, 2, 4; von Wening-Ingelheim, *op. cit.*, 205; F. L. von Keller, PANDEKTEN (1861), 213; Thibaut, *op. cit.*, II, 247.

121. Sintenis, *op. cit.*, I, 474; von Keller, *op. cit.*, 210.

122. *Op. cit.*, Sec. 167, note 3.

123. See Göschen, *op. cit.*, 20; Mühlenbruch, *op. cit.*, II, 245; Sintenis, *op. cit.*, I, 474; Dernburg, *op. cit.*, sec. 192; Thibaut, *op. cit.*, II, Sec. 699; K. A. von Vangerow, LEHRBUCH DER PANDEKTEN (7th ed., 1876), I, 540; L. Arndts Ritter von Arensberg, *op. cit.*, sec. 130. The term "an sich schrankenlos" was used by Vangerow, *op. cit.*, 50; Windscheid, *op. cit.*, sec. 167, note 5, writes: "An sich, das will eben sagen: solange das Recht den Spruch, den es in der Verleihung des Eigentums getan hat, nicht in dieser oder jeder einzelnen Beziehung zurückgenommen hat." See also Puchta, *op. cit.*, 207. A. Randa, *op. cit.*, 1 f., speaks of "Idee" and "innere Anlage" of property. Sintenis, *op. cit.*, I, 472, writes that "Eigentum heisst das Recht, welches seiner Natur nach die volle und ausschliessliche Unterwerfung einer Sache umfasst." (See also Thibaut, *op. cit.*, sec. 699.)

124. Göschen, *op. cit.*, 71; Mackeldey, *op. cit.*, I, 68 f.

125. Savigny, *op. cit.*, I, 370 f.

126. Mackeldey, *op. cit.*, 40 f. For similar opinions, see F. Förster, THEORIE UND PRAXIS DES HEUTIGEN GEMEINEN PREUSSISCHEN PRIVATRECHTS AUF DER GRUNDLAGE DES GEMEINEN RECHTS (1873), Sec. 167; Dernburg, *op. cit.*, 445; Windscheid, *op. cit.*, Sec. 169a; von Wening-Ingenheim, *op. cit.*, I, 209 f. Comp. also Arndt, *op. cit.*, 203; Sintenis, *op. cit.*, I, 474.

127. Schwender, *op. cit.*, 51.

128. We believe that Schwender's thesis was influenced by the anti-individualism of the national-socialist regime. Had the people opposed the liberal and individualistic concept of property, they would hardly have adopted the German civil code.

129. Henri Hayem, ESSAI SUR LE DROIT DE PROPRIÉTÉ ET SES LIMITES (1910), 357. As the word "c'était" implies, Hayem feels that at the time of his writing, the Code was no longer a "code of property."

130. For a refutation of Hayem's thesis, see George Ripert, LES FORCES CRÉATRICES DU DROIT (1955), 191 ff.

131. Raymond T. Troplong, DE LA PROPRIÉTÉ D'APRÈS LE CODE CIVIL (1848), 6. For Troplong's influence, see J. Charmont and A. Chausse, "Les Interprètes du Code Civil," LIVRE DU CENTENAIRE, I, 149 ff.

132. C. Demolombe, COURS DE CODE NAPOLÉON (2nd ed., 1860-64), IX, 479.

133. Jacques de Malville, ANALYSE RAISONNÉ DE LA DISCUSSION DU CODE CIVIL AU CONSEIL D'ÉTAT (1822), II, 27 ff.

134. Demolombe, *op. cit.*, IX, 479 f., writes: "Dieu, qui a créé l'homme sociable, lui a donné en même temps le moyen d'accomplir sa destinée; et c'est ainsi Dieu lui-même, qui a institué le droit de la propriété, celui de tous les droits peut-être qui se revèle le plus vivement par le seul instinct de la conscience, celui de tous, dont l'assentiment universel et le libre respect des peuples proclament, avec le plus d'énergie, l'inviolabilité indépendamment des lois positives, partout où les funestes doctrines et les détestable excitations des partis n'ont pas égaré leur bon sens et leur bonne foi.

Rien n'attestera mieux, devant l'histoire, l'état de perturbation morale, dans lequel la société française était tombé, dans ces derniers temps, que les monstreuses controverses auxquelles nous venons d'assister.

Chose étrange! c'est au nom du travail et la liberté, que la propriété individuelle a été audacieusement méconnue.

Et la propriété individuelle, c'est le travail! c'est la liberté elle-même!

. . . .

Il suffit, en effet, de la plus vulgaire raison pour reconnaître que la propriété individuelle et transmissible est le seul moyen qui ait été donné à l'homme de louir librement de la terre, que la nature a offerte à ses besoins, et qu'il n'y a, pour l'humanité en dehors de cette condition, d'autre alternative que la barbarie ou l'esclavage."

If public power does not guarantee private property in soil, he writes, "c'est que nul ne jouira de la terre; c'est que la possession, que j'aurai acquise, pourra m'être à tout instant arraché par un autre plus fort que moi, auquel un troisième encore plus fort viendra immédiatement l'arracher à son tour; c'est que tous, se disputant ainsi, de toutes partes, en même temps, les mêmes biens, ce sera la guerre! la guerre partout! la guerre sans fin et sans trève! Et alors, point de culture! point de travail! point de civilisation, mais le brigandage, la misère et le faim! et ces pillards se rejètent les uns sur les autres, . . . le monde restera barbare. (Thiers, de la propriété, p. 43)." Comp. also the longer statement on the ethics of property by Frédéric Mourlon, RÉPÉTITION ÉCRITES SUR LE PREMIER EXAMEN DU CODE NAPOLÉON, CONTENANT L'EXPOSÉ DES PRINCIPES GÉNÉRAUX, LEURS MOTIFS ET LA SOLUTION DES QUESTIONS THÉORIQUES (1866), I, 684 ff.

135. *Op. cit.*, II, 29.

136. V. Marcadé, COURS ÉLÉMENTAIRE DE DROIT CIVIL FRANÇAIS (1850), II, 391.

137. J. M. Boileux, COMMENTAIRE SUR LE CODE NAPOLÉON (6th ed., 1852-57), II, 655.

138. Charles Aubry and C. Rau, COURS DE DROIT CIVIL FRANÇAIS (1869-83), II, 171, 175.

139. *Op. cit.*, 490.

140. G. Baudry-Lacantinerie, PRÉCIS DE DROIT CIVIL (1885-86), I, 729.

141. F. Laurent, COURS ÉLÉMENTAIRE DE DROIT CIVIL (1881), I, 479 f.

142. Marcel Planiol, TRAITÉ ÉLÉMENTAIRE DE DROIT CIVIL (3rd ed., 1904), I, 476.

143. *Id.*, I, 746; Baudry-Lacantinerie, *op. cit.*, I, 729.

144. Laurent, *op. cit.*, I, 480.

145. Comp. Charmont and Chausse, *op, cit.*, 155 ff.

146. Comp. Friedrich Meinecke, WELTBÜRGERTUM UND NATIONALSTAAT (2nd ed., 1911).

147. Comp., for instance, the comments by Ed. Fuzier-Herman in his annotations to the CODE CIVIL (1885-98), I, 698, on two decisions of the Court of Cassation: "Le droit de propriété est tellement absolu que les tribunaux ne sauraient, sans excès de pouvoirs, le résoudre en une simple indemnité. Ainsi, d'une part, le propriétaire sur le fond duquel est commis un empiètement et sont faites des constructions nonobstant son opposition, peut, dans tous les cas, exiger la démolition des ouvrages, quelque léger que soit le dommage à lui causé par les constructions, et quelque grave que soit le dommage causé au constructeur par l'obligation de démolir; obliger le propriétaire à se contenter d'une indemnité, ce serait porter attente au droit de propriété. . . . De même, les juges qui reconnaissent un droit de propriété sur une part d'immeuble, ne peuvent, à défaut d'accord des parties, convertir ce droit en une indemnité pécuniaire sous prétexte que l'assiette de cette part n'étant pas précisée, la délivrance en nature en serait impossible."

148. See the author's "Judicial Review in Europe," *loc. cit.*, 539.

149. See Wright, THE CONTRACT CLAUSE OF THE CONSTITUTION, 53 ff., 82 ff.

150. Constitutions of Pennsylvania (1790), art. 9, sec. 17; Kentucky (1792), art. 12, sec. 18; Tennessee (1796), art. 11, sec. 20.

151. Constitutions of Ohio (1802), art. 8, sec. 16; Indiana (1816), art. 1, sec. 18; Mississippi (1817), art 1, sec. 19; Illinois (1818), art. 13, sec. 17; Alabama (1819), art. 1, sec. 19; Maine (1819), art. 1, sec. 11; Virginia (1830), art. 3, sec. 11; Michigan (1835), art. 1, sec. 17. With the exception of the constitution of Virginia, all these constitutions list the contract clause in their bills of rights.

152. Constitutions of Arkansas (1836), art. 2, sec. 18; California (1849), art. 1, sec. 16; Florida (1838), art. 1, sec. 19; Iowa (1846), art. 1, sec. 21; Kansas (1855), art. 4, sec. 20; Louisiana (1864), title VII, art. 109; Minnesota (1857), art. 1, sec. 11; New Jersey (1844), art. 4, sec. 7; Nevada (1864), art. 1, sec. 15; Oregon (1857), art. 1, sec. 22; Rhode Island (1842), art. 1, sec. 12; Texas (1845), art. 1, sec. 14; West Virginia (1863), art. 2, sec. 1; Wisconsin (1848), art. 1, sec. 12. Here again, with the exception of the constitutions of Kansas and Louisiana, all constitutions bring the contract clause in their bills of rights.

153. Comp. George Ripert, LES FORCES CRÉATRICES DU DROIT (1955).

154. It is doubtful whether even that distinction was too clearly drawn in the 19th century. The Austinian school came into being only in that century and an outstanding German positivist, Bergbohm, wrote only toward the end of the century. Legal positivism has to this day been unable to separate itself absolutely from higher law. Comp. Heinrich Rommen, DIE EWIGE WIEDERKEHR DES NATURRECHTS (2nd ed., 1947).

155. Kurt Rudolph, DIE BINDUNGEN DES EIGENTUMS (1960), writes on p. 7: "Der wahre Eigentumsbegriff hat sich freilich noch nie in einer formalen Definition erschöpft." See also Hans Peter, WANDLUNGEN DER EIGENTUMSORDNUNG UND DER EIGENTUMSLEHRE SEIT DEM 19. JAHRHUNDERT (1949), 108 ff.

CHAPTER IV

1. Comp. Erik von Kuehnelt-Leddihn, LIBERTY OR EQUALITY (1952), esp. ch. 2.

2. José Ortega y Gasset, LA REBELION DES LAS MASAS (1929).

3. No matter what kind of assault would be launched, property would suffer. For like freedom, property has various components. An infringement upon a part constitutes curtailment of the whole. In general, two types of property may be distinguished, namely, static property and dynamic property. Land lying waste, capital hoarded, a house uninhabited, a pencil not used, are examples of the former. Such "passive" property does not increase the proprietor's wealth. However, the moment it is used, it ceases to be merely static. Land cultivated netting fruit, money invested netting interest, a house inhabited netting rent or shelter, a pencil used netting a written product—all these are examples of more dynamic or active aspects of property. A situation could be imagined in which property is used so much and yields such great profits that its static aspects become overshadowed by the dynamic ones.

There also appear to exist merely dynamic aspects of property. When there is no static property to use, when the individual employs his faculties only to acquire property, property can be said to be merely dynamic. It can scarcely be doubted that this kind of property constitutes as much property as less dynamic or merely static types. The argument that no property rights can exist without tangible property misconceives the nature of property rights. Property rights are the rights not only *of* property, but also *to* property. They do imply not only the right to enjoy what one owns, but also the right to own. Consequently, those who do not yet own must have the right to employ their faculties in order that they may own. Logically, the right to acquire precedes the right to own what has been acquired. Without the right to acquire property there could be no property. To assert that property rights presuppose the existence of owned property does no less than maintain that such property came into existence through an unlawful act. At one time existing property must have been acquired by the owner, be it by gift, occupation, or work. If he had then no right to acquire, no right to receive or to occupy, his property must be illegal. But the argument that merely dynamic property is a contradiction in terms can be refuted from still another point of view. Even the seemingly exclusively dynamic type of property, i.e., the right to use one's faculties to acquire property, is not absolutely free from the static type of property, for what else if not properly inherent in man are his faculties to acquire property? Isn't the individual, when using his faculties, actually only activating forces latent in him, "dynamizing" static property, so to speak?

Static property is thus potentially dynamic property, just as dynamic property is based upon static property. As the examples mentioned show, it is difficult to draw a line between the two. They are more or less integrated. But, irrespective of what particular aspect of property predominates, there can be no doubt that an attack on any aspect —dynamic as well as static—must constitute an attack upon property as a whole. Therefore, an attack upon the freedom to acquire property must be as much an attack upon property as, for instance, an attack upon nearly exclusively static property, such as the right to waste property. This example makes obvious the relatively high position the freedom to acquire property occupies in the scale of property rights. It might easily be argued that an attack upon the right to waste property must be less objectionable than an attack upon the right to acquire property. For the former is directed only against waste and the right to be passive, whereas the latter is directed against progress and the right to be active. The former questions a right that derives from created property; the latter, the right to create property—a prior right.

4. Comp. Wilhelm R. Beyer, DER SPIELGELCHARAKTER DER RECHTSORDNUNG (1951).

5. Maurice B. Rickitt, "Christian Socialism," ENCYCLOPAEDIA OF THE SOCIAL SCIENCES, III, 450.

6. Hans Voelter, FRIEDRICH NAUMANN UND DER DEUTSCHE SOZIALISMUS (1950), 19.

7. "Liberty I am told is divine. Liberty when it becomes liberty to die by starvation is not so divine," Carlyle is quoted to have said. Canon Raven, CHRISTIAN SOCIALISM (1920),

31. Raven, *id.*, 54, writes that the English Christian socialists in some respect "owed their inspiration to Carlyle and their opportunity to the Chartists."

8. Stoecker's major work is CHRISTLICH-SOZIAL (1890). The best biography on him is Walter Frank, HOFPREDIGER ADOLF STOECKER (1928).

9. DAS SOZIALE PROGRAMM DER EVANGELISCHEN KIRCHEN (1891); DER ARBEITERKATECHISMUS ODER DER WAHRE SOZIALISMUS (1889).

10. DIE ARBEITERFRAGE UND DAS CHRISTENTUM (1864).

11. Hofstadter, *op. cit.*, 86 f. See also Charles Howard Hopkins, THE RISE OF THE SOCIAL GOSPEL IN AMERICAN PROTESTANTISM 1865-1915 (1940); James Dombrowski, THE EARLY DAYS OF CHRISTIAN SOCIALISM IN AMERICA (1936); Paine Gilman, SOCIALISM AND THE AMERICAN SPIRIT (1893).

12. Dombrowski, *op. cit.*, 14, 87. In his SOCIALISM AND CHRISTIANITY (1886), 133, Behrends wrote that "Christianity cannot grant the adequacy of the 'laissez-faire' philosophy, cannot admit that the perfect and permanent social state is the product of natural law and of an unrestricted competition." He cited the Belgian socialist Laveleye who said that the followers of the laissez-faire doctrine are the real and only logical adversaries at once of Christianity and of socialism. *Id.*, 64 ff. On the other hand, Behrends made it clear that he was not a radical socialist. The title of the fourth chapter of his book is "The Economic Fallacies of Modern Socialism."

13. Abbott's major work is CHRISTIANITY AND SOCIAL PROBLEMS (1896).

14. RULING IDEAS OF THE PRESENT AGE (1895), 63 ff., 73 f., 146, 150 ff.; APPLIED CHRISTIANITY (1886), 104 f., cf. also 111 f., 130. TOOLS AND THE MAN (1893), 3, 36, 176, 275 ff., cf. also 270, 287 f.; SOCIAL FACTS AND FORCES (1897), 2, 93, 220. For his favoring a 'genuine' free enterprise, see APPLIED CHRISTIANITY, 20.

15. RULING IDEAS OF THE PRESENT AGE (1895), 159 f. For Gladden's opposition to the state's taking possession of all and dividing it among its citizens, see APPLIED CHRISTIANITY, 15-21. "Certainly we want no more eleemosynary distribution of money by the state than we have now," he wrote. However, he added: "The time may come when the nation will be compelled to take under its control, if not into its ownership, the railroads and the telegraphy, and administer them for the common good." *Id.*, 17 f.

16. Dombrowski, *op. cit.*, 18. Throughout Dombrowski's work, the conservative character of the social gospel movement is evident.

17. See Heinrich Oppenheim, DER KATHEDERSOZIALISMUS (1872).

18. GRUNDLEGUNG DER POLITISCHEN OEKONOMIE (3rd ed., 1894), III, 3 ff., esp. 9 ff., 13 f., 36 ff., 183 ff., 197 ff., 209, 215 ff., 250 f., 262 ff., 265 ff., 269, 270 f.

19. SCHMOLLERS JAHRBUCH FÜR GESETZGEBUNG, VERWALTUNG UND VOLKSWIRTSCHAFT appeared from 1877-1919.

20. ÜBER EINIGE GRUNDFAGEN DES RECHTS UND DER VOLKSWIRTSCHAFT, EIN OFFENES SENDSCHREIBEN AN HERRN PROFESSOR DR. HEINRICH VON TREITSCHKE (1875, being an answer to Treitschke's "Der Socialismus und seine Gönner," PREUSSISCHE JAHRBÜCHER [1874, July and September]), 49 ff., 55 ff. On p. 55, Schmoller writes: "Ihre Eigentumstheorie ist eine überwiegend individualistische; Sie gehen ausschliesslich vom Individuum und dem sittlichen Zusammenhang der Individuen in der Familie, dem Erbrecht, aus. Die Zusammenhänge der Individuen, die ausserhalb der Familienbande liegen, kommen dabei zu kurz; die Schranken und Pflichten, die hieraus folgen, die staatlichen Seiten des Eigentums als allgemeiner Rechts- und Wirtschaftsinstitution, diese verkümmern dabei." Comp. also p. 58: "Jede Behauptung also, die irgend eine neue Sitte, eine gesetzliche Reform als in das Eigentum eingreifend verwirft, steht an sich auf einem schiefen Standpunkte. Sie verwechselt das formelle Recht mit den leitenden Ideen für die Schaffung eines neuen Rechts, das einzelne Stück Eigentum mit der Eigentumsordnung. Niemals folgt aus dem Prinzip des Eigentums, dass eine schädliche oder ungerechte Eigentumsverteilung für alle Zukunft unantastbar sein müsse, dass es erworbene Rechte in dem Sinne gebe, dass sie der Gesetzgebung entzogen wären. Die Gesetzgebung ist allmächtig; ihr Direktiv ist das Prinzip der Gerechtigkeit, sie wird zu jeder Zeit beherrscht von der Art, wie das Prinzip der Gerechtigkeit in den leitenden Geistern und der öffentlichen Meinung seiner Zeit aufgefasst wird." For Schmoller's attitude toward property, see also his GRUNDRISS DER ALLGEMEINEN VOLKSWIRTSCHAFTSLEHRE

(1900), esp. 380 ff., 387 f., 389 f. Schmoller maintains that with the increasing Vergesell-schaftung, the freedom of property would not disappear. *Id.* 122. For Schmoller's attacks on the Manchester school, see *id.*, 92 f.

21. SOCIALISM (1894), 306 f.; "Competition: Its Nature, Its Permanence and Its Bene-ficence," PUBLICATIONS OF THE AMERICAN ECONOMIC ASSOCIATION, Third Series (1901), II, 55.

22. THE PREMISES OF POLITICAL ECONOMY (1885), 121 ff.

23. The essentially conservative character of the "New School" is emphasized by Joseph Dorfman, THORSTEIN VEBLEN AND HIS AMERICA (1934), 61 ff. For a general account of American developments, see that author's THE ECONOMIC MIND OF AMERICAN CIVILIZATION (1946-59), III, and Sidney Fine, LAISSEZ-FAIRE AND THE GENERAL WELFARE STATE (1956).

24. Rudolf von Jhering, DER GEIST DES RÖMISCHEN RECHTS AUF DEN VERSCHIEDENEN STUFEN SEINER ENTWICKLUNG (4th ed., 1878), 7. It is interesting to note that this quotation can not yet be found in the first edition, published in 1852, but only from the second edition of 1866 on.

25. DER ZWECK IM RECHT (3rd ed., 1893), I, 443 ff., 535, 536 ff.

26. *Id.*, 524.

27. *Id.*, 515. Comp. also DER GEIST DES RÖMISCHEN RECHTS (3rd ed., 1874), 133 ff.

28. "Alle Rechte des Privatrechts, wenn sie auch zunächst nur das Individuum zum Zwecke haben, sind beeinflusst und gebunden durch die Rücksicht auf die Gesellschaft, es gibt kein einziges, bei dem das Subjekt sagen könnte, dies habe ich ausschliesslich für mich, ich bin Herr und Meister über dasselbe, die Konsequenz des Rechtsbegriffs erfordert es, dass die Gesellschaft mich nicht beschränke." DER ZWECK IM RECHT, I, 534. Jhering tries to show that the proprietor never was permitted an unlimited power over his property on a number of Roman institutions. *Id.*, I, 525 ff. On p. 523, he writes: "Es ist also nicht wahr, dass das Eigentum šeiner 'Idee' nach die absolute Verfügungsgewalt in sich schlösse. Ein Eigentum in solcher Gestalt kann die Gesellschaft nicht dulden und hat sie nie geduldet—die 'Idee' des Eigentums kann nichts mit sich bringen, was mit der 'Idee der Gesellschaft' in Wider-spruch steht. Diese Vorstellung ist noch ein Rest jener ungesunden naturrechtlichen Vor-stellung, welche das Individuum auf sich selber isolierte. Wohin es führen müsste, wenn der Eigentümer sich auf eine unzugängliche Burg zurückziehen könnte, wird nicht des Nachweises bedürfen." For support of Jhering's thesis that under Roman law the proprietor was ex-pected to take into account the interests of the community, see Gustav Hartmann, "Rechte an eigener Sache," JHERING'S JAHRBUCH (1879), XVII, 69 ff., 124 ff., 130 f.

29. DER ZWECK IM RECHT, I, 519 ff., 534.

30. *Id.*, I, 532 f.

31. DIE SOZIALE AUFGABE DES PRIVATRECHTS (1889); DER ENTWURF EINES BÜRGERLICHEN GESETZBUCHES UND DAS DEUTSCHE RECHT (1889).

32. DIE SOZIALE AUFGABE DES PRIVATRECHTS, 17 ff., 20.

33. DER ENTWURF, etc., 1 ff., 103, 183, 323 ff.; DIE SOZIALE AUFGABE DES PRIVATRECHTS, 4 ff., 17 ff.; DEUTSCHES PRIVATRECHT (1895), I, 26 ff., esp. note 40.

34. DER ENTWURF, 103.

35. Especially in LE DROIT SOCIAL, LE DROIT INDIVIDUEL ET LA TRANSFORMATION DE L'ÉTAT (1908, 3rd ed., 1920); LES TRANSFORMATIONS GÉNÉRALES DU DROIT PRIVÉ DEPUIS LE CODE NAPOLÉON (1912, 2nd ed. 1920); LES TRANSFORMATIONS DU DROIT PUBLIC (1913).

36. TRANSFORMATIONS DU DROIT PRIVÉ, 6 f., 12 f., 14, 15 ff., 16, 18, 24 ff., 29, 176.

37. LE DROIT SOCIAL, 7, 10.

38. TRANSFORMATIONS DU DROIT PRIVÉ, 8, 25.

39. *Id.*, 15, 153, 157, 158.

40. See Edward S. Corwin, "The Higher Law Background of American Constitutional Law," HARVARD LAW REVIEW (1928-29), XLII, 149, 365.

41. As the only one of the great representatives of sociological jurisprudence who sur-vived the New Deal and the Fair Deal, Dean Pound saw to what extremes sociological jurisprudence had led. In his later years, he emphasized conservatism.

42. 198 U. S. 45, 75-76 (1905).

43. McCulloch v. Maryland, 17 U. S. (4 Wheat.), 316, 407, 515 (1819).

44. It is often overlooked that the great Chief Justice brought forth the doctrine of

implied powers (McCulloch v. Maryland) and gave the commerce clause a nationalistic interpretation (Gibbons v. Ogden, 9 Wheat. 1 [1824]), only *after* having established judicial review as an effective means for the protection of the rights of the individual (Marbury v. Madison, 1 Cranch 137 [1803]) and *after* having given the contract clause a broad interpretation for the sake of property rights (Fletcher v. Peck, 6 Cranch 87 [1810]).

45. CURRENT LITERATURE, March 1911. Quoted by Alfred Lief, ed., THE BRANDEIS GUIDE TO THE MODERN WORLD (1941), 48.

46. Whitney v. California, 274 U. S. 357, 372 (1927).

47. Address before the Chicago Bar Association of Jan. 3, 1916. Lief, *op. cit.*, 99 f.

48. Boston Globe, March 9, 1905; "Life Insurance, the Abuses and the Remedies," an address delivered before the Commercial Club of Boston, Oct. 26, 1905. Reprinted in Louis D. Brandeis, BUSINESS—A PROFESSION (2nd ed., 1925), 158.

49. DAILY EASTERN ARGUS (Portland, Maine), April 19, 1905.

50. Argument in Stettler v. O'Hara, 243 U. S. 629, Dec. 17, 1914.

51. Erik Wolf, GROSSE RECHTSDENKER DER DEUTSCHEN GEISTESGESCHICHTE (3rd ed., 1951), 624 f., 649.

52. "Das Privateigentum und das Erbrecht werden stets bestehen bleiben und die auf seine Beseitigung gerichteten sozialistischen und kommunistischen Ideen halte ich für eine eitle Torheit." DER ZWECK IM RECHT (6th–8th ed., 1923), I, 416.

53. In his NATURRECHT UND DEUTSCHES RECHT (1883), 30, Gierke states that "in der Neuzeit, römisches Recht, Naturrecht, wirtschaftlicher Liberalismus, Individualismus und Kapitalismus als Zerstörer der organischen und sozialen Überlieferung des germanischen Rechts dastehen." On the other hand, he feared that "die in den sozialistischen Lehren zum System erhobenen Gedanken, welche den Menschen ausschliesslich als Glied der Gesellschaft begreifen und werten, alles Recht mit Umbildung in eine staatliche Verwaltungsordnung bedrohen." DIE SOZIALE AUFGABE DES PRIVATRECHTS, 11.

54. *Id.*, 12.

55. Duguit, LES TRANSFORMATIONS DU DROIT PRIVÉ, 160, 165.

56. Harold J. Laski, "Mr. Justice Holmes for his Eighty-Ninth Birthday," in Felix Frankfurter, ed., MR. JUSTICE HOLMES (1931), 152 f. For Holmes' opinion on the necessity of a protection of property, see his opinion in Hudson County Water Co. v. McCarter, 209 U.S. 349, 355-56 (1908).

57. Alpheus T. Mason, BRANDEIS—A FREE MAN'S LIFE (1946), 366.

58. See his "An Economic Exhortation to Organized Labor," an address before the Boston Central Labor Union, Feb. 5, 1905. Published in CIVIL FEDERATION REVIEW, March 1905. Reported in the BOSTON GLOBE, Feb. 6, 1905.

59. DAILY EASTERN ARGUS (Portland, Maine), April 19, 1905. Comp. also his address before the Economic Club of Providence, R. I., in which Brandeis saw trade unions as a force tending "toward conservatism." (Reported in PROVIDENCE NEWS AND PROVIDENCE EVENING BULLETIN, April 11, 1905).

60. "The greatest factors making for communism, socialism, or anarchy among a free people, are the excesses of capital." (BOSTON GLOBE, March 5, 1905); "In my opinion the extension of functions of the State to life insurance is at the present time highly undesirable. Our government does not grapple successfully with the duties which it has assumed, and should not extend its operations at least until it does. But whatever and however strong our convictions against the extension of governmental functions may be, we shall inevitably be swept farther toward socialism unless we curb the excesses of our financial magnates." In "Life Insurance, the Abuses and Remedies," *loc. cit.*, 158, Brandeis denounced insurance leaders as "the most dangerous of socialists and anarchists, because true conservatism necessarily involves progress." Quoted by Alpheus T. Mason, *op. cit.*, 167. Before the Committee on Interstate Commerce, Brandeis stated that "socialism has been developed largely by the power of individual trusts." HEARINGS BEFORE THE COMMITTEE ON INTERSTATE COMMERCE (1911), U.S. Senate, 62nd Congress, Sen. Res. 98, p. 1258.

61. Among American advocates of the social gospel, for instance, were also men like George Herron and William Dwight Bliss who were to the left of Peabody, Behrends, Abbott and Gladden. See Hofstadter, *op. cit.*, 90 ff. In England, the Anglo-Catholic move-

ment at the beginning of this century was further to the left than had been the Christian socialism of Ludlow and Maurice. Reckitt, *op. cit.*, 451. Friedrich Naumann was so far to the left from Stoecker that the latter advised him to restrain himself to emphasizing the evangelic element in the "evangelical-social." Among the socialists of the chair, Lujo Brentano was considerably to the right of the *Staatssozialist* Adolph Wagner.

62. Comp. the opinion of the two justices in Pennsylvania Coal Co. v. Mahon, 260 U.S. 393 (1922).

63. Letter to his brother of Aug. 19, 1909, after Governor Draper of Massachusetts had signed the holding company bill in accordance with the wishes of the New Haven railroad. Alpheus T. Mason, *op. cit.*, 198.

64. Ambroise Colin, in his introduction to Henri Pascaud, LE CODE CIVIL ET LES RÉFORMES QU'IL COMPORTE (1906), where he advocated a reform of the Napoleonic Code by a "legislation sociale," (vii), suggests that the French reform should take into account the reforms in other countries, maintaining that a "cosmopolitanisme juridique" is inevitable. As far as the jurists' new appreciation of property is concerned, such a "juridical cosmopolitanism" can indeed be said to exist.

65. "Le droit de propriété doit avoir pour mesure la satisfaction d'une intérêt sérieux et légitime," and "les principes de la morale et de l'équité s'opposent à ce que la justice sanctionne une action inspirée par la malveillance, accomplie sous l'empire d'une mauvaise passion, ne se jusifiant par aucune utilité personelle et portant un grave préjudice à autrui," the court said. Colmar May 2, 1855, D. P. 1856, 2.9.

66. Kurt Rudolph, DIE BINDUNGEN DES EIGENTUMS (1960), 78. After the decision of Colmar, French courts stigmatized "l'envie de nuire" (Lyon, April 18, 1856. D. 56, 2, 200), "les manoeuvres vexatoires pratiquées avec cette intention manifeste" (Paris, Dec. 3, 1871, D. 73, 2, 185), "la malice et l'intention usurpatrice" (Montpellier, July 16, 1866, S. 67, 2, 115), "l'entreprise faite par haine et par malice sans intérêt pour celui qui se la permet" (Civ. June 8, 1857, S. 58, 1, 305).

67. For an extensive interpretation of *abus de droit*, see Ambroise Colin, Henri Capitant and Léon Juillio de La Morandière, COURS ÉLÉMENTAIRE DE DROIT CIVIL FRANÇAIS (18th ed., 1942-50), I, 794 ff. For a criticism of extreme theories of *abus de droit*, see Georges Ripert, LE RÉGIME DÉMOCRATIQUE ET LE DROIT CIVIL MODERNE (2nd ed., 1948), 209 ff.; Marcel Planiol/Georges Ripert, TRAITÉ PRATIQUE DE DROIT CIVIL FRANÇAIS (2nd ed., 1952-57), III, 462, states on the courts' attitude toward *abus de droit*: ". . . la jurisprudence en a sagement limité l'application. Pour elle, abuser de son droit c'est l'exercer dans l'intention de nuire à autrui sans utilité pour soi-même, ou, à la rigueur, l'exercer sans motif sérieux et légitime." For a narrow interpretation of *abus de droit,* see Louis Josserand, DE L'ABUS DES DROITS (1905), 43 ff.

68. They made reference to the saying, qui iure suo utitur, neminem laedit. The abuse of that proverb is attacked by Leo Pininski, BEGRIFF UND GRENZEN DES EIGENTUMSRECHTS NACH RÖMISCHEM RECHT (1902), 114 ff.; Stanislaus Dnistrjanskyi, "Zur Grundlegung des modernen Privatrechts," JHERINGS JAHRBÜCHER (1930), LXXX, 220.

69. Peter, *op. cit.*, 97, referring to Windscheid/Kipp, *op. cit.*, I, 602, esp. note 3.

70. See Achilles, Spahn, Gebhard, editors, PROTOKOLLE DER KOMMISSION FÜR DIE ZWEITE LESUNG DES ENTWURFES EINES BÜRGERLICHEN GESETZBUCHES (1897-99), I, 238 ff. Comp. Sec. 226 BGB.

71. Rideout v. Knox, 148 Mass. 368; 19 N.E. 390 (1889).

72. Bordeaux v. Greene, 22 Mont. 254; 56 Pac. 218 (1899).

73. William J. Grange, REAL ESTATE (1937), 319.

74. Rideout v. Knox, 19 N.E. 390, 391, 392 (1889).

75. William L. Prosser, HANDBOOK OF THE LAW OF TORTS (1941), 32. On p. 33, this work contains an enumeration of state laws against spite fences and spite walls.

76. The first decision was that rendered by the Tribunal de la Seine of Aug. 22, 1840, S. 44, 1, 811. Later, the courts made no distinction as to the originator of the damage done to the neighbor, and restricted the baker who bothered his neighbor with his nightwork (Orléans, Nov. 22, 1889, D. 91, 2, 120), and the breeder of pigs and fowl (Trib. civ. de Tours, March 25, 1904, D. 1905, 2, 199; Req. Dec. 5, 1904, D. 1905, 1, 77), and the owner

of a coal depot (Req. April 19, 1905, 1, 256), and the big industrialist. Similarly, the owner of a theater was restricted "à raison des dommages résultant du bruit nocturne, des allées et venues des piétons et des voitures, des dangers plus considérable d'incendie" (Req. April 24, 1865, D. 66, 1, 35 S. 66, 1, 402; Bordeaux, March 21, 1867, D. 69, 2, 159; Marseilles, March 10, 1905, S. 1905, 2, 149), as well as the owner of a hospital with inmates suffering from tuberculosis, most of whom were incurably ill (Limoges, Feb. 5, 1902, *La Loi,* April 29, 1902), as well as the owner of a school whose students by their noise bothered a neighboring hotel. (Paris, Dec. 9, 1904, D. 1905, 2, 32, S. 1905, 2, 175).

77. See Farge, LE VOISINAGE INDUSTRIEL (Diss. Grenoble, 1924); Leyat, LA RESPONSABILITÉ DANS LES RAPPORTS DE VOISINAGES (Diss. Toulouse, 1935).

78. Windscheid/Kipp, PANDEKTEN, I, 863; Heinrich Dernburg, PANDEKTEN (6th ed., 1900), 77.

79. Already in 1883, the *Reichsgericht* had assumed that under Sec. 906 there existed a "Pflicht zur gegenseitigen Rücksichtnahme" among neighbors (RGZ. 11, 341, 343). In a decision of March 10, 1937, that court stated that in the case of locally customary, but dangerous immissions it was necessary "im Einzelfall den gerechten Ausgleich zu finden" (RGZ. 154, 161, 165 f.). In decisions of June 16, 1937 (RGZ. 155, 154, 159), and April 21, 1941 (RGZ. 167, 14, 24), the court adopted the policy of applying the general principle of good faith *(Treu und Glauben)* for the consideration of the relationship among neighbors. This, of course, gave broadest protection to the interests of the neighbor and correspondingly restricted the rights of the proprietor. The decisions, rendered during the Third Reich, are a demonstration of the nazis' antagonism against the liberal, individualistic conception of property.

80. Martin Wolff and Ludwig Raiser, SACHENRECHT (10th ed., 1957), 182. Decision of the Bundesgerichtshof, 6. Zivilsenat, of April 14, 1954, in Fritz Lindenmaier/Möhring, NACH-SCHLAGEWERK DES BUNDESGERICHTSHOFS (1951), No. 1 to sec. 906 BGB.

81. It is interesting to note that the other modern code in the German-speaking world, the Swiss Civil Code of 1907 (ZGB), goes even further in restricting the proprietor's rights for the sake of good neighborhood. It prohibits "alle übermässigen Einwirkungen auf das Eigentum des Nachbarn" (Art. 684). These "Einwirkungen" were interpreted to mean not only material immissions such as smoke, dust, odor or noise, but also so-called immaterial immissions, as they exist, for instance, when a hospital with incurably ill inmates is located in the proximity of a residential area. (BGE 42 II 446 ff.) For further examples of Swiss adjudication, see Robert Haab, KOMMENTAR ZUM SACHENRECHT DES SCHWEIZERISCHEN ZIVILGESETZBUCHS (1929-37), Nos. 9 and 13 on Art. 684 ZBG. For the different German practice, see Martin Wolff, DAS SACHENRECHT (9th ed., 1932), 164.

82. LE RÉGIME DÉMOCRATIQUE ET LE DROIT CIVIL MODERNE.

83. Lambert brought forth his suggestions for socialization in various prefaces he wrote for studies that were published by his Institute for Comparative Law in Lyon.

84. LE SOCIALISME JURIDIQUE (1928). Comp. also his LES FONDEMENTS DU DROIT (1934); LA VISION SOCIALISTE DU DROIT (1926). Lévy had many followers. De Monzie wrote of him: "Il aurait dû être un des guides de notre temps." (Quoted by Dolléans, PRÉFACE DE LE DROIT [n.d.], 17). H. M. de Mann stated of Lévy: "Il est de ceux dont la pensée et le sentiment préfigurent demain." Quoted by Lévy, LE DROIT (1934), 34.

85. SACHENRECHT (1924), esp. 52 ff.

86. Esp. Hans Fehr. He went further than Hedemann in his advocacy of a germanistic (more social) interpretation and evaluation of property. RECHT UND WIRKLICHKEIT (1928), esp. 92 ff.

87. Richard T. Ely, PROPERTY AND CONTRACT IN THEIR RELATIONS TO THE DISTRIBUTION OF WEALTH (1914), I, 144.

88. Morris R. Cohen, LAW AND THE SOCIAL ORDER (1933), 59.

89. See Rudolph, *op. cit.,* 95 ff.

90. *Id.,* 55 ff., 58 ff., 83 ff., 113 ff., 101 ff.

91. For a comparative survey, see the two volumes published on the occasion of its fiftieth anniversary by the Société de législation comparée, LES TRANSFORMATIONS DU DROIT DANS LES PRINCIPAUX PAYS DEPUIS CINQUANTE ANS (1869-1919) (1922-23).

92. Characteristically, the study on legislative development from 1869 to 1919, mentioned in the preceding note, starts out with an essay by Maurice Dufourmantelle, "La législation sociale en France," which is followed by Henri Capitant's "Les transformations du droit civil français depuis cinquante ans."

93. See Edwin E. Witte, "Labor Legislation," ENCYCLOPAEDIA OF THE SOCIAL SCIENCES, VIII, 658.

94. For the thesis that these features were not as bad as they might have appeared, see W. H. Hutt, "The Factory System of the Early Nineteenth Century," in F. A. Hayek, ed., CAPITALISM AND THE HISTORIANS (1954), 160.

95. Hammer v. Dagenhart, 247 U.S. 251 (1918); Bailey v. Drexel Furniture Company, 259 U.S. 20 (1922).

96. Laws of May 19, 1874, Nov. 2, 1892, March 30, 1900; *Code du Travail* of 1912. For a discussion of these laws, see Dufourmantelle, *op. cit.*, 16 ff.

97. Laws of June 17, 1913, and Aug. 5, 1917.

98. An argument advanced in favor of shorter working hours is that such hours spread the job load and secure full employment. This argument, being one of expediency merely, does, however, not constitute an excuse for infringing upon the right of the individual to work as long as he wants to, a right that might be essential for the very survival of himself and his family.

99. That desire, again, was not so much motivated by the idea of spreading the job load and of securing full employment, but, rather, by inclinations not to work too hard.

100. This term is preferred over "welfare" because it shows more clearly what welfare legislation has come to amount to.

101. See F. A. Hayek, THE CONSTITUTION OF LIBERTY (1960), 285 ff.

102. Enforced savings imply, of course, a restriction of the free use of property. However, such restrictions by which, after all, the person saving will profit in the end and by which he is not likely to be *deprived* of his property, are to be preferred over restrictions of the taxpayer's property, restrictions that actually deprive the taxpayers of their property in order that such property may be given to those that are being taken care of by the state.

103. It is realized that in many cases social security benefits given by employers constitute nothing but part of the contract between employer and employee and are thus more or less just part of wages.

104. The law of the survival of the fittest does not only apply in normal times, but also in times of emergency.

105. See Georges Ripert, LE RÉGIME DÉMOCRATIQUE, 122 ff. On p. 145, Ripert writes: "L'intervention constante des pouvoirs public dans les rapports entre les créanciers et leurs débiteurs est peut-être inspirée par l'idée généreuse de secourir les faibles, mais elle aboutit à une complaisance coupable pour les malheureaux. Cette faiblesse pour les débiteurs est source de désordre. "Il faut punir, écrivait Vauvenargues; la miséricorde rarement employée et avec jugement est une belle et singulière vertu, mais la clémence ordinaire, sans distinction et discipline, est l'entière subversion de tout ordre."

106. According to Ripert, LE RÉGIME DÉMOCRATIQUE, 123, the text of the tables permits that conclusion.

107. Imprisonment for debts was abolished by the Convention through the decree of March 9, 1793. "C'est une honte pour l'humanité, pour la philosophie, qu'un homme, en trouvant de l'argent, puisse hypothéquer et sa personne et sa sécurité. . . . Un tel emprisonnement est contraire à la saine morale, aux droits de l'homme, aux vrais principes de la liberté." (Quoted by Ripert, LE RÉGIME DÉMOCRATIQUE, 124). In spite of these aims of the Revolution, the Napoleonic Code still provided for imprisonment for debt. The French Code of Civil Procedure permitted imprisonment for debt for additional cases, and the Code of Commerce subjected all merchants to such imprisonment.

108. Ripert, LE RÉGIME DÉMOCRATIQUE, 129 ff. The situation in France is demonstrative of that in other countries.

109. When the mark was stabilized in November, 1923, one gold mark was worth one thousand billions paper mark. On the injustice of the principle "mark equals mark," see Ernst Heymann, "Schutz der Hypothekengläubiger," DEUTSCHE JURISTENZEITUNG (1923),

XXVIII, 211; Hans Fritz Abraham, "Die Gefährdung der Zivilrechtspflege," *id.*, XXVIII, 269; Richterverein beim Reichsgericht, "Ein Gesetzesentwurf nebst Begründung, betr. die Ausgleichung der Folgen wirtschaftlicher Änderungen, im besonderen der Veränderungen des Geldwertes," *id.*, XXVIII, 441; Manigk, "Geldentwertung und Zivilrechtsmethodik," *id.*, XXVIII, 532.

110. "Il faut exécuter l'auteur, et non le projet." Reported by F. Gentz, "Über die Hilfsquellen der französischen Regierung," HISTORISCHES JOURNAL (1799), III, 138. Gentz refers to progressive taxation as "nicht viel besser als eine Strassenraub."

111. "On the Complaints and Proposals Regarding Taxation," EDINBURGH REVIEW (1833), LVII, 164. Of course, the question arises whether proportional taxation is not also unfair and an unjust infringement upon property rights and the principle of equality before the law.

112. DE LA PROPRIÉTÉ (1848), 319.

113. PRINCIPLES OF POLITICAL ECONOMY (1848), II, 353.

114. "Die allerheiligsten politischen Grundsätze der Gleichheit werden sich aber untreu, wenn wir an die Frage der Progressivsteuer herangehen. Da verleugnet selbst die absolute Demokratie in Hunderttausenden von Stimmen ihre Grundsätze, wenn es sich darum handelt, den Reichen schärfer zu treffen." STENOGRAPHISCHE BERICHTE DER VERHANDLUNGEN. . . . DES PREUSSISCHEN ABGEORDNETENHAUSES (1898-99), II, 907.

115. Hayek, *op. cit.*, 311.

116. Comp. Georg Meyer, DER STAAT UND DIE WOHLERWORBENEN RECHTE (1895).

117. Gerhard Anschütz, DIE VERFASSUNG DES DEUTSCHEN REICHS VOM 11. AUGUST 1919 (13th ed., 1930), 606.

118. *Id.*, 607, 612.

119. Anschütz, *loc. cit.*, 620, was representative of the former view. Outstanding among the latter was Martin Wolff. See his "Reichsverfassung und Eigentum," BERLINER FESTGABE FÜR KAHL (1923), esp. 10 ff.

120. Hermann von Mangoldt, DAS BONNER GRUNDGESETZ (1950-53), 100.

121. *Id.*, 100 f. Mangoldt states: "Aber das Grundrecht ist nicht mehr ein rein individualistisches. Mit dem Eigentum sind die besonderen, in seinen sozialen Bindungen begründeten Grundpflichten des Abs. 2 verbunden. Diese Vorschrift kann keineswegs mehr nur als Richtschnur (so Anschütz) für oder ein Appell an den Gesetzgeber (so Schelcher) angesehen werden. Vielmehr fliessen aus ihr, wie auch schon zu Abs. 3 des Art. 153 von einigen Schriftstellern angenommen worden ist, unmittelbare Rechtspflichten. Der Eigentümer kann mit seinem Eigentum nicht mehr völlig frei "nach Belieben" verfahren (so 903 BGB.). Er hat vielmehr nach Abs. 2 Satz 2 nicht nur Rücksicht auf das Wohl der Allgemeinheit zu nehmen, sondern soll den Gebrauch so einrichten, dass er ausser seinen eigenen Interessen zugleich auch dem Wohl der Allgemeinheit dient. Zum mindesten jeder Gebrauch der diese Rechtspflicht verletzt, ist also ein Missbrauch und geniesst als solcher nicht den Schutz des Gesetzes. D. h. ein derartiger Missbrauch kann für sich nicht die Eigentumsgarantie des Art. 14 beanspruchen."

122. Art. 20 refers to it as a "sozialer Bundesstaat" and Art. 28 as a "sozialer Rechtsstaat." For the meaning of the word "social," comp. Helmut Rumpf, DER IDEOLOGISCHE GEHALT DES BONNER GRUNDGESETZES (1958), 27; Christian Friedrich Menger, ZUM BEGRIFF DES SOZIALEN RECHTSSTAATS IM BONNER GRUNDGESETZ (1953); Fechner, FREIHEIT UND ZWANG IM SOZIALEN RECHTSSTAAT (1953).

123. M. A. Lamartine, LE CONSEILLER DU PEOPLE (1849-50), I, 25.

124. Georges Vedel, MANUEL ÉLÉMENTAIRE DE DROIT CONSTITUTIONNEL (1949), 96.

125. Marcel Prélot, PRÉCIS DE DROIT CONSTITUTIONNEL (2nd ed., 1953), 333. Comp. also Jean Rivero and Georges Vedel, LES PROBLÈMES ÉCONOMIQUES ET SOCIAUX DE LA CONSTITUTION DE 27 OCTOBRE 1946 (1947).

126. The evolutionary character of English and American government is usually considered an asset. While, on the whole, one may agree with this proposition, it should not be overlooked that evolution can also be dangerous because it can bring about an undesirable situation without people being too much aware of it. Evolution, in distinction to revolution, blurs issues and conceals dangers. While a social interpretation of laws protecting property may be less dangerous to property than social legislation, it should not be over-

looked that interpretation—being of a rather evolutionary character—might be even more dangerous to property than legislation, because property rights might be gradually infringed upon with people being aware of what happens. Whereas the citizens usually have an opportunity to become acquainted with proposed legislation, they do not have such an opportunity in the case of proposed adjudication.

127. 19 Howard 393, 426 (1857).

128. See the author's "America and Europe—Decline and Emergence of Judicial Review," *loc. cit.*, 1259 ff.

CHAPTER V

1. This is stressed, in the case of the German pandectists, by Erich Molitor, "Zweckverbindungen des Eigentums," FESTSCHRIFT FÜR ALFRED SCHULTZE (1934), 33. On p. 37, note 2, Molitor writes: "Bei Licht besehen scheint die ganze Vorstellung von der grundsätzlichen Schrankenlosigkeit des Eigentums gerade darin zu bestehen, dass die Pandektendoktrin des 19. Jahrhunderts das Eigentum als das grundsätzlich unbeschränkte Recht in Gegensatz stellt zu den zu einem beschränkten Zweck begründeten sonstigen Rechten." See also Franz Wieacker, "Entwicklungsstufen des römischen Eigentums." in H. Berve, DAS NEUE BILD DER ANTIKE (1942), 157 ff. These two authors were writing during the nationalist-socialist regime under which their ideas were welcome. Therefore, they might overlook the fact that the pandectists, usually good liberals, also believed in a rather absolute protection of property rights. Molitor's and Wieacker's opinions are shared by a Swiss scholar, Hans Peter, WANDLUNGEN DER EIGENTUMSORDNUNG UND DER EIGENTUMSLEHRE SEIT DEM 19. JAHRHUNDERT (1949), 113 ff.

2. Quanto latius officiorum patet quam iuris regula? Quam multa pietas, humanitas, liberalitas, iustitia, fides exigunt, quae omnia extra publicas tabulas sunt." Seneca, DE IRA, Book 2, sec. 28. The Romans considered moral duties (officia) of the humanitas, fides, etc., as being as important for the individual as strict legal norms. Comp. Fritz Schulz, PRINZIPIEN DES RÖMISCHEN RECHTS (1934), 13 ff., 128 ff., 151 ff.; Pietro de Francisci, DER GEIST DER RÖMISCHEN KULTUR (German transl., 1941), 54 f., 68 f., 81 f., 191 ff.; Wieacker, *op. cit.*, 168 ff.

3. Whereas people who attacked the "excessive" use of property often asserted that those who made such use had acquired their property without much effort, it is here maintained that most people who became property owners in the nineteenth century did so on account of effort. In many cases they had no property to begin with and were literally starting from scratch. Often, they had to work their way up against adversity. It is scarcely surprising that these self-made men, pioneers in the best sense of the word, often would not be very meticulous in the use of their property against competitors. After all, they themselves had experienced the attempts of existing property owners to prevent their rise. This had hardened them. Having in the end come out on top, they were not likely to be very considerate toward others on their way up.

4. In the opinion of this author, an "abuse of rights" is a contradiction in terms.

5. It should not be overlooked, however, that German law was advocated by the proponents of unification not so much because it was more "social" than Roman law, but because it was more German. Advocacy of Germanic law was the result of romanticism and historicism, rather than socialism.

6. Especially in its general part, the law of family and inheritance.

7. An outstanding example of the subordination of rights of the individual to the patriotic cause is the clear and present danger rule, as announced in Schenck v. United States, 249 U.S. 47 (1919).

8. Bismarck's social legislation comes to mind. It was during the period prior to World War I that the idea of "Vater Staat" (the state as a caretaker) became more and more accepted.

9. Hobbes had argued that corporations were "like worms within the entrails of a natural man." Quoted by Harold Laski, "Freedom of Association," ENCYCLOPAEDIA OF THE SOCIAL SCIENCES, VI, 449.

10. *Id.,* 448 f.

11. Lucien Crouzil, LA LIBERTÉ D'ASSOCIATION (1907). Outstanding early advocates for the right of association were Guizot and Thiers. Tocqueville wrote: "The most natural privilege of man, next to the right of acting for himself, is that of combining his exertions with those of his fellow creatures and of acting in common with them. The right of association therefore appears to me also as unalienable in its nature as the right of personal liberty. No legislator can attack it without impairing the foundations of society." DEMOCRACY IN AMERICA (1945 ed.), I, 196.

12. Comp. Eugène Rostand in REVUE POLITIQUE ET PARLEMENTAIRE (1901), XXVIII, 259.

13. Whereas the constitutional project of April 19, 1946, guaranteed the right of association in articles 15-17, the constitution of the Fourth Republic protects it by implication in the preamble, as does the constitution of the Fifth Republic.

14. Prussian constitution of 1850, art. 29, and Prussian Vereinsgesetz of March 11, 1850; Bavarian Vereinsgesetz of Feb. 26, 1850; Vereinsgesetz of Saxony of Nov. 22, 1850. These laws, however, did not guarantee freedom of association as unequivocally as the Frankfurt constitution.

15. Articles 124 and 9, respectively.

16. Whereas associations like the Sons of Liberty and the Committees of Correspondence played an important role in the formation of the United States, constitutions were remarkably reluctant to guarantee a right of association. Freedom of assembly is guaranteed in the constitutions of North Carolina (1776), art. 18; Vermont (1777), art. 18; Pennsylvania (1776), art. 16; Massachusetts (1780), art. 19; New Hampshire (1784), art. 32. None of these constitutions, nor any other state constitution prior to 1789, guarantees freedom of association. The existence of associations is, however, mentioned in art. 6 of the constitution of Massachusetts of 1780.

17. First amendment. Similarly, state constitutions guaranteed the freedom of religious association, although that freedom cannot be as easily implied from their provisions as it can from the first amendment of the United States constitution. Comp. the constitutions of Delaware (1776), art. 29; Maryland (1776), art. 33; New Jersey (1776), art. 18, 19; Pennsylvania (1776), art. 3; Virginia (1776), sec. 16; Vermont (1777), III; Massachusetts (1780), art. 2, 3; New Hampshire (1784), art. 4-6.

18. Glenn Abernathy, THE RIGHTS OF ASSEMBLY AND ASSOCIATION (1961), 235, 173.

19. *Id.,* 180 ff.

20. De Jonge v. Oregon, 299 U.S. 353 (1937).

21. See Wieman v. Updegraff, 344 U.S. 183 (1952); Sweezy v. New Hampshire, 354 U.S. 237 (1957); N.A.A.C.P. v. Alabama, 357 U.S. 449 (1958).

22. We need think only of the pressure exercised by labor unions.

23. Comp. Abernathy, *op. cit.,* 240.

24. This is most evident in authoritarian regimes. However, even in free, so-called pluralistic societies, it can hardly be doubted that associations can be a means in the hands of the government to control individuals.

25. Comp. Tocqueville's observation on the Americans: "They cannot belong to these associations for any length of time without finding out how order is maintained amongst a large number of men, and by what contrivance they are made to advance, harmoniously and methodically, to the same object. Thus they learn to surrender their own will to that of all the rest, and to make their own exertions subordinate to the common impulse— things which it is not less necessary to know in civil than in political associations. Political associations may therefore be considered as large free schools, where all the members of the community go to learn the general theory of association." DEMOCRACY IN AMERICA (Reeve transl., 1889), II, 107. Arthur M. Schlesinger, "Biography of a Nation of Joiners," AMERICAN HISTORICAL REVIEW (1944), L, 1, writes: "At first thought it seems paradoxical that a country famed for being individualistic should provide the world's greatest example of joiners. . . . To Americans individualism has meant, not the

individual's independence of other individuals, but his and their freedom from governmental restraint. Traditionally, the people have tended to minimize collective organization as represented by the state while exercising the largest possible liberty in forming their own voluntary organizations. This conception of a political authority too weak to interfere with men's ordinary pursuits actually created the necessity for self-constituted associations to do things beyond the capacity of a single person, and by reverse effect the success of such endeavors proved a continuing argument against the growth of stronger government."

26. Dayton D. McKean, PARTY AND PRESSURE POLITICS (1949), 430, states that by the middle of this century, there existed in the U.S. some 8,000 trade associations, 30,500 associations concerned with agriculture, over 50,000 women's organizations, and about 500 professional associations. Though the figures are lower in other countries, there can be observed also an increase of associations and their membership.—See in this connection William H. Whyte, Jr., THE ORGANIZATION MAN (1956).

27. Comp. Gierke's major work, DAS DEUTSCHE GENOSSENSCHAFTSRECHT (1868-1913).

28. In Germany, for instance, there existed before 1871 only 235 joint stock companies. There were founded, between 1871 and 1880, 1,343 new ones; between 1881 and 1890, 1,681 new ones; between 1891 and 1900, 2,025 new ones. By 1925, that number had swelled to 13,010. MEYER'S KONVERSATIONSLEXIKON (1909), I, 240; DER GROSSE BROCKHAUS (1952), I, 135. In France, the average number of joint stock companies founded per year between 1856 and 1860 was 12; between 1861 and 1865, 16; between 1866 and 1870, 121; between 1871 and 1875, 202; between 1867 and 1880, 419. The number continued to grow. LA GRANDE ENCYCLOPÉDIE, XXX, 134. For the similar situation in the United States, see Adolph A. Berle and Gardiner C. Means, THE MODERN CORPORATION AND PRIVATE PROPERTY (1932).

29. DER KAMPF UMS RECHT (4th ed., 1874), esp. 24 f.

30. Comp. David C. Bayne, Mortimer M. Caplin, Frank D. Emerson, Franklin C. Latcham, "Proxy Regulation and the Rule-Making Process: The 1954 Amendments," VIRGINIA LAW REVIEW (1954), XL, 387.

31. For the assertion that the individual's "experience in various associations is virtually a guaranty of respect for the majority view," see Abernathy, op. cit., 240. Comp. also Tocqueville's statement, supra, note 25.

32. "Die Massen rücken vor." Quoted in BLÄTTER DES DEUTSCHEN THEATERS IN GÖTTINGEN (1959-60), X, 257.

33. "Auch die gegliederte Masse ist geistlos und unmenschlich. Sie kann alles zertreten, hat die Tendenz, keine Grösse zu dulden und keine Selbständigkeit, aber die Menschen zu züchten, dass sie zu Ameisen werden." Karl Jaspers, DIE GEISTIGE SITUATION DER ZEIT (1931), 37. This work contains an incisive analysis of the masses.

34. Comp. Hamilton's statement that the inequality of property constitutes "the great and fundamental distinction in society." Henry Cabot Lodge, ed., THE WORKS OF ALEXANDER HAMILTON (1904), I, 410.

35. Jaspers, op. cit., 37.

36. Friedrich Schiller, "Was ist die Mehrheit? Mehrheit ist der Unsinn! Verstand ist stets bei Wenigen nur gewesen!" Quoted in BLÄTTER DES DEUTSCHEN THEATERS IN GÖTTINGEN (1959-61), X, 257.

37. The argument of the Declaration is not that the colonists are the natural equals of other people, but that they were denied equality in the enjoyment of freedom, that they were denied the *rights* other people had. Although the Declaration avoids a reference to the "rights of Englishmen," this is probably due to expediency: "Being now committed to independence, the position of the colonies could not be simply or convincingly presented from the point of view of the rights of British subjects." (Carl L. Becker, op. cit., 21.) It would be strange indeed if the framers of the Declaration would not have thought of the rights of Englishmen, rights that had been in the foreground throughout the struggle between the colonies and the mother country.

38. Jefferson strongly denounced egalitarian tendencies in his "Notes on Virginia." He admitted that his idea of equality was compatible with the inequality that was due to legal office, i.e., to talent and virtue. (Letter to De Meusnier of 1786. WRITINGS (Mem. ed.),

XVII, 88). Even after his return from France, Jefferson believed that equality meant equality before the law only. In his First Inaugural Address, while calling it a "sacred principle" that the will of the majority should prevail, he emphasized that that will, to be rightful, must be reasonable, saying that "the minority possess their equal rights, which equal laws must protect, and to violate would be oppression." WRITINGS (Ford ed.), VIII, 2. Had Jefferson believed in natural equality, he could hardly have advocated a "natural aristocracy," based upon "virtue and talents." (Letter to John Adams of Oct. 28, 1814. *Id.* IX, 425 ff.)

39. Emphasis supplied.

40. The decline of the House of Lords, which could be expected ever since the Reform Act was passed in 1832, came about only with the Parliament Act of 1911.

41. The inscription on the Supreme Court building is, significantly, 'Equal Justice Under Law.' For the problems arising from that inscription, see Dietze, "America and Europe— Decline and Emergence of Judicial Review," *loc. cit.*, 1270.

42. See Maurice Deslandres, HISTOIRE CONSTITUTIONELLE DE LA FRANCE DE 1789 À 1870 (1932), I, 49 ff., 191 ff., 345 ff.; Robert K. Gooch, "France," in Shotwell, ed., GOVERNMENTS OF MODERN EUROPE (Rev. ed., 1952), 41 ff., 47 ff., 59 f.

43. The original constitution with its bill of rights had for its premise not only the natural inequality of men, but their legal inequality. The latter idea was only abolished during the Civil War.

44. The term "classic" is often used by continental authors. It expresses the original conception of democracy as a means for the protection of the individual, and has largely the meaning of "good." Unlimited or absolute democracy would then be a "bad," or "degenerated" democracy.

45. This statement was made by Chancellor James Kent. REPORTS OF THE PROCEEDINGS AND DEBATES OF THE CONVENTION OF 1821, ASSEMBLED FOR THE PURPOSE OF AMENDING THE CONSTITUTION OF THE STATE OF NEW YORK (1821), 222.

46. DE L'ESPRIT DES LOIS, Book 5, ch. 3.

47. "L'égalité est tout autre chose qu'une belle et stérile fiction de la loi." MANIFESTE DES ÉGAUX (1796).

48. Louis Auguste Paul Rougier, LA MYSTIQUE DÉMOCRATIQUE, SES ORIGINES, SES ILLUSIONS (1929), 80.

49. Hegel only said, "Die Massen rücken vor." Ortega y Gasset already speaks of "the revolt of the masses." *loc. cit.*

50. For a comparative description, see Georg Meyer, DAS PARLAMENTARISCHE WAHLRECHT (1901).

51. Book 11, ch. 6.

52. Which does not mean that other qualifications would not have existed. Thus minors were considered as "mean" and as having no will of their own, and so were women. As in the case of property qualifications, the tendency has been to broaden the suffrage by reducing age requirements and by extending the right to vote to women. With the abolition of property qualifications, more and more questions were opened about unfitness among men in general, and it was felt useful to introduce educational qualifications.

53. W. J. Shepard, "Suffrage," ENCYCLOPAEDIA OF THE SOCIAL SCIENCES, XIII, 448.

54. Comp. the article "Suffrage," in LA GRANDE ENCYCLOPÉDIE, XXX, 660.

55. For the expansion of the right to vote in France, see Meyer, *op. cit.*, 42 ff., 84 ff., 159 ff.; Lucien Delabrousse, "Cens," LA GRANDE ENCYCLOPÉDIE, IX, 1110 ff.

56. Meyer, DAS PARLAMENTARISCHE WAHLRECHT, 106 ff., 174 ff.

57. In his Easter Message of 1917, the King of Prussia proclaimed that the Dreiklassenwahlrecht would be abolished. However, the actual abolition came only with the revolution of 1918.

58. See, on the whole, Kirk H. Porter, A HISTORY OF SUFFRAGE IN THE UNITED STATES (1918).

59. 2nd ed., 1891, I, 464 f.

60. Comp. Ripert, LE RÉGIME DÉMOCRATIQUE, 83 ff. Ripert begins his discussion of equality

with the statement, "Une démocratie ne peut pas ne pas être égalitaire." He quotes Francesco Nitti, LA DÉMOCRATIE (1933), I, 31, saying, "la démocratie moderne est complètement, jalousement égalitaire."

61. Shepard, *op. cit.*, 449.

62. Significantly, the French declaration of 1789 is called the Declaration of the Rights of Man and Citizen, expressing the close connection between the rights of man and the rights of the citizen.

63. "Nos lois ne seront que le Code de la Nature . . . La nature est le seul oracle que nous ayons interrogé." (Rapport à la Convention, 23 Fructidor, An II.) Berlier declared in the Convention: "Le grand livre de la Raison s'ouvre et se développe à nos yeux. C'est à cette source pure que nous devons puiser." Quoted in Van Kan, LES EFFORTS DE LA CODIFICATION EN FRANCE, 366.

64. "Il existe un droit universel et immutable source de toutes les lois positives; il n'est que la raison naturelle." Comp. the statement by Portalis: "Le droit civil participe en quelque sorte par l'observance commune de quelques règles principales à l'universalité du droit naturel." Quoted by Ripert, LE RÉGIME DÉMOCRATIQUE, 45.

65. Ripert, LA RÈGLE MORALE DANS LES OBLIGATIONS CIVILES (3rd ed., 1935), 15. See also Julien Bonnecase, LA THÉMIS (2nd ed., 1914), 69. LA NOTION DE DROIT EN FRANCE AU XIXe SIÈCLE (1919), 48.

66. Ripert, LA RÈGLE MORALE DANS LES OBLIGATIONS CIVILES, 15, writes that throughout the nineteenth century the doctrine of natural law "s'affirme à la tribune parlementaire, et au barreau, dans les mercuriales des magistrats, dans les discours officiels." Bonnecase, LA NOTION DU DROIT, 54, note 1, lists these discourses. In 1848, the Académie des Sciences Morales proclaimed the doctrine of natural law as a doctrine of the French state. General Cavaignac appealed to the Academy to publish a series of studies on natural law. The first of these studies was Victor Cousin, JUSTICE ET CHARITÉ (1848); the most famous one, Thiers's LA PROPRIÉTÉ (1848).

67. See Mohl's STAATSRECHT DES KÖNIGREICHS WÜRTTEMBERG (1829-31); DIE POLIZEI-WISSENSCHAFT NACH DEN GRUNDSÄTZEN DES RECHTSSTAATES (1832); GESCHICHTE UND LITERATUR DER STAATSWISSENSCHAFTEN (1855-58). Mohl wrote also DAS BUNDESSTAATSRECHT DER VEREINIGTEN STAATEN VON NORDAMERIKA (1824), which earned him a good reputation in the United States. See AMERICAN JURIST (1835), XIV, 330. Significantly J. F. Stahl was the leading conservative *Staatsrechtler* of his time. Stahl's well-known definition of the Rechtsstaat can be found in his DIE STAATSLEHRE UND DIE PRINZIPIEN DES STAATSRECHTS (3rd ed., 1856), 137.

68. Carl Schmitt, DIE LAGE DER EUROPÄISCHEN RECHTSWISSENSCHAFT (1950), 25, writes: " 'Rechtsstaat' ist eine deutsche Prägung des 19. Jahrhunderts und liegt kurz vor 1848, also in dem kritischen Punkt der Aufspaltung des unproblematischen Rechts in Legalität und Legitimität."

69. Comp. Walter Jellinek, VERWALTUNGSRECHT (3rd ed., 1931), sec. 5; Carl Schmitt, "Was bedeutet der Streit um den 'Rechtsstaat'?" ZEITSCHRIFT FÜR DIE GESAMTE STAATS-WISSENSCHAFT (1935), XCV, 189. The change in the meaning of the term *Rechtsstaat* can even be seen in the writings of von Mohl. In the first edition of DIE POLIZEI-WISSENSCHAFT NACH DEN GRUNDSÄTZEN DES RECHTSSTAATES, published in 1832, von Mohl emphasizes the negative character of the *Rechtsstaat*. He maintains that the *Rechtsstaat* was based upon the idea that "the freedom of the citizen is . . . the supreme principle" (I, 7), and that the *Rechtsstaat* had the sole purpose of securing the greatest possible freedom for the individual (I, 6 ff., 8 ff., 14 ff.). The third, "considerably revised," edition, published in 1866, shows "essential changes in the fundamental beliefs" (I, ix) of the author. Less emphasis is put upon the negative character of the *Rechtsstaat*. We miss a statement that the freedom of the individual is the supreme principle. A more positive role of the state to secure the well-being of society is indicated (I, 3-19). Lorenz von Stein, DIE VERWALTUNGSLEHRE (2nd ed., 1869), I, 296 ff., stresses that the *Rechtsstaat* is a German rather than a liberal institution. He writes that it is no longer necessary to emphasize that the *Rechtsstaat* is based upon a contract which guarantees the rights of the individual, since these rights are protected

by the *Gesetze* (297). For von Stein, a *Rechtsstaat* is "das System von Rechtsgrundsätzen und Rechtsmitteln, durch welche die Regierung zur *Innehaltung des gesetzlichen Rechts* in ihren Verordnungen und conkreten Thätigkeiten gezwungen werden soll" (298). Rudolf Gneist, DER RECHTSSTAAT (1872), 180 ff:, denies that the *Rechtsstaat* is something negative, a *Juristenstaat* under which the citizens can be exclusively concerned with pursuing their professional aims and their pleasures. While Gneist recognizes the danger inherent in changing legislative bodies, he proposes a permanent organ of *Gesetzgebung*. He advocates a *Rechtsstaat* that is based upon the requirements of the present society, a government according to the laws. (*"Rechtsstaat auf dem Boden der heutigen Gesellschaft,"* . . . "eine Regierung nach Gesetzen.") (182).

70. James Goldschmidt, "Gesetzesdämmerung," JURISTISCHE WOCHENSCHRIFT (1924), LIII, 245, complained that the state of emergency laws (Gesetze) had developed into a state of the emergency of the law (Recht). Marschall von Bieberstein published a book, VOM KAMPF DES RECHTES GEGEN DIE GESETZE (1927).

71. Jacob Burckhardt, WELTGESCHICHTLICHE BETRACHTUNGEN (Kröner ed.), 97.

72. Romano Guardini, DIE MACHT (1951), 19.

73. It is interesting to note that, on the whole, the "generosity" of the people in making laws was about in proportion to the generosity of the government to broaden the suffrage.

74. Schmitt, DIE LAGE DER EUROPÄISCHEN RECHTSWISSENSCHAFT, 20, writes: "Man hat von der Verordnung gesagt, sie sei das 'motorisierte Gesetz'. . . . Wie die Verordnung ein 'motorisiertes Gesetz,' so konnte die Anordnung eine 'motorisierte Verordnung' genannt werden. Hier hört der Spielraum einer selbständigen, rein gesetzespositivistischen Rechtswissenschaft von selber auf. Das Gesetz verwandelt sich in ein Mittel der Planung, der Verwaltungsakt in einen Lenkungsakt." Comp. also Georg Daskalakis, DAS GESETZ ALS MITTEL DER PLANUNG (1938.)

75. See Schmitt, DIE LAGE DER EUROPÄISCHEN RECHTSWISSENSCHAFT, 18 ff.

76. Modern Library ed., 406.

77. VOM BERUF UNSERER ZEIT FÜR GESETZGEBUNG UND RECHTSWISSENSCHAFT (1814), and "Stimmen für und wider neue Gesetzbücher," ZEITSCHRIFT FÜR GESCHICHTLICHE RECHTSWISSENSCHAFT, No. 1 (1816).

78. HISTORISCHE FRAGMENTE (1942 ed.), 205.

79. PRINCIPES DE DROIT PUBLIC (1916), xi.

80. To complete the statement by Burckhardt just referred to: "The decisively new thing that was introduced by the French Revolution. . . . is the possibility of and the desire for changes for the public weal."

81. Ripert, LE DÉCLIN DU DROIT (1949); F. A. Hayek, THE CONSTITUTION OF LIBERTY (1960), 234.

82. Book 26, ch. 15.

83. "Discours préliminaire sur le projet de Code Civil," in DISCOURS, RAPPORTS ET TRAVAUX INÉDITES SUR LE CODE CIVIL (1844), 3.

84. Ripert, LE DÉCLIN DU DROIT, 44.

85. Comp. G. D. H. Cole, "Socialization," ENCYCLOPAEDIA OF THE SOCIAL SCIENCES, XIV, 221.

86. See Jaspers, *op. cit.;* Ortega y Gasset, *op. cit.*

87. Georg Jellinek, *loc. cit.*

88. Ripert, LE DÉCLIN DU DROIT, 192.

89. Joseph Barthélemy, LE PROBLÈME DE LA COMPÉTENCE DANS LA DÉMOCRATIE (1918), 251: "Une attraction profonde, mystérieuse, irrésistible, puissante et fatale comme une force de la nature, entraîne le peuple vers la démocratie. On est libre de critiquer le mouvement démocratique, mais il faut se rendre compte que c'est une oeuvre aussi vaine que de critiquer le cours des saisons ou l'attraction des astres."

90. Ripert, LE RÉGIME DÉMOCRATIQUE, 45.

91. Jean Lerminier, PHILOSOPHIE DU DROIT (1831, 3rd ed., 1853); Theodore Jouffroy, COURS DE DROIT NATUREL (1833, 5th ed., 1876); William Belime, PHILOSOPHIE DU DROIT (1843, 4th ed., 1881); Julien Oudot, PREMIERS ESSAIS DE PHILOSOPHIE DU DROIT ET D'ENSEIGNEMENT

MÉTHODIQUE DES LOIS FRANÇAISES (1846); Alfred Jourdan, LE DROIT FRANÇAIS (1875); Charles Beudant, LE DROIT INDIVIDUEL ET L'ÉTAT (2nd ed., 1891, 3rd ed., 1920); Glasson, ÉLÉMENTS DE DROIT FRANÇAIS (1875, 2nd ed., 1880).

92. Quotations from Ripert, LE RÉGIME DÉMOCRATIQUE, 45 f.

93. The *Ecole de l'Exégèse* was sceptical of judges, fearing that they might by way of interpretation alter the will of the legislator or the will of the people. It is interesting to note that the most emphatic advocates of a most narrow interpretation of the codes, Huc in France and Laurent in Belgium, were those among the jurists who believed most unequivocally in democracy. Comp. Bonnecase, PROBLÈME DU DROIT ET SCIENCE BELGE DU DROIT CIVIL (1931).

94. Joseph Charmont, LA RENAISSANCE DU DROIT NATUREL (1910). See also that author's LE DROIT ET L'ESPRIT DÉMOCRATIQUE (1908).

95. Ripert, LE RÉGIME DÉMOCRATIQUE, 47 f. Ripert even voices doubts about the sincerity of most jurists advocating natural law. Catholic defenders of natural law were in his opinion the only sincere advocates of that law. Among them were Tancrède Rothe, TRAITÉ DE DROIT NATUREL THÉORIQUE ET APPLIQUÉ (1885-1904); De Vareilles-Sommières, LES PRINCIPES FONDAMENTAUX DU DROIT (1889), Alphonse Boistel, COURS DE PHILOSOPHIE DU DROIT (1899).

96. See L'OEUVRE JURIDIQUE DE R. SALEILLES (1925).

97. Comp. Eugène Gaudemet, "L'oeuvre de Saleilles et l'oeuvre de Gény," RECUEIL JUBILAIRE GÉNY, II, 7.

98. Raymond Saleilles, "Ecole historique et droit naturel," REVUE TRIMESTRALE (1912), 80.

99. Ripert, LE RÉGIME DÉMOCRATIQUE, 57, writes: "Si on veut être classé parmi les hommes de progrès, il faut répéter sans cesse que le droit doit devenir social!" He states that "dans les thèses de doctorat soutenues dans ces toutes dernières années on trouvera incessamment répétée cette formule."

100. ÜBER DIE NOTWENDIGKEIT EINES ALLGEMEINEN BÜRGERLICHEN RECHTS FÜR DEUTSCHLAND (1814).

101. DIE WERTLOSIGKEIT DER JURISPRUDENZ ALS WISSENSCHAFT (1847), published by Gottfried Neesse (1938).

102. Kirchmann actually said: "Drei berichtigende Worte des Gesetzgebers und ganze Bibliotheken werden zu Makulatur." "Das positive Gesetz macht den Juristen zum Wurm im faulen Holz."

103. Quoted by Schmitt, DIE LAGE DER EUROPÄISCHEN RECHTSWISSENSCHAFT, 14.

104. DIE LEHRE VOM RICHTIGEN RECHTE (1902).

105. In his JURISPRUDENZ UND RECHTSWISSENSCHAFT (1892), Bergbohm stated that "from the point of view of juridical positivism every law, even the most base legal norm, must be recognized as binding, as long as it came about in the prescribed form."

106. HAUPTPROBLEME DER STAATSRECHTSLEHRE (1923); ALLGEMEINE STAATSLEHRE (1924), DIE PHILOSOPHISCHEN GRUNDLAGEN DER NATURRECHTSLEHRE UND DES RECHTSPOSITIVISMUS (1928).

107. HAUPTPROBLEME DER STAATSRECHTSLEHRE, 249. In a way, this statement backfired. Kelsen was one of the first victims of the Hitler regime, a regime that had come to power quite legally under the Weimar constitution, and did make ample and cruel use of the positivism that had been developed by the jurists under the Empire and the Weimar Republic.

108. Eric Voegelin, "Kelsen's Pure Theory of Law," POLITICAL SCIENCE QUARTERLY (1927), XLII, 268.

109. In "Law in Science and Science in Law" (1884), COLLECTED LEGAL PAPERS (1920), 225, Holmes stated that "everyone instinctively recognizes that in these days the justification of a law for us cannot be found in the fact that our fathers always have followed it." In 1897, he stated: "It is revolting to have no better reason for a rule of law than that so it was laid down in the time of Henry IV. It is still more revolting if the grounds upon which it was laid down have vanished long since, and the rule simply persists from blind imitation of the past." "The Path of the Law," *id.*, 187.

110. THE COMMON LAW (1881), 41; "Law in Science and Science in Law," *loc. cit.*, 225.

111. F. A. Hayek, *op. cit.*, 246.

112. A GOVERNMENT OF LAWS OR A GOVERNMENT OF MEN (1929), 37, 18.

113. LAW AND THE MODERN MIND (1930).

114. Thurman Arnold, "Judge Jerome Frank," UNIVERSITY OF CHICAGO LAW REVIEW (1957), XXIV, 635, writes that *"Law and the Modern Mind . . .* was a tremendously effective work. More than any other it cleared the way for a new set of conceptions and ideals with respect to the relationship of the citizens to his government."

115. Quoted by Hayek, *op. cit.*, 247.

116. See Dietze, "Judicial Review in Europe," MICHIGAN LAW REVIEW (1957), LV, 548 ff.

117. Comp. the statements of Justice Patterson in Van Horne's Lessee v. Dorrance, 2 Dall 304, 310 (1795); of Justice Chase in Calder v. Bull, 3 Dall. 386, 387, 388, 389 (1798); of Justice Story in Terrett v. Taylor, 19 Cranch 43, 51, 52 (1815), and in Wilkinson v. Leland, 2 Pet. 627, 657, 658 (1829); Justice Miller in Loan Association v. Topeka, 87 U.S. 655, 663, 664 (1874); Justice Brown in Holden v. Hardy, 169 U.S. 115, 122 (1915).

118. THE FEDERALIST, essay 78 (Modern Library ed.), 503, 505.

119. To John Dickinson on Dec. 19, 1801. WRITINGS (Mem. ed.), X, 302.

120. See Dietze, "America and Europe—Decline and Emergence of Judicial Review," *loc. cit.*, 1243 ff., 1262.

121. LE GOUVERNEMENT DES JUGES ET LA LUTTE CONTRE LA LÉGISLATION SOCIALE AUX ÉTATS-UNIS (1921). Frank used the term "cult of the Robe" as a title of an article in THE SATURDAY REVIEW OF LITERATURE of Oct. 13, 1945, p. 12.

122. "Law and the Court," COLLECTED LEGAL PAPERS, 295 f.

123. See Haines, "Political Theories of the Supreme Court from 1789-1835," AMERICAN POLITICAL SCIENCE REVIEW (1908), II, 221; THE CONFLICT OVER JUDICIAL POWERS (1909); "Judicial Criticism of Legislation by Courts," MICHIGAN LAW REVIEW (1912), XI, 26; THE AMERICAN DOCTRINE OF JUDICIAL SUPREMACY (1914). Frank, "The Cult of the Robe," *loc. cit.*, 192.

124. Comp. Madison statement, quoted *supra*, p. 152. In essay 27 (Modern Library ed.), 167, Hamilton makes a similar statement. In essay 85, *id.*, 568, Hamilton complains of "those practices . . . which have planted mutual distrust in the breasts of all classes of citizens, and have occasioned an almost universal prostration of morals."

125. See Peter, *op. cit.*, 73 ff.; Ripert, LE RÉGIME DÉMOCRATIQUE, 230 ff.

126. See Dietze, "America and Europe—Decline and Emergence of Judicial Review," *loc. cit.*, 1265 f.

127. Ripert, LE RÉGIME DÉMOCRATIQUE, 43 ff.

128. Maxime Leroy, LA LOI, ESSAI SUR LA THÉORIE DE L'AUTORITÉ DANS LA DÉMOCRATIE (1908), 51.

129. Ripert, LE RÉGIME DÉMOCRATIQUE, 33.

130. "Recht ist, was dem Volke nutzt," was the principle of national-socialist justice.

131. DE L'ESPRIT DES LOIS, Book 5, ch. 3.

132. Quoted by Ripert, LE RÉGIME DÉMOCRATIQUE, 83.

CHAPTER VI

1. See Dietze, "The Disregard for Property in International Law," NORTHWESTERN UNIVERSITY LAW REVIEW (1961), LVI, 96 ff.

2. CONTRAT SOCIAL (1762 ed.), 12. Portalis expressed a similar idea at the first sitting of the Conseil des Prises. See Latifi, EFFECTS OF WAR ON PROPERTY (1909), 5. These opinions do not imply that no infringements upon private property occurred at that time. One of the most flagrant cases was the deprivation of thousands of American loyalists of their property through the Treaty of Paris of 1783.

3. Dietze, "The Disregard for Property in International Law," *loc. cit.*, 96.

4. Comp. Alfredo B. Cuéllar, EXPROPRIACIÓN Y CRISIS EN MEXICO (1940); Gordon, THE

EXPROPRIATION OF FOREIGN OWNED PROPERTY IN MEXICO (1941); Ricardo Araya, NACION-
ALIZACIÓN DE LAS MINAS DE BOLIVIA (1952). The "Interhandel Case" is an example of confiscation by the United States. INTERNATIONAL COURT OF JUSTICE REPORTS (1957), 105;
(1959), 6. The case is digested in AMERICAN JOURNAL OF INTERNATIONAL LAW (1958), LII,
320, and (1959), LIII, 671.

5. Atlantic Charter, Aug. 14, 1941, 55 Stat. 1603, E.A.S. No. 236. The charter specifically
referred to freedom from fear and want. However, President Roosevelt, in his message
to Congress of Aug. 21, 1941, said that "it is . . . unnecessary for me to point out that the
declaration of principles includes of necessity the world need for freedom of religion and
freedom of information. No society of the world organized under announced principles
could survive without these freedoms which are a part of the whole freedom for which
we strive."

6. Meeting of Sept. 24, 1941. CMD. No. 6315 (Misc. No. 3, 1941), 6-7.

7. Declaration of Jan. 1, 1942. 55 Stat. 1600, E.A.S. No. 236, DEPARTMENT OF STATE
BULLETIN (1942), VI, 3.

8. Resolution 35 of the third meeting of Jan. 28, 1942. INTERNATIONAL CONCILIATION
(1942), CCCLXXVIII, 140.

9. The United Nations Declaration of Twenty-Six Nations, stressing the necessity of the
defense of "life, liberty, independence, and religious freedom" and the preservation of
"human rights and justice" is, with its omission of a reference to property, characteristic
of the general trend existing at that time. Quotations are from Hartmann, BASIC DOCUMENTS
OF INTERNATIONAL RELATIONS (1951), 144.

10. Id., 159. Moscow Declaration Regarding Italy, Nov. 1, 1943, Department of State,
A DECADE OF AMERICAN FOREIGN POLICY—BASIC DOCUMENTS 1941-49, S. Doc. No. 123, 81st
Cong., 1st Sess. 34 (1956).

11. Hartmann, op. cit., 245. The Berlin (Potsdam) Conference, July 17-Aug. 2, 1945,
Dept. of State, A DECADE OF AMERICAN FOREIGN POLICY—BASIC DOCUMENTS 1941-49, S. Doc.
No. 123, 81st Cong., 1st Sess. 34 (1956).

12. INTERNATIONAL LABOR REVIEW (1944), L, 37 f.

13. United Nations, ed., FOR FUNDAMENTAL HUMAN RIGHTS (1948), 66 f.

14. UNITED NATIONS CONFERENCE ON INTERNATIONAL ORGANIZATION (1945), I, 115.

15. Id., I, 123, 125 f.

16. Id., I, 177.

17. Art. 55.

18. As President Truman pointed out in his address to the closing session on June 26,
1945: "The Charter is dedicated to the achievement and observance of human rights and
fundamental freedoms. Unless we can attain those objectives for all men and women
everywhere—without regard to race, language or religion—we cannot have permanent
peace and security." U. N. CONFERENCE ON INTERNATIONAL ORGANIZATION, I, 717.

19. Sixth plenary session of May 1, 1945. Id., I, 425. A similar attitude was taken by the
representatives of Panama the next day at the eighth plenary session. Id., I, 560.

20. Id., I, 717.

21. U. N. ECOSOC COUNCIL OFF. REC. 1st Sess., 163 f. (E/20) (1946) (Res. 1/5 of Feb. 16,
1946); Id., 2nd Sess., Annex 14, at 400-02 (E/56°Rev. 1, E/84/14) (1946) (Res. 2/9 of
June 21, 1946).

22. The General Assembly adopted it on Dec. 10, 1948, by forty-eight votes to none,
with eight abstentions. See U. N. GEN. ASS. OFF. REC. 3rd Sess., part 1, Ad Hoc Pol. Comm.
71 (1948) (Res. 217 [III]A of Dec. 10, 1948).

23. Arthur N. Holcombe, HUMAN RIGHTS IN THE MODERN WORLD (1948), 92.

24. It should be kept in mind that the jus gentium originally was "the common element
in the jura of the several gentes. It was not, at any rate not at first, an ideal which all men
ought to follow but the body of common rules which gentes, however diverse, did actually
follow." Max Radin, "Jus Gentium," ENCYCLOPAEDIA OF THE SOCIAL SCIENCES, VIII, 502.
Later, the jus gentium developed into the jus inter gentes, i.e., the law different nations
had in common and actually practiced, and thus became the law among these nations, or
inter-national, law.

25. On the development of installment buying in various countries, see Hermann Berlak and Alfred Felix, DAS TEILZAHLUNGSGESCHÄFT (1928); Wirtschaftsverband Teilzahlungsbanken, ed., HANDBUCH DER TEILZAHLUNGSWIRTSCHAFT (1958); Werner Fischer, DAS TEILZAHLUNGSGESCHÄFT (1952). It is generally agreed that modern installment buying originated in the United States toward the end of the nineteenth century. (See Berlak/Felix, *op. cit.*, 13; Robert Nöll v.d. Nahmer, WIE IST UNTER VOLKSWIRTSCHAFTLICHEN GESICHTSPUNKTEN DER TEILZAHLUNGSKREDIT ZU BEURTEILEN [1957], 29). Thus the beginning of modern installment buying coincides with the beginning of the decline of property rights. It is interesting to quote in this connection a statement made by Jefferson in 1787, which is complementary to statements that were made in the Philadelphia Convention: "Among many good qualities which my countrymen possess, some of a different character unhappily mix themselves. The most remarkable are, indolence, extravagance, and infidelity to their engagements. Cure the two first, and the last would disappear, because it is a consequence of them, and not proceeding from a want of morals. I know of no remedy against indolence and extravagance, but a free course of justice. Everything else is merely palliative; but unhappily, the evil has gained too generally the mass of the nation, to leave the course of justice unobstructed. The maxim of buying nothing without the money in our pockets to pay for it, would make of our country one of the happiest upon earth. Experience during the war proved this; as I think every man will remember, that under all the privations it obliged him to submit to, during that period, he slept sounder, and awakened happier than he can do now. Desperate of finding relief from a free course of justice, I look forward to the abolition of all credit, as the only other remedy which can take place. I have seen, therefore, with pleasure, the exaggerations of our want of faith, with which the London papers teem. It is indeed, a strong medicine. It will prevent their crediting us abroad, in which case we cannot be credited at home." The thought comes to mind that the Constitution, favoring a protection of property, educated the Americans away from the installment buying of which Jefferson complained, and that only after the Constitution had become subject to social interpretation at the end of the nineteenth century, did Americans revert back to installment buying. An outstanding opponent of installment buying is Wilhelm Röpke, BORGKAUF IM LICHTE SOZIALETHISCHER KRITIK (1954), VORGEGESSEN BROT (1955). For a critique of Röpke, see v. d. Nahmer, *op. cit.*

26. In a retrospect on the first nine months of the Kennedy Administration, U.S. NEWS AND WORLD REPORT (Oct. 23, 1961), stated that "'neutrals' almost immediately showed their hand. . . . They'd been paid $6 billion, but they criticized the U.S., did not criticize Russia." At the Belgrade Conference of the so-called uncommitted nations, held shortly after the communists had built the Wall through Berlin, West Germany found out that many of the nations she had given financial aid did not back her against East Germany, although the latter nation had not given aid to them.

27. See Albert Hunold, ed., ENTWICKLUNGSLÄNDER—WAHN UND WIRKLICHKEIT (1961); Peter T. Bauer, ECONOMIC ANALYSIS AND POLICY IN UNDERDEVELOPED COUNTRIES (1957); INDIAN ECONOMIC POLICY AND DEVELOPMENT (1961); (with Basil S. Yamey), THE ECONOMICS OF UNDERDEVELOPED COUNTRIES (1957); Hans Morgenthau, "A Political Theory of Foreign Aid," AMERICAN POLITICAL SCIENCE REVIEW (1962), LVI, 301.

28. In the Belgrade conference of neutralist nations, held shortly after the construction of the Berlin wall, hardly any criticism of communist oppression was voiced. India, although she had just been invaded by the Chinese communists in the fall of 1962 and was waiting for American military aid after having received great amounts in economic aid throughout the preceding years, opposed the United States, as she had done previously, by supporting the admission of Red China to the United Nations.

29. Comp. John Plamenatz, ON ALIEN RULE AND SELF-GOVERNMENT (1960), 184 f.: "If all Asia and Africa were to go Communist, I doubt whether the West would be much less secure than it is now."

30. When the crisis between Italy and Yugoslavia over Trieste came to a head, a situation existed in which a communist nation, strengthened through American aid, threatened an ally of the United States. The Indian army, made strong through American aid, attacked possessions of Portugal, an ally of the United States.

31. This was well exposed by Max Weber, WISSENSCHAFT ALS BERUF (1919). A translation of that work can be found in H. H. Gerth and C. Wright, eds., FROM MAX WEBER: ESSAYS IN SOCIOLOGY (1958), 129. See esp. 132 ff. Weber does not exaggerate. Often the quest for mediocrity verges upon the ludicrous. Perhaps the reader will permit the author to relate one of his many experiences in that respect. He knows of a case where a young man who held doctorates from a good American and a good European university soon found out that this was a burden rather than an asset. His applications for teaching positions, sent to a number of departmental chairmen at various colleges, were consistently turned down. He then was given the advice to write directly to a college president and to circumpass the departmental chairman, since the latter might be afraid of having a man with two doctorates in his department. Following this advice, he was offered a position immediately. The story does not end here. It continues on the graduate level. Later, our young man was asked to teach at a graduate school for international studies. He did so for five years, and enrollment in his class increased from year to year. But then he made what was perhaps a *faut pas*. When he heard that the school's catalogue would be distributed also in Europe, he suggested that in the new catalogue not only his American degree, but also his European one, should be mentioned. Shortly after the catalogue with the new information had made its appearance, our young man became *persona non grata*, in spite of the fact that his latest book had just been received very favorably. He was, significantly, replaced by two gentlemen who together boasted of only one doctorate!

32. There are few scholars indeed who, like F. A. Hayek, can say: "I have never learned even to avail myself of the aid of a research assistant." CONSTITUTION OF LIBERTY, 416.

33. It happened to me not too long ago that I was asked by an instructor to think up a program with which some senior would stand a chance of winning a Fulbright grant. When I expressed surprise at this attempt to get money under false pretenses, the instructor was not in the least perturbed, and neither was the senior who was with him. The latter even said that everybody was doing that sort of thing. Unfortunately this is only too often true. Whenever I taught abroad, I came across Fulbright students who hardly studied at all, but just had a good time and showed off their money. Their background and intellectual capacity was often lamentable. This can perhaps be explained by the fact that for many professors and colleges, it has become a matter of prestige to win grants for their students. Strong letters of recommendation will often be written for mediocre applicants, who often submit projects they simply dreamed up and have no intention to pursue.

A question that ought to be raised in this connection is whether the Fulbright Act has not lost its *raison d'être*. It was passed to help nations out of their dollar shortage. By today, the situation has fundamentally changed. Many foreign nations have less reason to complain of a dollar shortage and gold shortage than the United States.

It would be a worthwhile undertaking to find out how many of the research projects that are supported by (often stupendous!) research grants were ever completed.

34. Comp. Karl Jaspers, DIE GEISTIGE SITUATION DER ZEIT (5th ed., 1932, reprinted 1953), 115 f.

35. Comp. Ortega y Gasset, "Meier-Graefe," OBRAS COMPLETAS (1946-47), I, 96. For the relation of impressionism to the *fin de siècle*, see his "Tiempo, distancia y forma en el arte de Proust," *id.*, II, 699. Significantly, the art historian Wickoff of Vienna referred to the impressionist school as "illusionism." Ortega y Gasset, "Del realismo en pintura," *id.*, I, 560.

36. See Paul Tillich, "The Destruction of Death," THE SHAKING OF THE FOUNDATIONS (1953), 169.

37. The anthem of the National Socialist German Labor Party *(Horst Wessel Lied)*, contained a passage lauding comrades that had been killed by communists and reaction:
    "Kameraden, die Rotfront und Reaktion erschossen,
    Marschier'n im Geist in unsern Reihen mit."

38. It is interesting to note that in the United States the word "liberalism" has, since the beginning of this century, a quite different connotation than before. More and more, it stands for the welfare state, social legislation, and socialism. Its meaning has thus become

as perverted as the meaning of "progressivism." Significantly, the change in the meaning of the word occurred at about the same time when the term "democracy" became palatable to the American people who, until the end of the nineteenth century, had considered "democracy" to be nearly as bad as communism.

39. Continental bills of rights usually permit infringements upon the rights of the individual by the legislator. Although American bills of rights prohibit such infringements, American practice hardly differs from that of Europe. Comp. Holmes's decision in Schenck v. U.S., 249 U.S. 47 (1919).

40. The Bonn Basic Law has drawn this lesson by adopting articles 9 and 18. For a discussion of that adoption, see JAHRBUCH DES ÖFFENTLICHEN RECHTS (1951) I (N.F.), 116 ff., 171 ff.

41. Schenck v. U.S., *loc. cit.*

42. See his famous "Jamaica Letter" of Sept. 6, 1815. Harold A. Bierck, Jr., ed., SELECTED WRITINGS OF BOLIVAR (2nd ed., 1951), I, 103.

43. ·This is evident not only in the case of Latin America, where the Alliance for Progress program is based upon the idea of social reform. (See *infra*, p. 196). In South Vietnam, for instance, there exists the paradoxical situation that "social reform" is not only advocated by the communists, but also by the United States government.

44. For a New Dealer's concept of the "vital center," see Arthur M. Schlesinger, Jr., THE VITAL CENTER (1949).

45. Comp. THE FEDERALIST, essay 9 (Hamilton), and essay 10 (Madison).

46. See the author's "America and Europe—Decline and Emergence of Judicial Review," *loc. cit.*, esp. 1256 ff.

47. See Friedrich Meinecke, DIE IDEE DER STAATSRÄSON IN DER NEUEREN GESCHICHTE (1924, 3rd printing 1929, reprinted 1951).

48. This is not the twisting of the concept of reason of state as it might appear at first sight. Meinecke himself says at the very outset of his work: "Staatsräson ist die Maxime des Handelns, das Bewegungsgesetz des Staates. Sie sagt dem Staatsmann, was er tun muss, um den Staat in Gesundheit und Kraft zu erhalten. Und da der Staat ein organisches Gebilde ist, dessen volle Kraft sich nur erhält, wenn sie irgendwie noch zu wachsen vermag, so gibt die Staatsräson auch die Wege und Ziele dieses Wachstums an." Consequently, since under democratic theory the freedom of the individual—including free property—is the prerequisite for keeping the state healthy and strong and able to grow, democratic reason of state, or the maxim of those interested in a survival of free government, requires to do everything possible for the protection of freedom and free property, including seemingly "illegal" acts.

49. Consider, in France, the shift of power from the prime minister who, under the Third and Fourth Republics, was at the mercy of the legislature, to the President of the Fifth Republic who holds office for seven years; in Germany, the institution of the "constructive veto," under which the lower house can force a chancellor to resign only after it has chosen his successor.

50. See Michel Debré, LA RÉPUBLIQUE ET SES PROBLÈMES (1952), 46 f.; Stanley H. Hoffmann, "The Areal Division of Powers in the Writings of French Political Thinkers," Arthur Maas, ed., AREA AND POWER (1959), 113.

51. See Taylor Cole, "Three Constitutional Courts: A Comparison," AMERICAN POLITICAL SCIENCE REVIEW (1959), LIII, 963; Dietze, "Judicial Review in Europe," MICHIGAN LAW REVIEW (1957), 539, esp. 558 ff. As compared with the Fourth Republic, judicial review was strengthened under the Fifth Republic.

52. See Dietze, "Natural Law in the Modern European Constitutions," NATURAL LAW FORUM (1956), I, 73.

53. Articles 9, 18, 19.

54. Art. 1. On the provision, "the dignity of man is inviolable," Friedrich Giese, GRUNDGESETZ FÜR DIE BUNDESREPUBLIK DEUTSCHLAND (1953), 12 f., comments, "Rechtserhebliches verfassungsmässiges Bekenntnis zum fundamentalen Menschenrecht. Dieses "materielle Hauptgrundrecht" . . . aller Menschen als solches ist grundlegend für alle einzelnen Grund-

rechte; es wirkt absolut und aktuell, ist unverletzlich (unentziehbar) und unveräusserlich (unverzichtbar), absolut unabänderlich . . . und unbedingt massgeblich für alle Staatsorgane und sämtliche Staatsfunktionen. . . ."

55. See Christian Friedrich Menger, ZUM BEGRIFF DES SOZIALEN RECHTSSTAATS IM BONNER GRUNDGESETZ (1953); Erich Fechner, FREIHEIT UND ZWANG IM SOZIALEN RECHTSSTAAT (1953); Helmut Rumpf, DER IDEOLOGISCHE GEHALT DES BONNER GRUNDGESETZES (1958), 29, 33.

56. See Theodor Maunz, "Das Ende des subjektiven öffentlichen Rechts," ZEITSCHRIFT FÜR DIE GESAMTE STAATSWISSENSCHAFT (1935), XCVI, 71. Already in an earlier study, Maunz had spoken of the "overcome" subjective public rights. "Die neue Gestalt des Verwaltungsrechts," DEUTSCHE VERWALTUNGSBLÄTTER (1934), LXXXII, 211, 213. After the fall of the Third Reich, German jurists favored not only a reinstitution of subjective public rights, but a restitution of private law. See Walther Hallstein, "Wiederherstellung des Privatrechts," SÜDDEUTSCHE JURISTENZEITUNG (1946), I, 1.

57. Comp. Albert Hunold, ed., WIRTSCHAFT OHNE WUNDER (1953).

58. See Dietze, "Natural Law in the Modern European Constitutions," loc. cit.

59. Comp. art. 95 of the constitution of the Fourth Republic, art. 139 of the constitution of the Republic of Italy, and art. 79 of the Bonn Basic Law.

60. Art. 5 provides that no state shall be deprived, without its consent, of its equal suffrage in the Senate.

61. For an account of the doctrine of duel federalism, see Alfred H. Kelly and Winfred A. Harbison, THE AMERICAN CONSTITUTION, ITS ORIGINS AND DEVELOPMENT (Rev. ed., 1955), 683 ff., 738 f., 786 ff.

62. George C. S. Benson, THE NEW CENTRALIZATION (1941); Felix Morley, FREEDOM AND FEDERALISM (1959).

63. Comp. Edward S. Corwin, THE PRESIDENT, OFFICE AND POWERS, 1787-1957 (4th ed., 1957); Clinton Rossiter, THE AMERICAN PRESIDENCY (1956); Rexford G. Tugwell, THE ENLARGEMENT OF THE PRESIDENCY (1960).

64. See the author's "America and Europe—Decline and Emergence of Judicial Review," loc. cit., 1264 ff.

65. André Siegfried, AMERICA COMES OF AGE (1927).

66. Complaint about the apathy of the nation was one of the key features of Mr. Kennedy's electoral campaign. It also figures prominently in his First Address on the Nature of the Union.

67. "Benjamin Rush and the American Revolution," Dickinson College, ed., THE BOYD LEE SPAHR LECTURES IN AMERICANA 1957-1961 (1961), III, 89 f.

68. See C. D. Dillon's statement "Alliance for Progress, A Program for the Peoples of the Americas," with a message from President Kennedy, DEPARTMENT OF STATE BULLETIN (1961), XLV, 355. For a defense of the Alliance for Progress, see John C. Dreier, ed., THE ALLIANCE FOR PROGRESS (1962).

69. For the expropriations in Mexico and Bolivia, see supra, p. 166. The most recent expropriations took place in Cuba.

70. In the opinion of this author, the importance of strategic and ideological conflict within the communist camp (Khrushchevism vs. Stalinism, Soviet Union vs. Red China, etc.) is being overemphasized by Western observers. Greater scepticism should be employed in our evaluation of the communist situation. Our evaluation all too often seems to be a result of wishful thinking. We should question whether communist admissions, and perhaps even propagations of quarrels and difficulties within the Soviet bloc, are not tactical retreats for the sake of strategic gains, as suggested by Lenin. Could not the so-called "split" in the communist camp be a communist device to make the West feel more secure and thus lessen its defense efforts? It will be argued that the Soviet Union is not willing to suffer the loss of prestige that is involved in the admission of disunity. However, it seems doubtful that a strong nation need worry about prestige. The Soviet Union, even when in a relatively weak position, demonstrated that she was willing to sacrifice prestige. During the winter war with Finland (1939-40), the Soviets gave the impression that they could not defeat a small nation. (Hitler later referred to that policy as "the greatest deceit in world history"—a deceit of which he himself had become a victim.) By admitting a "split,"

the Soviets can also officially wash their hands of involvement in aggressive acts which are committed by other communist nations, such as Red China or Cuba, while remaining in the background as instigators. The Soviet Union can parade as a *defensor pacis*, a role in which she obviously likes to see herself, as the many "peace campaigns" and "peace congresses" indicate.

71. The most tragic case of appeasement is probably that of Berlin, when the United States government not only put up with the building of the wall, but even agreed to negotiate the future status of that city with the Soviet Union. At the time of the construction of the wall, this author was in Germany. Many people, including himself, had the impression that in the election campaign then being waged in West Germany, the United States supported the candidate of the Social Democrats rather than her long-time unequivocal ally Chancellor Adenauer, because her government felt that the former would be more willing to make concessions to the Soviet Union over Berlin. (This policy, however, backfired. While Adenauer lost his majority, the Social Democrats did not win either. On the other hand, the Free Democrats increased their mandates and became Adenauer's coalition partners. While the Free Democrats are even more rigid on Berlin than are the Christian Democrats, they are less pro-American.)

As to Cuba, the dismantling of Russian missile bases shortly before the American elections in November, 1962, does not alter the fact that Cuba remains a beachhead of the Soviet Union. From this base, the Russians will be in a good position to continue their infiltration of Latin America, a process that has been very successful since World War II, as was pointed out by Salvador de Madariaga, LATIN AMERICA BETWEEN THE EAGLE AND THE BEAR (1962). Irrespective of how the Kennedy administration will tackle the Cuban problem in the future, it can hardly be absolved of the guilt of having permitted the deterioration of the Cuban situation up to the fall of 1962, when these lines went to press. For before the advent of that administration, a definitely communist Cuba had not yet come into existence. The invasion of the Bay of Pigs early in 1961 was nothing but an attempt to eliminate the *chances* of Cuba's turning communist. In the following months, however, the establishment and the consolidation of communism were permitted. President Kennedy's assurance, given during the missile crisis, not to attack Cuba if offensive weapons on the island were dismantled, amounts to no less than an official American sanction of a communist, coexisting satellite, something few people would have dreamed of two years ago, something that is unique in United States foreign policy ever since the Monroe Doctrine was pronounced, and makes the death of that doctrine undisputable. Whereas the Kennedy administration has been alerted, shortly before the American elections, by a Cuba that harbored direct threats to the United States, it shows considerably less concern over a Cuba that has come into being ever since, a Cuba that constitutes a less direct—though hardly less severe—danger to this nation. Communism, it seems, is feared mainly in so far as it amounts to an immediate, violent challenge to American security. It is not so much resented as a way of life *per se*, as a non-violent, evolutionary, challenge to the American way of life. This author would not be surprised if one day Castro—probably under orders from Moscow—would turn Titoist and receive American foreign aid. The whole attitude of the Kennedy administration is tragic indeed. For it must give comfort and incentive to communist movements in other parts of the world, just as it must make people living under communist dictatorship despair. That attitude is also suicidal. For it will promote the coexistential or evolutionary communization of the world.

72. Otherwise, section 4 of the second article of the Constitution, "The President, Vice President and all civil officers of the United States, shall be removed from office on impeachment for, and conviction of, treason, bribery, or other high crimes and misdemeanors," would be redundant. For the importance attached by the Founders to the provision, see Max Farrand, THE FRAMING OF THE CONSTITUTION (1913), 79, 118. For the Founders' arguments in favor of a clause providing for a removal of the executive, see Max Farrand, ed., THE RECORDS OF THE FEDERAL CONVENTION OF 1787 (1911), I, 86; II, 64 ff., 550.

73. The Swiss playwright Friedrich Dürrenmatt, in his comedy "Die Ehe des Herrn Mississippi" (KOMÖDIEN [1958], I), shows how a convenient method of getting rid of a

political opponent is to have him committed to a mental institution. When the former General Walker was recently committed to psychiatric observation in a federal institution because of his part in the riots at the University of Mississippi (indeed a strange coincidence of names!), concern was voiced lest he was sent there without due process of law in order to be eliminated as a political opponent of the administration.

CONCLUDING REMARK

1. Comp. the statements by Tocqueville, DEMOCRACY IN AMERICA (1898), I, 311; II, 210, 275. On the other hand, James Bryce noted two generations later that Americans "are now not more sensitive to external opinion than the nations of Western Europe, and less so than the Russians, though they are still a trifle more apt to go through Europe comparing what they find with what they left at home. A foreign critic who tries to flout or scourge them no longer disturbs their composure; his jeers are received with amusement and indifference." THE AMERICAN COMMONWEALTH (2nd ed., 1891), II, 651 f. Even Bryce's statement does, however, not refute what I said. For if Americans are as sensitive to external criticism as are the nations of Western Europe, then they *are* more sensitive to external than to internal criticism.

2. St. John VIII, 32: "Ye shall know the Truth and the Truth shall make you free."

3. See Louis Hartz, THE LIBERAL TRADITION IN AMERICA (1955).

4. In his introduction to an edition of the WEALTH OF NATIONS (1910), xiv, Edwin R. A. Seligman writes that "Adam Smith had his eyes opened to the shortcomings of the restrictive colonial policy by the discontent in America." Significantly, Smith was a friend of David Hume, who showed much sympathy for the American cause. See Charles W. Hendel, ed., DAVID HUME'S POLITICAL ESSAYS (1953), 1 ff.

5. For the idea that the protection of private property is conducive to peace, see *supra*, Chapter One.

6. Johannes Winckelmann, LEGITIMITÄT UND LEGALITÄT IN MAX WEBERS HERRSCHAFTS-SOZIOLOGIE (1952), 33, writes that according to Weber, a rule is charismatic "sofern sie auf der ausseralltäglichen Hingabe an die Heiligkeit, Heldenkraft oder Vorbildlichkeit einer Person und die durch sie offenbarten und gewiesenen Ordnungen ruht." Comp. Max Weber, "Die drei reinen Typen der legitimen Herrschaft," PREUSSISCHE JAHRBÜCHER (1922), 6 ff.; WIRTSCHAFT UND GESELLSCHAFT (1921), 124, 140, 227 f., 612, 753 f., 758 f. There is no apparent reason why the idea of charismatic leadership could not be applied to nations. Russia has been exercising such leadership for communist movements for a long time. The dilemma of the free world is possibly due to the fact that no nation has exercised such leadership.

7. The "Crusade for Freedom" is an American program against communism. Consult the ANNUAL REPORTS OF THE FREE EUROPE COMMITTEE. See also "They Fight Communism," CHANGING TIMES (March, 1953), 43. Harold Lord Varney, "Big Names in The Window," AMERICAN MERCURY (March, 1956), 97, comments upon those who endorsed the Crusade for Freedom as follows: "Only 'safe' names were selected for the top sponsorship. Although the program was one of anti-Communism, the most conspicuous anti-Communist names in the nation were significantly absent. The list was composed of reassuring middle-of-the-roaders with no Herbert Hoovers, no Gen. Douglas MacArthurs, no Gen. Albert C. Wedemeyers, no Charles A. Lindberghs. . . . A "Crusade" against Communism was being conducted by men, some of whom had records soggy with appeasement and past identification with Communist fellow-traveler movements. This blue-penciling of the outspoken anti-Communists unquestionably was a factor in the subsequent fizzing out of the movement when Eisenhower and his group, under the Geneva spell, switched to co-existence." *Id.*, 98 f.

8. For other aspects of America's manifest destiny, see Albert K. Weinberg, MANIFEST DESTINY (1935).

9. The American attitude toward Latin American independence is described by Samuel F. Bemis, THE LATIN AMERICAN POLICY OF THE UNITED STATES (1943), 31 ff.; William S. Robertson, RISE OF THE SPANISH-AMERICAN REPUBLICS (1918). For the American attitude during World War II, see Jacob Viner, THE AMERICAN INTEREST IN THE COLONIAL PROBLEM (1944); Emil J. Sadi, THE UNITED NATIONS AND DEPENDENT PEOPLES (1956), 13 f.; Ruth Russell, HISTORY OF THE UNITED NATIONS CHARTER (1958), 330 ff. Once the U.N. with its professed aim of ending colonialism (an aim that was supported by the United States) had come into existence, many colonies won independence so rapidly that it has been said that "it is doubtful that the rapidity of this development was anticipated at San Francisco." (Clark M. Eichelberger, UN: THE FIRST TEN YEARS [1955], 3.) Five years later, the same author, noting that another hundred million had become independent, wrote that "the rapidity of this development was not anticipated in San Francisco." (UN: THE FIRST FIF-TEEN YEARS [1960], 2.) Do we here have a case of a sorcerer's apprentice? Although it has been emphasized that after the war the United States took the interests of her European allies more into account (Sadi, *loc. cit.*; Lincoln P. Bloomfield, THE UNITED NATIONS AND UNITED STATES FOREIGN POLICY [1960], 192 ff.), she nevertheless continued to support movements for independence. See Grayson Kirk, "Declining Empires and American Interests," SURVEY (1949), LXXXV, 254. Though perhaps recognizing the problems involved in such movements, the United States was reluctant to openly show her doubts and of implementing these doubts. See Alastair M. Taylor, INDONESIAN INDEPENDENCE AND THE UNITED NATIONS (1960), 391 ff.; "What Should the United States do about Tunisia?" FOREIGN POLICY BULLETIN (July 15, 1952), 4; Mohammed Alwan, ALGERIA BEFORE THE UNITED NATIONS (1959), 45 ff.; Henry A. Byroade, "The World's Colonies and Ex-Colonies: A Challenge to America," UNITED STATES DEPARTMENT OF STATE BULLETIN (1953), XXIX, 655.

10. Comp. Viner, *op. cit.,* 8 ff.

11. Comp. Louis Hartz, *op. cit.,* 66.

12. In Ghana, for instance, a person can be held without trial for as long as five years. Undaunted by criticism, the government of that nation is now considering to extend that period to twenty years. See "Ghana and 'The Redeemer'," NEW REPUBLIC (May 7, 1962), 11. Assurances given to the colonial powers, that after independence the rights of individuals, including Europeans, will be respected, do not constitute a guaranty. Even if such assurances are a *conditio sine qua non* for the withdrawal of the colonial power, they are actually nothing but promises. Once the colony has become sovereign, it can under the rules of international law make its own laws concerning the rights of individuals living on its territory. See Eichelberger, UN: THE FIRST FIFTEEN YEARS (1960), 66.

13. In the General Assembly, which seems to be on its way to becoming the most important branch of the UN (see Sidney D. Bailey, THE GENERAL ASSEMBLY OF THE UNITED NATIONS [1960], 253 ff.; Benjamin V. Cohen, THE UNITED NATIONS [1961], 16 ff.), a combination of the so-called uncommitted nations (for the fact that these nations have a double standard and are tending to side with the Soviet rather than the Western bloc, see Eichelberger, UN: THE FIRST FIFTEEN YEARS [1960], 133) and the Soviet bloc can easily outvote the West. See "New Era of Change for UN," BUSINESS WEEK (Oct. 22, 1960), 95; "Changing World, Changing UN," COMMONWEAL (1961), LXXIII, 400.

14. THE WORLD AND THE WEST (1953).

15. For Jefferson's exposition of the concept of natural aristocracy, see his letter to John Adams of Oct. 28, 1814 (WRITINGS, Ford ed., IX, 424 ff.) While in Jefferson's opinion, those who acquire wealth through their own effort belong to the natural aristocracy, Jefferson also leaves no doubt that those who possess wealth that has not been acquired through their own effort may belong to that group: "There is a natural aristocracy among men. The grounds of this are virtue and talents. . . There is also an artificial aristocracy, founded on wealth and birth, without either virtue or talents; *for with these it would belong to the first class." (Id.,* 425. Emphasis supplied by the author). Jefferson then continues: "The natural aristocracy I consider as the most precious gift of nature, for the instruction, the trusts, and government of society. And indeed, it would have been inconsistent in creation to have formed man for the social state, and not to have provided virtue and wisdom enough to manage the concerns of the society. May we not even

say, that that form of government is the best, which provides the most effectually for a pure selection of these natural aristoi into the offices of government?" Consequently, if the natural aristocracy is eliminated—and it will be eliminated if a display of virtue and talent is discouraged by means of discriminations against the reward for such display, i.e. property—then the "most precious gift of nature," the very prerequisite of good government, will be eliminated. Comp. Jefferson's statement in his First Annual Message to Congress of Dec. 8, 1801, which vindicates that essential aspect of free property—free enterprise: "Agriculture, manufacturers, commerce, and navigation, the four pillars of our prosperity, are the most thriving when left to individual enterprise. Protection from casual embarrassments, however, may sometimes be seasonably interposed." *Id.*, VIII, 123.

16. Though during the presidential campaign Khrushchev never came out in favor of Kennedy, there was no doubt, especially after the U-2 incident, that he preferred a Democratic administration. He had a strong personal dislike of Vice-President Nixon. After the election, Khrushchev, in his congratulatory message, expressed hope that "relations between our two nations would again follow the line along which they were developing in Franklin Roosevelt's time."

17. See the remarks on the score of the Kennedy administration after six, resp. nine, months, in U.S. NEWS & WORLD REPORT (July 31, 1961), 26; (Oct. 23, 1961), 21. See also Robert P. Martin, "Southeast Asia on the Road to a Communist Take-over?" *Id.*, (April 10, 1961), 39. After the Cuban debacle, the Soviet ambassador in Washington told Attorney General Robert F. Kennedy at a reception on July 14, 1961: "The American people are not ready. They don't want to fight. In the final analysis, when the chips are down, the American people won't fight for Berlin." *Id.*, (July 31, 1961), 21. Newspapers at the time stressed how infuriated the President's brother was about that remark, claiming that Menshikov underestimated the Americans. Less than a month later, the United States did not oppose the building of the Wall in Berlin. Comp. *supra,* p. 255, note 71.

18. It is often overlooked that also the freedom of the people of West Berlin, said to be protected, was actually seriously restrained, since they no longer have the right to go to East Berlin. As a face-saving device, the Western powers maintained that their own rights in Berlin were not touched by the building of the Wall. Thus, it is often overlooked that prior to August 13, the U.S. government had maintained that it would not suffer *any* change in the status of the city.

19. See Raoul E. Desvernine, DEMOCRATIC DESPOTISM (1936).

20. The actual quotation reads: "I am certainly not an advocate for frequent and untried changes in laws and constitutions. . . But I know also, that laws and institutions must go hand in hand with the progress of the human mind. As that becomes more developed, more enlightened, as new discoveries are made, new truths disclosed, and manners and opinions change with the change of circumstances, institutions must advance also, and keep pace with the times. . . ." To Samuel Kercheval on July 12, 1816. WRITINGS, Mem. ed., XV, 40 f.

21. In his First Inaugural Address of March 4, 1801, Jefferson stated: "With all these blessings, what more is necessary to make us a happy and prosperous people? Still one thing more, fellow citizens, a wise and frugal government, which shall restrain men from injuring one another, shall leave them otherwise free to regulate their own pursuits of industry and improvement, and shall not take from the mouth of labor the bread it has earned. This is the sum of good government, and this is necessary to close the circle of our felicities." *Id.*, III, 320 f.

SELECTED BIBLIOGRAPHY
(Other sources can be found in the text and notes)

Günther Absalon, DIE GESCHICHTLICHE ENTWICKLUNG DES EIGENTUMS-BEGRIFFES UND SEINE GESTALTUNG DURCH DIE NATIONALSOZIALIS-TISCHE GESETZGEBUNG (Düsseldorf, 1936).

Heinrich Altrichter, WANDLUNGEN DES EIGENTUMSBEGRIFFS UND NEUERE AUSGESTALTUNG DES EIGENTUMSRECHTS (Marburg, 1930).

Ernest Beaglehole, PROPERTY (London, 1931).

Hilaire Belloc, AN ESSAY ON THE RESTORATION OF PROPERTY (London, 1936).

Adolf A. Berle, THE EQUITABLE DISTRIBUTION OF PROPERTY (New York, 1930).

Arwed Blomeyer, DIE AUSSERPOSITIVEN GRUNDLAGEN DES PRIVATEIGEN-TUMS (Jena, 1929).

Anton Burghardt, EIGENTUMSETHIK UND EIGENTUMSREVISIONISMUS (Munich, 1955).

Maurice Byé and Léon Francis Julliot de la Morandière, LES NATION-ALISATIONS EN FRANCE ET À L'ÉTRANGER (Paris, 1948).

Arthur J. Eddy, PROPERTY (Chicago, 1921).

Hermann Eichler, WANDLUNGEN DES EIGENTUMSBEGRIFFES IN DER DEUTSCHEN RECHTSAUFFASSUNG UND GESETZGEBUNG (Weimar, 1938).

Ludwig Felix, ENTWICKLUNGSGESCHICHTE DES EIGENTUMS (Leipzig, 1883-1903).

Joseph F. Fletcher, ed., CHRISTIANITY AND PROPERTY (Philadelphia, 1947).

Wolfgang Friedmann, LAW IN A CHANGING SOCIETY (Berkeley, 1959).

Georges Gurvitch, L'IDÉE DU DROIT SOCIAL; NOTION ET SYSTÈME DU DROIT SOCIAL (Paris, 1932).

Hans Haab, PRIVATEIGENTUM UND MATERIELLE ENTEIGNUNG (Bern, 1947).

Günther Hagenlocher, WANDLUNGEN DES EIGENTUMSBEGRIFFES IN DER DEUTSCHEN RECHTSAUFFASSUNG UND GESETZGEBUNG (Heidelberg, 1935).

Friedrich A. Hayek, THE ROAD TO SERFDOM (Chicago, 1944).

Justus Wilhelm Hedemann, DAS BÜRGERLICHE RECHT UND DIE NEUE ZEIT (Jena, 1919).

John A. Hobson, PROPERTY AND IMPROPERTY (London, 1937).

Günther Holstein, DIE LEHRE VON DER ÖFFENTLICH-RECHTLICHEN EIGENTUMSBESCHRÄNKUNG (Berlin, 1921).

Charles H. Hopkins, THE RISE OF THE SOCIAL GOSPEL IN AMERICAN PROTESTANTISM 1865-1915 (New Haven, 1940).

Lucien Jansse, LA PROPRIÉTÉ (Paris, 1953).

Alfred W. Jones, LIFE, LIBERTY AND PROPERTY (Philadelphia, 1941).

Max Kaser, EIGENTUM UND BESITZ IM ÄLTEREN RÖMISCHEN RECHT (Weimar, 1943).

Robert von Keller, FREIHEITSGARANTIEN FÜR PERSON UND EIGENTUM IM MITTELALTER (Heidelberg, 1933).

Frederik Vinding Kruse, DAS EIGENTUMSRECHT (Berlin, 1931-36).

Paul Lafargue, THE EVOLUTION OF PROPERTY FROM SAVAGERY TO CIVILIZATION (London, 1894).

Carla Laier, DER EIGENTUMSBEGRIFF IN DER ZEIT DES NATURRECHTES UND DER AUFKLÄRUNG (Düsseldorf, 1937).

Paschal Larkin, PROPERTY IN THE EIGHTEENTH CENTURY, WITH SPECIAL REFERENCE TO ENGLAND AND LOCKE (Cork, 1930).

Ferdinand Lassalle, DAS SYSTEM DER ERWORBENEN RECHTE (Leipzig, 1861).

Arnold Lindwurm, DAS EIGENTUMSRECHT UND DIE MENSCHHEITSIDEE IM STAATE (Leipzig, 1878).

Theodor Lorch, DIE BEURTEILUNG DES EIGENTUMS IM DEUTSCHEN PROTESTANTISMUS SEIT 1848 (Gütersloh, 1930).

William J. McDonald, THE SOCIAL VALUE OF PROPERTY ACCORDING TO ST. THOMAS AQUINAS (Washington, 1939).

Daniel B. Merino, NATURAL JUSTICE AND PRIVATE PROPERTY (St. Louis, 1923).

Walter Merk, DAS EIGENTUM IM WANDEL DER ZEITEN (Langensalza, 1934).

Ludwig von Mises, THE THEORY OF MONEY AND CREDIT (New ed., New Haven, 1953).

Emmanuel Mounier, DE LA PROPRIÉTÉ CAPITALISTE À LA PROPRIÉTÉ HUMAINE (Paris, 1936).

W. Nippold, DIE ANFÄNGE DES EIGENTUMS BEI DEN NATURVÖLKERN UND DIE ENTSTEHUNG DES PRIVATEIGENTUMS (The Hague, 1954).

Charles R. Noyes, THE INSTITUTION OF PROPERTY (New York; 1936).

Kirby Page, PROPERTY (New York, 1936).

Georges Renard and Louis Trotabas, LA FONCTION SOCIALE DE LA PROPRIÉTÉ PRIVÉE (Paris, 1930).

Karl Renner, DIE RECHTSINSTITUTE DES PRIVATRECHTS UND IHRE SOZIALE FUNKTION (Tübingen, 1929).

John A. Ryan, DISTRIBUTIVE JUSTICE (New York, 1916).

Adolph Samter, DAS EIGENTUM IN SEINER SOZIALEN BEDEUTUNG (Jena, 1879).

René Savatier, DU DROIT CIVIL AU DROIT PUBLIC (Paris, 1945).

Otto Schilling, DER KIRCHLICHE EIGENTUMSBEGRIFF (2nd ed., Freiburg i. Br., 1930).

Carl Schmitt, UNABHÄNGIGKEIT DER RICHTER, GLEICHHEIT VOR DEM GESETZ UND GEWÄHRLEISTUNG DES PRIVATEIGENTUMS NACH DER WEIMARER VERFASSUNG (Berlin, 1926).

W. G. Serra, PROPERTY, ITS SUBSTANCE AND VALUE (London, 1935).

Ferdinand Tönnies, DAS EIGENTUM (Wien, 1926).

Johannes Uhde, EIGENTUM, KAPITALISMUS, CHRISTENTUM (Leipzig, 1930).

Arthur F. Utz, FREIHEIT UND BINDUNG DES EIGENTUMS (Heidelberg, 1949).

Thorstein Veblen, ABSENTEE OWNERSHIP AND BUSINESS ENTERPRISE IN RECENT TIMES (New York, 1923).

INDEX

Abbott, Lyman, 97
Ability
  and equality, 63
  reward according to, 5, 68
Absolute democracy, 20, 22-25, 146-163,
  186-199, 209
Absolute monarchy, 20-22, 25, 57, 73,
  see "Ancien régime"
Absolute protection of property, 71-92
  attacks upon, 93, 127
Abus de droit, 109-112
Academe, 179
Adams, John, 33, 34, 80
Adams, Samuel, 31
Aegidius Romanus, 16
Ager publicus, 50
Agreement of the People, 215
Albertus Magnus, 16
Allgemeines Bürgerliches Gesetzbuch
  (ABGB.), 74-75, 77
  impact of, 78
Allgemeines Landrecht (ALR.), 73-74
Alliance for Progress, 196
Altruism of protection of property, 9, 15,
  16, 20, 23, 25, 67, 84
America, United States of
  adjudication in, 78-84, 110-111
  and Europe, 190-199, 200-202
  and France, 62
  anti-colonialism of, 65, 203-204
  apathy of, 194
  as defensor pacis, 201-203
  as leader of the West, 203, 205, 206

America, United States of (*continued*)
  as protector of property, 201-203
  attacks upon property in, 33, 34, 97-98,
    103-106, 107-108, 110-111, 113, 116-
    119, 122, 124-125, 194-198
  criticism of, 1-7, 192-199, 200-209
  decline of, 3-5, 194-199, 206
  Goethe on, 2, 3
  legislation in, 33, 91, 116-119, 122
  power of, 3, 192, 194, 201
  protection of property in, 6, 26, 29-34,
    59-61, 78-86
  rediscovery of, 3
  solved problem of democracy, 203
American century, 5
American Constitution, 41, 124-125
  as constitution of property, 34, 59, 60-61,
    78-86
  as transmutation of higher law, 104
  property rights and liberal rights in,
    60-61
American Economic Association, 99-100
American optimism, 5, 198
American overoptimism, 1-6
American Revolution
  and equality, 59, 60
  and property, 30-34, 59-61
  permanency of, 2
American state constitutions
  property and happiness in, 32-33
  property rights and liberal rights in, 60
American type, 3-5
American way of life, 3-4

263

Anabaptists, 17, 18, 20
Anarchy resulting from common owner-
    ship, 14, 18, 23, 28, 67
Ancien régime, 21, 24, 25, 64, 68, 71, 72,
    95, 136, 139, 140, 142, 149
Anglo-Catholic movement, 96
Anschütz, Gerhard, 241
Antiquity, property in, 12-15
Aristocracy
    artificial, 257-258
    natural, 7, 204, 205, 208-209
Aristotle, 13, 16, 32, 35, 37, 38, 66
Assembly, freedom of, 131, 133
Association, freedom of, 131-139
Atlantic Charter, 166
Aubry, Charles, 89
Austrian school of economics, 69

Babeuf, François-Emile, 25, 71, 141, 143
Baptists, 36
Barclay, William, 21
Barlow, Joel, 210
Barrow, Isaac, 214
Barthélemy, Joseph, 247
Bastiat, Frédéric, 69
Bavarian Maximilian Code, 73
Baxter, Richard, 19
Beard, Charles A., 217
Becker, Carl L., 217
Befreiungsgesetzgebung, 75-76
Behrends, A.J.F., 97
Belloc, Hilaire, 218
Benson, George C. S., 254
Belloy, Pierre de, 21
Bellum omnium contra omnes, 20, 21
Bemis, Edward, 100
Bentham, Jeremy, 66-67, 96
Bergbohm, Karl, 157
Berlin, 251, 255, 258
Bill of Rights (England), 58-59, 141-142
Bill of Rights (United States), 61, 169
Bills of rights
    property and equality in, 60
    property and liberal rights in, 60
Blackstone, William, 27-28, 221
Bodin, Jean, 20
Boileux, J. M., 89
Bolívar, Simon, 185-186
Bonn Republic, 123, 190, 219, 222
Bowen, Francis, 226
Bradford, Governor, 30
Brandeis, Louis D., 104, 105-106, 107, 116,
    125, 130, 159
Brentano, Lujo, 99
Brown, Robert E., 217

Bryce, James, 146, 256
Burckhardt, Jacob, 152
Bugnet, Jean-Joseph, 156
Bürgerliches Gesetzbuch (BGB.), 76-77,
    109, 111, 129-130
    impact of, 78
Burke, Edmund, 24, 38, 67-68, 225

Calvin, John, 18
Cambacérès, Jean-Jacques de, 149
Campanella, Tommaso, 26
Carlyle, A. J., 212, 213
Carlyle, Thomas, 96
Carpenter, William S., 216
Castro, Fidel, 186
Catholic thought on property, 15-17, 35,
    70-71, 96, 97
Challaye, Félicien, 225, 227
Charles River case, 81, 82, 85
Chartists, 96
Chicanery (malicious use of property),
    109-111
Child labor, 116-117
Christian socialism, 96-98
Church, W. F., 214
Cicero, 13-14, 29
Civil Code, see "Napoleonic Code"
Civil rights
    and democratic rights, 45-48
    and property rights, 45-48
Civilization
    and freedom, 93
    and progress, 93
    and property, 9, 16, 17, 20, 23, 25, 27, 34,
        38, 39, 40, 42, 45, 48, 64, 67, 68, 89
Cobdenism, 68
Cochran, Thomas C., 226
Code Boissonade, 227
Co-existence, 185
Colbertism, 68
Cole, Taylor, 253
Coleridge, Samuel T., 96
Collectivism, see "Common ownership"
Comforts of life, comfortable living, 3, 4,
    173, 177, 195
Commerce clause of U. S. Constitution, 83
Committee of Five (France), 62
Common ownership
    and anarchy, 18, 23, 28
    and family, 20
    and happiness, 18, 21, 85
    and incentive, 13, 70
    and justice, 9, 84
    and peace, 9, 13, 16, 18
    and progress, 9, 13, 18

Common ownership (*continued*)
and society's good, 20
contradiction in terms, 88
prior to private ownership, 50-51
unnatural, 38, 70, 85
utopian, 9, 13, 14, 15, 17, 18, 20, 22, 25, 26, 27, 28, 29, 30, 38, 67, 85, 95
Commons, John R., 100
Communism, 7, 13, 14, 16, 17, 28, 50, 174, 176
aid to, 196-197
hard line of, 185
impact upon international law, 164-172, 173-174
soft line, 185
split, 196, 254-255
Communist Manifesto, 95, 96
Communization of the world, gradual and radical, 185
Conant, John, 214
Condorcet, Marie Jean Antoine Nicolas de, 62
Conscience and property rights, 74, 88, 90, 102
Conservatism, 78, 181, 199
Constitutional action, 198-199, *see* "Reaction"
Constitutionalism, 25-34, 93, 94, 139-163
Constitutions
admitting social interpretation of property, 103-106, 122-125
conquered by legislation, 122-125
providing for adequate protection of property, 24, 25, 33-34, 60-61, 78-84
providing for contract clauses, 61, 78, 91
Constituent Assembly (France), 62
Continental Congress (U. S.), 31
Contract clause of the U. S. Constitution, 61, 78-82, 83, 85, 91
and state reservation clauses, 81
Contract clauses in American state constitutions, 61, 78, 91
Contract, freedom of, 83, 86, 104, 105
Cooke, John, 215
Corwin, Edward S., 220, 224, 228, 236
Coulanges, Fustel de, 222, 223
Cromwell, Oliver, 23
Crusade for Freedom, 203, 256
Cuba, 186, 197, 206, 255
Cumberland, Richard, 214
Cushman, Robert E., 221

Dakin, Arthur, 213
Danton, George Jacques, 24
Dartmouth College case, 80

Darwin, Charles R., 69
Debts
Jefferson on, 251
modern attitude toward, 5, 173
Debtors
increase in numbers of, 5, 173, 177
legislation favoring, 33, 120, 177
political power of, 146, 148-149, 171, 177
Decalogue, *see* "Ten Commandments"
Declaration of Independence, 1, 6, 34, 41, 221, 244
and equality, 59-60, 140, 145
and property, 31-32, 59-60, 140
property rights and liberal rights in, 59-60, 140
Declaration of the Rights of Man and Citizen, 41, 124, 144, 221, 224
and equality, 63, 140-141, 143
and property, 24, 140-141
property rights and liberal rights in, 24, 61, 62-63, 140-141
Democracy
absolute, 20, 22-25, 146-163, 186-199, 209
and civil rights, 45-48
and equality, 139-147, 147-149, 149-163
and freedom, 172-176
and higher law, 149-152, 156-160
and property, 22-25, 25-34, 57-63, 128-163, 164, 204, 208-209
conducive to freedom, 47, 64, 142-143, 144
destructive of freedom, 147-149, 149-163, 208-209
limited, 25-34, 139-142
march of, 128-163
working, 46
Democratic despotism, *see* "Absolute democracy"
Democratic revolutions
in America, 30-34, 59-61, 63-64
in England, 22-23, 57-59, 63-64
in France, 23-25, 61-63, 63-64
protection of property in, 22-25, 57-63
Democratic rights
and civil rights, 45-48
and liberal rights, 43-45, 146-149
and property rights, 42-48, 146-149, 160-161, 161-163
conducive to freedom, 44-45, 47
destructive of freedom, 146-149, 149-163, 204
no prerequisite for freedom, 44-45
Demeunier (often Desmeuniers), Jean Nicolas, 62
Depression, 4, 113, 125
Desvernine, Raoul E., 221

Dickinson, John, 216
Diggers, 22, 141
Divine right, 21, 22
Dominium, 20, 22, 26
Dred Scott Case, 82, 125
Due process under U. S. Constitution, 61, 78, 82, 85
  and liberty, 83
  procedural, 82
  substantive, 82-83
Duguit, Léon, 100, 102-103, 106, 112, 125, 216
Dunoyer, Barthélemy Charles Pierre Joseph, 69

Edict Concerning the Facilitated Possession and Free Use of Real Property as well as the Personal Conditions of the Rural Population (1807), 75
Edict for the Improvement of Land Culture (1811), 75
Education for the appreciation of property, 188
Egoism
  and protection of property, 87, 101
  and protection of rights other than property rights, 47-48
  see "Altruism of protection of property"
Eighteenth century, property in, 22-34, 65-66
Eisenhower, Dwight D., 192
Ely, Richard T., 99, 100
Encyclicals
  on freedom of religion, 52
  on property, 70-71
Engels, Friedrich, 50
England
  Agreement of the People, 215
  Bill of Rights, 58-59, 141-142
  Christian socialism in, 96
  common law in, 84, 85
  democratic revolutions in, 22-23, 57-59, 63-64
  Instrument of Government, 58
  Parliament, 21, 23, 29, 30, 54, 57, 58
  Petition of Right, 57-58
  property in the American colonies, 50
  Putney Debates, 23
Enlightenment, property in the
  under absolute democracy, 22-25, 61-63
  under absolute monarchy, 20-22, 57-58
  under limited government, 25-34, 58-63
Equality
  and democracy, 139-147, 147-149, 149-163

Equality (continued)
  and freedom, 139-149 (freedom over equality, 139-143; equality over freedom, 143-149)
  and property, 148-149
  and suffrage, 144-147, 171
  as a right for the masses, 143
  before the law, 140-141
  in the Declaration of Independence, 59-60, 140
  in the Declaration of the Rights of Man and Citizen, 63, 140
  in state constitutions, 60
  march of, 142-149, 149-161, 161-163, 171, 204
  not unalienable, 59-60, 63
  qualified by virtue and talent, 63
  through the law, 149, 162-163
Europe
  America and, 2, 3, 6-7, 190-199, 201-203
  feudal heritage of, 2, 3, 201
  Goethe on, 2, 3
  recent trends in, 190-192
Evolution, dangers of, 241-242
Exegesis, school of, 157
Expropriation
  eminent domain, 74, 160
  legislation favoring debtors, 120-121
  nationalization, 155, 196
  take-care legislation, 119-120

Fair balance among liberal rights, 42-43, 183-184
Fall of man, 15, 16
Fascism, 93, 130, 196, see National-socialism
Faust, 2, 3
Federal Convention (U. S.), 34, 79, 91, 222
Federalism, 189, 190, 192-193
  as means for the protection of property, 189
Federalist Papers, 5, 34, 79, 85, 152, 160
Feudalism, 24, 25, 67, 72, 75, 76, 201
Fifth Freedom, 166
Fifth Republic, 124, 190-191
Figgis, J. N., 218
Fin de siècle, 93
First Christians, life of, 15, 16-17
Fletcher v. Peck, 78, 80
Foreign aid, 174-177
Founding Fathers, 86, 199
  and contract clause, 79-82
  and democracy, 192
  and due process, 82
  and property, 5, 34, 61, 84

Four Freedoms, 166
Fourth Republic, 124, 190, 219
France
  adjudication in, 90-91, 111, 191
  and America, 62
  and Germany, 90, 190-192
  attacks upon property, 24-25, 102-103, 109, 111, 112, 117, 123-124
  constitutions in, 24, 25, 190-192
  Declaration of the Rights of Man and Citizen, 24, 41, 61, 62-63, 124, 140-141, 143, 144, 221, 224
  legislation in, 71-72, 117, 131-132, 144-145
  property in the American colonies of, 50
  protection of property in, 23-25, 61-63, 71-72, 88-90, 90-91
  recent trends in, 190-192
Fraenkel, Ernst, 211
Frank, Jerome, 158, 159
Franklin, Benjamin, 211
Frederick the Great, 73
Freedom
  and civil rights, 40, 45-48
  and civilization, 39, 45, 93
  and democracy, 172-176
  and democratic rights, 40-45
  and equality, 139-149 (freedom over equality, 139-143; equality over freedom, 143-149)
  and liberal rights, 43-44
  and liberties, 40, 41-48
  and property, 40-64
  as an individualistic right, 143
  of assembly, 46, 49, 54, 56, 61, 62, 64, 131, 133
  of association, 46, 47, 49, 131-139
  of religion, 42, 43, 44, 49, 51-54, 54-56, 61, 62
  of speech, 43, 44, 46, 47, 49, 54, 56, 60, 61, 62, 63, 64, 184-185
  no absolute protection of, 81
  to destroy freedom, 184-185
French Revolution, 121, 152, 162, 165, 222
  and equality, 24-25, 63, 66, 71
  and property, 23-25, 61-63, 71, 89
Friedrich, Carl J., 212, 227, 228

General will
  and liberal rights, 62
  and property rights, 23, 62
  representative of the masses, 182
  sublimity of, 23, 66, 161-163
Germany
  adjudication in, 90-91, 111, 112, 191

Germany (continued)
  and France, 90, 190-192
  attacks upon property, 96-97, 98-99, 100-102, 109-110, 111, 117, 121, 122-123
  constitutions in, 122-123
  legislation in, 73-78, 117, 132-133, 145
  protection of property in, 73-78, 86-88, 90-91
  recent trends in, 190-192
Germanic law, 88, 112, 129
Germanists, 102
Gersterding F. C., 86
Gesetz, 150
Gesetzesstaat, 150
Gierke, Otto von, 102, 106, 116, 125, 136-137
Giese, Friedrich, 253-254
Gladden, Washington, 97
Gneist, Rudolf von, 122
Goethe, Johann Wolfgang von, 2, 3
Golden, Harry L., 211
Golden age, 13, 15, 20, 23
Gonnard, René, 222, 223
Greek thought on property, 12-13
Grotius, Hugo, 26, 162
Guiraud, Paul, 222, 223

Haines, Charles Grove, 158, 159
Hamilton, Alexander, 2, 37, 78, 79, 244
Hartz, Louis, 256, 257
Hauriou, Maurice, 152
Haves and have-nots, 95
Hayek, F. A., 240, 241, 249
Hayem, Henri, 232
Hedemann, Justus Wilhelm, 112
Hegel, Georg Wilhelm Friedrich, 67, 95
Held, Adolf, 99
Historical school, 67-68, 69, 90, 92, 157
Hobbes, Thomas, 10, 21-22, 131
Hofstadter, Richard, 226, 235
Holcombe, Arthur N., 250
Holmes, Oliver W., 104-105, 107, 110, 116, 125, 130, 158, 159, 185, 248
Hooker, Richard, 18
Hoover, Herbert, 166
Hugo, Victor, 10
Huguenots, 20
Hume, David, 67
Hunold, Albert, 254
Hus, John, 17

Idealism, 9, 67, 69, 70, 73, 92, 94, 212
Imperium, 20, 26
Impressionism, 180, 207

Incentive and private property, 17, 18, 26, 27, 28, 30, 70, 84, 85, 89, 94, 126
Individual
  as citizen and subject, 38
  protection of property good for, 19, 22, 25, 26, 34, 38, 47
Individualism, 15, 20, 77, 92, 106
Individualistic rights, 133-135, 143, *see* "Mass rights"
Inflation, 121
Inherited wealth, 67-68, 194-195
Installment buying, 5, 173, 251
Instrument of Government, 58
International Labor Organization, 166-167
International Law, 165-172
Ireton, Colonel, 23
Ius abutendi, 14-15, 67, 72, 74, 90, 109-115
Ius fruendi, 14, 72, 74
Ius gentium, 171
Ius utendi, 14, 72, 74, 115

Jacobins, 24
James I, 21
Jefferson, Thomas, 2, 6, 7, 31, 32, 33, 37, 57, 80, 205, 206-208, 245
Jefferson Memorial, 206-207
Jellinek, Georg, 212, 219, 220
Jellinek, Walter, 246
Jhering, Rudolf von, 100-101, 106, 116, 125, 138
Judicial review, 79-84, 90, 159-160, 189, 191, 193
Jullian, Camille, 223
Juristenstaat, 247
Justice
  protection of property conducive to, 19, 28, 34, 38, 61, 67, 75, 84, 86, 87
  social, 94, 95-100, 100-108, 108-115, 115-125, 125-127

Kant, Immanuel, 67
Kelsen, Hans, 158
Kennedy, John F., 206
Kent, James, 84-85, 86, 221
Ketteler, Wilhelm, 97
Khrushchev, Nikita, 180, 185, 206
Kingsley, Charles, 96
Kipp, Theodor, 86
Kirchmann, Hermann von, 157
Knowlton, Jerome C., 231
Knox, Henry, 33
Kolping, Adolf, 97
Koschaker, Paul, 218
Kuehnelt-Leddihn, Erik von, 234

Lacombe, V., 222
Lafayette, Marie Joseph, 62
Laissez-faire, 92, 96, 97, 98, 99, 100, 104, 129
  is natural, 68, 69
Lamartine, Alphonse de, 123
Lambert, Edouard, 112, 159
Larkin, Paschal, 217
Laski, Harold, 107, 215, 243
Latin America, 185-186, 196, 206
Latouche, Robert, 223
Laughlin, J. Laurence, 226
Laveleye, Emile de, 50
Law
  abstract, 102, 103, 109
  common, customary, 13, 16, 20, 21, 38, 45
  decline of, 153-160
  divine, 17, 18-19, 20-21, 26, 34
  man-made, 15, 16, 17, 22, 24, 26, 27, 28, 29, 38, 45, 149-163
  natural, 13, 15, 16, 17, 20, 21, 26, 27, 29, 31, 38, 39, 45, 149-152, 156-159, 191
  private, 91-92, 153-160
  public, 91-92, 153-160
  socialization of, 99, 100-102, 102-103, 112
Lawmaker
  fallible, 149-163
  limited, 79, 80, 82, 83, 86, 91, 142-144
  qualitatively unlimited, 149-152
  quantitatively unlimited, 152-153
Legality and legitimacy, 189-190
Legislation
  detrimental to property, 160-161, 161-163
    in France, 24-25, 116-117
    in Germany, 116-117
    in the international community, 165-172
    in the United States, 33, 116-117
  favoring property
    in France, 71-72
    in Germany, 73-78
    in the United States, 91
  labor, 116-119
  social, 115-122
  take-care, 119-120
Leo XIII, 70
Lessius, Leonardo, 16, 37
Levellers, 22-23, 215
Lévy, Emmanuel, 112
Liberal rights, 42-44
  and civil rights, 45-48
  and democratic rights, 43-45, 146-149
  and property rights, 24, 45-48, 59-60, 61, 62-63
Liberalism, 76, 90, 92, 95, 128-129, 187-188

"Liberalism", 183-187, 199
Lichtenberger, André, 215
Life, liberty and property, 31, 32, 33, 61, 69, 82
  property important for liberty, 62, 66, 67, 77, 83, 86, 88
  propery vital for life and liberty, 48-51, 64, 89
Limited government, 25-34, 139-142
  and democratic rights, 43-45, 142-144, 144-146, 146-147
  and liberal rights, 43-45
  and property rights, 25-34, 43-45, 139-142, 142-144
Lochner v. New York, 104
Locke, John, 6, 10, 26-28, 31, 32, 37, 56
Louis XIV, 21
Lugo, Juan de, 16, 37
Luther, Martin, 17-18, 37
Luzerne, de la, 62

Madison, James, 152-153
Magna Carta, 41, 54-55, 56, 57
Maine, Henry, 50, 68
Malville, Jacques de, 89
Manchester school, 68, 96, 98
Mangoldt, Hermann von, 241
Manifest Destiny, 205
Manton, Thomas, 214
Marshall, John, 78-80, 81, 85, 91, 105
Marx, Karl, 95, 105, 125, 182
Mason, Alpheus T., 211, 237
Mass rights, 133-135, 143, see "Individualistic rights"
Masses
  advance of the, 138
  and equality, 143
  and property, 138-139, 146-147, 147-163
  revolt of the, 138, 178
McDonald, Forrest, 217
McKean, Dayton D., 244
Meinecke, Friedrich, 233, 253
Melanchthon, Philipp, 213
Mennonites, 36
Mercantilism, 29
Methodists, 36
Meyer, Georg, 220
Middle Ages, 15-17, 35, 37, 41, 52, 55
Mill, James, 68, 225
Mill, John Stuart, 56, 68, 121
Mirabeau, 24, 62
Mohl, Robert von, 150, 246
Molina, Luis de, 16
Monster Petition (England), 96
Montesquieu, 28-29, 37, 142, 144, 153, 165

More perfect Union, (U.S.), 61, 78
More, Thomas, 26
Morgan, J. P., 5
Morley, Felix, 254
Moscow Declaration Concerning Italy, 166
Münster, 20
Murphy, Carroll D., 212

Napoleonic code, 25, 71-72, 111, 149, 156
  as code of property, 25, 34, 72, 88, 89, 90, 104
  impact of, 73
National-socialism, 1, 7, 130
  opposed reaction as much as communism, 181
Natural importance of property, 48-51
Negative rights, see "Liberal rights"
Neurotic age, 179-180
New Alliance, 194-195, 199
New Deal, 4-5, 112, 158, 159, 192, 193, 199
New Freedom, 4, 199
New Frontier, 195-197, 199, 206
New Frontiers, 4, 196
New Generation, 5
New Jersey v. Wilson, 79, 80
New Testament, 15, 17
Nineteenth century
  adjudication favoring property, 78-84, 90-91
  as century of individualism, 66, 94, 156
  as century of liberalism, 66, 128
  as century of property, 66, 77, 92, 95, 104
  end of, 93
  jurisprudence favoring property, 84-90
  legislation favoring property, 71-78, 91
  schools of thought favoring property, 66-71
  social evaluations of property, 95-100, 100-103, 116-117
Noblesse of the masses, 155-156
Northwest Ordinance, 91
Notes on Virginia, 6, 33, 208, 244
Nulla poena sine lege, applicable to property rights, 46

Old Testament, 16, 17
Organic theory of the state, 130
Organization Man, 136
Ortega y Gasset, José, 178, 252

Paine, Thomas, 56
Pandektenwissenschaft, 86, 90, 104, 109

Paris Commune, 95
Parliament, 21, 23, 29, 30, 54, 57, 58
Participation principle, *see* "Democratic rights"
Paternalism, 86, 105, 158
Patten, Simon, 99
Patterson, Bennett B., 220
Patterson, James, 223
Pax Americana, 202, 203
Peabody, Francis G., 97
Peace, property conducive to, 9, 13, 16, 17, 26, 27, 34, 38, 61, 89
Persecution on grounds of race, 7
Pietists, 36
Planck, Gottlieb, 77
Planiol, Marcel, 90
Plato, 13, 16, 20
Plena in re potestas, 89
Perry, A. L., 226
Petition of Right, 57-58
Petrucci, Raphael, 222
Plymouth Rock, 29-30
Portalis, Jean Etienne Marie, 89, 153
Positive rights, *see* "Democratic rights"
Potsdam Conference, 166
Pound, Dean, 104
Prélot, Marcel, 241
Presbyterians, 18
Primitive societies, property in, 49-51
Prochnow, Herbert V., 212
Progress, property conducive to, 9, 13, 17, 18, 19, 20, 26, 27, 28, 34, 38, 40, 67, 69, 70, 76, 84, 85, 89, 94
"Progressivism", 187, 197
Property
  absolute right of, 72, 74, 87, 89
  acquisition of,
    free, 25, 26, 27, 28, 67, 72, 75, 94, 95
    regulated, restricted, 71-72, 75-77
    through labor or occupation, 38
    virtuous, 18-19, 36
  and civil rights, 45-48
  and democracy, 128-163
  and democratic rights, 42-48, 146-149, 160-161, 161-163
  and freedom, 40-64
  and liberal rights, 24, 45-48, 59-60, 61, 62-63 (more important than other liberal rights, 61, 63, 64, 68)
  and new liberal rights, 131-139
  and propriety, 9-12, 209
  appreciation in languages, 9-12
  as an arbitrary right, 74, 75, 77, 87
  as a natural right, 24, 25, 26, 27, 31, 38, 39
  decline of,
    a democratic phenomenon, 128-63, 164

Property
  decline of (*continued*)
    consequences of, 172-181
    in international law, 165-172
    in municipal law, 93-127
  definition of, 8, 87, 92, 233
  divided, 72, 88, 89
  dynamic and static, 8, 65, 68, 94, 105, 234
  good for,
    civilization, 9, 16, 17, 20, 23, 25, 26, 27, 34, 38, 39, 40, 42, 45, 48, 64, 67, 68, 89
    family, 18, 71, 85
    incentive, 17, 18, 26, 27, 28, 30, 70, 84, 85, 89, 94, 126
    individual's well-being, 19, 22, 25, 26, 34, 38, 47
    justice, 9, 19, 28, 34, 38, 61, 67, 75, 84, 86, 87
    law and order, 15, 16, 34, 61, 89
    liberality (charity), 13, 19, 70, 71, 85
    happiness, 9, 13, 29, 32, 33, 34, 38
    peace, 9, 13, 16, 17, 26, 27, 34, 38, 61, 89
    progress, 9, 13, 17, 18, 19, 20, 26, 27, 28, 34, 38, 40, 67, 69, 70, 76, 84, 85, 89, 94
    society's well-being, 15, 16, 20, 23, 25, 67, 84
  identical to
    fulfillment of the law, 87
    liberty, 83, 88
  implying duties, 87, 99, 112
  in antiquity, 12-15
  in Catholic thought, 15-17, 35, 70-71, 96, 97
  in England, 21-23, 26-28, 57-59, 96
  in France, 20-21, 23-25, 28-29, 61-63, 69, 71-72, 90-91, 95, 102-103, 109, 111, 112, 117, 121, 123-124, 190-192
  in Germany, 17-18, 67, 68, 73-78, 86-88, 90-91, 97, 98-99, 100, 100-102, 109-110, 111, 112, 117, 121, 122, 122-123, 190-192
  in the U.S., 29-34, 59-61, 69, 78-86, 91, 97-98, 103-106, 110-112, 116-117, 122, 124-125, 192-199, 200-208
  in intangible as well as tangible things, 38, 69, 83
  individualistic concept of, 94, 96, 98, 99, 102, 108, 109, 129
  inviolability, unalienability of, 70, 71, 76, 86, 89, 90, 91, 105
  protected under,
    common and customary law, 13, 16, 20, 21, 38, 64, 68

Property
  protected under (*continued*)
    higher and natural law, 13, 15, 16, 17,
      20, 21, 22, 26, 27, 29, 31, 38, 39,
      64, 68, 70, 85
    man-made law, 15, 16, 17, 22, 24, 26,
      27, 28, 38, 70
    protection not an end in itself, 42
    protection the end of government, 14,
      18, 20, 24, 27, 31, 33, 61
    social concept of, 94, 96, 101, 102, 103,
      108, 109
Propriety, property and, 9-12, 209
Protection principle, *see* "Liberal rights"
Protestant thought on property, 17-19, 36,
  96-98
Proudhon, Pierre Joseph, 69
Public interest, 95-100, 100-106, 112-115,
  153-154
Puritans, 18-19
Pursuit of happiness, 3, 5, 31-32, 59, 62
  and property, 31-33
Putney debates, 23

Quakers, 36
Quod Apostoli Muneris, 70

Reaction, 181
Reason of state, 189-190
Rau, C., 89
Raven, Canon, 234-235
Reception of Roman law, 35, 218
Recht, 150
Rechtsstaat, 122, 150, 246-247
Reformation, 17-19, 65
Relativization of the rights of man, 172-173
Religious freedom, 42, 43, 44, 49, 51-54,
  54-56, 61, 62
Rerum Novarum, 70
Res communis, 50
Res nullius, 50
Revolution
  American, 30-34, 59-61
  English, 22-23, 57-59
  French, 23-25, 61-63
  right of, 62, 63, 198-199
Rhédon, 62
Ricardo, David, 68
Rights of man, *see* "freedom"
Rights of Englishmen, 140
Rivière, Mercier de la, 68
Robespierre, Maximilien de, 24
Röpke, Wilhelm, 251

Roman law
  favors free property, 14-15, 73, 86-88,
    98-99, 100-102
    but no absolute protection of prop-
      erty, 101
    impact of, 35-36, 86-88, 98-99, 100-102,
      129
Romanticists, 94
Rommen, Heinrich, 233
Roosevelt, Franklin D., 211-212
Rousseau, Jean Jacques, 23-24, 94, 131,
  165, 182, 215
Rudolph, Kurt, 233
Rufinus, 16
Rush, Benjamin, 33

Saleilles, Raymond, 157, 158
San Francisco Conference, 167
Savigny, F. C. von, 68, 88, 92, 152, 157
Schiller, Friedrich, 244
Schlatter, Richard, 212, 213, 214, 215, 216,
  225
Schlesinger, Arthur M., 243-244
Schmitt, Carl, 220, 246, 247, 248
Schmoller, Gustav, 98
Schulz, Fritz, 213
Schwender, H. W., 227-228
Seagle, William, 231
Sée, Henri, 214, 222
Ségal, V. L., 222
Separation of powers, 141, 189, 191, 193
  means for protection of property, 189
Shays's Rebellion, 34, 141, 229
Siegfried, André, 254
Siéyès, 62
Smith, Adam, 65, 68, 202, 225
Social gospel, 96-98, 100
Social insurance, 119-120
Social justice, 94, 163
Social legislation, 24-25, 33, 116-117, 160-
  161, 161-163, 187
Socialism, 70, 93, 94, 95, 97
  and "liberalism", 183-184
  Christian, 96-98
  gradual and radical achievement of, 182-
    184, 185-187
  of the chair, 98-100
  orthodox, 99
  revisionist, 95, 99
  "sweet water," 99
Socialization
  of international law, 165-172
  of municipal law, 153-160
Sociological jurisprudence, 100, 103-108,
  130

Sohm, Rudolf, 77
Southey, Robert, 96
Spencer, Herbert, 68, 69, 104, 226
Spite walls etc., 75, 109, 110
Stahl, J. F., 150
Stammler, Rudolf, 157, 158
Stamp, Josiah, 225
Stamp Act Congress, 31
State
    as caretaker, 5, 119-120, 120-121, 126-127
    as means for the protection of property, 14, 18, 20, 24, 27, 31, 33, 61
    as regulator of property, 115-122, 160-161, 161-163, 187
Stein, Lorenz von, 246
Stenton, Doris M., 223
Stoecker, Adolf, 97, 100
Stoics, 13
Story, Joseph, 78
Struggle for the law, 138
Suffrage
    expansion of, 141-146
    meaning for democratic government, 146-149
Summum ius, summa iniuria, 162
Supreme Court (U.S.), 78-84, 104-106, 125, 159-160, 221

Talmon, J. L., 211
Taney, Roger B., 80-82, 85, 91, 125
Tawney, R. H., 213
Taxation
    for foreign aid, 175
    for social legislation, 119-120
    progressive, 121-122, 127
Ten Commandments, 51, 53-54, 55
Terrett v. Taylor, 79-80
Thibaut, A. J. F., 157, 231
Thiers, Adolphe, 121
Third International, 185
Third Reich, 88, 181, 190
Third Republic, 124
Thomas of Aquinas, 16, 52
Thompson, J. M., 215
Tillotson, John, 214
Tocqueville, Alexis de, 69, 243, 256
Toutain, J. F., 222
Toynbee, Arnold, 204
Treitschke, Heinrich von, 98
Trial by jury in civil as well as criminal cases, 61
Tronchet, 62
Truman, Harry S., 167, 168, 169

Tunc, André, 227
Twelve Tables, 120
Twentieth century
    adjudication detrimental to property, 108-115
    as century of authoritarianism, 93-94
    as century of the masses, 94
    jurisprudence detrimental to property, 103-106, 112
    legislation detrimental to property, 117, 121-122, 122-124, 165-172

Unions, 136
United Nations, 167-169, 174, 186, 187, 204
Universal Declaration of Human Rights, 169-171, 174
Utilitarianism, 66-67, 69, 96

Vichy regime, 190
Vital center, 188
Voegelin, Eric, 248
Volenti non fit iniuria, 118
Volney, Constantin François, 163
Vox populi vox dei, 152, 161

Wagner, Adolph, 98, 100
Wallace, Henry A., 211
Wayland, Francis, 226
Wealth of Nations, 65, 202
Weber, Max, 213, 218, 252
Weeks, O. Douglas, 231
Weimar Republic, 122-123, 145, 151, 190, 222
Welfare state, 5, 93, 94, 173-178, see "State"
Whigs, 61
Whitgift, John, 18
Wichern, Johann Hinrich, 96, 97
William II, 1
Wilson, Woodrow, 4
Windscheid, B., 86, 157, 231
Winstanley, Gerrard, 22
Women labor, 117
Wood, H. G., 213, 214
World War I, 112, 124
World War II, 4, 113, 124, 190, 192
Wright, Benjamin F., 229, 233
Wycliffe, John, 17

Zeiller, Franz von, 74

BIOGRAPHICAL SKETCH

Gottfried Dietze graduated from the University of Heidelberg Law School. After further studies in Germany and the United States, he received doctorates in law from Heidelberg, in politics from Princeton University, and in juridical science from the University of Virginia.

He is a professor of political science at the Johns Hopkins University and teaches comparative government. His major interest is in Western constitutionalism. Mr. Dietze was a visiting professor at Heidelberg for four semesters, and at the Brookings Institution. He has lectured at European and Far Eastern universities, and often spends his summers abroad lecturing, doing research, and writing.

His first major work, *Über Formulierung der Menschenrechte* (1956), suggests new techniques for the formulation of bills of rights, and won him election to the Academy of Human Rights.

The Federalist—A Classic on Federalism and Free Government (1960) brought Mr. Dietze further acclaim. The first book published on the Federalist Papers, it has been reprinted several times. Mr. Dietze has also contributed many articles to American and European professional journals, and is now completing the first volume of a comparative study of judicial review. The central theme in his writings has been that of the protection of the individual from the government, be it that of one, the few, or many.